# Reading the Bible Theologica

Theological interpretation of the B

debates within theology today. Yet what exactly is theological reading? Darren Sarisky proposes that it requires identification of the reader via a theological anthropology, an understanding of the text as a collection of signs, and reading the text with a view toward engaging with what it says of transcendence. Accounts of theological reading do not often give explicit focus to the place of the reader, but this work seeks to redress this neglect. Sarisky examines Augustine's approach to the Bible and how his theological insights into the reader and the text generate an aim for interpretation, which is fulfilled by fitting reading strategies. He also engages with Spinoza, showing that theological exegesis contrasts not with approaches that take history seriously, but with naturalistic approaches to reading.

DR. DARREN SARISKY is currently Departmental Lecturer in Modern Theology at the Faculty of Theology and Religion, University of Oxford. His publications on scriptural interpretation include *Theology, History, and Biblical Interpretation: Modern Readings* (2015) and *Scriptural Interpretation: A Theological Exploration, Challenges in Contemporary Theology* (2013).

CURRENT ISSUES IN THEOLOGY

**General Editor:**
Iain Torrance
*Pro-Chancellor of the University of Aberdeen*

**Editorial Advisory Board:**

David Ford *University of Cambridge*
Bryan Spinks *Yale University*
Kathryn Tanner *Yale Divinity School*

There is a need among upper-undergraduate and graduate students of theology, as well as among Christian teachers and church professionals, for a series of short, focussed studies of particular key topics in theology written by prominent theologians. Current Issues in Theology meets this need.

The books in the series are designed to provide a "state-of-the-art" statement on the topic in question, engaging with contemporary thinking as well as providing original insights. The aim is to publish books which stand between the static monograph genre and the more immediate statement of a journal article, by authors who are questioning existing paradigms or rethinking perspectives.

Other titles in the series:

*Holy Scripture* John Webster
*The Just War Revisited* Oliver O'Donovan
*Bodies and Souls, or Spirited Bodies?* Nancey Murphy
*Christ and Horrors* Marilyn McCord Adams
*Divinity and Humanity* Oliver D. Crisp
*The Eucharist and Ecumenism* George Hunsinger
*Christ the Key* Kathryn Tanner
*Theology without Metaphysics* Kevin W. Hector
*Reconsidering John Calvin* Randall C. Zachman
*God's Presence* Frances Young
*An Incarnational Model of the Eucharist* James M. Arcadi
*The Providence of God* David Fergusson

DARREN SARISKY
*University of Oxford*

# Reading the Bible Theologically

CAMBRIDGE
UNIVERSITY PRESS

**CAMBRIDGE**
**UNIVERSITY PRESS**

University Printing House, Cambridge CB2 8BS, United Kingdom

One Liberty Plaza, 20th Floor, New York, NY 10006, USA

477 Williamstown Road, Port Melbourne, VIC 3207, Australia

314-321, 3rd Floor, Plot 3, Splendor Forum, Jasola District Centre, New Delhi - 110025, India

79 Anson Road, #06-04/06, Singapore 079906

Cambridge University Press is part of the University of Cambridge.

It furthers the University's mission by disseminating knowledge in the pursuit of education, learning and research at the highest international levels of excellence.

www.cambridge.org
Information on this title: www.cambridge.org/9781108734097
DOI: 10.1017/9781108609296

© Darren Sarisky 2019

This publication is in copyright. Subject to statutory exception and to the provisions of relevant collective licensing agreements, no reproduction of any part may take place without the written permission of Cambridge University Press.

First published 2019
First paperback edition 2020

*A catalogue record for this publication is available from the British Library*

*Library of Congress Cataloging in Publication data*
NAMES: Sarisky, Darren, author.
TITLE: Reading the Bible theologically / Darren Sarisky, University of Oxford.
DESCRIPTION: 1 [edition].. | New York : Cambridge University Press, 2019. | Series: Current issues in theology
IDENTIFIERS: LCCN 2018030109 | ISBN 9781108497480 (hardback)
SUBJECTS: LCSH: Bible–Hermeneutics. | Theology. | Bible–Criticism, interpretation, etc.
CLASSIFICATION: LCC BS476 .S269 2018 | DDC 220.601–dc23
LC record available at https://lccn.loc.gov/2018030109

ISBN 978-1-108-49748-0 Hardback
ISBN 978-1-108-73409-7 Paperback

Cambridge University Press has no responsibility for the persistence or accuracy of URLs for external or third-party internet websites referred to in this publication, and does not guarantee that any content on such websites is, or will remain, accurate or appropriate.

For David Ford and the late John Webster,
for whose guidance, encouragement,
and inspiring examples I will be forever grateful.
By the time I finished this book
David had retired and John had died,
but I could not have written it without both of them.

# Contents

*Preface* *page* ix
*Acknowledgments* xiv
*List of Abbreviations* xix

**Introduction** 1

PART I THE MODEL OF AUGUSTINE 73

1 **The Reader, Redemption, and Signs** 75

2 **Between *Scientia* and the Trinity** 105

PART II A CONSTRUCTIVE PROPOSAL 141

3 **In Contradistinction to Naturalism** 151

4 **Faith and the Ecclesial Community** 188

5 **The Bible and Theological Semiotics** 239

6 **Exegetical Ends and Means** 284

**Conclusion** 328

*Works Cited* 366
*Index* 402

# Preface

I was guided by two convictions when I began the research that stands behind this book about theological exegesis. The first conviction holds firm, while the other also remains with me, though in a qualified form. The belief that remains with me is that in the current discussion it is often quite unclear what *theological interpretation* signifies, even as its merits, demerits, history, and promise are all the subject of vigorous debate. As W. T. Dickens has recently and rightly said, "The term theological interpretation needs some explanation."[1] This book aims to explicate what theological reading entails with a view toward clarifying the issues at stake.

I also set out with the intuition that the main ideas underlying the current discussion of theological reading marked out a territory in which interesting and valuable work might be done.[2] From my point of view now, this still seems true, but with a caveat, namely that some of the principles animating aspects of the discussion need to be brought to light and critically examined.[3] A key issue needing

[1] W. T. Dickens, "The Uses of the Bible in Theology," in *The New Cambridge History of the Bible*, ed. John Riches, Vol. 4: From 1750 to the Present (Cambridge: Cambridge University Press, 2015), 184.

[2] This is despite there being quite a variety of ideas in the debate, and in spite of the unfortunate reality that recently published theological commentaries are only sometimes compelling. For critique of both the commentaries themselves and the associated literature, see Mark W. Elliot, *The Heart of Biblical Theology: Providence Experienced* (Farnham: Ashgate, 2012), 3–36.

[3] I thus do not entirely agree with Stephen E. Fowl when he says, "As a relatively recent arrival on the scholarly scene, there was a period of time when theological interpreters

reconsideration is the very understandings of theology that many in the discussion of theological exegesis are presupposing. Discussion about theological interpretation can advance by giving close attention to what theology is and what tasks it may properly perform within an account of interpretation. In this connection, John Webster is right to insist that it is crucial to attend to the way that debates about the Bible and its interpretation are framed and to give close examination to some of the assumptions that are most deeply embedded within them, all the while allowing oneself freedom to question the adequacy of the terms by which debates are conducted.[4] I intend to pursue such questions here. I consider the issues that the current ferment raises by setting the discussion in the larger context of the history of biblical interpretation and hermeneutical reflection, thus decentering the present discussion and offering new insights to it.[5]

needed to engage in a period of self-definition. A part of this self-definition included a good deal of criticism of other more established interpretive methods, as well as rigorous marking of disciplinary boundaries. It is my view that such a period is now over." See "Editor's Notes" *Anglican Theological Review* 99 (2017): 645. Fowl makes it clear that he does not see it as *entirely* out of place now to continue to reflect on what theological interpretation is, for he also says "the boundaries of theological interpretation should be contestable, flexible, and porous" ("Editor's Notes," 645). Yet his point seems to be that the *main* time during which it was necessary to consider fundamental questions of self-definition has passed. I concur that part of what makes necessary a discussion of the nature of theological reading is ensuring that there is institutional space in which it can be pursued, and it is good that there have been positive developments recently here – thanks in part to the efforts of Fowl himself. However, a major working assumption of this book is that further discussion of what theological reading is becomes justified if additional light can be shed on its nature.

4 John Webster, "Biblical Reasoning," *Anglican Theological Review* 90 (2008): 734. The way this project is set up owes something to the suggestive remarks about the nature of theological reading in John Webster, "One Who Is Son: Theological Reflections on the Exordium to the Epistle to the Hebrews," in *The Epistle to the Hebrews and Christian Theology*, ed. Richard Bauckham et al. (Grand Rapids: Eerdmans, 2009), 69–70.

5 I draw the term *decentering* from Rowan Williams, *Why Study the Past?: The Quest for the Historical Church* (London: Darton, Longman, and Todd, 2005), 110.

This book is distinctive in that it is (at the time of writing this preface) the first monograph to deal with theological reading against the background of the current discussion. More importantly, the substance of my argument is distinctive: I argue that understanding theological reading requires coming to grips with the deep difference it makes for biblical interpretation to be based on a theological construal of reality itself. If one understands existing things, and especially the realities involved most directly in reading – the reader and the text above all else – in the light of their relation to God, rather than eliminating theological description in order to think from an exclusively immanent point of view, then certain entailments follow as a matter of course. In *A Secular Age*, Charles Taylor rightly says: "Belief in God is no longer axiomatic. There are alternatives."[6] I contend that the direction reading takes is a consequence of the reader's beliefs about God (or denial of God's existence): one's stance here carries implications for the aim of interpretation as well as for the interpretive strategies that seek to fulfill that goal. Theological exegesis is an interpretive response to the Bible that is the product of construing the reading subject and the object to be read in connection with God. A crucial aim of this book is to argue that there are such entailments, and therefore that the doctrinal perspective on the reader and text is not simply pious language invoked at the outset of thinking about interpretation, but a way of understanding the reading subject and the interpreted object that has substantial hermeneutical implications.

The case I make in this book should be of interest to anyone wanting to think about theological reading, whether or not such readers think of themselves as part of the Christian tradition. Offering a proleptic summary of the argument in the form of three bare-bones propositions will assist in explaining how this is so. I contend, first, that the reader is one who responds to the text's

[6] Charles Taylor, *A Secular Age* (Cambridge, MA: Belknap Press of Harvard University Press, 2007), 3.

mediation of divine self-disclosure in faith; second, that the text of the Bible constitutes a set of signs pointing beyond itself to the God who opens the eyes of the interpreting subject; and third, *because* of the prior two points, the text should be read with reference to God. Quite a bit more than this needs to be said, and is in fact said, in the following pages to unpack and defend each of the three propositions that form the core of the constructive argument; this bald summary will not accomplish a great deal by itself. Yet what I intend for this summary to do is simply to indicate something crucial about the *form* of the overall argument. In the constructive chapters of this work, I argue for both of the first two propositions, and I seek to demonstrate that norms for reading do indeed follow from these ontological affirmations. One reading audience, then, is those who themselves have a faith commitment matching up to the initial two affirmations, or at least something very much like them. Such readers will be engaged by the argument I am making because they can identify with its starting points: they see them as true or at least verisimilitudinous, for they operate within the same tradition of thought. However, anyone can engage in what I am saying about the first two propositions with a view toward critically considering whether the interpretive entailments actually do follow from them. Anyone can assess whether the hermeneutical implications are genuinely implications. Readers seeking to evaluate the argument in this way will at least learn how one proposal for a Christian biblical hermeneutic works. Both of these audiences are important for me, just as in writing this book I have learned important things from those who are within my own tradition as well as those who are not.

This project is a sequel to my first monograph, *Scriptural Interpretation: A Theological Exploration.*[7] In this second book, I am building on some of the research into patristic and modern theology that I did for the first volume, and in both I make a

[7] Darren Sarisky, *Scriptural Interpretation: A Theological Account*, Challenges in Contemporary Theology (Oxford: Wiley-Blackwell, 2013).

determined effort to think theologically about reading the Bible. However, the two books deal with different focal questions, and this second one does more to develop its constructive position. In *Scriptural Interpretation*, the query is: What is happening, in theological terms, when the Bible is read in the church, and what presuppositions does this make about the text and the reader? In the present book, I ask what theological reading is and pursue questions of how reading strategies ought to fulfill the aim of interpretation.

To be sure, a great deal more remains to be done in the whole area of theological exegesis. Roughly thirty years ago, Joseph Ratzinger said that giving theology a greater role in exegesis, while not falling into a docetic view of the Bible – in his words, finding "a better synthesis between the historical and theological methods" – was the work of at least a generation.[8] My inclination is to say that this will surely take several generations. It is no easy task. I hope that the proposal here to anchor reading strategies in theological ontology represents one step forward along that path. There are some signs that theological interpretation is entering a new phase, in which it is less reactive to perceived opponents and increasingly able to speak constructively. Only time will tell what this will finally amount to, but this book is written with the confidence that, however much this or that venture appears to be a mere fad, the ultimate issues at stake are worthy of careful attention and deep consideration.

[8] Joseph Ratzinger, "Biblical Interpretation in Crisis: On the Question of the Foundations and Approaches of Exegesis Today," in *Biblical Interpretation in Crisis: The Ratzinger Conference on Bible and Church*, ed. Richard John Neuhaus, The Encounter Series (Grand Rapids: Eerdmans, 1989), 5–6.

# Acknowledgments

I started this project during a postdoctoral fellowship at the University of Cambridge. I discussed the ideas around which the book revolves in a number of seminars there, and I extend my thanks to the members of these seminars for the intellectual stimulation they provided. Daniel Weiss and I co-led a seminar called "Scripture and Modernity," which was originally envisaged to take only a single term but which ended up expanding into three because of all the interest the topics generated among the participants, who came from an interesting mix of disciplinary and religious backgrounds. The rigor of Daniel's thinking was a continual and helpful challenge for me to clarify my take on the texts we were discussing. In addition, it was my privilege to organize a series of MPhil seminars with Janet Soskice around the theme of "Text and Interpretation." We designed the new seminars with a view to offering our postgraduates additional teaching, but I am sure that I gained as much from the sessions as any of the students, especially because of Janet's wise guidance of the discussions. Finally, exploring John's Gospel with David Ford and Simeon Zahl, in connection with David's excellent undergraduate course "Theological Interpretation of the Gospel of John," helped me see what theological exegesis can look like in practice. In the midst of writing a book oriented toward theory, it was good to engage in the practice of biblical interpretation. I am glad that I had this opportunity to work with David, and a valued postdoctoral colleague who has now become a lecturer, as David was preparing his commentary on the Fourth Gospel and the set of Bampton lectures he gave in Oxford. I have plans to write my own theological commentary in due course, and I will be better able to do so because I have both seen good examples and settled in my own mind what the nature of the task is.[1]

I also benefited from being able to talk through relevant texts and themes with students who enrolled in courses I taught during a brief stint as a fixed-term lecturer in Systematic Theology at King's College London. I appreciate Susannah Ticciati entrusting me with her courses while she was away on leave. The seminars at King's, together with all of the seminars in Cambridge, provided me with indispensable opportunities to plough up the ground and to prepare for writing this book.

Many less formal but still quite instructive discussions in recent years have also helped my thoughts about Augustine and theological exegesis to mature. David Ford pointed out some of the major conceptual obstacles that would need to be overcome for this book to prove successful. James Andrews and Jonathan Teubner were helpful in orienting me to Augustine and Augustine scholarship at the outset of my research; as I progressed, they were both constant dialogue partners with whom I could mull over slowly developing ideas. I appreciate the conversations I have been able to have about how to think in light of Augustine with a few senior scholars: Michel Barnes, Ivor Davidson, Paul Griffiths, Andrew

[1] There is a parallel here with what David Tracy says about theology: "*The* problem of the contemporary systematic theologian, as has often been remarked, is actually to *do* systematic theology. The major attempt of this book has been to propose a model which may perform some initial spadework for that larger enterprise and to interpret certain familiar instances of contemporary theologizing in what one hopes is the clarifying light of the model proposed." See *Blessed Rage for Order: The New Pluralism in Theology* (Chicago: University of Chicago Press, 1996), 238. As with theology, so with theological interpretation of the Bible: what is offered here is a formal account or a prolegomenon, which can serve the practice of theological reading by clarifying the nature of the endeavor. With Robert Morgan and John Barton, who speak with reference to theological interpretation of Scripture as they see it, I thus say, "The aim of this book is to clarify the task, not actually to perform it." See their *Biblical Interpretation*, Oxford Bible Series (Oxford: Oxford University Press, 1988), 274.

Louth, and Charles Mathewes. Karla Pollmann graciously sent me a scan of one of her essays that was proving terribly difficult to track down. Though we did not discuss Augustine, but rather other aspects of biblical exegesis and the history of reception, Markus Bockmuehl, Clayton Croy, Nathan Eubank, Joel Rasmussen, Ross Wagner, Kevin Vanhoozer, and N. T. Wright have all been illuminating interlocutors for me.

I owe a debt of gratitude to all of those who heard me present pilot papers at conferences and at university seminars, and who spurred me to hone my ideas before setting them down in final form. I presented material related to this book at conferences of the Society for the Study of Theology, the Society of Biblical Literature, and the British Early Career Association for Theologians. I also appreciate the invitation to present research at Duke University, King's College London, Trinity College Bristol, the University of Aberdeen, Wheaton College, the University of Virginia, and the University of Oxford. This book is far better than it would otherwise have been because I was able to float a number of trial balloons.

Several people have read at least part of this work, and I am greatly in their debt for them doing so. Never one to shy away from a task of forbidding difficulty, Daniel Treier waded through an early draft of the entire book and offered copious and spiritedly critical feedback, which convinced me that the manuscript was not as far along then as I had hoped. Lewis Ayres, on returning from literally circumnavigating the globe speaking at various conferences, managed to work through the introduction as well as the Augustine chapters and encouraged me to undertake one more round of revisions to sharpen and clarify my presentation. Brad East, Michael Legaspi, Angus Paddison, and Susannah Ticciati each read a chapter and asked many perceptive questions. I also received feedback on draft material from two research assistants, Julian Borda and Nikolaas Deketelaere. Colleen Sarisky's comments greatly improved the text. Mine is the only name on the cover of this book, but I am keenly aware of just how much I have learned from others in writing it.

Receiving a Junior Research Fellowship from Homerton College, Cambridge made possible much of the research for this book, as well as the writing of its initial chapters. Though it is a secular college, and the college community does not join together for services of worship, I am grateful for the significant investment that Homerton is making in the field of Theology and Religious Studies, not only by virtue of having had two theologians as part of its fellowship, but also by having the largest contingent of theology students of any Cambridge college. I also appreciate the many opportunities I have had to discuss theology with Thomas Graumann, Peter O'Donnell, Olivier Tonneau, and many others at high table. I have wonderful memories of walking around the apple orchards of Homerton during the summer months thinking about this book. Who would not feel fortunate to have had a position where they are given three years to do whatever they wanted to do? Though in many ways my situation was different, I resonated with what Augustine says about being able to study and think without the pressure of having to attend to other responsibilities: "Nobody could outdo me in enjoying such anxiety-free leisure. There's nothing better, nothing more pleasant than to search through the divine treasure chest with nobody making a commotion."[2]

I owe a great deal to the many people who helped me craft the original research proposal that was the blueprint for this book and part of the Cambridge fellowship application. Thanks are due to John Webster for suggesting that I work on this topic. Sadly, he suddenly died as I was revising a draft of the manuscript. His absence leaves a large void in the theological scene. I am particularly disappointed that I could not get his opinion on the completed version of a work he commissioned, so to speak. However, I will be

[2] *Sermon* 339.4 (SPM 1, 115; WSA III/9, 282).

forever grateful for all that he taught me when I was his student and for his support as I began my academic career; I appreciate the comments he offered on a very early draft of the conclusion, to the effect that it was original in content and "calmly confident" in tone. I also appreciate the feedback I received on proposal drafts from Carol Harrison, Paul Dafydd Jones, Andrew Louth, Nathan MacDonald, Walter Moberly, Angus Paddison, Joachim Schaper, and Phil Ziegler. Their critical questions have been ringing in my ears as I have worked on the book. I must leave it to them to render judgment on the extent to which I have successfully addressed the objections they raised to the project's initial conceptualization. What I can say for certain is that this book is much better because I received their input at an early stage.

I wrote the final chapters of this book as I took up a position at Wycliffe Hall in Oxford and put the finishing touches on the manuscript as a Departmental Lecturer in the Faculty of Theology and Religion. It has been a boon to me to discuss the argument and related issues with both teaching staff at Wycliffe and with other members of the Oxford Faculty. I appreciate the warm welcome they have all given me, and I have profited from my discussions with them.

I appreciate Beatrice Rehl and Ian Torrance accepting this book into the Current Issues in Theology series with Cambridge University Press. They are a truly outstanding team, and it was my pleasure to be able to work with them as my manuscript underwent review and entered the production process.

Finally, I must thank my family. Working through the early years of an academic career can be a wild ride at times – or, it would be more accurate and forthright to say that it can occasionally be calm and peaceful, because it ends up being a wild ride most of the time in the current economic and political climate. My wife and children have tolerated admirably well the difficulties and uncertainties of being on this journey with me. I also very much appreciate the help that my parents have provided along the way.

# Abbreviations

| | |
|---|---|
| ACW | Ancient Christian Writers |
| CCSL | Corpus Christianorum Series Latina |
| CSEL | Corpus Scriptorum Ecclesiasticorum Latinorum |
| FOC | Fathers of the Church |
| LCL | Loeb Classical Library |
| OWC | Oxford World's Classics |
| SPM | Stromata Patristica et Mediaevalia |
| WSA | Works of Saint Augustine |

# Introduction

All responsible readers of Scripture attend closely to the words on the page, learning what they can about the text's vocabulary and grammar; they also look into the historical background of biblical books in order to illuminate their meaning. "In this sense interpreting a biblical text is no special and exceptional hermeneutical situation."[1] The present work considers whether the many readers of the Bible who have a Christian theological commitment read differently for this very reason. Does such allegiance affect the interpretation that they give to texts? If so, what difference does belief make? How does faith relate to studying a text's vocabulary, grammar, and historical background? Christians, as such, come to the text with a web of theological convictions about the nature of God and his revelatory activity as well as about Christ, the Holy Spirit, salvation, and a great many other things. The claim at the heart of this work is that a reader's faith in such matters does indeed (properly) alter the way in which she reasons exegetically. This means that the doctrine of God, together with the whole package of related beliefs about how God reveals himself and so on, is not simply dormant in interpretation. Within biblical interpretation, the doctrine of God should not hold "a rather isolated position" in an interpreter's outlook on reading; once the topic is raised, it should not be the case that the subject "is never brought up again"; it ought not be that "even after it has been made known to us, it

[1] Hans Georg Gadamer, "Religious and Poetical Speaking," in *Myth, Symbol, and Reality*, ed. Alan M. Olson (Notre Dame: University of Notre Dame Press, 1980), 96.

remains, *as a reality*, locked up within itself," as Karl Rahner says with reference to how the Trinity is irrelevant to the outlook of many Christians.[2] Instead, God actually matters.

How so? This book considers the place of commitment within interpretation, proposing an account of theological interpretation of Scripture from the vantage point of systematic theology. Systematics explores not simply the content of Christian beliefs, but the logical interconnection between different articles of belief. That is, it traces out the links between discrete theological loci, attending to each item of belief as if it were a piece in a jigsaw puzzle, one shaped such that it interlocks with other pieces to form a full picture.[3] In a limited sense, this book concerns itself with quite a wide range of convictions and how they impinge on reading, yet the book is, of course, by no means about everything. The interlocking topics that come into focus here, and are the book's main concern, are the reader of Scripture, the text itself, and the practice of interpretation – as all three are seen in light of God. When the reader is understood theologically, the interpreter has the capacity to exercise faith in the God who discloses himself through the text of the Bible. The correlative view of Scripture is that it consists of a set of signs directing the reader's attention to its subject matter, the triune God. Reading with commitment generates a trajectory or an aim for interpretation, within the context of which it makes sense to consider what reading strategies are most fitting to employ. This purpose is to ascertain what the text signifies about divine reality and how this reality enfolds readers themselves. That interpretation has this aim or purpose is not to comment at all on what certain readers *can* or *cannot* do; rather, it

[2] Karl Rahner, *The Trinity* (London: Burns & Oates, 1970), 14.

[3] See A. N. Williams's compelling point that theology is not systematic only when it is found in a genre of work that treats Christian doctrine comprehensively locus by locus, but whenever it traces out the logical interrelationship between doctrines: *The Architecture of Theology: Structure, System, and Ratio* (Oxford: Oxford University Press, 2011), 1–4.

pertains to what interpreters with theological commitment *should* or *must* do. There is a parallel here with the way that material commitments generate styles of writing: for example, of course anyone can write so as to unsettle the status quo or challenge the establishment, but there is a certain necessity to do so for those committed to liberation theologies. Likewise, anyone can read with the aim of engaging with what the text says about God. However, those committed to the views of the reader and the text on which this book concentrates should, as a matter of course, interpret the Bible with this aim in view.[4]

This work thus explores the consequences for reading of believers believing their own beliefs and thinking their own thoughts about interpretation. The book foregrounds theological thinking, rather than forcing it to remain forever only in the background; it aims to put theological ideas to work such that they are active at the most important points in the account of reading. The project assumes a doctrine of the Trinity right from the beginning, working *from* it rather than trying to get *to* it by establishing its legitimacy. It starts from a doctrine of God in the sense that it frames the notions of the reader and the text in relation to God: the reader is one who expresses faith in the triune God who discloses himself through the text, which is itself a pointer to divine reality. An account of these created realities is thus incomplete without reference to God: this makes the

4 The main aim of this text is to consider such commitments as affirmations of faith that individuals or communities make more or less consciously. I note a few times in the text, however, that differentiating cleanly between this sense of commitment and a reader simply having Christianity as their cultural or intellectual language is not particularly easy. In this connection, see the comments of Hans Georg Gadamer, "Kant and the Question of God," in *Hermeneutics, Religion, and Ethics* (New Haven: Yale University Press, 1999), 4. This project is not heavily invested in any such differentiation, so I do not pursue this issue extensively. The book is more focused on the content of theological commitment and the work that it does than precisely how it is acquired.

operative view of the reader and text specifically Christian rather than secular in its orientation. This work nowhere seeks to justify or provide warrant for the doctrine of God to which its exposition of the reader and the text is intrinsically related, and this is for two reasons. Partly, it is because no book, including this one, is about its own assumptions. And partly, this is impossible even in principle – at least if justifying a Christian doctrine of God means generating an argument for subscribing to it that appeals to something else that itself carries more weight or is more ultimate than God himself. Nothing can have that status. Since it starts with a doctrine of God, the whole book depends on an assumption for which no argument is ever presented, though that is as it must be. The only question then is about the precise role of language about God, and this introductory chapter dwells at length on that query.

What this book does is to suggest that theological reading be conceived differently than it usually is, as an interpretive response that inevitably results from thinking theologically about the reader and the text, thus challenging readers to reconsider their self-conception, their view of Scripture, and how both impinge on interpretation. By outlining a whole account starting from a theological ontology, this book proposes that reality itself sets the conditions for interpretation and impels the reader to proceed in a certain way. The book does not ask the entire Christian tradition to reconstitute itself around a set of novel interpretive methods that are being proposed here for the first time. It is necessary to face the critique that committed reading is not genuinely *reading*. Perhaps, as the objection goes, the reader's beliefs corrupt the effort to understand, such that the degree to which commitment is present is the extent to which an engagement with a text should be considered an exercise in self-assertion as opposed to listening. After developing the positive proposal, this work entertains and responds to this question. The book as a whole asks what entailments follow, not from readers identifying in a facile way the text being read with theological views they hold, but from belief functioning as a substructure that deeply shapes the course of interpretation.[5]

## Varieties of Theological Interpretation

This work frames the above issue against the backdrop of the current discussion of theological interpretation of Scripture, as well as the much longer history of interpretation in which it is a recent episode. The book makes a contribution to or an intervention in the lively current debate about theological reading of Scripture, and it comes into dialogue with major participants in this discussion. As the ongoing discussion forms the background of the present work, it is worth surveying it at the outset as a way to set the stage for the positive proposal this book develops. The examples of theological reading from the debate canvassed immediately below count as instances of theological exegesis in a rough-and-ready sense that would be broadly recognized within scholarly discussion. The cases all have a special concern to focus biblical interpretation around an overriding interest in what the Bible says about God, that is, how the text has been, can be, and even perhaps should be read with special reference to him. My own more precise analysis of the meaning of theological reading will come in due course.

The current discussion includes a whole range of different approaches, which makes it misleading to describe the debate using terms such as *movement*; such language could easily suggest it is unified by strong methodological or substantive commitments. For

[5] As I have said above, I offer this work as a systematic theological account of theological reading of the Bible. It is not an effort in phenomenology in any strong sense, though the theological description of reader and text is given from the point of view of Christian belief. In that way, it is thus, unavoidably, a book about the realities involved in reading as they appear within a certain perspective. Later in this chapter, in the section on the functions of theological discourse, I further distinguish my position on theological ontology from phenomenology.

instance, the glossary to a work considering how to marry theological and historical reading in a number of religious traditions defines theological exegesis as "a recent *movement* to recapture the theological relevance of Scripture for the church rather than focusing exclusively on historical-critical and other academic issues."[6] Perhaps this definition is trying, with the unfortunate word *movement*, to convey the intense level of energy surrounding the discussion of these issues.[7] Still, terms like *debate* or *discussion* are preferable because the phenomenon is so diffuse and varied. This brief explanation may also be misleading, were readers to construe it as claiming that the current discussion is *only* a recent phenomenon, one that does not connect to a long previous history of debate. At minimum, it is important to underline the variety of current thinking on this topic and even the conflict between genuinely different paradigms. It is possible to indicate some of the variety in the discussion with a brief mapping of key points of divergence within it and upon it.

First, theological reading can proceed in markedly different modes depending on the relative weight assigned to concepts and ideas that derive from within the Christian tradition vis-à-vis frameworks of thought drawn from the broader culture. For instance, Gordon Kaufman allows philosophical concepts and other contemporary modes of thought to have complete priority over the theological language which is the native tongue of the Christian church, such that the former displaces the latter whenever conflicts

[6] Marc Zvi Brettler, Peter Enns, and Daniel J. Harrington, *The Bible and the Believer: How to Read the Bible Critically and Religiously* (Oxford: Oxford University Press, 2012), 200; cf. 12. Emphasis added.

[7] The discussion is especially vigorous in English-speaking theology. For a few examples of discussions in German, see a loose collection of essays concerned with the openness of the biblical text to various sorts of reception: Stephen Chapman, Christine Helmer, and Christof Landmesser, eds., *Biblischer Text und theologische Theoriebildung*, Biblisch-theologishche Studien (Neukirchen-Vluyn: Neukirchener, 2001); and the more doctrinally focused reflections from a Roman Catholic point of view: Adel Théodore Khoury and Ludwig Muth, eds., *Glauben durch Lesen? Für eine christliche Lesekultur*, Quaestiones Disputatae (Freiburg: Herder, 1990).

occur. For Kaufman, the Bible is a special text in that its representations of God have wielded an unparalleled influence over Western culture for many centuries. The Bible is the text par excellence for the quest to discover the sources for our culture's thinking about the divine. This gives theological questions an undeniable importance in the interpretation of the Bible. Yet can a modern reader actually believe the things that the Bible says about God? Kaufman boldly and forthrightly answers in the negative, "Talk of God's historical activity cannot be made intelligible so long as, and in the respects that, we appropriate our experience and attempt to conceive our world (both nature and history) without reference to him. Our customary modes of thought – scientific, historical, philosophical – make no reference to God or his activity and seemingly find no need to do so."[8] He continues: "For a world totally secular (i.e., grasped entirely in this-worldly terms), God is dead,"[9] which is to say that a modern thinker cannot believe in God as he has traditionally been conceived. There is thus a direct clash between the way God is portrayed within the biblical text, on the one hand, and the way that reality is understood by modern forms of knowledge, on the other. The proper conclusion to draw, given the priority of the latter over the former, is that God does not exist: belief (in any traditional form) becomes literally unbelievable. This volume takes theological commitment much more seriously, not ceding entirely to secular disciplines the fundamental task of depicting all of reality, but allowing theology to play a key part in conversations about what reality is like, with the result that other forms of knowledge may be reshaped in light of theology's influence. Kaufman's approach to biblical interpretation is admirably clear and deeply thoughtful, but his first principles differ from the ideas at the heart of this book.

[8] Gordon D. Kaufman, "What Shall We Do with the Bible?," *Interpretation* 25 (1971): 110–11.

[9] Kaufman, "What Shall We Do with the Bible?," 111.

David Tracy, by contrast, insists that both the Christian-specific content of Scripture and the conceptuality of the reader's culture have a significant place within the interpretation of the Bible. On his view, which displays a significant debt to general hermeneutical theory, the text makes a theological claim to truth that arrests the attention of the reader. At the same time, the reader also comes to the text with a certain understanding of the questions the text addresses, a set of views delimiting the possibilities for how he might construe what the Bible says. Both the subject matter of the text and the reader's prior commitments are constitutive elements of interpretation, and neither has a clear priority over the other, such that it can dominate the practice of reading. Interpretation thus takes the form of a conversation between text and reader, in which both partners can question the views of the other. For Tracy, the task of biblical interpretation involves establishing "*mutually critical correlations* between an interpretation of the Christian tradition and an interpretation of the contemporary situation,"[10] so that "neither text nor interpreter, but only the conversation between both can rule."[11] Readings of the Bible have to be both fitting to the text and intelligible to the reader and his culture because scriptural interpretation is an ongoing negotiation between these two poles.[12] While no theologian can demur from the truth that all theology is marked by the context in which it originated, this book is not based on an in-principle commitment to give so much relative weight to whatever ideas are current in one's context. The strategy behind this version of theological reading is to invest heavily in the resources theology provides and to draw in ad hoc ways on other disciplines.

A recent collection of essays called the *Art of Reading Scripture*, which is the work of a group of scholars and pastors called the

[10] Robert M. Grant and David Tracy, *A Short History of the Interpretation of the Bible*, 2nd ed. (Minneapolis: Fortress, 1984), 170. Emphasis added.

[11] Ibid., 172.

[12] Ibid., 175–76.

"Scripture Project," gives a more determinative role to theological conceptuality in its account of interpretation. The collection opens with a frequently discussed set of theses providing parameters for theological interpretation,[13] the first of which gives biblical interpretation a definite theocentric aim by stating that the subject matter of the Bible is God's creation, judgment, and salvation of the world.[14] Most of the essays in the volume are written by authors who think forthrightly on the basis of a Christian theological framework, without an a priori commitment to correlate their beliefs with the broader culture,[15] or to allow the thought forms from outside the tradition to trump and reconstitute it. Indeed, some of the contributors are quite sanguine about utilizing resources found in ancient tracts of the Christian tradition to train readers today in the practice of biblical interpretation. According to the seventh thesis, "The saints of the church provide guidance in how to interpret and perform Scripture."[16] The volume is animated by the conviction that today's interpreters have a great deal to learn from their forebears, and there is little anxious hand-wringing about whether thinking with the tradition about the topic of biblical interpretation remains possible in the

[13] The Scripture Project, "Nine Theses on the Interpretation of Scripture," in *The Art of Reading Scripture*, ed. Ellen F. Davis and Richard B. Hays (Grand Rapids: Eerdmans, 2003), 1–5. Lewis Ayres develops a tenth thesis in his "The Soul and the Reading of Scripture: A Note on Henri de Lubac," *Scottish Journal of Theology* 61 (2008): 188–90. David F. Ford works a set of variations on all of the theses and contributes his own tenth principle in *Christian Wisdom: Desiring God and Learning in Love* (Cambridge: Cambridge University Press, 2007), 79–89.

[14] Scripture Project, "Nine Theses on the Interpretation of Scripture," 1.

[15] The collection is by no means monolithic, however. For instance, William Stacy Johnson expounds some key postmodern themes – opposition to foundationalism, skepticism toward metanarratives, and an orientation toward the other – and Christian doctrinal teachings with a view toward bring the two into harmony with each other. See his "Reading the Scriptures Faithfully in a Postmodern Age," in *The Art of Reading Scripture*, ed. Ellen F. Davis and Richard B. Hays (Grand Rapids: Eerdmans, 2003), 109–24.

[16] Scripture Project, "Nine Theses on the Interpretation of Scripture," 4.

contemporary world. The authors contributing to this volume write in conversation with various "others" from outside of the church (see thesis eight[17]), yet their contribution is framed as a helpful auxiliary, rather than as an utterly crucial resource for establishing the aim of interpretation or for determining which reading strategies are appropriate.

As this example and the previous two show, contemporary culture may subordinate itself to specifically Christian testimony (Scripture Project), or today's milieu may have a clear priority over biblical testimony (Kaufman), or the two can be brought together in an interplay where neither partner has a decided precedence over the other (Tracy). It will become clear as the introduction unfolds that the present work is closest in ethos to that of the Scripture Project, because of the role it affords theological language and because of the way its constructive proposal builds on past tracts of the Christian tradition.

The above authors are all examples of theological readers from a single community of faith, the Christian tradition, despite their divergent views on how the tradition should relate to the broader culture. A second distinction, then, which will provide further orientation to the current discussion, is between intrafaith and interfaith reading. There are now significant works that have come out of the discussion of Scriptural Reasoning, an interfaith venture in which Christians, Jews, and Muslims read and debate the implications of each other's scriptures. Scriptural Reasoning does not presume that distinct religious traditions – here the three major traditions that look back to Abraham as a leading figure – share a great deal of common ground below the surface of putative disagreements. Instead, Scriptural Reasoning revolves around an exploration and articulation of abiding differences, which are preserved in the respective scriptures of each tradition and in the

[17] Ibid., 4–5.

history of interpretation that forms the identity of those who read them.[18] In each session of Scriptural Reasoning, a small group selects a passage from the scripture of each tradition that speaks to a shared theme, and those gathered discuss how the texts are read within each tradition. As the three texts are ruminated over in turn, Scriptural Reasoners seek a deeper understanding of three things: their own traditions, which they can often see in sharper relief when they are compared to two others; the traditions of which they are not a part, and which they therefore may know less well than their own; and common goods that the traditions may work together to preserve or foster. Scriptural Reasoning manifests a special focus on God insofar as each tradition testifies to God and the form of life that God requires, and each tradition opens itself up to receiving insights about God from the others taking part in the discussion.

This book is primarily concerned with the reading practices of a single tradition, so it is an intrafaith endeavor, not an interfaith one; it is a work about biblical reasoning, not Scriptural Reasoning. Yet it nevertheless contributes in its own manner, and on a modest scale, to the work of understanding that Scriptural Reasoning sponsors.

[18] There is no single definitive account of Scriptural Reasoning, and none is likely to be forthcoming, given the overall de-emphasis on theory among the leading lights of Scriptural Reasoning, and given that many different practitioners have their own accounts of the practice, none of which seeks to dominate how all others view the evolving operation of the practice. For a succinct and quite probing interpretation, see Nicholas Adams, *Habermas and Theology* (Cambridge: Cambridge University Press, 2006), 239–55. Other programmatic statements include the Jewish, Muslim, and Christian perspectives collected in David F. Ford and C. C. Pecknold, eds., *The Promise of Scriptural Reasoning* (Oxford: Blackwell, 2006); Tom Greggs, *Theology against Religion: Constructive Dialogues with Bonhoeffer and Barth* (London: T. & T. Clark, 2011), 196–216. Insights from a couple of other important works by Peter Ochs have helped to shape Scriptural Reasoning, though they are not accounts of the practice itself: *Peirce, Pragmatism, and the Logic of Scripture* (Cambridge: Cambridge University Press, 2004); Peter Ochs, ed., *The Return of Scripture in Judaism and Christianity: Essays in Postcritical Scriptural Interpretation* (New York: Paulist, 1993).

Scriptural Reasoning involves what has insightfully been called "the making explicit of 'deep reasoning'"[19] or "making deep reasonings public."[20] This refers to the rehearsal by members of each tradition of their tradition's history of interpretation of the passages under consideration for the sake of the others gathered. Adherents of each tradition articulate their own community's history of encounter with, and arguments over the sense of, a scriptural passage, as an expression of their own communal identity, and as an explanation of their tradition to the gathered outsiders. Discussion usually takes a concrete form, and revolves around historically important chains of exegetical reasoning about texts, rather than focusing on more formal and abstract issues, such as the logics and rules that govern such reasoning.[21] For instance, the Nicene Creed of 325 CE and the documents that influenced its formulation preserve the Christian church's "deep reasoning" about the status of Jesus Christ, and the church's conclusion that he is of the "same substance" as God the Father. Scriptural Reasoning discussions usually center on the history of exegesis (asking how specific interpreters read particular texts), rather than hermeneutics (dealing with the system of exegetical rules they employed), while this work concentrates on the latter. Yet insofar as the two categories relate closely – the rules govern practice and practice embodies rules – shedding light on the logic of Christian reading is a complementary way of expounding to a religious other how Christian reading takes place. This work seeks to illuminate methods of reading and the commitments that generate them, and thereby opens up a window onto the working of one of the traditions involved in Scriptural Reasoning. Though it does not bring a plurality of traditions into conversation, this book's exposition of hermeneutical theory works in concord with the more

[19] Adams, *Habermas and Theology*, 241.

[20] Nicholas Adams, "Making Deep Reasonings Public," *Modern Theology* 22 (2006): 398–400.

[21] Adams, *Habermas and Theology*, 242.

concrete focus of Scriptural Reasoning in shedding light on a tradition by using reading as a lens.

A third distinction worth registering about the current discussion is that the debate itself can be construed either quite narrowly or more broadly. A narrower approach would focus only on works that identify themselves explicitly as efforts at theological exegesis, such as biblical commentaries published in series dedicated specifically to theological interpretation. Most of the major English-language theological publishers now have a commentary series with a focus that is in some way theological, either by having systematic theologians engage with the Bible, or by having biblical scholars give concerted attention to theological questions that emerge from the text, or some combination.[22] Monograph series, journals, and reference works devoted to theological reading would also qualify according to this narrow view.[23] However, thinking about this issue exclusively with reference to material that owns the label *theological reading*, or some equivalent, obscures the long history of debate

[22] R. Michael Allen and Scott Swain, eds., *T. & T. Clark International Theological Commentary* (London: T. & T. Clark, 2016–); Joel B. Green and Max Turner, eds., *The Two Horizons New Testament Commentary* (Grand Rapids: Eerdmans, 2005–); J. Gordon McConville and Craig Bartholomew, eds., *The Two Horizons Old Testament Commentary* (Grand Rapids: Eerdmans, 2008–); William C. Placher and Amy Plantinga Pauw, eds., *Belief: A Theological Commentary* (Louisville: Westminster John Knox, 2010–); R. R. Reno, ed., *Brazos Theological Commentary on the Bible* (Grand Rapids: Brazos, 2005–); C. L. Seow, ed., *Illuminations* (Grand Rapids: Eerdmans, 2013–).

[23] Craig G. Bartholomew, Joel Green, and Christopher R. Seitz, eds., *Studies in Theological Interpretation* (Grand Rapids: Baker, 2006); *Ex auditu: An International Journal for Theological Interpretation of Scripture*; *Journal of Theological Interpretation*; *Jahrbuch für biblische Theologie*; Kevin J. Vanhoozer et al., *Dictionary for Theological Interpretation of the Bible* (Grand Rapids: Baker, 2005). There is also a collaborative manifesto, though there is some variety within the essays included, a number of which contain significant insights: Craig G. Bartholomew and Heath A. Thomas, eds., *A Manifesto for Theological Interpretation* (Grand Rapids: Baker, 2016).

about the role of theological belief in biblical interpretation,[24] and it rules out a great deal of valuable work dealing with the same issues.[25] The idea that this is the primary or only way to think about theological reading owes a great deal to aggressive marketing campaigns by certain publishers. Discussions of theological reading have seldom been at their best when there come to be roll calls for TISers, those who are affiliated with a so-called theological interpretation of Scripture movement, or those who operate as if there is a trademark after the phrase TIS.[26] Because of the value of material to be found outside of our own milieu, and of works generally unconcerned with labels, this work does not restrict itself to engaging with theological reading narrowly construed.

Considering the discussion from a wider, more flexible perspective entails including, in addition to the sort of work already mentioned, the whole range of ways in which theologians frame their own constructive theological proposals on exegetical grounds, and biblical scholars give serious attention to what the Bible says about God.[27] A broader take on the discussion would also embrace historical studies on the interplay between theological convictions

[24] For selected highlights in the history of the discussion, see the range of texts collected in Darren Sarisky, ed., *Theology, History, and Biblical Interpretation: Modern Readings* (London: T. & T. Clark, 2015).

[25] There are other book series that are well worth noting in this connection. For instance, see James D. G. Dunn, ed., *New Testament Theology* (Cambridge: Cambridge University Press, 1991–2003). And there are other reference works: Samuel E. Balentine, ed., *The Oxford Encyclopedia of the Bible and Theology*, 2 vols, The Oxford Encyclopedias of the Bible (Oxford: Oxford University Press, 2015).

[26] I owe the trademark idea to conversation with Markus Bockmuehl.

[27] Among theologians, see especially Oliver Davies, *The Creativity of God: World, Eucharist, Reason*, Cambridge Studies in Christian Doctrine (Cambridge: Cambridge University Press, 2004); Ford, *Christian Wisdom*; David F. Ford, *John's Gospel Now*, Bampton Lectures (Oxford: Bampton Trust, 2015); David H. Kelsey, *Eccentric Existence: A Theological Anthropology*, 2 vols. (Louisville: Westminster John Knox, 2009); Friedrich Mildenberger, *Biblische Dogmatik: Eine biblische Theologie in dogmatischer Perspektive*, 3 vols. (Stuttgart: W. Kohlhammer, 1991–1993); Susannah Ticciati, *Job and the Disruption of Identity: Reading Beyond Barth* (London: T. & T. Clark International,

and biblical interpretation in the history of interpretation. It is important to acknowledge the significance of the broad conception of theological reading, because the way that the theological reading debate has altered the landscape of whole fields of research is what most powerfully demonstrates the importance of the discussion. It is in this connection that Miroslav Volf comments that contemporary interest in theological reading constitutes the single most significant theological development in the last two decades.[28] It has contributed to the softening of disciplinary boundaries, especially between systematic theology and biblical studies, and it has provoked historians to appreciate more fully the Bible's role as a text with unparalleled influence in the theological tradition. The present work attempts a focused task, offering an account of the nature of theological reading, but it does so by entering into conversation with texts from other historical periods as well as with several theologians and some biblical scholars, most of whom are blithely unaware of where they stand in relation to a supposed movement.[29]

2005); Susannah Ticciati, *Job and the Disruption of Identity: Reading Beyond Barth* (London: T. & T. Clark International, 2005); Michael Welker, *God the Spirit* (Minneapolis: Fortress, 1994). There is also an illuminating collection of essays by established theologians, most of whom are British, reflecting on how the Bible factors into their theological work: Angus Paddison, ed., *Theologians on Scripture* (London: Bloomsbury T. & T. Clark, 2016).

Among scholars of the Bible, there are too many works to name individually, but some of the leading recent efforts come from authors such as Gary Anderson, John Barclay, Richard Bauckham, Ellen Davis, Richard Hays, Larry Hurtado, R. W. L. Moberly, Marianne Meye Thompson, Francis Watson, and N. T. Wright. Because of just how much it straddles disciplinary divisions, synthesizing biblical texts under the topical headings of traditional systematic theology, specific mention should be made of Dale B. Martin, *Biblical Truths: The Meaning of Scripture in the Twenty-First Century* (New Haven: Yale University Press, 2017).

28 Miroslav Volf, "Reading the Bible Theologically," in *Captive to the Word of God: Engaging the Scriptures for Contemporary Reflection* (Grand Rapids: Eerdmans, 2010), 14. This essay includes a bibliography I have found useful in working on this chapter.

29 If the discussion of theological reading is to continue to develop and mature, it will surely need to engage increasingly with practices of interpretation that originate from

## Literature on the Nature of Theological Interpretation

Theological reading in its many forms – explicitly so-called or not, intrafaith or interfaith, primarily deferential to the ecclesial tradition or more indebted to philosophy in the broadest possible sense – constitutes a significant discussion in theology and biblical interpretation today, and there is some literature that addresses the fundamental query of what theological reading actually is. Sometimes this literature aims mainly to describe the current state of play, thus providing an explanation of what a certain set of instances of theological r5eading, such as those surveyed above, have in common. More often, the goal is to put forth recommendations about the form theological reading should take and the grounds for this. It is possible to find comments about what theological interpretation is in short works, such as reference works, critical reviews of commentaries, chapters in edited volumes, and journal articles.[30]

outside the established Western tradition. In this connection, Michael J. Gorman's new collection is noteworthy for the way that it brings the current discussion of theological reading into dialogue with voices from other parts of the world: *Scripture and Its Interpretation: A Global, Ecumenical Introduction to the Bible* (Grand Rapids: Baker, 2017). Also important in this connection is Bungishabaku Katho, "Idolatry and the Peril of the Nation: Reading Jeremiah 2 in an African Context," *Anglican Theological Review* 99 (2017): 713–28. The whole discussion of theological reading takes place against the background of modern curricular divisions that position theology and biblical studies in different compartments. This arrangement for teaching and research is a modern Western phenomenon, so to some extent the debate is framed as a set of reflections on and reactions to what currently exists in the West. But it is certainly the case that thinking spurred by the curricular structure of the West will be greatly enriched by taking into account views from others outside the West as well as marginalized voices within the Western tradition.

30 Here is a selective list of some especially insightful essays from Protestant, Roman Catholic, and Orthodox authors: Lewis Ayres, "The Word Answering the Word: Opening the Space of Catholic Biblical Interpretation," in *Theological Theology: Essays in Honour of John Webster*, ed. R. David Nelson, Darren Sarisky, and Justin Stratis (London: Bloomsbury T. & T. Clark, 2015), 37–53; Brevard S. Childs, "Toward Recovering Theological Exegesis," *Ex auditu* 16 (2000): 121–29; Richard B. Hays, "Reading the Bible with Eyes of Faith: The Practice of Theological Exegesis," *Journal*

It is also possible to find perceptive reflection on this topic in works that are concerned primarily with other subjects.[31] There are, in addition, textbooks that introduce students to the debate by

*of Theological Interpretation* 1 (2007): 5–21; Kaufman, "What Shall We Do with the Bible?," 95–112; George Lindbeck, "The Story-Shaped Church: Critical Exegesis and Theological Interpretation," in *Scriptural Authority and Narrative Interpretation*, ed. Garrett Green (Philadelphia: Fortress, 1987), 161–78; Andrew Louth, "Inspiration of the Scriptures," *Sobornost* 9 (2009): 29–44; R. W. L. Moberly, "What Is Theological Interpretation of Scripture?," *Journal of Theological Interpretation* 3 (2009): 161–78; Angus Paddison, "Who and What Is Theological Interpretation For?," in *Conception, Reception and the Spirit: Essays in Honor of Andrew T. Lincoln*, ed. J. Gordon McConville and Lloyd Pietersen (Eugene: Cascade, 2015), 210–23; Stanley E. Porter, "What Exactly Is Theological Interpretation of Scripture, and Is It Hermeneutically Robust Enough for the Task to Which It Has Been Appointed?," in *Horizons in Hermeneutics: A Festschrift in Honor of Anthony C. Thiselton*, ed. Stanley E. Porter and Matthew R. Malcolm (Grand Rapids: Eerdmans, 2013), 234–67; Francis Schüssler Fiorenza, "The Crisis of Scriptural Authority: Interpretation and Reception," *Interpretation* 44 (1990): 353–68; David Tracy, "On Reading Scripture Theologically," in *Theology and Dialogue: Essays in Conversation with George Lindbeck*, ed. Bruce Marshall (Notre Dame: University of Notre Dame Press, 1990), 35–68; Kevin J. Vanhoozer, "Theological Commentary and the 'Voice from Heaven': Exegesis, Ontology, and the Travail of Biblical Interpretation," in *On the Writing of New Testament Commentaries: Festschrift for Grant R. Osborne on the Occasion of His 70th Birthday*, ed. Stanley E. Porter and Eckhard J. Schnabel, Texts and Editions for New Testament Study (Leiden: Brill, 2013), 269–97; Volf, "Reading the Bible Theologically," 3–40.

It is also worth consulting a couple of pieces that critically review an early theological commentary and consider the wider question of the nature of the genre: Brian E. Daley, "The Acts and Christian Confession: Finding the Start of the Dogmatic Tradition," *Pro Ecclesia* 16 (2007): 18–25; C. Kavin Rowe and Richard B. Hays, "What Is a Theological Commentary?," *Pro Ecclesia* 16 (2007): 26–32.

31 Ford, *Christian Wisdom*, 52–89. There is an account of reading canonical holy Scripture laid out with extraordinary analytical power in Kelsey, *Eccentric Existence*, 1: 132–56. See also the explication of the Eucharistic hermeneutic in Jean-Luc Marion, *God without Being: Hors-Texte* (Chicago: University of Chicago Press, 1991), 139–58. There is a chapter on theological interpretation in a text on how the Bible is taught within institutions dedicated to theological training in Dale B. Martin, *Pedagogy of the Bible: An Analysis and Proposal* (Louisville: Westminster John Knox, 2008), 71–91. In addition, see the exposition of "depth exegesis" in Thomas F. Torrance, *The Christian Doctrine of God: One Being, Three Persons* (Edinburgh: T. & T. Clark, 1996), 32–72. A text that has already been mentioned is a history of the interpretation of the Bible

summing it up in an illuminating way.[32] There are also monographs that treat related issues, for instance what it might mean to undertake a theological reading of non-biblical texts, such as literary, philosophical, and even legal writing.[33] And, of course, there is a whole literature that questions the legitimacy of claiming that theological commitments might shape reading in positive ways.[34]

which ends with a constructive proposal on theological reading: Grant and Tracy, *A Short History*, 167–87. There is a brief treatment of "biblical reasoning" in Kevin J. Vanhoozer, *Remythologizing Theology: Divine Action, Passion, and Authorship*, Cambridge Studies in Christian Doctrine (Cambridge: Cambridge University Press, 2010), 187–94. What Nicholas Wolterstorff calls the second hermeneutic – seeking to appropriate the divine discourse from the mediating human discourse of the Bible, to which it is not identical – is another way of speaking about theological reading: *Divine Discourse: Philosophical Reflections on the Claim That God Speaks* (Cambridge: Cambridge University Press, 1995), 202–22.

[32] J. Todd Billings, *The Word of God for the People of God: An Entryway to the Theological Interpretation of Scripture* (Grand Rapids: Eerdmans, 2010); Christopher Bryan, *Listening to the Bible: The Art of Faithful Biblical Interpretation* (Oxford: Oxford University Press, 2014); Stephen E. Fowl, *Theological Interpretation of Scripture*, Cascade Companions (Eugene: Cascade, 2009); Daniel J. Treier, *Introducing Theological Interpretation of Scripture: Recovering a Christian Practice* (Grand Rapids: Baker, 2008); Scott R. Swain, *Trinity, Revelation, and Reading: A Theological Introduction to the Bible and Its Interpretation* (London: T. & T. Clark, 2011). See also a text which envisions all of theology as funded by theological reading: Kevin J. Vanhoozer and Daniel J. Treier, *Theology and the Mirror of Scripture: A Mere Evangelical Account*, Studies in Christian Doctrine and Scripture (London: Apollos, 2016).

[33] Alan Jacobs, *A Theology of Reading: The Hermeneutics of Love* (Boulder: Westview, 2001). More distantly related to the topic at hand, there is a monograph on how, over the course of history, Christian theology shaped the canon of Western literature: David L. Jeffrey, *People of the Book: Christian Identity and Literary Culture* (Grand Rapids: Eerdmans, 1996).

[34] The basic criticism that theological commitment should have no role in interpretation is quite common, especially among certain biblical scholars. For example, James Barr pointedly criticizes those who advocate a version of theological reading that allows faith commitment to do anything more than foster empathy with the material content of the Bible. See, for instance, the culminating work of his career: *The Concept of Biblical Theology: An Old Testament Perspective* (Minneapolis: Fortress, 1999), 189–208. John Barton sums up succinctly the familiar criticism that theological reading amounts essentially to eisegesis, an illegitimate projection of one's views onto the text

Yet most of the material dealing directly with theological reading, seeking to expound and defend it, comes in brief form. There is room for a more expansive consideration of what theological

of Scripture: *The Nature of Biblical Criticism* (Louisville: Westminster John Knox, 2007), 137–86. For a focused and sharp polemic against Richard Hays's summary account of theological exegesis, see Joachim Schaper, "Historical Criticism, 'Theological Exegesis,' and Theology amongst the Humanities," in *Theology, University, Humanities: Initium Sapientiae Timor Domini*, ed. Christopher Craig Brittain and Francesca Aran Murphy (Eugene: Wipf and Stock, 2011), 75–90. Philip Davies advocates a mode of reading that declines to take its bearings from the Bible itself, and he finds fault with those he feels have been seduced by the Bible's rhetoric and have adopted its point of view, yet have draped themselves with the historian's mantle: "Two Nations, One Womb," in *Whose Bible Is It Anyway?* (London: T. & T. Clark, 2004), 17–55. For Robert Oden, the residual influence of theological belief within biblical scholarship inevitably leads to making value judgments on the material studied, and blocks efforts at fair comparative studies of the Bible and other literature: *The Bible without Theology: The Theological Tradition and Alternatives to It* (Urbana: University of Illinois Press, 2000). As a final example, Heikki Räisänen provides a running critique of those whose interpretive work he sees as warped by an inclination to synthesize diverse passages into a uniform whole, or by the related inability on the part of readers to differentiate between the content of texts and their own theological views: *Beyond New Testament Theology: A Story and a Programme*, 2nd ed. (London: SCM Press, 2000); *Neutestamentliche Theologie? Eine religionswissenschaftliche Alternative*, Stuttgarter Bibelstudien (Stuttgart: Katholisches Bibelwerk, 2000).

Other biblical scholars have been both sympathetic and critical of theological reading. In a recent essay, Markus Bockmuehl asks probing questions about what theological reading is and whether it has anything of value to offer: "Bible Versus Theology: Is 'Theological Interpretation' the Answer?," *Nova et Vetera* 9 (2011): 27–37. This essay guards against excesses in the current debate, thus supplementing and qualifying the more positive discussion in his *Seeing the Word: Refocusing New Testament Study*, Studies in Theological Interpretation (Grand Rapids: Baker, 2006). One finds a combination of sympathy toward many of the root motivations behind theological reading and intemperate ranting on a whole range of subjects, both ancient and modern, not least the present state of the theological interpretation discussion itself, in D. A. Carson, "Theological Interpretation of Scripture: Yes, But. . .," in *Theological Commentary: Evangelical Perspectives*, ed. R. Michael Allen (London: T. & T. Clark, 2011), 187–207.

If every translation is a sort of interpretation – and surely that is the case – then perhaps David Bentley Hart's fresh rendering of the New Testament belongs with those works above which reject the idea of doctrine rightly playing any role in interpretation. As he describes his aim, Hart seeks to translate from Greek into English

interpretation is. Recently, calls have appeared for greater clarity on this topic.[35]

Alongside the material just mentioned, there are monographs that deal with questions in the vicinity of what theological reading is, but in these works analysis of interpretive practices proceeds via relatively generic categories, rather than by the theological terms that structure the practice of reading from the point of view of its practitioners.[36] In these texts, the primary operative categories

without advancing "any theological or ideological agenda," though he concedes that he can only approach this goal asymptotically; he wants to "capture in English as much of the suggestiveness and uncertainty and mystery of the original Greek as possible, precisely in order to prevent any prior set of commitments from determining for the reader in advance what it is that the text *must* say (even when it does not)." See the concluding reaffirmation of his purpose statement in *The New Testament: A Translation* (New Haven: Yale University Press, 2017), 577. While Hart forcefully opposes the use of some commonplace Western doctrines, seeing them as distorting lenses, he clearly wants to do more than to remove particular doctrines he considers impediments. He is verging on a categorical rejection of doctrine per se as useful in interpretation. The claim that theology should not affect interpretation does not cohere in an obvious way with one of his earlier lectures on biblical interpretation: "The Second Naiveté? Allegorical and Critical Readings of Scripture" (paper presented at the Christian Scholars' Conference, Pepperdine University, 2011), www.youtube.com/watch?v=EOShHXaqtoM. The promise to deliver an unprecedentedly transparent view on the original text is sure to draw a great deal of attention to the book, whether or not readers actually find there something that matches the promotional rhetoric.

35 For instance, Markus Bockmuehl, "Introduction," in *Scripture's Doctrine and Theology's Bible: How the New Testament Shapes Christian Dogmatics*, ed. Markus Bockmuehl and Alan J. Torrance (Grand Rapids: Baker, 2008), 7–13. Bockmuehl places his own edited volume within this wider discussion and rightly claims that the book contributes to it, but he notes (again, correctly) that much remains to be done.

36 Paul J. Griffiths, *Religious Reading: The Place of Reading in the Practice of Religion* (Oxford: Oxford University Press, 1999); John B. Henderson, *Scripture, Canon, and Commentary: A Comparison of Confucian and Western Exegesis* (Princeton: Princeton University Press, 1991); Wesley A. Kort, *Take, Read: Scripture, Textuality, and Cultural Practice* (University Park: Pennsylvania State University Press, 1996). A book that stands somewhere between a textbook and a monograph, and that expounds theological interpretation by leaning heavily on a theory of religion is Morgan and Barton, *Biblical Interpretation.*

come from religious studies, and are intended to encompass multiple traditions under universal headings, or from literary studies, and so are even more distant from theology.[37] These are substantial works, from which any reader is bound to glean a great deal: my own debt to them will be obvious to anyone who reads the footnotes of this book. Work in this area shines a light on what is distinctive about reading within a set of religious traditions, and what unifies these practices over against approaches that lack a religious grounding. However, attempting to describe the nature of a tradition-specific practice on its own terms is a subtly different endeavor from attempting to coordinate this practice with those of genuinely different religious traditions; it is a third distinguishable endeavor to limit the depiction of one tradition or multiple traditions to categories culled from outside the sphere of religious traditions altogether. If one inquires about the nature of theological exegesis and then develops an answer that does not use theological categories, one is "changing the subject"[38] rather than actually answering the question precisely as posed. This work proceeds on the assumption that the Christian tradition has, within itself, resources that shed light on its own practices, and that this interpretive practice can be expounded on its own terms in an illuminating way. It builds on insights from neighboring disciplines, but does not limit itself to dialoguing with them. What is needed is an analytical account of just this sort which is developed at the length of a monograph. This book proposes to develop an account

[37] A partial exception, a monograph in which theology becomes a bit more operative, is Klaas Huizing, *Homo legens: Vom Ursprung der Theologie im Lesen*, Theologische Bibliothek Töpelmann (Berlin: W. de Gruyter, 1996). The work is, essentially, a Reformed account of Scripture inflected through Derrida, Levinas, Ricoeur, and other contemporary philosophers: because of heavy reliance on philosophy, the deployment of traditional theological categories is a negotiated and not untrammeled one.

[38] Donald Davidson, "Mental Events," in *Essays on Actions and Events* (Oxford: Clarendon Press, 1980), 216.

of theological exegesis on the basis of its "immanent meanings – that is, in terms of the meanings immanent in the religious language of whose use the text [i.e., the Bible] is a paradigmatic instance."[39] The book's primary query is: What is Christian theological interpretation of Scripture?[40] Answering precisely that question requires recourse to theology.

A final category of literature consists of a few books dealing with the interpretation of the Bible from a more theological angle: these works are theological in a certain sense, but they might be more deeply theological.[41] Something else is needed here, in part because the most recent of these texts is almost two decades old, and the

[39] George Lindbeck, *The Nature of Doctrine: Religion and Theology in a Postliberal Age*, 25th anniversary ed. (Louisville: Westminster John Knox, 2009), 102.

[40] Cf. works that focus on the form that biblical interpretation takes within the Jewish tradition: Michael A. Fishbane, *Biblical Interpretation in Ancient Israel* (Oxford: Clarendon Press, 1985); Jon D. Levenson, *The Hebrew Bible, the Old Testament, and Historical Criticism: Jews and Christians in Biblical Studies* (Louisville: Westminster John Knox, 1993); Benjamin D. Sommer, "Dialogical Biblical Theology: A Jewish Approach to Reading Scripture Theologically," in *Biblical Theology: Introducing the Conversation*, ed. Leo G. Perdue, Robert Morgan, and Benjamin D. Sommer, Library of Biblical Theology (Nashville: Abingdon, 2009), 25–48. Many of the pertinent issues are explored in a novel about a young Jewish student who wrestles with the tensions between his community's habits of textual interpretation and practices that do not take his communal location for granted: Chaim Potok, *In the Beginning* (New York: Fawcett/Ballantine, 1997).

[41] See R. W. L. Moberly, *The Bible, Theology, and Faith: A Study of Abraham and Jesus*, Cambridge Studies in Christian Doctrine (Cambridge: Cambridge University Press, 2000); Elisabeth Schüssler Fiorenza, *Bread Not Stone: The Challenge of Feminist Biblical Interpretation* (Edinburgh: T. & T. Clark, 1990); Stephen E. Fowl, *Engaging Scripture: A Model for Theological Interpretation* (Oxford: Blackwell, 1998); Sandra M. Schneiders, *The Revelatory Text: Interpreting the New Testament as Sacred Scripture*, 2nd ed. (Collegeville: Liturgical Press, 1999). Moberly's book exemplifies theological reading through a set of case studies, and he articulates the theocentric hermeneutical principles that hold together his sample interpretations. This book is, however, stronger in setting forth examples of actual readings – certainly something valuable in itself, at which few are better than Moberly – than it is in articulating a unified account of what theological reading is.

discussion going on in the background has moved forward in that period of time. More importantly, though, theology's role is limited in these works. To consider one example, for Elisabeth Schüssler Fiorenza, theological reading of the Bible is about interpreting the text not *as* revelation, or even as *conveying* it without exception, but *in relation to it*, for revelation is located first and foremost in the experience of communities struggling to achieve equality, and the task of interpretation is to promote rather than encumber the quest for freedom.[42] On this view, the text must be read with reference to God, not because it is understood according to a theological ontology, but because it is a foundational text with enduring power in contemporary communities, one whose influence will necessarily be oppressive if it is not reclaimed for the purpose of liberation.[43] The text shapes community life in a salutary way when interpreters read it to render liberating images of the divine and of human response to God. On this view, theological language depicts the purpose of interpretation, though not the object being interpreted (or for that matter the interpreting subject[44]). Social and political coefficients are basic to describing the realities involved in interpretation. Theological terms enter in at a later stage, once the overall trajectory of the account has already been set. Thus, theology does not perform the task that is most basic to the account of theological reading, namely, offering description of the realities involved. It does not do all it potentially can do. Furthermore, while the goal of liberation is surely important, Schüssler Fiorenza's approach is not the only means by which to achieve it. Sandra Schneiders and Stephen Fowl come closer to offering theological description at this

[42] Schüssler Fiorenza, *Bread Not Stone*, xi, 1, 60, 140.

[43] Ibid., xvi.

[44] See, for instance, the account of human salvation in ibid., 13–14.

basic level, but neither entirely achieves it.[45] This is therefore a lacuna in the discussion.[46]

In light of what is missing from the current discussion, a promising way to consider the nature of theological interpretation is to inquire into the difference it makes to have in place a resolutely theological description of the realities involved in reading. If theology depicts who the reader is and what the text is, how would that change what happens when the reader encounters the text? If theological commitment is built into how the process of reading is understood at this very basic level, how should the reader's engagement with the text proceed? How does it affect exegesis? Exegesis of scriptural texts means providing interpretation or analysis of them that allows readers to access their sense.[47] That is to say, exegesis allows interpreters to read biblical texts and understand what they say. Does theological belief change how readers access the text's sense (exegesis in a narrow sense)? Or does it affect how they understand and evaluate the text's meaning, or how they make use of it (exegesis in a broader sense[48])? This book's way of pursuing

[45] Schneiders structures her account around a notion of the text, as the title of her book suggests, but the reader enters into the total picture as well. See her *The Revelatory Text*, 3. What keeps her work from being more deeply theological is that the main outlines of the account are set by phenomenological theory, with theological concepts fitted into an overall structure that is determined on other grounds. For an analysis of Stephen Fowl's view, see the next section of this chapter.

[46] The role of theological language has been addressed at essay length in the following works: Brian E. Daley, "'In Many and Various Ways': Towards a Theology of Theological Exegesis," *Modern Theology* 28 (2012): 597–615; Donald Wood, "The Place of Theology in Theological Hermeneutics," *International Journal of Systematic Theology* 4 (2002): 156–71.

[47] Throughout the course of this book, I use the terms exegesis and interpretation interchangeably. Thus I intend for *theological exegesis* and *theological interpretation* to be essentially synonymous.

[48] There exist differences of opinion about whether this second set of activities qualifies as exegesis or whether it falls outside its scope. For a view according to which it is artificial to create a division between application and the supposedly prior phases of interpretation, see Hans Georg Gadamer, *Truth and Method*, 2nd ed. (London:

what theological interpretation is, is to consider this query. In this way, the book takes forward a key question that emerges from the current debate. There is ultimately a programmatic or normative thrust to the argument this book proffers. The book makes a case that a certain set of faith commitments brings with it implications for reading, but the argument is not merely conditional in form: if a reader believes a set of things *x*, hermeneutic *y* is the consequence of these beliefs when taken together. Because the antecedents of the conditional are also affirmed, the hermeneutical consequences of the faith commitments are of logical necessity espoused as well. For this reason, the book is about how reading *ought* to take place, though it certainly builds on a good deal of descriptive work en route to propounding this position.

As I said in the preface, the question on which this book centers will be of interest to different readers for different reasons. For those who read the Bible with a faith commitment of some sort, exploring this question will present them with an opportunity to examine the logic of their own beliefs, or how the theological premises of this account of reading might bear interesting analogies to their own fundamental commitments. Those who read in faith will thus find that they have a personal resonance with the argument, on some level at least. Others will construe the case presented here differently, as the unpacking of the rationale for an interpretive practice that is foreign to them, however much it informs the reading of a large percentage of those who regularly engage with the Bible. For readers in this second group, the present proposal will still deal essentially with the logic of faith commitments, but nothing in their own framework of beliefs will be identical with or analogous to those beliefs. Even for readers without faith, this book

Continuum, 2004), 306–10. For the beginning of an attempt to maintain stricter divisions, see Friedrich Schleiermacher, *Hermeneutics: The Handwritten Manuscripts, Texts and Translation* (Missoula: Scholars, 1977), 1. My own usage of the term *exegesis* accords with the broader sense.

presents an opportunity for understanding – not for self-understanding, but for understanding the thought and practice of others. These readers will need imaginatively to project themselves into a framework of thinking and reading that is not their own, so that they can come to terms with it and appreciate how it operates. Yet once they have done so, they are well-placed to reach a verdict on whether the faith commitments under discussion here make the difference the book claims they make for reading. They are fully able to evaluate the internal coherence of the position this book stakes out and to understand the conditional aspect of the argument, even if they are not persuaded of the legitimacy of the faith position with which the argument commences.

## The Functions of Theological Discourse

To make clear what is involved in allowing theology to describe the realities involved in reading,[49] it will prove illuminating to sketch a miniature typology of positions on the relationship between theology and the Bible. The typology offers analysis and comparison of four distinct positions. Its modest scale will make it entirely clear that the classificatory scheme does not aim to provide a comprehensive survey of all of the contemporary scene's competing views on theology and the Bible. It therefore does not count as an objection against it that it does not offer a slot in which any given current type of reading would comfortably fit. Readers seeking more comprehensive mappings are directed to the relevant literature.[50] This typology's purpose is primarily to bring out the distinctiveness and

[49] The two realities with which this book is mainly concerned are the reader and the text. The book is not trying to develop a general theological ontology of *all* things, though the aim of doctrine in one of the types below is to reach toward comprehensive description using theological categories.

[50] See especially Hans Frei's classic typology of five different views on the relationship between theology and philosophy and the implications of the first three for

contribution of the final position: its uniqueness stands out in sharp relief when seen in relation to the other views. In other words, this exposition charts out three influential trajectories that are tellingly different from the one this book develops and elaborates, and then it gives an outline of that way forward.

## *Theology as Passive in Relation to Biblical Interpretation*

First, theology might be passive insofar as it does not play an integral role in any exegetical argument. If a biblical passage is theologically substantive, which is to say that it says something about God or may shape theological belief at least indirectly, then a proper reading of such a text explicates that theology, but theological commitment on the part of the reader is not necessary in order for that explication properly to take place. Interest in theological issues can stimulate the reader to ask theological questions of the text, and a modest level of empathy with the text will facilitate grasping its subject matter, but this does not require the reader's assent to the text's claims. Readers themselves need not believe in order properly to describe the beliefs of others. Theology is essentially passive in the sense that it is what receives interpretive

approaches to Scripture: *Types of Christian Theology* (New Haven: Yale University Press, 1992), 56–69. There are also more recent works worth consulting. Daniel J. Treier offers two types of orientations, the first of which relates theological interpretation to biblical theology: "Biblical Theology and/or Theological Interpretation of Scripture?," *Scottish Journal of Theology* 61 (2008): 16–31; the second describes the role of ecclesiology in the thinking of several major figures: "What Is Theological Interpretation? An Ecclesiological Reduction," *International Journal of Systematic Theology* 12 (2010): 144–61. On the tendency among theologians and biblical scholars to stress *either* the divine *or* human element of the Bible and its interpretation, see Mark Alan Bowald, *Rendering the Word in Theological Hermeneutics: Mapping Divine and Human Agency* (Aldershot: Ashgate, 2007). Finally, a more popular-level charting of a range of positions on history's place within interpretation is Edward W. Klink and Darian R. Lockett, *Understanding Biblical Theology: A Comparison of Theory and Practice* (Grand Rapids: Zondervan, 2012).

description, just as when a passive verb is employed, the subject receives the action of the verb.

James Barr, a scholar of the Hebrew Bible/Old Testament, provides an example of this first way of relating theology and the Bible. In the inaugural lecture for his Oriel chair at the University of Oxford, he aims to set out what he tellingly calls an "inner philosophy . . . of modern biblical study,"[51] distinguishing two ways that theology can be used in this context. In the first sense, theology refers to statements of personal faith, such as a believer's affirmation that "God is love," or that one should confess that God is love. Theology can, however, take a more straightforwardly and purely descriptive form, one that Barr sees as a direct report on the textual data of the Bible. In this second sense, theology includes any statement of the following form: whoever wrote the words of 1 John 4:8 *thought* that God is love. In this latter sense, theology does not speak forthrightly of God, but is essentially concerned with describing the subjectivity of a human being, that is, what the author of a biblical text thought, or what he tried to express in his writing. So, in the first sense, theology means statements of personal faith, while in sense two it refers to depictions of the faith or religious practices of others.

Having made this distinction, Barr contends that theological commitment (theology in the first sense) is not necessary to elucidate the content of theological texts (theology in the second sense).[52] Successfully describing a text's theology can be done by those with or without a faith commitment, since the critical interpretations that a reader offers – the reasoned arguments which conclude that a text should be read in a certain way – do not include any reference one way or another to what the reader

[51] James Barr, "Does Biblical Study Still Belong to Theology?," in *Bible and Interpretation: The Collected Essays of James Barr*, ed. John Barton, Vol. I: Interpretation and Theology (Oxford: Oxford University Press, 2013), 8.

[52] Ibid., 10.

affirms.[53] Exegetical arguments do not include as any part of their grounds the subjective state of the interpreters who proffer them, whether they affirm or deny belief in God. Interpretive reasoning keys on the relevant facets of the text itself – such as its grammatical, lexical, and literary features and its historical backdrop – and contends for construing these features (and these features alone) as together giving the text a certain meaning.

Theology does not enter directly and explicitly into the articulation of a critical exegesis on this view, and neither does it influence exegetical arguments by serving as an underlying presupposition of the argument. This is not to say that readers will not hold theological presuppositions – many who read the Bible will indeed have an allegiance to some form or other of theology. Yet this is only a psychological or biographical fact about readers, for their presuppositions exert no normative force to steer the course of their exegetical reasoning about how to construe the sense of a biblical text. Barr says: "Presuppositional criticism is essentially negative. It can help us to understand how and why certain wrong turns in the discipline have taken place; it does not tell us how to do it [i.e., to read the Bible] rightly."[54] In other words, by identifying a reader's presuppositions, one can criticize his argument by showing where a conclusion is really coming from, that is, the reader's

[53] For more on the structure of arguments, the warrants used within them, and the impossibility of the affirmations of a faith tradition serving as starting points for reasoning, see Van Harvey, *The Historian and the Believer: The Morality of Historical Knowledge and Christian Belief* (New York: Macmillan, 1966), 43–54; Tracy, *Blessed Rage for Order*, 6–7.

In using *critical* simply in the sense of reasoned, I do not use the term in the sense it is employed in the frequently cited essay by David C. Steinmetz, "The Superiority of Pre-Critical Exegesis," in *Taking the Long View: Christian Theology in Historical Perspective* (Oxford: Oxford University Press, 2011), 3–14. In that essay, critical exegesis is the basic form of interpretation that became prominent around the Enlightenment. Thus, in my usage, an uncritical exegesis would simply be an assertion of an exegetical judgment without any defense of it.

[54] Barr, "Does Biblical Study Still Belong to Theology?," 14.

theological viewpoint, rather than the text itself. However even at a subterranean level, in the form of presupposition, theological belief does not have a more positive role to play: "it does not tell us how to do it rightly."

Reasoned interpretations of Scripture will operate on the basis of other sorts of presuppositions, for instance assumptions about how language works or about the course of history.[55] These sorts of commitments are built into exegetical reasoning at a deep level, even though they often remain tacit. The situation with theological belief is different though, and what is crucial about theological assumptions is not that they pressure reading in a certain direction, but that a reader is willing to reform her presuppositions in the light of what the text actually says. "The theological fruitfulness of exegesis derives not from the existence of theological presuppositions but from the liveliness of the impact of the text upon these presuppositions."[56] At the level of presupposition, theology is passive in the sense that theological belief ought to respond to exegetical results, while it ought not influence what those results come to be. Theological belief does not have normative force within a piece of critical exegesis of the Bible either at the level of being an explicitly stated element of the case for a certain reading, or by serving as an implicit assumption of such reasoning.

That theology is essentially passive in the work of exegesis has two corollaries. First, it means that, with respect to the exegetical task, theological belief is privatized. A reader's theological allegiance, or disbelief in any established form of theology, does not

[55] Barr's first book encourages biblical scholars to appropriate the insights that modern linguistics makes available to them, and chides those whose interpretations do not take these advances into account: *The Semantics of Biblical Language* (Oxford: Oxford University Press, 1961).

[56] James Barr, "Exegesis as a Theological Discipline Reconsidered, and the Shadow of the Jesus of History," in *Bible and Interpretation: The Collected Essays of James Barr*, ed. John Barton. Vol. I: Interpretation and Theology (Oxford: Oxford University Press, 2013), 130.

enter into the discourse about how rightly to read a passage of the Bible, and should therefore remain one's own business, respected as the reader's deeply held convictions, but not pertinent to the task at hand. As Barr has it:

> Inherited denominational theological attitudes are manifest among scholars and are not to be deprecated or disparaged. But what scholars have found is that, in the actual work of biblical scholarship, though these attitudes are present and perhaps both necessary and creative, they cannot be logically determinative. You can't say, this interpretation is right because I am a Presbyterian and I know what is right. You may think it, but you can't say it.[57]

Second, because exegesis is not driven, influenced, or shaped by the interpreter's religious outlook – or at least theological factors do not make an exegetical argument any stronger than it already is on other grounds – reasoned interpretations about the sense of a passage can attain a relatively high degree of objectivity. It may not prove possible to eliminate biases entirely, but it is possible to eliminate their influence on exegetical work to a significant degree, one approximating complete success, and the interpreter should always strive to attain that goal as fully as possible. As Barr says, "It is true that complete objectivity is not attainable, but a high degree of objectivity is attainable, and a high degree of it is very much better than a low degree."[58]

What should one make of this view? It is certainly right to stress that readers should by no means make texts into mouthpieces for their presupposed theological viewpoints. The history of exegesis contains far too many examples of theology, in the sense of a reader's own commitment, running roughshod over the process of

[57] James Barr, "Biblical Scholarship and the Unity of the Church," in *Bible and Interpretation: The Collected Essays of James Barr*, ed. John Barton. Vol. I: Interpretation and Theology (Oxford: Oxford University Press, 2013), 22.

[58] Barr, "Does Biblical Study Still Belong to Theology?," 11.

explicating the text's theological content.[59] However, Barr portrays theology (in sense one) as essentially a mode of human subjectivity,[60] and this is unduly restrictive. It narrows the scope of theology to claim, "'Believing' is what religious people basically do," for this reduces "religion in general to a subjective concept in (other) people's minds."[61] This book explores the idea that theology might play an altogether different role by depicting what the Bible and its reader are. Such a move would reorient reading by having consequences for its overall course, with the key to the whole account being a construal of theology as something more than simply a mode of human subjectivity. What if theology played a comparatively active role in reading, this time not by making its presence felt in an obvious way, as a stated premise in an argument, or even as a presupposition, but instead much deeper down, as part of a framework that structures the overall practice of reading?[62] Following through on these suggestions would fundamentally alter the character of the relationship between theology and Scripture. It would hardly be felicitous to call this alternative view an inner philosophy of biblical interpretation; at least its primary categories would not be generic ones. It would be more apt, rather, to say that such an option takes its cue from a theological perspective on scriptural interpretation. These issues recur in what follows. At any rate, the first point in this typology is now in place.

[59] I explore this point in greater depth in the Conclusion of this book.

[60] See his comment about human relations in Barr, "Does Biblical Study Still Belong to Theology?," 10.

[61] Wilfred Cantwell Smith, *What Is Scripture? A Comparative Approach* (London: SCM Press, 1993), 223.

[62] There are times when Barr comes close to portraying theology as active in reading, but even when he does so, it is less in ascertaining meaning where theology has a crucial role than in reflecting on the content of the text within the parameters of the post-biblical theological tradition ("The Bible as a Document of Believing Communities," in *Bible and Interpretation: The Collected Essays of James Barr*, ed. John Barton. Vol. I: Interpretation and Theology [Oxford: Oxford University Press, 2013] 61; "Exegesis as a Theological Discipline Reconsidered," 137).

*Theology as Active in Relation to Biblical Interpretation, Version 1*

For the next three points of the typology, theological discourse becomes active in biblical interpretation. Here, theological language has not gone "on holiday,"[63] nor is it "like an engine idling,"[64] as opposed to when it is doing work. For each point, though, theological discourse relates to the Bible in a distinguishable way.

The second position focuses on a view of interpretation that sees the Bible's effective history (*Wirkungsgeschichte*) as utterly crucial to its interpretation. While those who insist that doctrine must remain passive think that "understanding is possible only if one keeps oneself out of play,"[65] that is not the aim here: stressing the effective history of the Bible means that the text is conceived as a work that reaches out beyond its circumstances of origin via the impact it has had on the reader's current context, which influence in turn shapes the reader's first-hand engagement with the text. There is, thus, for this second position not a binary relationship between the text and the interpreter. Instead, the two are seen as interpenetrating one another: the text is in the reader via its history of effects shaping her and her situation, and the reader is also in the text in that there is no such thing as an explication of the text that prescinds entirely from questions about how the text may come to bear on the reader. When the text in question is the Bible, breaking down the dualism between interpreting subject and the object to be understood tends toward making doctrine active, for the reader is involved in some way with the content of the Bible. Yet doctrinal belief is conceived here as a species of a reader's particularity, an imprint on his thinking that marks him out as an individual of a certain background. This construal of doctrine highlights how beliefs or commitments distinguish one human being from another,

[63] Ludwig Wittgenstein, *Philosophische Untersuchungen = Philosophical Investigations*, Rev. 4th ed. (Chichester: Wiley-Blackwell, 2009), 23e.

[64] Wittgenstein, *Philosophical Investigations*, 56e.

[65] Gadamer, *Truth and Method*, 330. Gadamer here describes a view he does not support.

and therefore how reading is not an utterly generic practice that all human beings undertake in the same way, arriving at identical results. This conceptualizes doctrine in a fundamentally mundane way.

Doctrine does not, on this view, define what either the reader or the text actually are. For this reason, it is entirely fair for Ulrich Luz to say, "My approach . . . does not contain the hidden agenda of a special 'sacred hermeneutic.'"[66] Instead, the basic terms that characterize the interpreter and the Bible are ones that Luz borrows from the hermeneutics of Gadamer, though the critical appropriation is inevitably Luz's own.[67] As has already been suggested briefly, the Bible, or for that matter any classic text – one with a noteworthy history of effects – is not well suited to being analyzed by a reader who holds the text at a distance, as if it could be read with reference only to the life it first had in the past, and without any concern for its present pertinence.[68] Any classic text, as such, does in fact have an influence over the reader's language, thinking, patterns of action, and historical situation. In its history of effects, the text reaches out and envelops the reader. This is especially true for interpreters who live in Western culture, where the Bible has exercised a deep shaping influence for millennia. For their part, readers are seen as subjects whose patterns of language and thought, and whose situation in history, put an imprint on any interpretive question they ask regarding the Bible. The inseparability of explication and application does not mean that whatever the text urges readers to do is something that becomes obligatory for them, but rather that their background factors into reading and

[66] Ulrich Luz, "Reflections on the Appropriate Interpretation of New Testament Texts," in *Studies in Matthew* (Grand Rapids: Eerdmans, 2005), 270.

[67] Luz's debt to Gadamer is deep, but the New Testament scholar explains how he differs at points from Gadamer: "Hermeneutics of 'Effective History' and the Church," in *Studies in Matthew* (Grand Rapids: Eerdmans, 2005), 351–52.

[68] Ulrich Luz, "The Significance of Matthew's Jesus Story for Today," in *Studies in Matthew* (Grand Rapids: Eerdmans, 2005), 373.

ought to be brought to explicit consciousness as much as possible.[69] History is, thus, like a river which carries a passenger on a journey in a boat. The passenger in the vessel can make observations about the river, but whether she does so or not, she is carried forward by its current, moved this way and that.[70] Explaining the illustration of history's power, Luz says, "Whatever we say about the biblical texts presupposes that we already have a relationship with them – directly, because we already know, love, or hate them; or indirectly, because we take part in a culture dominated by Christianity and speak a language formed by the Bible."[71]

While the text and reader are, at their most basic level, thought of in phenomenological rather than doctrinal terms, this conception of their relationship does allow doctrine to come into play in interpretation. For type two, *all* of the reader's particularities count within interpretation. This is because it is not only the text that is historically situated; so is the reader. Luz comments: "The epistemological significance of Gadamer's concept of 'effective history' lies for me in the fact that it gives the human being back to history."[72] The way in which textual meaning is perceived by readers is a function of the text itself, of course, and the text has a relative stability, but it is also a product of the location of the reader, whether man or woman, worker or professional, African, American, or European.[73] Religious affiliation is not excluded from this list of particularities. Readers who are members of a religious tradition interpret differently, whether they realize it or not, by virtue of their location within their specific community. They should not conceal this aspect of their

[69] Luz, "Reflections on the Appropriate Interpretation of New Testament Texts," 273.

[70] Ulrich Luz, *Matthew in History: Interpretation, Influence, and Effects* (Minneapolis: Fortress, 2007), 25.

[71] Ibid., 25.

[72] Ulrich Luz, "Can the Bible Still Be the Foundation for a Church Today? The Task of Exegesis in a Society of Religious Pluralism," in *Studies in Matthew* (Grand Rapids: Eerdmans, 2005), 325.

[73] Luz, *Matthew in History*, 26.

identity from themselves or others, but ought to bring it to consciousness,[74] so as to be able to assess how it influences them, and they should read in dialogue with others who bring their own distinctive preconceptions to the task of reading.

Because doctrine is conceived as being of a piece with other aspects of our "personal, cultural, and political situations,"[75] it functions within reading in at least two major ways. Readers' commitments, beliefs, and interests shape the interpretive queries that they put to the text, thus driving them to focus on certain aspects of the text more than others, and conditioning how those focal features are understood. Being part of a certain religious tradition can sensitize readers to aspects of a biblical passage that other readers may miss. Perhaps an example will help here. According to Luz's research, it was only in the Greek Orthodox tradition that interpreters of Matthew's story of the transfiguration (17:1–13) were able to perceive that the disciples actually participate in the vision of Jesus' glory on the mountain.[76] For the Orthodox, the transfiguration is observed as one of the great annual festivals of the church, in which participants proceed liturgically with Jesus, as it were, onto the mountain, only to return to day-to-day existence thereafter.[77] Perhaps it is because of taking part in this practice that interpreters from this tradition were able to see in the text things that others failed to see, especially if they were preoccupied with other concerns, such as whether the narrated events really took place and could be verified as historical. There are also instances where confessional allegiance can make it more difficult, rather than easier, to see certain things that are present in the text.[78]

[74] Luz does just this in the opening chapter of his constructive synthesis of hermeneutical theory: *Theologische Hermeneutik des Neuen Testaments* (Neukirchen-Vluyn: Neukirchener Theologie, 2014), 1–28.

[75] Luz, *Matthew in History*, 30.

[76] Ibid., 32.

[77] Ibid., 32.

[78] Ibid., 31.

In either case, the reader's theological particularity has efficacy by pushing interpretation toward or away from certain conclusions. The dynamics of effective history are explored through the entire text of Matthew in Luz's magisterial three-volume commentary on the Gospel text.[79]

Construing theological belief as an aspect of selfhood, even as a deep and ineradicable part of the human person that reflects the subject's historical inheritance and connects a single individual with others in both the past and present, makes it seem rather less than what most believers consider it to be. At one level, of course, belief simply is an aspect of the self, and holding too tightly to one's own views can impede growth and a broadening of horizons. Yet claiming that doctrine is *essentially* a form of the particularization of subjectivity and indeed intersubjectivity shortchanges the believer's own sense that these beliefs give him a purchase on reality and provide him with a sense of transcendence. This book aims to approach theological belief in the way that believing communities do, thinking in solidarity with the self-interpreters of Christianity, and thus developing a hermeneutic of restoration.[80] It recognizes that of course not all readers approach belief in this way, but the aim of this particular project is to base itself on an articulation of theology's role that takes theological commitment on its own terms, rather than transposing it into a register determined by generic explanatory language. In light of that goal, linking doctrine and interpretation in the way that this position does seems to miss something, though it certainly counts as an advance for doctrine to be acknowledged as playing an often positive role in reading. What is needed is a clearer sense that doctrine can enter into how

[79] Ulrich Luz, *Matthew: A Commentary*, 3 vols. Hermeneia: A Critical and Historical Commentary on the Bible (Minneapolis: Fortress, 2001, 2005, 2007).

[80] I owe the term *restoration* to Paul Ricoeur, *Freud and Philosophy: An Essay on Interpretation*, The Terry Lectures (New Haven: Yale University Press, 1970), 28–36; this source also contains a discussion of the value of suspicion.

the hermeneutical situation itself is construed; on the view just reviewed, that situation is described by phenomenology, which allows doctrine to become a factor only at a later stage.

### *Theology as Active in Relation to Biblical Interpretation, Version 2*

Doctrine is active once again for the third view, though what drives this viewpoint is not a phenomenology of classic texts in general, but the ecclesial location of reading Scripture. Here, the particularities of the reader's identity have relevance because discrete acts of interpretation, or actual exegetical judgments about how to construe passages, relate to the ongoing life of the Christian community. To state the matter more formally: "Given the ends toward which Christians interpret their scripture, Christian interpretation of scripture needs to involve a complex interaction in which Christian convictions, practices, and concerns are brought to bear on scriptural interpretation in ways that both shape that interpretation and are shaped by it."[81] That convictions, practices, and beliefs both shape reading and are shaped by it is a summary of Stephen Fowl's program of reading. There is not a detailed set of rules that prescribe a priori how the life of the community ought to relate to reading, but rather a firm insistence that the two belong together, as well as a sense of buoyant optimism that the actual interactions that take place in the community are, in fact, salutary ones. Fowl declines to lift himself out of the domain where ecclesial practices influence theological reflection in order to judge these interactions, for his hermeneutical ideal is precisely that of an engaged form of exegetical rationality. There is a complex diachronic dialectic between interpretation and practices, which means interpreters ought to trust the way in which ecclesial location forms them and disposes them to apply the Bible to genuinely Christian ends. That

[81] Fowl, *Engaging Scripture*, 8.

is, past interpretation of the Bible has influenced the practices that constitute church life at present, and in which the reader is immersed by virtue of being part of an ecclesial body. In turn, these practices shape and direct the reader's present interpretive endeavors. Yet certain ecclesial practices were written into the original interpretation as well, though these practices never existed apart from generating interpretation. In general, reading should never ground itself in the absence of practice and beliefs, nor should practices and beliefs find a justification for themselves that cuts them off from the influence of the text. The ideal is a continuing reciprocity between practices and reading.[82]

Neither this view nor position two aspires to fulfill the ideal of disengaged reason. For the second position, underscoring the location of the reader within history is of a piece with acknowledging that there are no truly universal, ahistorical canons of rationality applicable to all interpreters. On the third view, disengaged rationality is not the norm because theological beliefs can and indeed should factor into interpretative deliberations in the church. They can enter directly into critical exegetical reflection on how to read texts, and this rules out simple appeals to objectivity in adjudicating exegetical disputes.[83] For position three, it is not just that it is de facto impossible for interpreters to detach themselves from their religious convictions and predispositions for the sake of developing an objective rendering of the sense of the text, though they should attempt this, and can expect to achieve a significant measure of success, as on the first view. Rather, all reasoning, including all

[82] See his comments about the rule of faith as an example of this: Fowl, *Engaging Scripture*, 7–8; Stephen E. Fowl, "Theological and Ideological Strategies of Biblical Interpretation," in *Scripture: An Ecumenical Introduction to the Bible and Its Interpretation*, ed. Michael J. Gorman (Peabody: Hendrickson, 2005), 169–71.

[83] It is because Fowl disallows a theory of textual meaning to have hegemony over the practice of reading that he can give this scope to specifically Christian beliefs and practices. See the explication of "underdetermined" interpretation in Fowl, *Engaging Scripture*, 56–61.

deliberation about how to interpret biblical texts, is caught within and conditioned by the projects and purposes of interpreters and their communities.[84] Reflection on interpretation is always engaged with these sorts of concerns. There is no such thing as exegesis tout court, and "*the* interpretation does not exist";[85] there are only various species of exegesis with a definite end in view. Christian readers should seek to be deeply, fully, and openly Christian in their interpretive work, rather than claiming a neutrality that actually masks the ends for which they read.

An example of the interplay between practices and interpretation will serve to illustrate this view. Fowl commends to present-day Christian readers the example set by the apostles in the book of Acts: their practice of befriending Gentiles allowed them to discern the work of the Spirit within a community from which they had presumed God to be permanently absent. This practice-driven judgment, that God actually was present among the Gentiles in the power of the Spirit, catalyzed a whole new reading of the Old Testament's portrayal of non-Jewish people. The practice of befriending Gentiles thus made possible a revolution in reading, one that did not take the original intent of the authors of the Old Testament texts as its guiding criterion.[86] Refusing to make scholarly objectivity an ultimate value may seem to be a high cost for this approach to pay. However, the driving motivation behind this decision is to keep the Christian practice of interpretation from being forced into a mold it was never meant to fit. Something more than the Old Testament read according to its original sense was

[84] Ibid. 56–58. Fowl makes clear his significant debt to Jeffrey Stout, "What Is the Meaning of a Text?," *New Literary History* 14 (1982): 1–12.

[85] Wolfgang Iser, *The Range of Interpretation*, The Wellek Library Lecture Series (New York: Columbia University Press, 2000), 7.

[86] Fowl, *Engaging Scripture*, 97–127. There is a similar, and indeed even greater, stress on the efficacy of church practices in Stanley Hauerwas, *Unleashing the Scripture: Freeing the Bible from Captivity to America* (Nashville: Abingdon, 1993); Stanley Hauerwas, *Matthew* (Grand Rapids: Brazos, 2006).

needed to authorize the Jews to reach out to and include the Gentiles within their community. And if this additional necessary element is actually trammeled by the search for historical intention, it follows that intention should be less than ultimate.[87]

There is, to be sure, virtue in this position, which constitutes the third locus of the typology. Relating theology and biblical interpretation in this way, so as to define a specifically Christian style of reading, blocks any appeal to a general theory as a means to ground a specifically Christian approach in an encompassing view of textuality, readers, and readerly activity that purports to be a universal epistemic criterion. Thus, theological exegesis is not constrained by a generic, theology-free framework that serves as its model or standard. Fowl effectively prohibits general categories from coming to dominate an account of reading. When this problem happens, theology is necessarily marginalized because its categories are tradition-specific. Sidelining theology hardly seems to be the way to frame an account of theological exegesis, and Fowl has taken care to ensure that this dynamic does not occur in his own work, which is to his great credit.

The concern has to do, once again, with the implied understanding of the nature and task of theology. For this position, relating theology and biblical interpretation means making a judgment about whether specific interpretive arguments should admit and incorporate the reader's identity as a member of a religious community. The first position provides a nice contrast: from this point of view, such concerns are, strictly speaking, irrelevant to the task at hand. Readers may confess Christian beliefs or they may not, and they may perform certain practices or they may not. Neither of these things are operative within an exegesis that seeks the text's historical

[87] For much more extended examples of Fowl's exegesis, see his recent commentaries: *Philippians*, The Two Horizons New Testament Commentary (Grand Rapids: Eerdmans, 2005); *Ephesians: A Commentary*, The New Testament Library (Louisville: Westminster John Knox, 2012). Fowl explains clearly the ways in which the commentaries are shaped by theological concerns: see especially *Philippians*, 1–8; and also *Ephesians*, 2.

sense, so this whole category of concerns can be bracketed out of consideration – and indeed it must be bracketed out, lest it warp exegetical work. The third position deems it necessary to bring together what the first position holds apart; for position three, this is necessary, not to grasp meaning qua historical intention, but for the sake of securing the text's role within the process of Christian discipleship. Yet if theology is to provide an understanding of God and of all things in relation to him, then theology might perform a fundamentally different task than it does here, which is to offer an analysis of the beliefs, aims, and ritual devotion of the ecclesial community. Whether or not doctrines intend to refer to reality is a critical issue, one that has generated a great deal of discussion regarding the sources that inform and shape Fowl's position.[88] However these sources are read, that Fowl declines in practice, at least in his influential monograph on theological reading, to use doctrinal language to provide an account of the Bible or the interpreting subject does little to dispel doubts about whether doctrine might in principle be used for this purpose on Fowl's view.[89]

88 A key figure influencing Fowl's operative view of doctrine is George Lindbeck. See his reflection on religion and truth in Lindbeck, *The Nature of Doctrine*, 49–55. For a compelling interpretation of Lindbeck as seeing first-order theological statements by individuals as making truth claims, see Bruce Marshall, "Aquinas as Postliberal Theologian," *Thomist* 53 (1989): 357–70. On the other hand, for a nuanced and equally persuasive case for a countervailing point, that official church doctrinal statements, or second-order statements, do not make such claims straightforwardly in Lindbeck, see Reinhard Hütter, *Suffering Divine Things: Theology as Church Practice* (Grand Rapids: Eerdmans, 2000), 52–59.

89 For brief and not entirely convincing comments on the interpretation of Lindbeck, see Fowl, *Engaging Scripture*, 24. See also the functional view of the Bible in ibid., 3–6. There is more about the nature of Scripture in Stephen E. Fowl, "Scripture," in *The Oxford Handbook of Systematic Theology*, ed. John Webster, Kathryn Tanner, and Ian Torrance (Oxford: Oxford University Press, 2007), 345–61; Fowl, *Theological Interpretation of Scripture*, 1–12. See the comments in the following section on this slightly more evolved position. I discuss *Engaging Scripture* here because of its abiding presence in the current debate, because Fowl's new position is not as fully developed as the one he articulates in his monograph, and because the purpose of this typology is

A whole different way for theology to be active in relation to interpretation would be for it to provide a dense characterization of the nature of the subject and object involved in reading, that is, the reader and the biblical text. Though his position shifts a bit later, at least in *Engaging Scripture*, Fowl has a theological perspective on *how* the text functions, or the way in which it is *used* in the church, but not on what the text actually *is*. Nor does he use theological language to sketch the nature and end of the reader of Scripture, though he does often discuss the various aims and purposes that readers may have. The concise summary he offers of his view begins with the phrase, "given the ends toward which Christians interpret their scripture,"[90] but nowhere does Fowl indicate that interpretive aims are implications of a theological consideration of the situation of the reader. He is clear that general theories should not so control how the Bible is read that theological and church-practical considerations can have no influence on interpretation's course. What is missing is a clear sense that theology depicts the nature of the realities that interact in the practice of reading, together with the implication that theology might set reading's overall aim.[91] This silence is a pregnant one: because of this, it is unclear how the doctrines and practices that are brought to bear on the Bible have norms or limits. Where do they come from, and to which criteria of adequacy are they answerable? These criteria need not be ones that cramp Christian confession if they are generated by a specifically Christian ontology.

In one respect, this book's proposal builds on that of Fowl, which has an unquestionable importance within the current debate; however, it departs from his view in an important respect. It is crucial

ultimately to provide conceptual clarification of the fourth view by contrasting it with other options that are clearly distinct from it, not to give comprehensive coverage of the current scene. For my purposes, *Engaging Scripture* is still *the* book by Fowl.

90 Fowl, *Engaging Scripture*, 8.

91 My interpretation of Fowl is reinforced by Wood, "The Place of Theology in Theological Hermeneutics," 164–65.

that substance comes first for this position on the typology. Substance is prior in that there never takes place an interpretive operation on the text of the Bible that is uninfluenced by the reader's doctrinal commitments and the religious practices that shape her. (To say that substance comes first does not mean that it is more important than interpretive practices, only that reading never occurs without the reader already having been influenced by substantive commitments. As indicated above, the aim of establishing a dialectic means that there is not a clear ultimate priority for either reading, on the one hand, or doctrine and practice on the other.) For the proposal that this book advances, substance is also first in that interpretation takes its cue from an allegiance to definite theological content. The key difference is that the constructive position of this work takes theological ontology as its starting point and infers interpretive norms from this, rather than seeing the reading community's aims and purposes as freestanding, or perhaps worth crediting because the church is taken to be basically on track. Starting with ontology marks a real difference from saying, "Good commentary is whatever serves our interests and purposes,"[92] with the intent of using *our* to refer to the ecclesial community, and thereby allowing commentary to answer to no higher norm than the aims of this particular association. The goal of this book is not to put substance first in some generic way, but to put it first by basing the whole constructive proposal around theological ontology. This brings the discussion to expanding on theological ontology in the final point of the typology.

### *Theology as Active in Relation to Biblical Interpretation, Version 3*

Theology is here, once again, active in the interpretive process. However, now theology is not, in the first instance, related to

[92] Stout, "What Is the Meaning of a Text?," 6.

specific interpretive decisions about how to handle certain texts, though as a corollary theological commitment has a bearing on reading. Its primary role is, rather, to provide a theological depiction of what is involved in reading, with the text itself being the most obvious place to begin. Here theology does not just say *whose* text Scripture is, or *how* it functions within the Christian community, but *what* the text is.[93] This fourth position is thus best termed theological ontology, for it relates theology and biblical interpretation by having theology describe those things that are involved in interpretation.[94] Though ontology might be considered a philosophical term, it is employed here to describe the crucial work that theology does in depicting reality, and it would therefore be implausible to claim that it gives this view a philosophical rather than theological character.

This reflects a different vision of theology than we have seen previously. Thomas Aquinas is an example of a theologian who sees doctrine working essentially to provide a description of all that exists in relation to God. He writes, "Now all things are dealt with in holy teaching in terms of God (*sub ratione Dei*), either because they are God himself or because they are relative to him as their origin and end."[95] Thomas has a theological ontology, that is, a description of the nature of things that employs theological categories to do descriptive work by referring to God as that on which the relevant entities depend for their existence, and the one in relation

[93] The single most powerful extended statement of a functional view is David H. Kelsey, *Proving Doctrine: The Uses of Scripture in Modern Theology* (Harrisburg: Trinity Press International, 1999). A concise and updated version of the same, which draws significantly on the work of Fowl, is to be found in Kelsey, *Eccentric Existence*, 1: 132–56.

[94] My usage of theological ontology closely tracks John Webster's employment of the term *metaphysics*: "Resurrection and Scripture," in *The Domain of the Word: Scripture and Theological Reason* (London: Bloomsbury T. & T. Clark, 2013), 33.

[95] Thomas Aquinas, *Summa Theologiae*, Vol. I: Christian Theology (Ia. I) (Cambridge: Cambridge University Press, 2006), 26–27.

to whom these things have their purpose.[96] Theological ontology is in play when descriptions of reality employ, rather than suspend, theological discourse. Within this fourth type, it is not assumed that any particular doctrinal arrangement is necessarily true, but that the purpose of theological language is to describe reality in a veridical manner. That is, theological language at least makes claims to truth. What is requisite for this point on the typology, minimally, is viewing existing things so as to presuppose the existence of God and to build divine reality into the definition of the items in question: not by reducing God to a mere ingredient in the essence of another thing, but by making reference to the one who transcends all else, and on whom all else is contingent, part of a full description of an existing thing. Applying a theological ontology to existing realities frustrates all attempts to settle on a fixed and simple description of them, for it is the incomprehensible God in light of whom these things are seen.[97]

An example we might consider is Jean-Luc Marion, who operates with a theological ontology of Scripture in his account of theological reading. Now, at first glance it may seem exceedingly odd to claim that Marion is working with an ontology of any sort, for he is outspokenly critical of ontologies that might confine God within

[96] My use of *theological ontology* is not far from what Hans Boersma calls "sacramental ontology": *Nouvelle Théologie and Sacramental Ontology: A Return to Mystery* (Oxford: Oxford University Press, 2009), 4–9. Both my terminology and Boersma's reflect a desire to integrate "natural" and "supernatural" by denying that they represent fundamentally autonomous realms.

[97] Speaking of created things in light of God assumes that God can in some sense be known. Inhabiting this final position on the typology thus implicitly challenges the critique that God cannot be an object of knowledge at all. For useful responses to Immanuel Kant's version of this critique, and some discussion of its meaning, see Karl Barth, *Protestant Theology in the Nineteenth Century: Its Background & History* (London: SCM Press, 1972), 266–312; Alvin Plantinga, *Warranted Christian Belief* (Oxford: Oxford University Press, 2000), 3–30; Nicholas Wolterstorff, "Is It Possible and Desirable for Theologians to Recover from Kant?," *Modern Theology* 14 (1998): 1–18.

human categories. This provides an opportunity to clarify what ontology means in this book. What concerns Marion is ontology as a general theory of what it means to exist, for he thinks that such grand visions risk construing God as one existing entity among others, thereby squeezing him into a preexisting framework of representation so as to bring it to closure. Ontology in this sense corresponds to the notorious "defaming criterion of ontotheology."[98] My sense of *theological* ontology does not refer to what it means to be real as such, but indicates that something is being asserted about what is contingently real, namely, that it cannot be understood without reference to God. A theological ontology is thus a view of something as real in which the item in question is seen in light of God – though, again, God's existence is by no means restricted to being just a component part within an account of said item. God is not reduced in this way because making reference to him by thinking of created things in relation to him, and thus invoking his immanence, does not stand in tension with divine transcendence: by virtue of being creator, God exists in a noncontrastive relationship with the world of finite things.[99] He is not one being among many others, albeit one that allows for a complete description of finite objects, such as the text of the Bible, since he does not exist in the same order of discrete objects. That they are contingent realities, while he is necessary, means that they depend on him for their very existence, while he neither depends on them, nor is reduced in his otherness by being present to them as something in light of which they can be seen. If this study seems fundamentally nonplussed by pressure from critiques of ontotheology to relegate theology to its place of origin, rather than acceding

[98] Paul Ricoeur, "From Interpretation to Translation," in *Thinking Biblically: Exegetical and Hermeneutical Studies*, ed. André Lacocque and Paul Ricoeur (Chicago: University of Chicago Press, 1998), 356.

[99] Kathryn Tanner, *God and Creation in Christian Theology: Tyranny or Empowerment?* (Oxford: Basil Blackwell, 1988), 37–48.

to its more universalizing drive[100] – for the present work involves theology in its account of what is real – that is because of research concluding that major figures from the Christian tradition have often been read poorly by those advancing the critique.[101] The point about the non-contrastive relationship between God and the world is regularly missed.[102]

This clarification brings us back to Marion more directly. What allows him to fit into the theological ontology type is simply that he has a view of what Scripture is that makes reference to God. For him, the text is a *signum* pointing to Jesus Christ, a set of written words that directs attention to the Word made flesh: because Jesus is the *verbum Dei*, seeing the text as a pointer to the incarnate Word is a genuinely theological ontology. To utilize Marion's memorable image, the coming of Jesus Christ left traces on the text in the same way that a nuclear blast leaves burns and shadows on a wall.[103] The text is by no means identical with the event to which it testifies, which is itself the focus of ultimate concern, nor does it even, by

[100] See Ricoeur, "From Interpretation to Translation," 357.

[101] See Ibid., 355–61. In addition, see David Bentley Hart, who rightly says that the late Heidegger does not understand well the difference between God and creation in the theologies he targets: *The Beauty of the Infinite: The Aesthetics of Christian Truth* (Grand Rapids: Eerdmans, 2003), 183–84. For his part, Marion eventually came to realize that Thomas Aquinas does not actually fall into the problems typically associated with ontotheology. See "Thomas Aquinas and Onto-Theo-Logy," in *Mystics: Presence and Aporia*, ed. Michael Kessler and Christian Sheppard, Religion and Postmodernism (Chicago: University of Chicago Press, 2003), 38–74. For references to further relevant literature on ontotheology, see Sarisky, *Scriptural Interpretation*, 23–27.

[102] It is not just that certain philosophers have failed to become as deeply acquainted with the tradition of classical Christian theology as they should have been in order to mount a successful critique of it. It is also true that modern theology has often not operated with a non-contrastive understanding of God's relationship to the world. See Tanner, *God and Creation in Christian Theology*, 121–22. Thus, if this non-contrastive view is correct, theology must take some of the blame for portraying things as lining up with the terms of the ontotheological critique.

[103] Marion, *God without Being*, 145.

itself, permit a reader actually to encounter the event; it does, however, provide crucial indicators that gesture toward it and bring it to the reader's attention. If the text *is* a sign directing its reader toward the *Logos*, then it follows that reading can only properly proceed in one way. A purely literary reading of a divine sign cannot be adequate, for "literature dispenses with having recourse to an event in order to find its referent in that event."[104] Exclusively literary readings dispense with considering the event, but a theological reading should relate sign and referent to one another. More specifically: "The theologian must go beyond the text to the Word, interpreting it from the point of view of the Word."[105] How does this occur? Marion's account takes a traditionally Roman Catholic turn as he makes the divine disclosure at the Eucharist hermeneutically crucial. While the text alone does not suffice in order to access the Word, the privileged disclosure of the Word occurs at the Eucharist, which confers an anticipatory understanding of the referent (the Word) on readers, in light of which the text of Scripture can then be reread.[106] If all of this recalls Luke 24 and the disciples' epiphany there, followed as it was by a new ability to discern signs of Jesus in the Old Testament, that is exactly as it should be.[107] Christian worship services are weekly replays of the disciples' experience on the road to Emmaus.

There is tremendous promise in theological ontology and indeed of an ontology of the text specifically, for this way of conceiving of theology takes belief on its own terms, declining to transpose it into a different idiom. The problem here is that Marion's account has an artificially narrow focus on the text alone. To state the point more

104 Ibid., 146.

105 Ibid., 149.

106 Ibid., 149–52.

107 Ibid., 149–52. In this connection, see Marion's theologically sensitive reading of Luke's Gospel: "'They Recognized Him; and He Became Invisible to Them'," *Modern Theology* 18 (2002): 145–52.

fully and accurately: keying an account of reading to the text alone, and not making explicit reference to the other element involved in the practice of reading – namely, the reader – is to offer something incomplete. Reading is, after all, a matter of a reader encountering and making sense of a text: both subject and object are involved, and a theological explication of reading will not succeed without due consideration of *both* that which is read *and* the one who reads. As David Tracy notes: "Any act of interpretation involves at least three realities: some phenomenon to be interpreted, someone interpreting that phenomenon, and some interaction between these first two realities."[108] The issue is not that Marion is operating with an implicitly secular notion of the reader, which would have troubling implications for his account of theological reading. It is clear enough that Marion is operating with a theological anthropology of the reading subject, because he discusses the transformation of readers during the worship service as they partake of the Eucharist and read Scripture. The critical issue is that the theological anthropology remains implicit; it is not thematized and made central to the account of theological reading. At least for the purpose of this book, whose whole aim is to provide an account of theological reading, it is necessary for the role of the reader to rise to the surface and receive the same close attention that the text receives. (It is worth noting, in order to ward off misunderstanding early on, that reading should not be construed as a lone reader encountering and decoding a written text, as if in a vacuum. That this is so for Marion is clear because he locates reading within the liturgy, but the point has applicability throughout the whole course of this book. The entire discussion of readers assumes, and makes explicit at certain junctures of both Parts I and II, that readers exist in a social context which has an influence on interpretation itself. Reading is

[108] David Tracy, *Plurality and Ambiguity: Hermeneutics, Religion, Hope* (Chicago: University of Chicago Press, 1994), 10.

thus "the negotiated construction of meaning within a particular sociocultural context."[109])

There is special value in offering to the current broader discussion of theological reading a systematic account of theological exegesis. The reason for this is that it is not only Marion's account of theological reading which highlights the text to the neglect of the reader. There is a much wider pattern of accounts drawing attention to something theologically distinctive about the text as the main identifying mark of theological reading as such, as the literature mentioned in the footnote below demonstrates.[110] The general

[109] William A. Johnson, *Readers and Reading Culture in the High Roman Empire: A Study of Elite Communities*, Classical Culture and Society (Oxford: Oxford University Press, 2010), 17. Emphasis removed. Johnson means for his point to apply to reading in both ancient and modern contexts.

[110] For instance, what Alvin Plantinga calls "Traditional Biblical Commentary," as opposed to "Historical Biblical Criticism," is defined according to three notes about the text: "Two (or More) Kinds of Scripture Scholarship." In *Oxford Readings in Philosophical Theology*, ed. Michael C. Rea, Vol. 2: Providence, Scripture, and Resurrection (Oxford: Oxford University Press, 2009), 270–73. In Eleonore Stump's differentiation between a medieval drama based on a harmonization of the Gospel accounts and Raymond Brown's historical-critical commentary on John, a great deal turns on whether the biblical accounts are assumed to be true or false: "Visits to the Sepulcher and Biblical Exegesis," in *Oxford Readings in Philosophical Theology*, ed. Michael C. Rea, Vol. 2: Providence, Scripture, and Resurrection (Oxford: Oxford University Press, 2009), 255. T. F. Torrance's depth-exegesis program is built around three theological observations about the text of the Bible: *The Christian Doctrine of God*, 35–47. Rowan Williams's exploration of different modes of reading focuses in similarly on the text: "Historical Criticism and Sacred Text," in *Reading Texts, Seeking Wisdom: Scripture and Theology*, ed. David F. Ford and Graham Stanton (Grand Rapids: Eerdmans, 2004), 217–28. Hans Frei's broad historical account of the decline of a specifically Christian interpretive framework and its displacement by other overarching schemes focuses quite sharply on the fate of the biblical text and its construal as a unified narrative: *The Eclipse of Biblical Narrative: A Study in Eighteenth and Nineteenth Century Hermeneutics* (New Haven: Yale University Press, 1974). A full explanation of the decline of determinately Christian modes of engagement with the Bible should have something to say about other factors as well, though as, on Frei's view, the biblical story reaches out so as to include present-day readers, the reader of the Bible is to some extent included in Frei's concentration on

tendency is that the role of the reader is often omitted completely; sometimes, this role is implicit, but it is not a core part of the existing extended accounts of theological reading. The distinctive contribution of this book is to characterize theological reading by giving due attention to both reader and text, and on the basis of a

the text. For insightful comments on the reader as being absent in Frei's hermeneutic, with the consequence that it is difficult to see reading as transformative for interpreters, see David Dawson, *Christian Figural Reading and the Fashioning of Identity* (Berkeley: University of California Press, 2002), 213–14.

Basically the same pattern obtains within some major Jewish accounts. All four of James Kugel's assumptions that distinguish ancient interpreters from modern ones are observations about how the text of Scripture is viewed: *How to Read the Bible: A Guide to Scripture, Then and Now* (New York: Free Press, 2008), 14–16, 31–32. Likewise, Jon D. Levenson's contrast between religious and historical reading corresponds to two different contexts in which the text can be read, that is, the literary context of a canon or the historical context from which the documents emerged: *The Hebrew Bible, the Old Testament, and Historical Criticism*, xiv.

In many of these cases, distinctive views of the reader lurk just below the surface, as I have pointed out with reference to Frei. Plantinga provides clear and insightful discussion of how Historical Biblical Criticism limits itself to what can be known by unassisted reason, while Traditional Biblical Commentary includes the deliverances of faith in its structuring principles. Yet he neither organizes his discussion around different views of the reader, nor builds a notion of the reader into his definition of Traditional Biblical Commentary. See Plantinga, "Two (or More) Kinds of Scripture Scholarship," 270–77.

The structure of Griffiths's "religious reading" paradigm is similar to the systematic account at the center of this book, in that Griffiths highlights features of the reader, the text, and reading: for readers to attain full humanity, they must take part in religious reading; the text is a vast resource, one so full of meaning that no interpretation can exhaust its riches; and reading is a reverential handling of the text. See *Religious Reading*, 40–54. As was pointed out above, however, the operative categories are fairly generic; specifically theological terms have a low profile in his account. It might be possible to consider Ernst Troeltsch as having an awareness of the reader in the way he contrasts the historical and dogmatic methods of interpretation with reference to the different notions of the history in which each embeds the text and the reader: the first depending on history as an unbroken nexus of cause and effect, the second on the history of salvation. But the theme of the reader does not receive a great deal of explicit development. See "On the Historical and Dogmatic Methods in Theology," in *Religion in History* (Edinburgh: T. & T. Clark, 1991), 20–21.

conception of theology whereby it ventures claims about reality in light of God. If one construes both the reader and the text of Scripture in theological terms, what are the implications for reading that follow? What does the aim of reading become? And what reading strategies become fitting in light of that goal? The theological depictions of the text and reader come together to confer an overall trajectory on reading: the twofold ontology shapes the norm for interpretation, and particular reading strategies take their cue from and fulfill that aim. Though this work makes several interdisciplinary connections, it is very much a systematic theological work in that it is keenly interested in how such ideas interconnect.

Because this call is precisely for an ontology of the reader, the requirement is not met by Fowl's existing work. Right at the center of Fowl's major writing lies a commitment to the communal location of the reader, not a theological ontology of the interpreting subject. In *Reading in Communion*, Fowl and Jones helpfully criticize individualistic views of interpretation, according to which a set of well-defined rules governs interpretation and leads to the resolution of interpretive disputes. A great deal here turns on which interpretive strategies are applied to texts, and the reader's situation in a community of interpretation drives strategy selection: "Our claim is that an answer [to which strategy is appropriate] will only be found within the political constitution of the various contexts in which interpretation takes place."[111] Similarly, in his more mature *Engaging Scripture*, and especially in his well-known discussion of "underdetermined interpretation,"[112] Fowl refuses to allow any theory of textual meaning to have hegemony within interpretation, lest this were to disallow the work specifically Christian beliefs and practices should do in interpretive deliberations. It is the Christian community that inducts readers into these beliefs and practices,

[111] Stephen E. Fowl and L. Gregory Jones, *Reading in Communion: Scripture and Ethics in Christian Life* (Eugene: Wipf and Stock, 1991), 16.

[112] Fowl, *Engaging Scripture*, 56–61.

thus forming them to read well: "For Christians, scriptural interpretation should shape and be shaped by the convictions, practices, and concerns of Christian communities as part of their ongoing struggle to live and worship faithfully before God."[113] Proper interpretation thus happens only in this polarity between text and community. This is a statement about the wider field in which readers exist, but the emphasis is on its social aspect, as opposed to the capacities that readers employ in interpreting the Bible. The point is not to make anthropology the center of gravity for this account, but to make direct language about God more central by underscoring the reader's response to divine self-revelation.[114] Fowl's most recent work on theological reading includes a chapter on the ontology of the Bible, though it does not provide the same extended analysis of a theological anthropology of the reader.[115] This newer work, furthermore, is a brief textbook, and therefore its argument is not as fully developed as is that of his monograph on theological reading.

In this section, I have taken the first step in indicating what is necessary in an account of theological reading by sketching a typology of four positions on how theological doctrine and biblical interpretation relate to one another. For the first type, theology does not enter into exegetical reasoning, though the theology of a particular biblical text is that with which exegetical reasoning concerns itself. In the next type, theology motivates the reader's particular

[113] Ibid., 62.

[114] The aim is to honor the principle that a "theological 'anthropology of reading' has to be undertaken indirectly, beginning, not with a theory of [autonomous] hermeneutical selfhood, but with the work of faith as an implicate of what is said about the triune economy." See John Webster, "The Domain of the Word." In *The Domain of the Word: Scripture and Theological Reason* (London: Bloomsbury T. & T. Clark, 2013), 27.

[115] Fowl, *Theological Interpretation of Scripture*, 1–12. This step toward thinking in terms of ontology does not merit mention in Fowl's discussion of his intellectual development: *Theological Interpretation of Scripture*, xiii–xv.

interests and shapes the queries the reader asks of the text, though it does not define what the text or reader are. Theology is active again in the third type, though this time in the capacity of supplying the community's beliefs that influence how the church reads, thus entering into the heart of the exegesis of particular texts and standing in the foreground more than in the second type. Yet in none of these cases is theology unambiguously offering description of the reader and the text being read; in the first three positions, it is a matter of accounting for identity, either of an individual reader, of cultural conditions on a larger scale, or of the ecclesial community. To conceive of theological reading without giving sustained attention to both of the realities involved risks allowing nontheological views of these topics implicitly to set the agenda. As Louis Dupré rightly says, in certain contexts it often happened that "religion became transformed by intellectual and moral principles conceived independently of faith and often against it."[116] The proposal here for theological exegesis counters this dynamic by insisting that the function of doctrine in relation to interpretation is to depict reality with reference to God. The purpose is not to analyze the subjectivity of an individual believer, while those beliefs remain in the private realm; nor is it to account for how theological belief is an aspect of identity that conditions all perception; nor is it simply to describe the beliefs and form of life that mark the ecclesial community. The whole constructive proposal this book advances is an instantiation of this fourth type, and the purpose of this typology is to bring clarity to a point that helps to frame the argument.

Later chapters of this book move beyond formal matters and fill out the material content of the relevant doctrines, but this chapter takes the logically prior step of specifying closely the essential work that doctrine does. It is crucial to weigh in on this point first of all, for everything else that is said depends on the role of

[116] Louis K. Dupré, *Religion and the Rise of Modern Culture* (Notre Dame: University of Notre Dame Press, 2008), 2.

doctrine, and the function of doctrine commended here is by no means taken for granted across the board in the current debate, as should be clear by now from the survey of other views.[117]

## Contra the Dualism of Doctrine and History

The previous section having taken the first step in setting out what is needed for an account of theological reading, this section takes the second. The present task is to work on the basis of the typology just developed, extending it to deal with the text of Scripture. Like a view of the reader, a construal of the Bible must do nothing less than see the text in light of God. The goal of this part of the introduction is not fully to articulate a theological view of the Bible, but more modestly to outline what such a view involves, and thereby to set out a criterion for a successfully theological view of

[117] It may seem that framing this project in these terms calls up a rather generic understanding of doctrine, one that is somehow too general. Markus Bockmuehl is understandably concerned about discussions of theological reading that proceed without much theological specificity: see his *Seeing the Word*, 58–59. On the one hand, every actual implementation of doctrinal language is, without exception, the employment of a particular language. Going into more detail on the material content of the reader, the text, and reading later on will allow me to fill out my own position in a much more specific way than is possible now in this introductory chapter. Part II will make it clear that this is an orthodox Protestant way of thinking about theological reading. Yet, on the other hand, the nature of the question being pursued in this book means that the doctrinal issues that receive the most attention are ones that set this form of reading off from those that require the bracketing of all forms of Christian faith commitment, or that commence on the basis of their negation. If there is a primary clash with which this book is concerned, it is that between reading with and without a commitment to the Christian tradition, rather than that between hermeneutical frameworks generated from within different strands of the Christian tradition. The aim of this work is to set out what it means to read with faith, in the face of the criticism that faith has no proper place in reading. The book leaves it as a thought experiment for any interested reader to consider the analogies that exist between the theological framework employed here and different iterations of Christian commitments that have relevance for reading.

Scripture. The question of what it means for a view of the biblical text to be genuinely theological turns out to be a subtle one, which is challenging to answer.

A discussion of the text is important, not because the text is often omitted from discussion, as the reader is, but due to the prevalence of a particular problem that often bedevils views of the text in considerations of theological reading. This section brings the text into the foreground with a view toward guarding against a misinterpretation of what a theological view of the text entails. The crucial point requiring clarification is this: seeing the Bible in relation to God, as a sign or witness to him, *cannot* imply denying, even implicitly, that the Bible is nevertheless, in a real sense, an ancient text. To establish a zero-sum game between a theological view of the Bible and the reality of its historical origin invokes a problematic dualism between doctrine and history. What a theological view of Scripture should mean is that precisely *as* a text that originated and was first read many centuries ago, the Bible today still says something about God for those who read it with the eyes of faith. If interpretation amounts to seeking the "inversion of the movement of thought [recorded in the text], which now addresses itself to me and makes me a subject that is spoken to,"[118] if the text is a present act of communication, then one can afford neither to ignore nor to minimize the way in which the text's origin in the past conditions the meaning it has for those who read it now. A danger in invoking transcendence and insisting that it has a role to play, as this project does with its view of doctrine, is that the transcendent realm might come to appear cut off or isolated from the mundane world. The two realms should be seen as intrinsically linked, however, with immanent realities construed in light of God rather than apart from him. There is a risk of dualism when transcendence is highlighted as distinct from the mundane, yet this

[118] Ricoeur, *Freud and Philosophy*, 31.

section cautions against allowing the immanent world to be separated from God in a dualistic manner.[119] To distinguish is not necessarily to separate.

As a way to develop this cautionary note, consider some reflections on Søren Kierkegaard and his interpretation of the Bible. There is a danger of dualism, or at least the prima facie appearance of it, in his most explicit treatment of how to read the Bible, which occurs in *For Self-Examination*.[120] What creates the danger of dualism is Kierkegaard's fierce polemic against the historical-critical stance toward the Bible, which was firmly established in university contexts in his own nineteenth-century European context.[121] As Kierkegaard sees it, this objectivizing mode of engaging with the Bible involves putting questions to the text about its background, and even sometimes about its substantive teachings, but always so as to factor out of the process how those questions bear on the reader of the text. It is, thus, not asking historical questions in and of themselves that bothers Kierkegaard, but rather the posture toward the text one assumes if they are the only interpretive questions one ever poses. This style of reading is fundamentally a process of *observation*, one that holds the claim of the text at a distance, so as to forestall any appropriation of its teaching.[122] The

[119] I am indebted for this way of putting things to Miroslav Volf, *Flourishing: Why We Need Religion in a Globalized World* (New Haven: Yale University Press, 2015), 68.

[120] Timothy Polk brings out well the deep similarities between Kierkegaard and Augustine, who becomes important for this project, highlighting especially how love is central to the biblical hermeneutics of both figures: *The Biblical Kierkegaard: Reading by the Rule of Faith* (Macon: Mercer University Press, 1997), 7–15. It is also true, though, that Polk assimilates Kierkegaard all too much to a postliberal theological outlook.

[121] For useful background on biblical study in this period, see Morgens Müller, "Kierkegaard and Eighteenth- and Nineteenth-Century Biblical Scholarship: A Case of Incongruity," in *Kierkegaard and the Bible*, ed. Lee C. Barrett and Jon Stewart, Vol. 2: The New Testament (Farnham: Ashgate, 2010), 285–327.

[122] Søren Kierkegaard, *Concluding Unscientific Postscript to Philosophical Fragments*, Kierkegaard's Writings (Princeton: Princeton University Press, 1992), 24–34.

text is an object to study with diligence and in exquisite detail, which process Kierkegaard compares to looking carefully at the surface of a mirror, all the while making sure not to focus on seeing one's reflection in it.[123] That is, one must look *at* the text, not *through* it.

From Kierkegaard's point of view, the problem with insisting that an in-depth understanding of the text's history is necessary for a proper reading is that doing so puts the reader permanently in an objectivizing relation to the text, for there is no end to historical queries. To require that historical questions receive satisfying answers before the text can be understood means the reader will never shift to interpretation for the sake of appropriation. As Kierkegaard famously says:

> "God's Word" is indeed the mirror – but, but – oh, how enormously complicated – strictly speaking, how much belongs to "God's Word"? Which books are authentic? Are they really by the apostles, and are the apostles really trustworthy? Have they personally seen everything, or have they perhaps only heard about various things from others? As for ways of reading, there are thirty thousand different ways. And then this crowd or crush of scholars and opinions, and learned opinions and unlearned opinions about how the particular passage is to be understood . . . is it not true that all this seems to be rather complicated! God's Word is the mirror – in reading it or hearing it, I am supposed to see myself in the mirror – but look, this business of the mirror is so confusing that I very likely never come to see myself reflected – at least not if I go at it this way.[124]

To say that historical knowledge is required thus seems to lead to readers being swamped by a multitude of historical questions.

123 Søren Kierkegaard, *For Self-Examination; Judge for Yourself!*, Kierkegaard's Writings (Princeton: Princeton University Press, 1990), 25–35.

124 Ibid., 25–26.

If posing historical queries makes it impossible to read the text as a work that allows readers to see themselves in its light, and if Christians are under an obligation to read the Bible so that it speaks to them specifically, then perhaps they should simply put out of their minds questions about the Bible's background.[125] This is the main thrust of *For Self-Examination*. In it, there are several analogies by which reading the Bible is portrayed as a communicative exchange between agents in a relationship where one of the parties incurs an obligation to the other. The Bible is like a letter from one lover to another with requests for action, a set of instructions from a teacher to a student on what lessons the student should complete, and an edict from a king to his subjects.[126] As Kierkegaard develops these analogies, the will of one agent is expressed either in written form or orally, at least the majority of the wish is sufficiently clear to be followed by the recipient, and raising interpretive questions about the finer points of the text serves essentially as a way to avoid, for the time being or perhaps indefinitely, complying with the wish. On this view, it is not necessary to expend effort to decipher the basic message; such effort is really a pretense for avoiding another kind of work, that which is required to abide by the message. "It is only all too easy to understand the requirement contained in God's Word ('Give all your goods to the poor.' 'If anyone strikes you on the right cheek, turn the left' . . . etc.). It is all just as easy to understand as the remark 'The weather is fine today.'"[127] Here, the Bible is a text that expresses clear imperatives directly to present-day readers, and readers should get on with doing what they already know that they must do.

[125] On how there is, precisely for this reason, little to be gained from historical study, see Iben Damgaard, "Kierkegaard's Rewriting of Biblical Narratives: The Mirror of the Text," in *Kierkegaard and the Bible*, ed. Lee C. Barrett and Jon Stewart, Vol. 1: The Old Testament (Farnham: Ashgate, 2010), 219.

[126] Kierkegaard, *For Self-Examination*, 26–35.

[127] Ibid., 34.

Though it is close, Kierkegaard's position is not quite dualistic. He pushes a specific polemical agenda quite hard and does little to guard himself against being misunderstood, yet all that he says is consistent with historical knowledge having some value toward a Christian reading. Granted, such knowledge is not necessary to understand the central message of the biblical text. Yet he does acknowledge (albeit in the context of a tentative concession) that there *might* in theory be passages of the Bible that are obscure in the sense that they require some historically informed interpretive work before their meanings are rendered clear.[128] He does not say that there definitely are such passages, only that they could exist, all the while guarding himself by saying, "Before I have anything to do with this objection, it must be made by someone whose life manifests that he has scrupulously complied with all the passages that are easy to understand."[129] If one could manage not to become overwhelmed by historical issues, it might prove possible to integrate historical understanding into a reading stance that seeks to appropriate the message of the text for oneself – and it may well be important to do this for texts that are initially unclear in meaning.[130] Thus, readers might after all need some level of historical knowledge for the sake of understanding what the text has to say to them ... possibly ... in the case of some texts.[131] It would

[128] Ibid., 29.

[129] Ibid., 29.

[130] It further substantiates this that Jolita Pons is able to cite instances of Kierkegaard integrating painstaking philological study into his biblical reflections: *Stealing a Gift: Kierkegaard's Pseudonyms and the Bible*, Perspectives in Continental Philosophy Series (New York: Fordham University Press, 2004), 62, 65. A contemporary commentary that integrates historical scholarship on and an appropriative reading of James, in dialogue with Kierkegaard, is Richard Bauckham, *James: Wisdom of James, Disciple of Jesus the Sage*, New Testament Readings (London: Routledge, 1999).

[131] See, for instance, Murray Rae's reflections, which extend the line that Kierkegard himself establishes: *Kierkegaard's Vision of the Incarnation: By Faith Transformed* (Oxford: Clarendon Press, 1997), 101–08.

therefore be unfair to classify Kierkegaard as dualistic, though seeing the role that historical knowledge has within his outlook requires reading him rather carefully.

For the task of framing a formal theological view of the biblical text, there is value in being altogether clearer and more forthright on this count than Kierkegaard is. There is a certain dualistic tendency with a presence in modern culture, to the effect that history is an independent domain of pure nature that stands on its own in isolation from any transcendent reality, which exists "above" nature, being cut off from it.[132] The challenge for theological commentators is to break out of the residual influence of this pattern of thinking. The issue is that for a theological view of what Scripture is to succeed, a theological construal must be applied to the Bible, which does contain historical features. These aspects of the text factor into how it conveys its meaning. For this project, it is worth being straightforward and direct about this. Otherwise the danger of dualism is an abiding threat, though surely its appearance arises in Kierkegaard's case in large part because he feels an intense need to counter an opposing view, according to which attempts to read the text as a message from God stall out at the preliminary stage of handling the supposedly necessary historical questions.[133] The dualism with

[132] These tendencies in modern culture are described, in various ways, by the following: Louis K. Dupré, *Passage to Modernity: An Essay in the Hermeneutics of Nature and Culture* (New Haven: Yale University Press, 1993); Henri de Lubac, *Surnaturel: Études historiques*, Théologie (Paris: Aubier, 1946); Eberhard Jüngel, *God as the Mystery of the World: On the Foundation of the Theology of the Crucified One in the Dispute between Theism and Atheism* (Grand Rapids: Eerdmans, 1983). How these trends bear on the Bible is sketched in John Webster, *Holy Scripture: A Dogmatic Sketch* (Cambridge: Cambridge University Press, 2003), 19–22.

[133] Cf. Joel Rasmussen's judicious judgment that aspects of Kierkegaard's response to the objectivizing study of history represent an overcorrection: "Kierkegaard's Biblical Hermeneutics: Imitation, Imaginative Freedom, and Paradoxical Fixation," in *Kierkegaard and the Bible*, ed. Lee C. Barrett and Jon Stewart, Vol. 2: The New Testament (Farnham: Ashgate, 2010), 277–79.

which Kierkegaard flirts is problematic because "just when it imagined that it was most successfully opposing the negations of naturalism, [it] was most strongly influenced by it, and the transcendence in which it hoped to preserve the supernatural with such jealous care was, in fact, a banishment."[134] What is needed is a more obviously integrated approach. This involves acknowledging the value of historical consciousness and drawing an awareness of how historical location influences thought into a conception of how the biblical text communicates. This work engages with early Christian texts, seeking to appropriate important principles from them, but it is built on the assumption that modern historical consciousness has value for biblical interpretation – as long as it is integrated with theological concerns. It would be far too grand an ambition for this book to seek a complete integration of theology and history: the goal is more limited and focused than that. The aim of Part II, in this connection, is only to articulate a view of Scripture that does not in principle exclude either side, and thereby to depict the big picture in a balanced manner.

From this section and the previous one, two major conditions have emerged that an account of theological interpretation of Scripture must meet. First, it is necessary for an explanation of theological reading to give explicit, considered attention to the embedded view of the reader of the Bible in the context of treating doctrine as a description of reality. Second, it is also necessary for a satisfying account of theological reading to construe the Bible theologically without depicting historical description as superfluous, or even as detrimental to proper reading of the Bible. The constructive proposal regarding theological reading that this book advances seeks to meet both of these conditions.

[134] Henri de Lubac, *Catholicism: A Study of Dogma in Relation to the Corporate Destiny of Mankind* (London: Burns & Oates, 1958), 167.

## Reading Augustine with a Hermeneutic of Restoration

Where might one locate resources with which to fund such a proposal? To find inspiration for an effort to think afresh about the Bible and its interpretation, Part I turns to the theology of Augustine. These two chapters reflect on a number of his writings, giving special focus to *On Christian Teaching*, together with texts that serve as background to it. *On Christian Teaching*, as well as Tyconius's treatise on interpretation – a text known to subsequent history mostly because aspects of it were assimilated by Augustine and rearticulated with commentary in his own text – is the first single work within the Christian tradition that provides a cohesive account of biblical interpretation. Prior to Augustine (and Tyconius), reflections on how to read the Bible generally occurred within the course of works dedicated primarily to other subjects, and often had a practical cast, for such reflection was intended to address questions about how to understand a particularly difficult text or a set of challenging texts. Augustine's work considers interpretation itself, and it does so in a broad perspective. It provides a theological framework within which to think about reading, setting biblical interpretation in "the widest possible learning context."[135] Augustine's text has definite goals and limits, but an operative assumption of the present work is that there are, even today, insights worth retrieving from this early Christian depiction of biblical interpretation. The first standalone Christian account of reading still speaks to those with an interest in what is involved in Christian theological interpretation of the Bible.

There are a number of reasons Augustine is helpful for this project. First, he gives considerable attention to the topic of biblical interpretation, writing about it in broader perspective than many

[135] Michael Cameron, *Christ Meets Me Everywhere: Augustine's Early Figurative Exegesis*, Oxford Studies in Historical Theology (New York: Oxford University Press, 2012), 218.

other figures of his time.[136] Second, the broad perspective in which he views the issues is deeply theological, qualifying as an example of the fourth type sketched in the previous chapter, in that he relates theology and biblical interpretation by viewing both the reader and the text *sub specie divinitatis*.[137] Michael Cameron comments rightly on *On Christian Teaching*: it "addresses not only the biblical text to be interpreted or the act of interpreting but also the character of the interpreter: Right reading depended not only on *what one reads* but also on *the one who reads*."[138] A close reading of this text, together

[136] On Augustine having a well-developed perspective on reading the Bible, see Carol Harrison, "Augustine," in *The New Cambridge History of the Bible*, ed. James Carleton Paget and Joachim Schaper, Vol. 1: From the Beginnings to 600 (Cambridge: Cambridge University Press, 2013), 696; R. A. Markus, "World and Text in Ancient Christianity I: Augustine," in *Signs and Meanings: World and Text in Ancient Christianity* (Liverpool: Liverpool University Press, 1996), 2; Brian Stock frames the issue in a slightly more general manner, as Augustine having a theory of reading per se: *Augustine the Reader: Meditation, Self-Knowledge, and the Ethics of Interpretation* (Cambridge, MA: Harvard University Press, 1996), 1.

[137] The Latin term *doctrina* in the title *De doctrina christiana* does not mean the same thing as doctrine in modern theological contexts, but it is clear that its sense – teaching as a cultural ideal – includes making claims about reality. See Gerald A. Press, "*Doctrina* in Augustine's *De doctrina christiana*," *Philosophy and Rhetoric* 17 (1984): 98–120. Karla Pollmann situates her excellent and frequently cited commentary on *On Christian Teaching* within a trajectory of recent work on Augustine that is "less dogmatically focused": "To Write by Advancing in Knowledge and to Advance by Writing," *Augustinian Studies* 29 (1998): 131. There is certainly much to be gained from interdisciplinary study of Augustine, but given how central theological considerations are to Augustine's work, it is crucial not to deflect attention from them. A work that concludes theology is utterly crucial to *On Christian Teaching* is Tarmo Toom, *Thought Clothed with Sound: Augustine's Christological Hermeneutics in De doctrina christiana*, International Theological Studies (Bern: Peter Lang, 2002), 244.

[138] Cameron, *Christ Meets Me Everywhere*, 220. Others have also noticed Augustine's emphasis on the reader, and the connection he makes between this topic and language; for instance, Rowan Williams, "Language, Reality and Desire in Augustine's *De Doctrina*," *Literature and Theology* 3 (1989): 139.

There is some precedent in Origen scholarship for seeing connections between interpretation and anthropology. In the most recent such major work, Peter Martens treats the reader as a lens through which to view Origen's whole project of

with related works, makes clear the role of theology in relation to biblical interpretation: the reading strategies that Augustine recommends make sense against the background of his theological views of the entities involved in the act of reading. Today's interpreters of the Bible often expect a theory of interpretation to lay out a system of rules that together designate *how* to read, without those principles being influenced by a set of strong substantive commitments, especially ones that are theological in content.[139] Augustine does indeed provide discussion of the procedures to follow in order to interpret well, but the value of his text for this project is that he situates his reflections on method within a theological framework, thereby demonstrating the function of theology, and providing a resource for thinking about what a contemporary theological reading might be. This book is Augustinian in that the constructive case follows Augustine in thinking about biblical interpretation as tied up with theological and religious concerns, rather than neutral with

interpretation, arguing successfully that the mode of reading Origen follows incorporates both scholarly skills and elements of the ideal reader's Christian commitment: "loyalties, guidelines, disposition, relationships, and doctrines." See his *Origen and Scripture: The Contours of the Exegetical Life*, Oxford Early Christian Studies (Oxford: Oxford University Press, 2012), 6. Martens argues that Origen's contextualization of interpretation within the economy of salvation is what makes him significant in the history of biblical interpretation, though this risks underplaying how Origen was part of a much broader pattern among Christian readers, including Augustine.

[139] For the general stress on method in contemporary culture, see Jacques Ellul, *The Technological Society* (New York: Knopf, 1964). For comparisons between what contemporary readers expect from a treatment of interpretation and what they get from Augustine, see Frances M. Young, *Biblical Exegesis and the Formation of Christian Culture* (Cambridge: Cambridge University Press, 1997), 272, 274. Of course there are a few thinkers who have deemphasized method, for instance Hans Georg Gadamer, whose most important work should, according to Paul Ricoeur, have been titled *Truth OR Method* instead of *Truth and Method*. See Paul Ricoeur, "The Task of Hermeneutics," in *Hermeneutics and the Human Sciences: Essays on Language, Action, and Interpretation* (Cambridge: Cambridge University Press, 1981), 60. Ricoeur seeks to build on the work of Gadamer, but to redress the lack of focus on process that he perceives in Gadamer's work.

respect to them.[140] A third feature that makes Augustine attractive is that his thinking is not dualistic in orientation.[141] Though Augustine will certainly not provide direct solutions to specifically modern problems, his example of not isolating "natural" and "supernatural" from one another, as separate spheres of reality, can inspire contemporary theological readers to move past disjunctions between historical reality and reference to transcendence.

Scholars of Augustine often note the limits of Augustine's focus in *On Christian Teaching*, but the boundaries of Augustine's text, real though they are, do not present a problem for the way that this book employs it. It is true that *On Christian Teaching* does not contain the entirety of Augustine's hermeneutic; for instance, he says little about certain topics, such as how to read the prophetic texts contained within the Old Testament.[142] It is also true that the work is addressed to a specific audience, namely, people who are already committed to Christianity, who have acquired some knowledge of the Bible, who are seeking to learn as much as possible themselves, and who are actively involved in teaching others.[143] This book turns especially to *On Christian Teaching* not because

140 This work is thus Augustinian in a sense spelled out in Alvin Plantinga, "Science: Augustinian or Duhemian?," *Faith and Philosophy* 13 (1996): 368–94.

141 See, for instance, Lubac, *Surnaturel.*

142 Cameron, *Christ Meets Me Everywhere*, 239–40.

143 Ibid., 218–40. For a compelling rejoinder to Cameron's effort to make a great deal of the limits of *On Christian Teaching*, see Isabelle Bochet, "Réflexions sur l'exégèse figurative d'augustin: *Christ Meets Me Everywhere: Augustine's Early Figurative Exegesis* de M. Cameron," *Augustinian Studies* 45 (2014): 288–89. For a reading of the text that maximizes its significance, portraying it as approaching a hermeneutic of universal import in a number of ways – it formulates an overall theory of interpretation rather than resting content with enumerating rules or dealing with particular difficult texts, interpretation encompasses and utilizes a vast range of other scholarly disciplines, and the work does less than many of Augustine's other texts to address a narrow target audience – see Karla Pollmann, *Doctrina christiana: Untersuchungen zu den Anfängen der christlichen Hermeneutik unter besonderer Berücksichtigung von Augustinus, De doctrina christiana*, Paradosis (Freiburg: Universitätsverlag, 1996), 66–244.

it treats biblical interpretation in an utterly comprehensive way. Augustine is too restless and adaptable to say everything that he thinks about a major topic in one place, never to revisit the issue again.[144] Appropriating insights from Augustine for the sake of an account of theological reading does not require a single summary statement of Augustine's approach to the Bible. What it does require, and what *On Christian Teaching* provides at least as well as any work in Augustine's massive oeuvre, is a clear statement of theology's role in interpretation. In no other text does Augustine explicate his semiotics so fully in relationship to Scripture. And in no other text does he set out as amply as he does in *On Christian Teaching* an account of the human person in interconnection with reading. These become important themes in Part I.

I apply to Augustine a hermeneutic of restoration. The investigation has a focus on particular aspects of Augustine's theological thought, that is, what he "can still give us to think"[145] with regard to the Bible and its interpretation.[146] This book's engagement with Augustine is hermeneutical in the sense that it is a reading for the sake of appropriating insights that open up new possibilities for reflection. Contemporary theology has seen an increasing number of theological statements based on an intensive reading of history, in which past texts serve as an interruption to the theological status quo, and as a set of possibilities from well outside the scope of a

[144] David Tracy fittingly likens reading thinkers such as Augustine to exploring an ancient city in which one never gets a comprehensive overview of the layout of the winding streets, as opposed to climbing to the summit of a mountain, from which height it is possible to see the overall layout of the surrounding terrain. See "Augustine's Christomorphic Theocentrism," in *Orthodox Readings of Augustine*, ed. George E. Demacopoulos and Aristotle Papanikolaou (Crestwood: St. Vladimir's Seminary Press, 2008), 263–89.

[145] Jean-Luc Marion, *The Idol and Distance: Five Studies*, Perspectives in Continental Philosophy (New York: Fordham University Press, 2001), 22.

[146] I have found useful guidance on integrating patristic sources into theological proposals in Lewis Ayres, "On the Practice and Teaching of Christian Doctrine," *Gregorianum* 80 (1999): 83–89.

contemporary outlook.[147] What makes a hermeneutic of restoration worth pursuing is what a contemporary theologian can glean from the past for the sake of the present, and indeed for the future.[148] As Friedrich Nietzsche says in his essay "On the Uses and

[147] Kathryn Tanner, "Shifts in Theology over the Last Quarter Century," *Modern Theology* 26 (2010): 39–44. For two distinguished examples of systematic theologies that utilize a range of patristic resources, see: Sarah Coakley, *God, Sexuality, and the Self: An Essay "On the Trinity"* (Cambridge: Cambridge University Press, 2013); Frances M. Young, *God's Presence: A Contemporary Recapitulation of Early Christianity*, Current Issues in Theology (Cambridge: Cambridge University Press, 2013). An older, magisterial example of the treatment of a single locus is Yves Congar, *Tradition and Traditions: An Historical and a Theological Essay* (London: Burns & Oats, 1966).

A few of the notable recent Christian appropriations of Augustine in particular include Jason Byassee, *Praise Seeking Understanding: Reading the Psalms with Augustine*, Radical Traditions (Grand Rapids: Eerdmans, 2007); Charles T. Mathewes, *A Theology of Public Life*, Cambridge Studies in Christian Doctrine (Cambridge: Cambridge University Press, 2007); Ian A. McFarland, *In Adam's Fall: A Meditation on the Christian Doctrine of Original Sin*, Challenges in Contemporary Theology (Chichester: Wiley-Blackwell, 2010); John Milbank, "'Postmodern Critical Augustinianism': A Short Summa in Forty Two Responses to Unasked Questions," *Modern Theology* 7 (1991): 225–37; Susannah Ticciati, *A New Apophaticism: Augustine and the Redemption of Signs* (Leiden: Brill, 2013). A work that is less scholarly but still deeply insightful is Paul J. Griffiths, Lying: *An Augustinian Theology of Duplicity* (Grand Rapids: Brazos, 2004).

For an example of a secularizing appropriation, which seeks to leave behind some of Augustine's theological commitments even as it draws on other aspects of his thinking, see Jean Bethke Elshtain, *Augustine and the Limits of Politics*, Frank M. Covey, Jr. Loyola Lectures in Political Analysis (Notre Dame: University of Notre Dame Press, 1995). She concludes that Augustine offers a "way of thinking and being in the world, a way that is in many vital respects available to those who are not doctrinally Augustine's brothers and sisters" (*Augustine and the Limits of Politics*, 114).

[148] Michel R. Barnes rightly chides modern thinkers, and especially contemporary systematic theologians, for drawing on Augustine without having read him closely. See "Augustine in Contemporary Trinitarian Theology," *Theological Studies* 56 (1995): 237–50. The essay is animated by a sense that Augustine is a theologian with a great deal to offer, that it represents a great loss for theologians to handle him in such a slipshod way, and that they should divest themselves of whatever commitments occlude Augustine from their view. Such problematic views include a penchant for

Disadvantages of History for Life," "He [the student of history] learns from it that the greatness that once existed was in any event once *possible* and may thus be possible again; he goes his way with more cheerful step, for the doubt which assailed him in weaker moments, whether he was not perhaps desiring the impossible, has now been banished."[149] This does not mean simply imitating historical models, for Nietzsche is right also to stress that thinking with historical sources is precisely *thinking with*, not simply copying: "And yet – to learn something new straightaway from this example – how inexact, fluid and provisional that comparison would be! How much of the past would have to be overlooked if it was to produce that mighty effect!"[150] In light of this consideration, Part II opens up a much wider dialogue in which modern thinkers and specifically modern issues – or at least issues with a modern twist – play an utterly central role.[151] The constructive

handling ideas in a highly schematized, abstract way which lifts them out of their originating cultural circumstances and Augustine's process of development as a thinker, and fails to relate them to the polemical targets Augustine formulated them to address. Barnes convincingly establishes that many contemporary theologians have made extravagant and false claims about Augustine without engaging responsibly with him. That said, it seems as if Barnes is implicitly claiming that systematic theologians should just become historical theologians. What place is there for constructive appropriations of Augustine today? In this piece, Barnes borders on making a totalizing assertion that his own discipline should have hegemony over foundational Christian texts. The door opens a crack in a later essay, in which Barnes is willing to use the label *Augustinian* not just to denote views that Augustine holds but also, and even with cautious approval, to refer to views that are like Augustine's, or that have been influenced by him: "Ebion at the Barricades: Moral Narrative and Post-Christian Catholic Theology," *Modern Theology* 26 (2010): 545n55.

149 Friedrich Nietzsche, "On the Uses and Disadvantages of History for Life," in *Untimely Meditations*, Cambridge Texts in the History of Philosophy (Cambridge: Cambridge University Press, 1997), 69.

150 Ibid., 69.

151 For systematic analysis of strategies by which Augustine has been appropriated, with a stress on the diversity of the ways in which he has been used through the centuries in different contexts, see these pieces by Karla Pollmann: "How to Do Things with Augustine. Patristics and Reception Theory," *Journal of Church Studies* 5 (2008):

proposal here takes inspiration from broad features of Augustine's view, though it by no means imitates him in every detail, nor does it limit itself to drawing on only him.

## Summary of the Argument

Theological exegesis is a view of interpretation that considers the two realities involved in reading, both the reader and the text, from the standpoint of two sets of categories, theological and immanent ones. The interpreting subject and interpreted object should be seen in light of God: the reader is one who responds to the text and the God it discloses, and the text constitutes a set of *signa* pointing to the divine *res*. Such explicitly theological language does not displace immanent categories, but operates in a noncompetitive relationship with them. The text and the reader exist in space and time: the reader is an agent whose identity is shaped crucially by various contingent factors, and the text is a set of documents with a complex natural history, by which it was formed and subsequently received. *This* reader receives the text's testimony, and *this* text is a collection of signs that direct the reader's attention beyond the immanent realm to God. Understanding the key realities involved in interpretation in this way has implications for the character of

31–41; "Alium sub meo nomine: Augustine between His Own Self-Fashioning and His Later Reception," *Zeitschrift für antikes Christentum* 14 (2010): 409–24; "Augustine's Legacy: Success or Failure?," In *The Cambridge Companion to Augustine*, 2nd ed., ed. David Vincent Meconi and Eleonore Stump (Cambridge: Cambridge University Press, 2014), 331–48. The present work treats Augustine as what Michel Foucault calls one of the "founders of discursivity." "They are unique in that they are not just the authors of their own works. They have produced something else: the possibilities and the rules for the formation of other texts." See Michel Foucault, "What Is an Author?," in *Textual Strategies: Perspectives in Post-Structuralist Criticism*, ed. Josué V. Harari (Ithaca: Cornell University Press, 1979), 154. Foucault deems the church fathers less generative than this and slots them into a different category. At any rate, I borrow his category, rather than the judgment he makes with it.

interpretation, prompting interpreters to read with a view toward grasping what the text has to say about the triune God, and pressing them to employ reading strategies that help them to fulfill this aim. The techniques that a theological interpreter employs are often the most easily identifiable aspect of a specifically theological reading program, but they derive from an ontology which often remains tacit – though that is, importantly, not the case with a work at the center of Part I, and which serves as a model for the constructive proposal of Part II.

As has been indicated, the book falls into two parts. The first part provides analysis of Augustine: Chapter 1 focuses on his theological view of the text and the reader, and Chapter 2 on the approach to interpretation that flows from these commitments. Drawing inspiration from Augustine's example, and seeking to follow him by having an ethics of interpretation that derives from a theological ontology, the second part proposes a constructive, contemporary view of theological reading. Part II expands its treatment of the reader and the text by having dedicated chapters for each topic, as well as a chapter on interpretation. The opening move in Part II, however, is to sketch out an example of what theological reading is not, in order to lend greater clarity to the effort to specify what is distinctive about a theological hermeneutic of the Bible, and to highlight that theological reading does not exist in contradistinction to a historically grounded approach to reading, but rather to one that is driven by metaphysical naturalism. While not naturalistic in orientation, the case that Part II advances integrates a concern for history into interpretation, intending to bring it together with theology. The book closes by grappling with the objection that theological reading is misguided because it really amounts to reading one's own views into the Bible, rather than understanding the text's content. The book explores hermeneutical viewpoints that have no room for a transcendent God, but it calls for those that do to allow doctrine to have the deepest possible impact on interpretation.

# Part I | The Model of Augustine

The archaeologist who lovingly seeks to make the Minoan civilization live again in our imaginations or the one who is filled with wonder in recreating the religious life of the cities of upper Asia during the time of the great Buddhist pilgrims, certainly has no desire to take us back to the customs of King Minos or to the beliefs of the monks of Khotan. They nevertheless have the sense of being moved by something other than futile curiosity. Is not the fruit of these investigations into the human past that of enriching the mind, of giving it a new fertility by making, so to speak, rich, ample humus for it? In proportion as he explores and tastes the varied creations of the genius of his race, man better perceives his own potentialities, and each cast of the sounding line into ancient culture thus makes one more source spring up through which his own culture will be fed.

Henri de Lubac[1]

[1] Henri de Lubac, *History and Spirit: The Understanding of Scripture according to Origen* (San Francisco: Ignatius, 2007), 428.

# 1 | The Reader, Redemption, and Signs

This chapter presents Augustine's views of the reader and the text, beginning with the former. Both chapters in Part I concentrate on Augustine and make almost no reference whatsoever to the present ferment over theological reading. The purpose of turning to Augustine is not to draw straightforwardly from him an account of the nature of reading the Bible theologically, in the sense that our own contemporaries have come to use that terminology. This he simply will not provide. Rather, as indicated in the Introduction, what Augustine does provide is a stimulating example of how to think theologically about who the reader of Scripture is, what Scripture itself is, and how strategies for reading can become fitting in light of specifically theological construals of the interpreting subject and the interpreted object. The objective of the first part of this book, then, is to synthesize what Augustine says about these connected topics from some of his most telling and pertinent texts, with a view toward drawing together what he offers that may be of value to today's reader, all the while noting ways in which his own context was genuinely different than our own. So I echo here the words of Yves Congar: "My immediate aim, then, is historical; but my ultimate intention remains strictly theological"[1] – where theological means *constructively* theological. Or, with Nietzsche: "We want to serve history only to the extent that history serves life."[2] That is to say, the interpretive work on Augustine presented in Part

[1] Congar, *Tradition and Traditions*, xix.

[2] Nietzsche, "History for Life," 59.

I will finally serve as a stimulus for the constructive theological position developed in Part II.[3]

Since Part I stresses that Augustine views both the reader and the text theologically, and that this in turn has implications for interpretation, it is worth clarifying what is meant by claiming that he is thinking in theological terms. In other words, what does the phrase *in theological terms* actually mean? To say that something is being depicted theologically is to say that describing that item, and getting to the heart of what it is, requires theological language. David Kelsey rightly says that in reflection on anthropology prior to modernity, examinations of what constitutes a human being were derived from beliefs about God, which were themselves more ultimate. Kelsey writes regarding the structure of anthropological thinking in Augustine's period:

> Beliefs about God and the ways in which God relates to all that is not God are logically more basic than many other beliefs, including anthropological beliefs. Hence the anthropological proposals made as part of a project exploring the logic of Christian beliefs were structured as secondary beliefs implied by, derived from, and conceptually dependent on more basic beliefs about God and God's ways of relating to all that is not God.

He continues:

> Consequently such anthropological proposals ... had in common that their internal logic was theocentric. God's relation to human beings and human beings' relation to God was structurally essential to such proposals, and not a topic to be raised after (conceptually "after") the anthropological proposals had been framed in a way that bracketed the God-relation.[4]

[3] In the present volume, when I myself cite biblical texts, I use the NRSV translation to do so. When I cite the works of Augustine, I cite his texts in both Latin and English translation, but I omit his name, lest it be needlessly repeated.

[4] Kelsey, *Eccentric Existence*, 1: 28–29. One of the major aims of Kelsey's own proposal is to be theocentric in the way that older anthropologies were. For the point that

The notion of the human person is "conceptually dependent" on prior beliefs about God in the sense that God is the person's origin and end, without reference to which the person cannot be understood fully.[5]

Two nuances need to be added here. First, setting out this explanation of what makes a descriptive term theological does not involve reducing God's identity to his role in filling out the denotations of the finite realities involved in reading. This was mentioned briefly in the Introduction, but the point should be expanded here, for where concerns about ontotheology are deeply felt,[6] any project that emphasizes the role of theological terms in the way that this book does is bound to provoke this sort of worry. It is indeed important to avoid instrumentalizing God, employing him as a mere tool in a conceptual mapping project, and thus making him serve a human desire to comprehend. Such a "God" would not be God at all. What can one say in response to this worry? It is necessary to underscore that God is transcendent and thereby greater than the role he plays in these and all concepts. Even as he serves a key role within a concept, God's alterity is safeguarded, "provided at least that the concept renounce comprehending the incomprehensible."[7] Properly understood, theological terms do not

Augustine's anthropology is theocentric, see Isabelle Bochet, *Le firmament de l'écriture: l'herméneutique augustinienne*, Collection des études augustiniennes série antiquité (Paris: Institut d'études augustiniennes, 2004), 320.

[5] For this reason, reading the Bible is indispensable for Augustine's understanding of human nature, a point of fundamental importance to Brian Stock, *The Integrated Self: Augustine, the Bible, and Ancient Thought*, Haney Foundation Series (Philadelphia: University of Pennsylvania Press, 2017), 1–2.

[6] For lyrical expression of this concern with reference to Augustine, and especially his *Confessions*, see Joseph S. O'Leary, *Questioning Back: The Overcoming of Metaphysics in Christian Tradition* (Minneapolis: Winston, 1985), 165–201. For an extended, sympathetic reading of Augustine in relation to this concern, which presents a more careful and persuasive reading of *Confessions*, see Jean-Luc Marion, *In the Self's Place: The Approach of Saint Augustine, Cultural Memory in the Present* (Stanford: Stanford University Press, 2012).

[7] Marion, *God without Being*, 22–23.

minimize God, making him too familiar or too close to us; they register the distance that exists between God and human beings and open our gaze up to a reality that can never be fully known. The concept must "welcome the distance of infinite depth."[8] This makes a theological ontology of the reader anything but an account of a simple essence that is easy to pin down. One should expect Augustine to think theologically about humanity, as the only alternative to thinking about the human interpreting subject with reference to God is, obviously, not doing so – conceiving of the reader in a way that does not inscribe the interpreter's origin in and vocation in relation to God into the concept of being human. This would be to frame a view of the reader in secular terms, and Augustine does not operate in this way. That theological terms do not cut God down to size, but rather expand the concepts of reader and text, is the first nuance that must be introduced here.

The second nuance that needs to be made in this discussion of theological terms is that there is no bright line in Augustine between theological and philosophical modes of thought. Twenty-first-century readers of Augustine are accustomed to a clear demarcation between theology and philosophy of religion as two different curricular subjects, the former concerned with systematic articulations of faith commitments and their interconnections, and the latter with examination of the rational basis of religious belief. They will certainly not, however, find any such distinction in Augustine's writings.[9] All the way through his corpus, Augustine integrates conceptuality of philosophical provenance into his thinking and puts these concepts to his own ends, even in discussing God himself. If the philosopher is one who loves wisdom, and true wisdom is ultimately to be found in Christ, modern interpreters

[8] Ibid., 23.

[9] There are useful reflections on the relationship between Augustine and modern notions of theology in the following, though Marion pushes beyond the threshold of plausibility the idea that Augustine has no place for ontology (*In the Self's Place*, 7–10).

of Augustine must recognize that the curricular divisions to which they themselves are accustomed do not match up with Augustine's own thinking because from his point of view the pursuit of wisdom is inseparable from knowing Christ.[10] The upshot of this is that terms that may have originated in philosophical contexts, even non-Christian philosophical contexts, can potentially still count as theological terms in Augustine's usage if they refer to God, whether directly or indirectly. Thus, for the purpose of this chapter, what is and is not a theological term depends, finally, not on the origin of the term but on the referent of the language.

For example, the term wisdom (*sapientia*) has a genealogy that includes being part of non-Christian philosophical thought, but it becomes a crucial category for Augustine's Christology, and thus has an important place in the discussion that follows. Having clarified the role of theology in Augustine's account of the reader and the biblical text, I turn to outlining what he has to say about these two topics, beginning with the reader.

## Reader: Interpreter in the Economy of Salvation[11]

### *Who Is the Reader? Parsing the Question*

There are several possible ways to ask about who the reader of the Bible is, but this section pursues just one of those paths. The aim

[10] See Goulven Madec, "Christus, scientia et sapientia nostra. Le principe de cohérence de la doctrine augustinienne," *Recherches augustiniennes et patristiques* 10 (1975): 77–85; Goulven Madec, "Verus philosophus est amator Dei. S. Ambroise, S. Augustin et la philosophie," *Revue des Sciences philosophiques et théologiques* 61 (1977): 560.

[11] Bochet is right to say that reading's location in the economy of salvation is implicit for much of *On Christian Teaching*, but that the theme holds together many of the text's other themes. See her "Place de l'écriture dans l'économie du salut," in *La doctrine chrétienne = De doctrina christiana*, ed. Madeleine Moreau et al., Bibliothèque augustinienne 11/2 (Paris: Institut d'études augustiniennes, 1997), 474. Where interpretation's situatedness in the economy becomes most clearly explicit is in the

here is not to ask about the *real reader* of the Bible, a reader who is known to us by "his documented reactions" to the biblical text.[12] Nor is the question about who was able to read in Augustine's milieu and what their reading habits were, as those practices can be reconstructed by scholarship on the history of this period, or even what Augustine knew about the reading practices of those under his ecclesial leadership. What is at issue is to understand the paradigm of what Augustine thinks the reader should be. Paul Griffiths gives attention to something like this, what he calls *ideal readers*.[13] However, what he means by ideal reader is still not precisely the topic at issue here. Griffiths inquires into comparatively practical questions, such as whether the ideal reader of a commentary would have been expected to have the text being commented on physically to hand while reading a commentary or hearing the text read aloud, or whether the work being commented on would be one that the ideal reader should have committed to memory. The focus of this section is closer to what Wolfgang Iser calls the *implied reader*, one who "embodies all those predispositions necessary for a literary work to exercise its effect – predispositions laid down, not by an empirical outside reality, but by the text itself."[14] Some adaptation of this definition is necessary because this chapter concentrates on the Bible rather than novels, the primary genre of texts that Iser has in mind. Yet what is important is the set of predispositions that Augustine views as key to reading, and the underlying human capacities together with the work of divine grace that make this

ascent text of book 2: *On Christian Teaching* 2.10 (CCSL 32, 37; OWC Green, 34). For more on this text, see the discussion of it in Chapter 2.

[12] Wolfgang Iser, *The Act of Reading: A Theory of Aesthetic Response* (Baltimore: Johns Hopkins University Press, 1978), 27.

[13] For the category of ideal readers, see Griffiths, *Religious Reading*, 94–97; on Augustine and other Latin Christians as examples, see ibid., 148–81.

[14] Iser, *The Act of Reading*, 34. Cf. Wolfgang Iser, *The Implied Reader: Patterns of Communication in Prose Fiction from Bunyan to Beckett* (Baltimore: Johns Hopkins University Press, 1974).

orientation possible. Asking about the nature of the reader in this way is akin to considering the elements of theological anthropology that are embedded in his treatment of scriptural readers. That is the sense in which this section focuses on the reader.[15]

Because this is the substance of the current query, and because literacy in Augustine's time was much more limited than it is today in the developed world, it follows that Augustine's "reader" might not actually have been able to read independently. That is, such a "reader" might have been illiterate – paradoxical though this may sound. If being literate refers to the ability to read (and write) comfortably in at least one language, then the extent of literacy in the Greek and Roman imperial periods hovered around 10 percent and at no time exceeded 15–20 percent of the total population.[16] Yet this did not keep reading, defined in a loose sense, from being a deeply significant part of thc lifc of Christian communities in this same period. Harry Gamble rightly says: "If most Christians were illiterate, it did not prevent them from participating in literacy or from being familiar with Christian texts."[17] Even illiterate Christians were able to partake of literacy because much of the textual interpretation in Christian communities was public and communal.

[15] My use of the term *reader* is thus close to that of David Dawson, who stresses that the interpreter *On Christian Teaching* assumes is an embodied soul whose affections become shaped by reading: "Sign Theory, Allegorical Reading, and the Motions of the Soul in De doctrina christiana," in *De doctrina christiana: A Classic of Western Culture*, ed. Duane W. H. Arnold and Pamela Bright, Christianity and Judaism in Antiquity (Notre Dame: University of Notre Dame Press, 1995), 124. My usage is somewhat broader than what Michael Cameron means by the *implied reader* of the treatise *On Christian Teaching*, whom he rightly takes to be a Christian who has advanced beyond the beginning stages of the Christian life (*Christ Meets Me Everywhere*, 220–21). I employ a wider sense for the term in an effort to find a rubric that will hold together a range of texts.

[16] William V. Harris, *Ancient Literacy* (Cambridge, MA: Harvard University Press, 1989), 3–25.

[17] Harry Y. Gamble, *Books and Readers in the Early Church: A History of Early Christian Texts* (New Haven: Yale University Press, 1995), 8.

People who could not read the Bible for themselves would have been exposed indirectly to the text in catechesis; in addition, even after the catechetical teaching that initiated new members into the ecclesial community, Christians would have been exposed to the Bible indirectly through homiletical exposition and the liturgy that structured their regular services of worship.[18] A further factor that meant that firsthand engagement with the Bible was not the only means of internalizing the text was the high premium that was placed on memorization of biblical passages during this period. For all of these reasons, it makes good sense to use the term *reader* in a broad sense, designating one who was familiar with the substantive content of the Bible, even if that content was mediated communally in various ways.[19]

## *Who Is the Reader? A Synopsis*

Who, then, is the reader on whom Augustine thinks the Bible will exercise its intended effect? Human beings are embodied souls.[20] Body and soul both have their origin in God. The body is the physical aspect of the human subject, and is bound to suffer the dissolution of death; the soul, while it will separate from the body at

[18] For a detailed account of the oral/aural dimensions of catechesis and preaching, see Carol Harrison, *The Art of Listening in the Early Church* (Oxford: Oxford University Press, 2013), 87–179.

[19] What I mean by *reader* is thus close to what Ingolf Dalferth intends by *hearer*, a term he prefers to *reader* because of the way it highlights that the communicative event is a personal encounter, and because it more obviously suggests Scripture's embeddedness in homiletical and liturgical contexts. See Ingolf Dalferth, "Von der Vieldeutigkeit der Schrift und der Eindeutigkeit des Wortes Gottes," in *Die Zukunft des Schriftprinzips*, ed. Richard K. Ziegert, Bibel im Gesprèach (Stuttgart: Deutsche Bibelgesellschaft, 1994), 158. Though what Dalferth preserves with his terminological choice is also significant to maintain with reference to Augustine, I persist with the term *reader* due to its clear connection with the topic of interpretation, which is central to the present work.

[20] *On the Greatness of the Soul* 1.2 (CSEL 89, 132; FOC 2, 60).

death, will always exist in some form.[21] The soul enlivens the body; it is the center of sensory perception and the facility of memory; it has the capacity for abstract thinking, prospective planning, and the production and interpretation of language.[22] Quite significantly for this chapter, the soul is also the center of emotion or affection. Human beings experience a whole range of feelings – joy, grief, desire, and fear among them – and what makes a specific feeling proper or improper is the underlying love generating it.[23] Love of God and neighbor, on the one hand, and love of self on the other are the two fundamental emotions of the soul,[24] in that they underpin and drive all the other feelings a person might have. For example, it is virtuous for a person to feel joy as a function of loving God, but a joy based simply on love of self is sinful. Emotions are thus forms of volition that are tied closely with one's movement toward or away from God. (To say that the person consists of body and soul is to give a bipartite anthropology. Augustine sometimes employs a tripartite division to describe human beings, including spirit as the third element, alongside a soul and a body.[25] However, the difference that a potential third aspect makes for the present discussion is negligible.)

Human beings are reliant on language to apprehend reality, and to this extent their acquaintance with things is indirect and therefore less than ideal. By comparison, for the primordial human being of whom Augustine speaks in his commentary *On Genesis, against the Manichees*, engagement with God was direct and unmediated by language, either written or oral/aural, thus entirely bypassing the challenges of interpretation that the reception of language

[21] *On the Immortality of the Soul* (CSEL 89, 101–28; FOC 2, 15–47).

[22] *On the Greatness of the Soul* 33.70–76 (CSEL 89, 217–25; FOC 2, 136–44).

[23] Dawson, "Sign Theory, Allegorical Reading, and the Motions of the Soul in *De doctrina christiana*," 124.

[24] *On Christian Teaching* 3.16 (CCSL 32, 87; OWC Green, 76).

[25] For example, see *On Faith and the Creed* 23 (CSEL 41, 28; WSA I/8, 171).

necessarily entails.[26] Augustine comments on the human condition before the fall, construing various objects mentioned in the creation narratives of Genesis in a figural manner:

> Before he [Adam] sinned, however, when God had made the greenery of the field and the fodder, which we have said mean the invisible creature, he was watering this creature from an inner spring, speaking directly to its understanding, so that it would not have to take in words from outside, like rain from the aforementioned clouds, but would be drenched from its own spring, that is, from the truth welling up from its innermost being.[27]

This reference to Adam's "innermost being" as a source of truth should not be pressed too hard: it is not that he himself constituted the ultimate source of truth, quite apart from God, but rather that he was, prior to sin, not dependent on external media to understand God's will. He was, instead, able to intuit divine direction immediately and to access God via a reliable conscience.[28] Thus, even this turn within reflects an anthropology with a fundamentally eccentric orientation: it remains theocentric in its portrayal of inwardness as a turning to oneself, not for the purpose of getting in touch with oneself as an ultimate end, but for the sake of engaging with the divine other.

The ideal of direct engagement with God, once but not presently available, becomes the eschatological goal Augustine holds out to human beings as what comes at the end of negotiating their way through a life marked by mediated understanding. In this way,

[26] *On Genesis, against the Manichees* 5 (CSEL 91, 123–24; WSA I/13, 73–74).

[27] *On Genesis, against the Manichees* 5 (CSEL 91, 123–24; WSA I/13, 74). In his later exegesis of the creation narrative, *On the Literal Interpretation of Genesis*, Augustine's position shifts such that language is possible but not necessary for communication between God and human beings: *On the Literal Interpretation of Genesis* 8.37–50 (CSEL 28.1, 257–67; WSA I/13, 368–75).

[28] *On Genesis, against the Manichees* 5 (CSEL 91, 123–24; WSA I/13, 74).

redemption is restoration, rather than starting utterly from scratch.[29] Reading is important during the transitional phase in human life, though not after that. The knowledge that reading provides, and the formation of the human person it effects, will be superseded by the immediacy of the *eschaton*. To draw once more from *On Genesis, against the Manichees*:

> For humanity toiling away on the land, confined that is to say in the parched earth of its sins, divine teaching is essential from human words, like rain from the clouds. This sort of knowledge, however, *will be done away with* (1 Cor 13:8). *For we see now in a riddle*, as if seeking satisfactory nourishment in the clouds; *but then it will be face to face* (1 Cor 13:12).[30]

Human existence, when encountering God directly, will thus approximate the present condition of the unfallen angels, about whom Augustine says: "They have no need to look up to this firmament [which stands metaphorically for Scripture] and to read so as to know your word."[31] Augustine's many sermons, commentaries, and biblically funded treatises bear witness to his earnestness about biblical interpretation as a key mode of relating to God for those who are *in via*. As important as the biblical text is for Augustine, a blinkered perspective results if it is forgotten that the knowledge reading provides is only penultimate, not ultimate.

The reader's existence is caught between the dark origins of language, which became necessary after an aboriginal rupture, and the immediate vision of God that becomes available in the *eschaton*. Reading takes place within this tension, so to consider the reader is to consider one who is in the process of becoming and is anything

[29] Oliver O'Donovan rightly comments: "Our being-as-we-are and our being-as-we-shall-be are held together as works of the One God who is both our Creator and Redeemer." See *The Problem of Self-Love in St. Augustine* (New Haven: Yale University Press, 1980), 159.

[30] *On Genesis, against the Manichees* 6 (CSEL 91, 125; WSA I/13, 75).

[31] *Confessions* 13.18 (CCSL 27, 251; OWC Chadwick, 283).

but static: the reader's life is "a struggle, a brokenness, a gift, a process of healing, a resistance to healing, an emptiness, a reference that impels one not to concentrate on oneself, in the end, but on that to which one's self-awareness propels one, to God."[32] In *On Christian Teaching*, Augustine depicts human life as a journey: those who read the text are "like travelers away from our Lord (*peregrinantes a domino*)";[33] progress is not made by moving through physical space "but through integrity of purpose and character,"[34] for people ought to love God above all else, though this proves to be a struggle in practice. Proper reading – interpretation that does not allow the practice to be overcome by the same dynamics that created the need for language in the first place – can serve as a conveyance by means of which human beings are restored to a fitting relation with God. Textual knowledge must play a part in this process: reading necessarily involves sensory contact with the text, whether it is read by the eyes in written form, or heard by the ears in oral presentation. However, the acquisition of textual data, and even deep ruminative reflection on the content of the text, are both a subordinate part of the journey, while what is primary is to love the *res* of the text. The journey is essentially about the reorientation of the soul from loving most what is inherently less valuable to arriving at the point where one loves most that which is best: namely, God.[35]

In addition to the imagery, Augustine uses a pair of technical terms in order to discuss how items outside oneself participate in

[32] John C. Cavadini, "The Darkest Enigma: Reconsidering the Self in Augustine's Thought," *Augustinian Studies* 38 (2007): 123. Also worth consulting on the dynamic and outwardly oriented nature of the self is Marion, *In the Self's Place*.

[33] *On Christian Teaching* 1.4 (CCSL 32, 8; OWC Green, 10).

[34] *On Christian Teaching* 1.10 (CCSL 32, 12; OWC Green, 13).

[35] For a more wide-ranging account of language's implication in both fall and redemption than is possible here, together with the results this has for how readers relate to Scripture, see Carol Harrison, *Beauty and Revelation in the Thought of Saint Augustine*, Oxford Theological Monographs (Oxford: Clarendon Press, 1992), 54–96.

the process of human transformation. The terms bearing a precise meaning appear in book 1 of *On Christian Teaching*, in a passage that combines them with the journey image: "Suppose we were travelers who could live happily only in our homeland, and because our absence made us unhappy we wished to put an end to our misery and return to our homeland: we would need transport by land or sea which we could use (*utendum esset*) to travel to our homeland, the object of our enjoyment (*fruendum erat*)."[36] As Augustine applies the terms to a whole range of potential objects, some infelicities begin to emerge, but the distinction between use and enjoyment is essentially this: one *uses* something by treating it as a means toward some end, and one *enjoys* whatever brings satisfaction in and of itself.[37] The idea of "transport by land or sea" is parallel to use, arrival at one's homeland the imaginative equivalent to enjoyment. As has been suggested already, the only thing that human beings ought to enjoy, in the sense just specified, is God.[38] "God alone is the end of desire; and that entails that there

[36] *On Christian Teaching* 1.4 (CCSL 32, 8; OWC Green, 9).

[37] In addition to the first book of *On Christian Teaching*, see also the very similar use of the pair of terms in *On Eighty-Three Varied Questions* 30 (CCSL 44A, 38–40; WSA I/12, 43–45).

[38] Gerald Press claims that the difference between use and enjoyment is "not a metaphysical or physical distinction; it is a moral one. It is drawn with reference to the attainment of happiness (*beatitudo*), the idea of obligation ... is clearly expressed by the gerundives *fruendum* and *utendum*, and the rest of the Book 1 maintains the imagery of the moral journey introduced here. And this moral orientation and motivation of the argument is sustained throughout the entire work." See "The Content and Argument of Augustine's De doctrina christiana," *Augustiniana* 31 (1981): 171n14. As he notes, Press is here following Gerard Istace, "Le livre Ier du De doctrina christiana de Saint Augustin. Organisation synthétique et méthode de mise en oeuvre," *Ephémérides theologicae Lovanienses* 32 (1956): 292. Pollmann also stresses that the concept of *caritas*, which she reads as essentially ethical in orientation, is determinative for the first book of the treatise: *Doctrina christiana*, 128–35. It is certainly true to say that this distinction pertains to ethics or morality – the domain of choices – but Augustine is presenting the grounds for valuing things as ontological, in the sense that one ought to love most that which is best, that is, God. Likewise, the basis for loving others as oneself is that other human beings fall in the same

is no finality, no 'closure', no settled or intrinsic meaning in the world we inhabit."[39] God is not an item within the world, an individual entity among the other finite things that together constitute the complete set of things that exist. Rather, everything that exists derives from God and is contingent on him, and he himself stands outside the entire series as the condition of its possibility.[40]

That people have misguided affections, being inclined to prefer lower things to higher ones, is their deeply ingrained condition, and central to the solution to this is the incarnation. It is at the single point of the incarnation that God entered earthly, human existence: in the person of Jesus Christ, God gives himself over to be known *as part* of the world, not simply *by means* of it. The entire world is a semiotic system that speaks of God for those who have the eyes to see, but the incarnation is a divine condescension to humanity's fixation with the created world: "And although wisdom is everywhere present to the inner eye that is healthy and pure, it deigned to appear even to the carnal eyes of those whose inner eye was weak and impure."[41] How should the incarnation be understood? In *On Christian Teaching*, Augustine says that people should be "hastening eagerly" through the humanity of Christ in order to perceive, and indeed to enjoy, his divinity.[42] This way of making the point risks suggesting that the deity of Christ is something distinct, lurking behind the humanity, when it would be better to say – as Augustine does in the mature configuration of his Christology – that there is nothing to the humanity apart from the deity.[43] It is not that one should look through the humanity *as if to something else*, which is the deity; for apart from the humanity of

ontological/axiological category as oneself. Hence, it is a false dichotomy to claim that Augustine is operating in a register that is ethical rather than metaphysical.

39 Williams, "Language, Reality and Desire," 140.

40 *On Christian Teaching* 1.5 (CCSL 32, 9; OWC Green, 10).

41 *On Christian Teaching* 1.11 (CCSL 32, 12; OWC Green, 13).

42 *On Christian Teaching* 1.39 (CCSL 32, 29; OWC Green, 26).

43 Cameron, *Christ Meets Me Everywhere*, 229.

Jesus, there is not anything else that exists in addition to it. One should see the humanity itself as divine, such that when one sees the humanity and discerns its significance, one is seeing the divinity.[44] Through biblical interpretation, readers should come to enjoy Jesus Christ, so understood.

Though the use/enjoyment terminology is important in *On Christian Teaching* for the way Augustine calls on readers to relate to the Bible, it is awkward in certain ways. Stressing strongly that one should not enjoy what one is using can make it easy to forget that even use is a form of love – just one that does not result in ultimate satisfaction. This is why Augustine must issue the qualification that it is possible to delight in things that serve as "conveyances," but only in such a way as to appreciate them for the sake of the journey they facilitate, not in their own right.[45] In addition, there is at least one collision between the technical sense that Augustine stipulates for enjoyment and biblical usage of the same language, which he feels is binding on him. The example comes from Paul's affectionate comment to his addressee Philemon, when the apostle says, "So, brother, I shall enjoy you in the Lord."[46] Augustine's strategy is to say that the enjoyment that is specifically in the Lord counts as use according to his definition, for the love Paul has for Philemon does not terminate on him, but opens up to include the God whom both Paul and Philemon serve.[47] The solution works well enough, but that his usage does not mesh obviously with that of the Bible itself means that Augustine has to defend his chosen terminology. Augustine is able to anticipate both of these ways in which the language he employs is susceptible to

[44] Cameron is right that Augustine is not entirely clear about these matters in *On Christian Teaching*, and it is only with later works, such as *Against Faustus, a Manichee*, that he reaches a more satisfactory formulation on the relationship between Christ's humanity and divinity (*Christ Meets Me Everywhere*, 227–31, 258–81).

[45] *On Christian Teaching* 1.39 (CCSL 32, 29; OWC Green, 27).

[46] *On Christian Teaching* 1.37 (CCSL 32, 27; OWC Green, 25).

[47] *On Christian Teaching* 1.37 (CCSL 32, 27; OWC Green, 25–26).

being misunderstood. While the qualifications make his terminological scheme less elegant and more cumbersome, they serve adequately to clarify his overall purpose.

There is one final awkward implication of saying that one must use everything except God, but this one serves especially well as a reminder that the language's purpose is to discuss reading the Bible. If human beings are to enjoy God alone and use all else, that must include using other people, which makes it sound as if human beings are instrumentalized in a given person's own projects, being forced to serve one's own purposes and amounting to little more than tools to be employed, rather than having an inherent value that needs to be respected. At least this language, taken by itself, could suggest this, apart from Augustine's explicit critique of seeking to acquire power over others as disrespecting the fact that other people fall in precisely the same spot on the grand scale of value as oneself does.[48] Rowan Williams provides a deeply sympathetic summary of Augustine's treatment of this issue:

> To "use" the love of neighbor . . . is simply to allow the capacity for gratuitous or self-forgetful *dilectio* opened up in these and other such loves to be opened up still further. The language of *uti* is designed to warn against an attitude toward any finite person or object that terminates their meaning in their capacity to satisfy my desire, that treats them as an end of desire.[49]

This is a convincing reading, but Augustine's language has to be justified with this sort of vindicatory gloss to compensate for what, at least on a hasty interpretation, might appear to be an endorsement of selfishly using one's fellow human beings. Because of the comprehensiveness of Augustine's use/enjoyment scheme, he must explain where human beings fall within it, but his language

[48] *On Christian Teaching* 1.23 (CCSL 32, 18–19; OWC Green, 18).
[49] Williams, "Language, Reality and Desire," 140.

is much more naturally applied in the context of the main thrust of his discussion.

Augustine deploys the language of use and enjoyment mainly for the sake of expounding biblical interpretation, where it makes his overall point clearly. It is perhaps for this reason that Augustine does not seem overly concerned about the problems just discussed, though the tangles he has to fight through to clarify his terms may serve as reasons that he does not recur to this language often in later writing. Be that as it may, the main focus of *On Christian Teaching* is biblical interpretation, and to speak of using the Bible to foster the love of God, of reading the text with that purpose in view, does not create the same sort of difficulties that are generated by applying this terminology to other human beings, because the Bible presents itself to be used in this way.[50] Construed as the "face of God for now,"[51] the Bible can be used by readers as a means to engage with God via a linguistic medium, which became necessary due to sin, and which has the capacity to form readers in divine and human love in the present life, thus reversing sin's effects and moving readers in the direction of being who they ought to be. The next section of this chapter provides an explanation of how the Bible does these things. The purpose of this section has been to sketch out the nature of the one in relation to whom the text has this effect.

When readers interpret the biblical text, they reach out toward their telos. This telos is the loving contemplation of wisdom

[50] What is missing from Oliver O'Donovan's generally quite useful essay on the first book of *On Christian Teaching* is a clear sense that the single book under discussion is part of a larger work with a literary integrity, whose subject is the interpretation of the Bible. Though he criticizes others for allowing their interpretation of the text to be controlled by how key concepts are used in other contexts, O'Donovan himself ought to reflect greater awareness that the use/enjoyment language is introduced into the treatise primarily to discuss the Bible. See "Usus and Fruitio in Augustine, De doctrina christiana I," *Journal of Theological Studies* 33 (1982): 361–97.

[51] *Sermon* 22.7 (CCSL 41, 297; WSA III/2, 46).

(*sapientia*), reflection that moves beyond the realm of the senses to eternal and immutable truths. Wisdom makes itself available in the present world in the person of Jesus Christ, who becomes the focal point of the reader's interpretive efforts. Readers are on a journey to the one abode which can fully satisfy their desires, and the whole drive of reading is to move them in this direction. Qua readers, they cannot finally achieve this state, for it occurs only in the, *eschaton*, not in the present life. Yet in the *eschaton*, they will no longer depend on a text that points them to God, for they can experience the *visio Dei* without the aid of created auxiliaries. In the present life, readers should be seeking to move in the direction of that experience as they reflect on the subject matter of the text. For this reason, reading is akin to what Michel Foucault calls a technology of the self. Technologies of the self "permit individuals to effect by their own means or with the help of others a certain number of operations on their own bodies and souls, thoughts, conduct, and way of being, so as to transform themselves in order to attain a certain state of happiness, purity, wisdom, perfection, or immortality."[52] Yet the influence that reading has on them is not so much a function of what they do to themselves, as what they experience by allowing the text to direct them to God's gracious self-disclosure. Whether readers engage the text directly, or hear it read to them, this experience is what makes it important to them.

## Text: Signs Evoking Love of God

### *The Nature of the Text: Initial Distinctions*

Augustine also has a theological view of the text. To bring this issue into focus, the question of how Augustine views the Bible

[52] Michel Foucault, "Technologies of the Self," in *Technologies of the Self: A Seminar with Michel Foucault*, ed. Huck Gutman, Patrick H. Hutton, and Luther H. Martin (Amherst: University of Massachusetts Press, 1988), 18.

theologically needs to be distinguished from another issue, that of which words constitute the text. Any given text is a "bounded verbal artifact," a sequence of words with a beginning and an end,[53] but for Augustine the question of which words constitute the Bible cannot receive a simple answer. Augustine did not know the Bible as a single unified volume, but rather in various manuscript versions of individual books and sets of books.[54] One reason that the issue of the words constituting Scripture is complex is the controversy over which books make up the Bible. There are places in his writing where Augustine lists the books of the Bible seriatim. He stood in basic agreement with other Christians of his period about which works belonged in the biblical canon, but his lists also indicate that there was a penumbra of doubt about certain books, regarding whether or not they properly belonged to the privileged set of texts that were to be read in public worship and that were to regulate belief and conduct.[55] Augustine's operative canon of texts included the works that came to be known as deuterocanonical. Another cause of complexity is the issue of the language in which the books of the Bible were written. Augustine most often made use of the Old Latin translations of the books of the Old and New Testaments, though he gradually warmed to the more sophisticated translation produced by Jerome, which came to be known in later history as the Vulgate. The Greek Septuagint, rather than the Hebrew text of the Old Testament, was for him the authoritative

[53] Paul J. Griffiths, "Which Are the Words of Scripture?," *Theological Studies* 72 (2011): 703.

[54] For extensive cataloging of his use of biblical texts, together with some analysis, see Anne-Marie La Bonnardière, *Biblia Augustiniana*, 7 vols. (Paris: Études augustiniennes, 1960–1975).

[55] For more on how Augustine understands the canon, see Anne-Marie La Bonnardière, "The Canon of Sacred Scripture," in *Augustine and the Bible*, ed. Pamela Bright, The Bible through the Ages (Notre Dame: University of Notre Dame Press, 1999), 26–41.

version of the first part of the Bible.[56] While Augustine did not have absolute certainty about which books belonged in the canon of Scripture, and though he often accessed the text via translation, with his view on which rendering was best evolving over time, he nevertheless observed a crisp in-principle distinction between texts that were part of Scripture and those that were not. The question on which this section concentrates – how Augustine views the text theologically – concerns the theological categories through which he construes the text, not the precise set of words to which he applies that category, as important as the latter question is in its own right.

In what follows, what it means that the text of the Bible is a set of signs directing the reader's attention to the triune God and continually reorienting the reader's affections will be unpacked. Because this is the perspective from which Augustine views the text, his ontology of the Bible is intricately tied up with a further issue, and it is worth making this distinction explicit. While the text is a privileged group of signifiers, the entire existing universe is a semiotic system that ultimately points to the same *res* as the text does. For Augustine, the created world can be seen as a poem or a beautifully ordered speech, which reveals to us that all things are providentially ordered.[57] Scripture is needed in order to see the world in this light, but the patterns that Scripture points to in the world do offer testimony to the triune God, and they can be understood in this way.[58] Thus, it is not only the Bible that has this semiotic capacity, but the entirety of the world: "To enlighten us and enable us, the whole temporal dispensation was set up by divine providence for

[56] For additional background on Augustine's developing preferences regarding textual versions of the Bible, see Anne-Marie La Bonnardière, "Did Augustine Use Jerome's Vulgate?," in *Augustine and the Bible*, ed. Pamela Bright, The Bible through the Ages (Notre Dame: University of Notre Dame Press, 1999), 42–51.

[57] For analysis of relevant passages, see Harrison, *Beauty and Revelation in the Thought of Saint Augustine*, 116–22.

[58] Ibid., 114–16.

our salvation."[59] While the text and the world both have a semiotic function that converges on identical subject matter, the text is privileged in the sense that it trains its readers to discern the world's value as a signifier by providing the concepts and narratives through which to construe it as such. While the text is not absolutely unique in being a set of signs, it has a certain priority above the other signifiers in that all other signifiers are interpreted on the basis of the text. It is also true, however, that an understanding of a whole range of auxiliary disciplines is important for the interpretation of the Bible, as these constitute background knowledge that is necessary to read well some texts that would otherwise remain obscure. There is thus complex interplay between textual and non-textual signifiers. The section below hones in on the text itself in its signifying capacity.

### *Semiotics as Theological Ontology*

One of Augustine's original contributions to the history of Christian reflection on interpretation is to apply semiotic insights to biblical hermeneutics by construing the Bible as a set of signs.[60] It is not Augustine's intention to offer a comprehensive semiotic theory, though sometimes commentators discuss what he says about semiotics in isolation from the overarching concerns to which he relates it.[61] His treatments of signs are circumscribed,

[59] *On Christian Teaching* 1.39 (CCSL 32, 29; OWC Green, 27).

[60] See Isabelle Bochet, "Les signes," in *La doctrine chrétienne = De doctrina christiana*, ed. Madeleine Moreauet et al., Bibliothèque augustinienne 11/2 (Paris: Institut d'études augustiniennes, 1997), 483–84, who is building on B. Darrell Jackson, "The Theory of Signs in St. Augustine's De doctrina christiana," in *Augustine: A Collection of Critical Essays*, ed. R. A. Markus, Modern Studies in Philosophy (Garden City: Anchor Books, 1972), 136.

[61] For instance, see Christopher Kirwan, *Augustine*, The Arguments of the Philosophers (New York: Routledge, 1989), 35–52. B. Darrell Jackson also breaks Augustine's semiotics out of the context of his other concerns, but he does so with much greater awareness of the limits of doing so: "The Theory of Signs in St. Augustine's *De doctrina christiana*," 92–147.

especially in *On Christian Teaching*, where he is clearly concentrating on Scripture. The aim of this discussion is to come to grips with Augustine's view of signs and to see, more specifically, how theological language functions within his semiotics of the scriptural text.

By the term *sign*, Augustine means something that signifies something for someone.[62] Within this signifying network, there are thus three elements that relate to one another: the sign that signifies, for instance a passage from the Bible; the subject matter the text says something about; and the interpreter of the sign who understands it as making sense, rather than it being simply a group of marks on a page that do not combine in any meaningful way. Sometimes the final component of this set is elided in certain discussions of what it means for something to be a sign, with the result that all that Augustine highlights in those contexts is the other two parts, signifier and signified.[63] In the overall framework he develops, however, the third element plays a prominent part: its significance is to point out that the way in which an interpreter makes sense of the signs that constitute the Bible, or decodes their meaning, is at least in part a function of conventions which the interpreter observes and participates in by virtue of arriving at an understanding of the meaning of the signifiers. That Augustine's view of signs is tripartite underlines the way in which the interpreter is enmeshed in a wider semiotic field, which is structured by conventions, and which connects up with certain patterns of willing and loving that relate to both the interpretive intentionality that reading the text on its own terms requires, and the formative influence that interpretation has on the reader.

All the signs making up the Bible belong to a particular classification or subdivision within the more general category of signs. Biblical words belong to the species of signs that are "given" (*data*)

[62] *On Christian Teaching* 2.1 (CCSL 32, 32; OWC Green, 30).

[63] *On Christian Teaching* 1.2 (CCSL 32, 7; OWC Green, 9).

rather than "natural" (*naturalia*). Natural signs, to begin with the category that is less important to Augustine, signify something quite apart from any intention on the part of the giver of the sign; for instance, the facial expression of an angry or depressed person makes their emotional state known, whether or not the person with that feeling wishes to communicate to others how they feel inside.[64] These signs allow something to be known – in that sense they signify – but what they make known is not a function of the intentionality of the agent who gives the sign, but rather what interpreters of the signs are able to infer from the object that produces the sign.[65] Smoke indicates fire because a fire is required to produce smoke.[66] In this case, inferring what can be inferred from the sign is not contingent on any socially determined signifying conventions, but simply on knowing about the operation of the natural world. By contrasting natural signs with the category that he actually brings to bear on the Bible, given signs, Augustine underscores what is most important about the latter for the endeavor of biblical interpretation, namely, how they communicate a certain intention. The purpose of given signs is for authors "to show, to the best of their ability, the emotions of their minds, or anything they have felt or learned."[67] For this class of signifiers, grasping meaning is tied closely to becoming involved with and affected by the intention of the giver. What makes Scripture important for the Christian reader is that the intention with which the signs are presented is aligned with the Christian's overriding obligation to love God and neighbor above other things that compete for one's allegiance. As Paul Kolbet explains, "Since this intention is properly

[64] *On Christian Teaching* 2.2 (CCSL 32, 32–33; OWC Green, 30).

[65] R. A. Markus, "Augustine on Signs," in *Signs and Meanings: World and Text in Ancient Christianity* (Liverpool: Liverpool University Press, 1996) 88.

[66] *On Christian Teaching* 2.2 (CCSL 32, 32–33; OWC Green, 30).

[67] *On Christian Teaching* 2.3 (CCSL 32, 33; OWC Green, 30).

ordered, the more deeply one is involved with these given signs, the more one's affections begin to conform to those of the givers."[68]

The prior part of this chapter argued that Augustine's view of what it means to be a human being cannot be articulated without reference to God. Just as this is the case, so also theology is part of his account of the Bible as a set of signs, and therefore the application of semiotics to Scripture yields a theological ontology of the text. The first way in which God is written into his hermeneutical system – or, to frame the matter more accurately, the capacity in which God remains outside the system, though it points in his direction and reaches out toward him – is that the triune God is the subject matter of the biblical text. He is the *res* that the biblical text signifies, but God is a necessarily and permanently elusive subject, whom readers of the Bible will by no means ever comprehend, since the language in which the text is written, like any human language, is incapable of revealing him in such a way that he could possibly be mastered.[69] Though God is a thing in the sense that he is that to which signs point, and is therefore at least distinguishable from the signs themselves, he is not a finite thing, a single item among others within the universe of contingent being.[70] Everything in the created realm depends for its existence and goodness on him, and creaturely language can only gesture toward him without being fully adequate to his nature. God is properly speaking ineffable, though he has sanctioned language to

[68] Paul R. Kolbet, *Augustine and the Cure of Souls: Revising a Classical Ideal*, Christianity and Judaism in Antiquity Series (Notre Dame: University of Notre Dame Press, 2010), 148.

[69] In a slightly later text, Augustine counsels a catechist that even if he cannot speak as well as he would like, and even if he cannot engage his audience as deeply as he would wish, nothing he could say or understand could match up to the reality of the God about whom he is speaking, and so he must proceed with a realistic assessment of what he is seeking to accomplish: *On the Instruction of Beginners* 2.4 (CCSL 46, 123; ACW 2, 16–17).

[70] *On Christian Teaching* 1.5 (CCSL 32, 9; OWC Green, 10).

serve as an instrument that refers to him in a relatively adequate way, and that has an effect on the minds and hearts of those who use it.[71] And *use* it is what human beings must do in the precise sense Augustine assigns that term: they cannot presume that any human language, even the languages in which the biblical text was written and into which it was translated, is fully transparent to divinity, as if the vantage point it provides matches up perfectly with the reality of which it speaks, such that there is nothing more to know of God once the text has received an appropriate interpretation. The text is sufficient to give its readers a provisional understanding of God and to shape their affections in relation to him. In this way, one of the three elements of the definition of signs (*res*) is, when brought to bear on the Bible, theological in the strongest possible sense, in that it is God himself.

The second way the sign framework is theologically oriented is, as has already been suggested, that the effect of engaging with such signs is that the interpreter's stance toward God is shaped by reading. As a set of given signs, the text gives expression to its author's intention or emotion with respect to some object: in that way, the written work is saying something about something. However, it also says something *to someone*, and grasping the signifying force of a sign activates a set of conventions between the reader and the producer of the text, together with the wider social context from within which the author wrote. These conventions are twofold. First of all, making sense of the text obligates the reader to be able to navigate the natural language in which the text was composed or, if that language differs from the one in which the text is accessed, the language of the translation.[72] Much more important for the purpose of this discussion is the second set of conventions in which readers

[71] *On Christian Teaching* 1.6 (CCSL 32, 9–10; OWC Green, 10–11).

[72] On the text existing in various versions and human unity being broken up by the different linguistic communities that make up the world, see *On Christian Teaching* 2.5–6 (CCSL 32, 34–35; OWC Green, 32).

take part, to the extent that they read with the grain of text, or in accord with its purpose. Those who interpret the intention-expressive signs constituting the Bible engage them as representing properly ordered expressions of the divine will, although the way in which the text offers that representation is often anything but transparent.[73] When readers engage the text in a receptive posture toward this expression of the divine will, which is summarized in the double command to love God above all else and one's neighbor equally with oneself,[74] the will's engagement in this signifying convention works on the reader's affections such that they increasingly line up with this leading principle of Scripture. Because of this second level of conventions, readers are not only focused on the *res* of the text, but are also shaped by the way in which textual signifiers hold out a vision of relating fittingly to it.

An example of Augustine's exegesis will help illustrate how the text has this effect on the reader. Consider this passage from Song of Songs: "Your teeth are like a flock of shorn ewes ascending from the pool, all of which give birth to twins, and there is not a sterile animal among them."[75] Augustine reads this as presenting truths about the church in the form of imagery that rouses more delight in these truths than a more abstract doctrinal rendering of them could.[76] Augustine relates this text to the double love command by seeing in it a representation of how the church incorporates into itself new members who shed their burden of sin (they have set aside their fleeces), and as they ascend from the baptismal pool, they give birth to twins, which is to say they manifest the love of God and neighbor, and none is sterile or fails to display such affection.[77] The text clothes its message in a form that gives the

[73] *On Christian Teaching* 2.6–7 (CCSL 32, 35; OWC Green, 32–33).
[74] *On Christian Teaching* 1.39 (CCSL 32, 28–29; OWC Green, 26–27).
[75] *On Christian Teaching* 2.7 (CCSL 32, 35; OWC Green, 33).
[76] *On Christian Teaching* 2.7–8 (CCSL 32, 35–36; OWC Green, 33).
[77] *On Christian Teaching* 2.7 (CCSL 32, 36; OWC Green, 33).

reader who comes to understand it great pleasure in this truth, but it also conceals the lesson in metaphorical dress, thus pressing the reader to exert greater effort and therefore to rejoice all the more in discovering a truth that proves to be hard-won. The basic doctrines of the Christian faith are not so thoroughly concealed in the Bible that they cannot be found in its relatively lucid passages, but difficult passages each shed further light and reward those who are willing to work hard to understand them.[78] All biblical signs embody a "peculiar dialectic of presence and absence"[79] in that the sign is readily available on a written page or is read aloud and therefore heard by those listening, while what it signifies is made available only to the mind of the interpreter and so is absent in a sense. However, certain signs have the effect they do because that which is signified is harder to detect than it is in passages where the meaning lies on the surface of the text, and because they are vivid and indeed delightful illustrations of important principles. In these ways, the text works on the reader's affections, and understanding it in relation to the double love command, by reading it figurally, invokes a set of communicative conventions that tie this passage to its *res*.

There are similar forms of communication outside biblical texts that draw interpreters into conventions that redirect the interpreter's will, but that do so by tugging the will in the opposite direction the Bible does. Such signifying practices serve to illuminate how the Bible operates by communicating similarly in one respect, while at the same time being radically different in another way. Examples include communicative exchanges that Augustine would consider superstitious practices, such as consulting astrologers for a knowledge of the future. Astrological predictions connect the timing of a baby's birth to the character of the child's life, and are predicated on

[78] *On Christian Teaching* 2.8 (CCSL 32, 35; OWC Green, 33).

[79] Umberto Eco, *Semiotics and the Philosophy of Language*, Advances in Semiotics (Bloomington: Indiana University Press, 1984), 19.

the assumption, which must be shared by the one offering the prediction and the one who receives it with confidence in it, that the moment of the baby's birth correlates with events that will occur later in life.[80] These agreements are socially shared by those who place stock in astrology, and are not a set of meanings that attach of necessity to the events themselves: the meaning these signs have is conventional. As Augustine says, "Likewise the signs by which this deadly agreement with demons is achieved have an effect that is in proportion to each individual's attention to them."[81] Apart from the fundamental principle of correlation on which the system is based being a false belief,[82] the reason that it is wrong to take part in this signifying system is that it works toward precisely the opposite end as the economy of biblical signs: "They [astrological signs] are not publicly promulgated by God in order to foster the love of God and one's neighbor, but they consume the hearts of wretched mortals by fostering selfish desires for temporal things."[83] Such signs do this by virtue of assigning ultimacy and influence to created things that are not worth the faith people put in them.[84] They foster an undue love of temporal things.

In sum, theological language is indispensable for thinking about what the text is as a field of signifiers, for God is the text's referent, and readers participate in the mode of willing the text expresses in the way that they decode its communicative intention. Theological language is thus a constitutive element of what the text is because it represents a key component to two of the three elements within the

[80] *On Christian Teaching* 2.32–37 (CCSL 32, 55–60; OWC Green, 49–53).

[81] *On Christian Teaching* 2.37 (CCSL 32, 60; OWC Green, 53).

[82] For Augustine, the false basis of the system is not the most important reason to forsake it: *On Christian Teaching* 2.35 (CCSL 32, 58; OWC Green, 51).

[83] *On Christian Teaching* 2.36 (CCSL 32, 58–59; OWC Green, 52).

[84] *On Christian Teaching* 2.32 (CCSL 32, 55; OWC Green, 49). On this whole issue, I am indebted to R. A. Markus, "Augustine on Magic: A Neglected Semiotic Theory," in *Signs and Meanings: World and Text in Ancient Christianity* (Liverpool: Liverpool University Press, 1996), 125–46.

fundamental definition of signs. It might be said that the final aspect of Augustine's three-part view of signs, the signifier itself, is also theological in that it has its origin in God, though Augustine does not develop this point to anywhere near the same degree that he elaborates and expounds the other two. Nevertheless, this account of the text is a deeply theological one; language relating the text to God is right at the core of what makes this set of signs the scriptural text that it is. It is insufficient to say that theology represents a limiting factor to what would otherwise be a universalizing hermeneutical framework, a tradition-specific element that stands in the way of a system that is moving in the direction of being applicable to the broadest imaginable audience and keeps it from attaining the scope it could otherwise have.[85] Rather than being an encumbrance to a fundamentally different conception of signs, theology is a defining feature of this way of thinking about them.

## Conclusion

The two main points made in this chapter, the first about the reader and the second regarding the text, set up the discussion about interpretation that will take place in Chapter 2. The reader of the Bible is an embodied soul who has distorted affections that can be continually reformed and redirected by training themselves on Christ, who is at the center of all of the Bible's signifying activity. The incarnation is the single point in the created order that is transparent to divinity, and the text is a set of signs which engage the reader's will in a process of coming to know its *res*, as the reader

[85] For her commentary's treatment of signs, see Pollmann, *Doctrina christiana*, 147–96. For her clearest and most distilled depiction of theology as a limiting particularity for Augustine's whole hermeneutical framework, see "Augustine's Hermeneutics as a Universal Discipline!?," in *Augustine and the Disciplines: From Cassiciacum to Confessions*, ed. Karla Pollmann and Mark Vessey (Oxford: Oxford University Press, 2005), 224–31.

relates to the text with an intention that fits what the text itself is. Theological language is thus indispensable for depicting both text and reader: these realities cannot be described adequately without reference to God. Augustine makes an original contribution to the history of biblical hermeneutics in applying semiotics to the Bible, and he is expansive as well in his consideration of the reader's involvement in the interpretive task. Given who the reader is, and what the text is, one would expect that reading should center around interpreting the text with respect to Jesus Christ as a formative practice with both cognitive and affective components. That is, considering these two ideas in their interconnection would lead a reader of Augustine to assume his treatment of interpretation will take this broad form. Chapter 2 argues that this is exactly what we find in Augustine's texts. All interpretive work has a theological aim, and he tailors the strategies for reading he inherits such that they work to fulfill the goal of interpretation.

# 2 | Between *Scientia* and the Trinity

Augustine's thinking about what constitutes proper "interpretation of Scripture" (*tractandarum scripturarum*), which he mentions in the opening lines of *On Christian Teaching*,[1] has what we might call an essentially substantive rather than procedural character, despite the extensive treatment he gives to rules and procedures for reading. This terminology is adapted from discussions of epistemology and ethics and can be extended into the context of biblical interpretation.[2] Calling a hermeneutical theory substantive designates the criterion of proper reading by specifying what is central to interpretation. What makes for proper reading here is not, in the first instance, whether the interpreter follows certain rules, but whether the reader arrives at views about the text that are considered correct. The emphasis falls, thus, on the outcome or the interpretive conclusion instead of the process of reading. Writing about ethics, Charles Taylor says: "To make practical reason substantive implies that practical wisdom is a matter of seeing an order which is in some sense in nature. This order determines what ought to be done."[3] Likewise, viewing hermeneutical rationality in substantive terms means that procedures do have some importance, but in such a way that they are responsive to the agenda set by substantive commitments. In order to arrive at approved results,

[1] *On Christian Teaching* Prooemium 1 (CCSL 32, 1; OWC Green, 3).

[2] Charles Taylor, *Sources of the Self: The Making of the Modern Identity* (Cambridge: Cambridge University Press, 1989), 85–86.

[3] Ibid., 86.

certain sorts of preconceptions are ruled out from the beginning because they start interpretation off on the wrong track.

By contrast, a procedural approach to biblical interpretation prescinds from making any requirements at all about what the results of reading will be, and instead insists firmly that a set of rules or interpretive principles be followed rigorously, without their being shaped by consideration of what the results of reading might turn out to be. A procedural approach to interpretation takes truth out of the equation in order to define the enterprise around following a certain course or employing right operations. It may well be the case that following correct interpretive procedures will, in the end, deliver the truth, yet that is not what defines an approach to interpretation as procedural. Procedural approaches "sideline a sense or vision of the good and consider it irrelevant"[4] to how reading ought to take place. That is to say, no view of the good influences interpretation; any such vision that is attractive to the reader has to be bracketed out for the sake of applying the rules properly. Procedural approaches to interpretation thus fit nicely with skeptical questioning of holistic religious views of reality, and often take such critical questioning as their point of departure, though all that they require is that such systems play no part within the process of reading. In Part II of this book, we will see an example of a fundamentally procedural approach to interpretation in the figure of Benedict de Spinoza: he stands as a major figure in the history of interpretation who thinks in a fundamentally different way than Augustine does about what makes for a good reading of the Bible.

For Augustine, a theological ontology leads to an ethics of biblical interpretation: how the reader and text are understood in relation to God determines how the text ought to be read. As has already been mentioned, a substantive view does not relegate procedures to the

[4] Ibid., 86.

margins of its account of interpretation; rules have an important place, and Augustine mentions that there are indeed certain rules for interpretation that can be passed on to readers and are profitable for them to employ.[5] Yet the nature of these procedures is shaped by the work that they do in relation to a theological vision of the good: approved interpretive procedures become a means toward an end, a way of getting readers to understand and to love what they should. The rules do not finally make sense in the abstract, outside of this particular theological framework,[6] or outside of any substantive framework altogether.[7] This chapter makes three interconnected main points about Augustine's substantive approach to reading. The first has to do with how human beings acquire a sense of what the ultimate good is. According to Augustine's view of biblical interpretation, at least by the time that his perspective has matured to the point represented in *On Christian Teaching*, human beings are inducted into a determinate view of what is good by affiliating with an ecclesial community, though the content of what they learn is also articulated within the Bible itself. Second, there is

[5] *On Christian Teaching* Prooemium 1 (CCSL 32, 1; OWC Green, 3).

[6] There are, of course, further constraints on interpretive rules, such as cultural and practical considerations that will enter into the discussion of this chapter as well. The point at present is to highlight the role of theological content.

[7] A discussion of a similar pattern in pre-modern ethics can be found in Henry Sidgwick, *The Methods of Ethics*, 7th ed. (Chicago: University of Chicago Press, 1962), 1–14. There is useful commentary on this text in John Rawls, *Lectures on the History of Political Philosophy* (Cambridge, MA: Belknap Press of Harvard University Press, 2007), 1–3. For other examples of ethical rules that make sense against the background of specific frameworks, see G. E. M. Anscombe, "Modern Moral Philosophy," *Philosophy* 33 (1958): 1–19; Alasdair C. MacIntyre, *After Virtue: A Study in Moral Theory*, 2nd ed. (Notre Dame: University of Notre Dame Press, 1984), 51–61. For an objection against continuing to think that ontology has implications for ethics, see Pierre Hadot, *Philosophy as a Way of Life: Spiritual Exercises from Socrates to Foucault* (Oxford: Blackwell, 1995), 283, who considers ontological frameworks to be contrived justifications for certain practices. Hadot takes for granted that these viewpoints are articulated as after-the-fact rationales for practices that already have achieved acceptance, such that practices really ground beliefs, rather than vice versa.

an aim or purpose for interpretation that is identical with the telos of all human life and activity. Third, this aim sets in context what interpretive strategies should seek to achieve.

## Theology and the Hermeneutical Circle

For Augustine, there is a certain circularity to the process of reading: the better one understands the subject of the text, the more adequate the interpretation that becomes possible; the greater one's skill in reading, the more fully one understands the *res* of Scripture. In the history of hermeneutical discussion, there are two major versions of the hermeneutical circle. Circularity can mean that a reader's understanding of what any given part of a text means depends on the accuracy with which he construes the sense of the whole, as all the parts cohere, perhaps in a complex way, and constitute the text in its (differentiated) unity.[8] The second sort of circularity pertains to the self's involvement with and knowledge of the subject matter of the text. There is, once again, a dialectic in play which can seem like a paradox if it is pushed to an extreme: the reader can only interpret the text properly if she has a viable provisional understanding of its content, though this proleptic knowledge is subject to constant adjustment and change under the pressure of further acquaintance with the text. Though Augustine does attempt to fit the parts of the Bible into a certain sort of whole, and this becomes an important consideration in how he reads certain passages, it is the second type of circularity that is more fundamentally important for this chapter, because it pertains more directly to the way readers acquire substantive commitments which determine how they engage texts from the Bible.

[8] See, for instance, Friedrich Schleiermacher, *Hermeneutics and Criticism and Other Writings*, Cambridge Texts in the History of Philosophy (Cambridge: Cambridge University Press, 1998), 24, 27.

Contemporary scholars will be familiar with the second version of circularity mainly through Gadamer, whose influence is sufficiently strong on the current scene that almost any discussion of this sort of circularity takes place via the vocabulary he provides. Gadamer is not concerned exclusively with the biblical text, but focuses on a more general category of texts into which the Bible is sometimes made to fit, that is, the classic. Classics are works of gravitas, those that are rich enough to defy all simple summaries and that attract the attention of readers from well beyond the texts' own contexts of origin. As Gadamer explains: "When we call something classical, there is a consciousness of something enduring, of significance that cannot be lost and that is independent of all the circumstances of time – a kind of timeless present that is contemporaneous with every other present."[9] Such texts reach out to each subsequent generation of interpreters by means of their history of effects: they shape language and culture to the point that even those who have not yet read them and encountered them firsthand are influenced by them indirectly, especially when they think about the text's subject matter. Readers come to these texts with an established pre-understanding of them, even if they do not recognize it as such. What makes reading with understanding possible, though it may also distort understanding in some circumstances, is that classical texts transmit themselves to readers and quietly establish a pre-understanding, which forms the starting point for a conversation between the reader and the text about the text's claims. For Martin Heidegger, as also for Gadamer, such circularity is not essentially problematic: "What is decisive is not to get out of the circle, but to get in it in the right way. . . . The circle must not be degraded to a *vitiosum*, not even a tolerated one. A positive possibility of the most primordial knowledge is hidden in it."[10]

[9] Gadamer, *Truth and Method*, 288.

[10] Martin Heidegger, *Being and Time*, Suny Series in Contemporary Continental Philosophy (Albany: State University of New York Press, 1996), 143.

Gadamer's way of developing a view of circularity is distinct from Augustine's, though the two are sometimes conflated. Augustine does indeed reflect on the same broad type of circularity – the coinherence of the self and the subject matter of the text – and that is crucial for this chapter.[11] However, the difficulty with assimilating Augustine to this outlook is that the proper way to enter the circle is different for Augustine than it is for Gadamer.[12] Augustine's views evolve over the course of his career, but what facilitates understanding for him is a set of variables that are clearly theological in their

[11] In this connection, see the work of Robert Markus, who highlights the "triadicity" of Augustine's theory of signs, or the involvement of the human subject as well as the sign and its referent, thereby understanding Augustine's work by means of categories inspired by the pragmatism of C. S. Peirce. See his essays: "World and Text in Ancient Christianity I," 22–29; "Augustine on Signs," 101–4. An even more directly theological way of highlighting this interconnection is present within Ayres's discussion of dual-focus purification vis-à-vis interpretation: Lewis Ayres, *Nicaea and Its Legacy: An Approach to Fourth-Century Trinitarian Theology* (Oxford: Oxford University Press, 2004), 325–42.

[12] Bochet notes briefly, though she does not expand on the point, that neither Gadamer nor Paul Ricoeur retain the theological element of Augustine's circularity, despite Augustine's influence on them. See "Le cercle herméneutique," in *La doctrine chrétienne = De doctrina christiana*, ed. Madeleine Moreau et al., Bibliothèque augustinienne 11/2 (Paris: Institut d'études augustiniennes, 1997), 441–43. Pollmann glosses Augustine in a way that is inspired by Gadamer without noting the differences: "Augustine's Hermeneutics as a Universal Discipline!?," 211. For an approach that is both alive to the similarities between Augustine and the twentieth-century masters of hermeneutics, and that is utterly clear on the ways in which Augustine allows theology a role that the latter do not, see David Tracy, "Charity, Obscurity, Clarity: Augustine's Search for Rhetoric and Hermeneutics," in *Rhetoric and Hermeneutics in Our Time*, ed. Walter Jost and Michael J. Hyde (New Haven: Yale University Press, 1997), 271. Thus, Tracy grasps Bochet's essential point. For Gadamer's own confession of Augustine's impact on some of the deepest reaches of his thinking about hermeneutics, see the comments in Jean Grondin, *Introduction to Philosophical Hermeneutics*, Yale Studies in Hermeneutics (New Haven: Yale University Press, 1994), xiii–xiv. There is a more detailed discussion of these issues than is possible here in Darren Sarisky, "Reading Augustine in Light of Gadamer: Reflections on the Character of Prior Understanding," *International Journal of Systematic Theology* (Forthcoming).

basic orientation. This differs from Gadamer's main focus, which is on the historical contextualization and connectedness of both the text and reader. The remainder of this section briefly traces out Augustine's evolving theological thinking on this sort of circularity, beginning with a work in which it is Christ as God who imparts understanding to the human knowing subject, and moving into later works where he integrates ecclesiology more into his outlook, first treating it in general terms, and finally in *On Christian Teaching* unpacking its significance in formal, creedal fashion. Augustine does not use the terminology of hermeneutical circle, but he clearly uses theological concepts to portray how learning requires that there not be a simple binary relationship between the self and the subject matter about which the human subject is learning. With the caveat that this is what the terminology means, it is not inappropriate to use the language of hermeneutical circle in connection with him.

In an early dialogue, *On the Teacher*, Augustine's first dedicated explication of signs and their interpretation, Augustine wrestles directly with the issue of the circularity that understanding involves.[13] The question is a vexing one: a person encountering signs must be able to relate them to their referent to understand them properly, but if the person already understands the referent, what precisely is the contribution of the signs themselves? What is the role of prior understanding, and how do signs factor into the process of coming to understand the subject matter of the signs? In Augustine's own words, "For when I am shown a sign, it cannot teach me anything if it finds me ignorant of the reality for which the sign stands; but if it finds me acquainted with the reality, what do

[13] On the hermeneutical circle in relation to *On Christian Teaching*, see Bochet, "Le cercle herméneutique," 438–49; Kathy Eden, *Hermeneutics and the Rhetorical Tradition: Chapters in the Ancient Legacy & Its Humanist Reception* (New Haven: Yale University Press, 1997), 58–63; Mark D. Jordan, "Words and Word: Incarnation and Signification in Augustine's De doctrina christiana," *Augustinian Studies* 11 (1980): 191. In relation to a wider range of texts, see Bochet, *Le firmament de l'écriture*, 91–115.

I learn from the sign?"[14] In the dialogue, most of the discussion between Augustine and his interlocutor, especially early on, is given over to the idea that the purpose of giving signs is, in one way or another, to teach something to someone.[15] At the outset, the stress is thus on signs having a certain pedagogical efficacy. Yet as the discussion progresses, Augustine comes to emphasize the opposite point, the impotence of signs: "Now if we examine the matter more carefully, perhaps you will discover that nothing is learned by means of its signs."[16] This shift is surprising if the drift of the previous discussion about the effectiveness of signs is taken to suggest that those who were taught learned from their instruction.[17] However, teaching and learning differ from one another, and the former does not necessarily lead to the latter: to teach is to present something to another, while to learn means, not simply believing the instruction one has received, but grasping the content with one's own mind so as to understand it for oneself.[18] To understand or know, rather than simply to believe, requires a firsthand acquaintance with that which is known; this may be acquired by seeing an object one can perceive visually, or by conceptualizing an abstract idea.

Because knowing or understanding entails more than second-hand engagement with an item of potential knowledge, the perception of signs alone cannot effect this state. Augustine illustrates this

[14] *On the Teacher* 10.33 (CCSL 29, 192; FOC 59, 46–47).

[15] *On the Teacher* 10.31 (CCSL 29, 190; FOC 59, 44). For helpful reflections on how this thesis relates to contemporary questions, especially the so-called linguistic turn in twentieth-century philosophy, see Myles F. Burnyeat, "Wittgenstein and Augustine's De Magistro," in *The Augustinian Tradition*, ed. Gareth Matthews (Berkeley: University of California Press, 1999), 286–303; Andrew Louth, "Augustine on Language," *Journal of Literature and Theology* 3 (1989): 152.

[16] *On the Teacher* 10.33 (CCSL 29, 192; FOC 59, 46).

[17] *On the Teacher* 10.33 (CCSL 29, 192; FOC 59, 46–47).

[18] *On the Teacher* 10.36–37 (CCSL 29, 194–195; FOC 59, 49–51).

by reflecting on the interpretation of an obscure word drawn from the book of Daniel:

> When I read this, for example: "And their saraballae were not changed," the word "saraballae" does not convey to me the thing it signifies. If it is some kind of head-covering that goes by this name, did I, upon hearing the word, come to learn either what "head" or "covering" means? These things I knew before, and I came to know them, not when they were called these names by others, but when I saw them by myself. Indeed, when the sound of the two-syllable word *caput* [head] first struck my ears, I was just as ignorant of what it signified as when I first heard or read the word "saraballae." But, after frequent repetitions of the word "head," I discovered, by paying careful attention at the time it was used, that this was the word for something that was well known to me by sight. Before discovering it, the word was only a sound so far as I was concerned. I came to know it as a sign when I discovered the reality of which it is a sign. And I learned what this reality was, not, as I have said, by any sign, but by looking at it. Hence, it is more of a matter of the sign being learned from the thing we know, than it is of knowing the thing itself from the manifestation of its sign.[19]

Verbal explanation of an unknown sign, such as the term *saraballae*, is not entirely pointless, but it is ultimately impossible to know what a word means unless one actually sees that to which the word refers, for truly knowing requires firsthand acquaintance. If the meaning of the sign is learned from the thing we grasp, interpreting becomes impossible without such prior knowledge. Given that signs do not confer prior understanding in and of themselves, and that they are interpreted in light of one's direct understanding of a matter (and are thus subordinate to that which the mind sees directly), how then is this understanding achieved?

[19] *On the Teacher* 10.33 (CCSL 29, 192; FOC 59, 47).

Theological concepts make their presence felt most strongly in the dialogue in the way that Augustine answers this question. Acquiring knowledge is possible only because of the activity of Christ within the mind, for he illuminates the human subject's understanding. "Now He who is consulted and who is said to 'dwell in the inner man,' He it is who teaches us, namely, Christ, that is to say, 'the unchangeable Power of God and everlasting wisdom.'"[20] Thus, it is Christ who is the teacher referred to by the title of the dialogue. His pedagogical role in granting understanding consists in allowing the human subject to conceptualize, and therefore to grasp with the mind, an item of knowledge by seeing a particular thing in relation to a universal that it instantiates. This divine activity is the basis of the prior knowledge that the interpretation of signs requires. While Christ's work is indispensable, signs still have a genuine, if circumscribed, efficacy within the production of knowledge: "The most I can say for words is that they merely intimate that we should look for realities; they do not present them to us for our knowledge."[21] Signs indicate where to focus the mind's attention; divine illumination is what allows the mind actually to understand that to which it attends. Thus, illumination is necessary for signs to be understood, while signs themselves are at least often useful, if not absolutely necessary in every case, for the acquisition of knowledge.[22] An example of signs not being necessary within the

[20] *On the Teacher* 11.38 (CCSL 29, 195–196; FOC 59, 51).

[21] *On the Teacher* 11.36 (CCSL 29, 194; FOC 59, 49).

[22] For a reading of Augustine that sees strands of Platonic philosophy as the context in which he needs to be interpreted, and that takes words as having almost no power at all within his outlook, see Phillip Cary, *Outward Signs: The Powerlessness of External Things in Augustine's Thought* (Oxford: Oxford University Press, 2008), 17–151. Cary is significantly indebted in this connection to the work of C. P. Mayer, though one of Mayer's more temperate pieces on Augustine's hermeneutics does not draw Cary's attention. See an essay in which Mayer concludes that Platonism's influence does not distort the specifically Christian content of Augustine's work: "Prinzipien der Hermeneutik Augustins und daraus sich ergebende Probleme," *Forum Katholische Theologie* 1 (1985): 210–11. On the power of signs in Augustine, it is better to see words

establishment of knowledge is a person considering and coming to understand an abstract object simply by means of calling it to mind and musing on it, quite apart from written or spoken words bringing it to his attention.

It is, thus, Christology that inducts people inside the hermeneutical circle in *On the Teacher*. It is by means of Christ's illuminating work that people enter into the circle of understanding. Though unpacking this Christology accounts for only a modest percentage of the treatise itself, it is the element of the text that Augustine highlights in the critical retrospective assessment of his published works that he undertook at the end of his life.[23] In fact, the Christology is the only feature of *On the Teacher* that seems to deserve being singled out for comment, as Augustine leaves entirely unmentioned the extensive and sometimes technical discussion of semiotics that constitutes the bulk of the work. The Christology of the treatise portrays Jesus as a divine, disembodied agent who is immediately present to the mind of the knowing subject, providing the illumination that makes knowledge possible. He is potentially present to all, but only those who are properly disposed toward him actually receive illumination.[24] Those who turn to Christ for illumination thus reestablish, on a small scale, and perhaps only momentarily, the interior link to God that was a constant reality for human beings prior to sin. According to this view, the humanity of Jesus hardly factors into the process, nor is the social mediation of knowledge highlighted: Christ encounters a solitary mind, not

as being quite often necessary but of themselves insufficient to achieving understanding, in accord with John M. Rist, *Augustine: Ancient Thought Baptized* (Cambridge: Cambridge University Press, 1994), 32.

[23] *Reconsiderations* 1.12 (CSEL 36, 56–57; WSA I/2 58). The entirety of Augustine's evaluative comment on his work reads thus: "During the same period I wrote a book entitled *On the Teacher*, in which there is discussed and sought and found that there is no teacher except God who teaches man knowledge, in accordance with what is written in the gospel: *One is your teacher, the Christ* (Mt 23:10)."

[24] *On the Teacher* 11.36–38 (CCSL 29, 194–96; FOC 59, 49–51).

one that is linked together with other members of a community in a way that makes a difference for how they acquire understanding. While *On the Teacher* deals with knowledge formation tout court, the role of the ecclesial community becomes much more important in later works, in which Augustine considers what establishes the prior understanding needed for knowledge of God.

Augustine raises the issue of circularity again in *On the Advantage of Believing*, which probably originates from 391–92, thus coming a few years after *On the Teacher*, and is the first written work he composed once he was ordained as a priest.[25] In it, Augustine argues that it is acceptable in principle, and even desirable, to believe some things that have not been proven with certainty by means of rigorous and explicit argumentation.[26] Taking the opposite position would present enormous obstacles in dealing with practical matters in everyday life. For instance, it would be impossible to have friends without being willing to believe certain things about one's friends,[27] and, likewise, it would be impossible for children to obey their parents, for they cannot be entirely sure on the basis of reason alone, apart from all testimony, who their parents actually are.[28] When it comes to weightier questions that challenge the capacity of reason, such as the understanding and worship of God, it becomes even less feasible to contend that apodictic certainty is always required, and that one should never rely on assent to testimony from others.[29] There is thus even

[25] For astute commentary on the text, see Bochet, *Le firmament de l'écriture*, 116, who argues persuasively that *On the Advantage of Believing* as a whole, including its discussion of Old Testament interpretation and the need for faith in the Christian church, as well as its biographical elements and even the prayer found within it, coheres around the theme of the hermeneutical circle.

[26] *On the Advantage of Believing* 24 (CSEL 25/1, 30; WSA I/8, 136).

[27] Ibid.

[28] *On the Advantage of Believing* 26 (CSEL 25/1, 34; WSA I/8, 138).

[29] *On the Advantage of Believing* 27 (CSEL 25/1, 34; WSA I/8, 138).

more reason to think that if God can be known by human beings, it will not be exclusively by means of discursive proof.

Though there are certain factors that recommend belief in God, coming to such belief is not completely straightforward. Augustine demonstrates the difficulty of acquiring what he refers to as wisdom, an understanding of the most significant truths, with a logical puzzle. If the wise are those who understand both human nature and God as well as a human being possibly can, while the foolish do not, then it would make good sense for the foolish to follow the wise, to defer to them in speculative questions as well as in practical matters, in order to glean from them the understanding they already possess.[30] The foolish, as such, do not understand well what constitutes a good life, yet they could find out wherein it consists by learning from those who know. For this learning to take place, it is necessary for the foolish to be able at least to identify which people are wise, as the assumption is that not all are wise. However, unlike in physical perception, where to perceive an object by means of the senses is distinguishable from actually possessing it, in intellectual matters (and neither God nor the good life are perceptible to the senses) there is no difference between perception and possession: "What the intellect apprehends . . . is within the mind, and perceiving it is the same as having it."[31] With respect to the foolish, who are defined as lacking understanding in these crucial matters, Augustine says: "They cannot recognize something by any of its signs, if they have no knowledge of the thing itself whose presence they indicate."[32] Those who lack wisdom are thus at an impasse: they are incapable, on their own, of acquiring that which they lack. They are locked into their present position. Though understanding wisdom, and being enabled to live in light of it, is very nearly a moral matter, the point here is precisely that

[30] *On the Advantage of Believing* 27 (CSEL 25/1, 34–35; WSA I/8, 138–39).
[31] *On the Advantage of Believing* 28 (CSEL 25/1, 36; WSA I/8, 139).
[32] Ibid.

those who lack wisdom are not able to understand it, not that they are able to grasp it but find it unbecoming. Where they need assistance is not with respect to their will, though Augustine's later works come to focus on this much more, especially as he engages with the Pelagians, but rather their faculty of understanding.

How can those who lack wisdom find it? The solution echoes that of *On the Teacher*, though Augustine integrates ecclesiology this time. Once again, it is God himself who grants understanding of the truth. "As our inquiry has to do with religion, the cure for this immense problem can only come from God."[33] By means of a certain prevenience, which Augustine does not expand on or explain in this treatise, God confers understanding, thus giving to human beings what they cannot attain by themselves. Yet understanding God is hardly an easy or quick task that a person can finish immediately after having received an initial hint of understanding. Coming to understand is a process of gradual learning that unfolds over time, for it involves becoming acclimated to an entirely new outlook and mode of life.[34] Faith is necessary if human beings expect ever to achieve a robust understanding of God because of the diachronic dimension of coming to understand. Belief means deferring to the testimony of others, specifically the ecclesial community, and holds one in assent to the truth while one's mind divests itself of prior modes of thought and assimilates an entirely new outlook.[35] Trust in another is indispensable during the "lifting of our mind from its earthly habitat, this turning from the love of this world to the true God."[36] Faith in the sense of assent based on the testimony of others would be unnecessary if direct knowledge or understanding had already been achieved. However, people would lose their focus on the truth if their loving attention were not held

[33] *On the Advantage of Believing* 29 (CSEL 25/1, 36; WSA I/8, 140).
[34] *On the Advantage of Believing* 29 (CSEL 25/1, 37; WSA I/8, 140).
[35] *On the Advantage of Believing* 34 (CSEL 25/1, 43; WSA I/8, 144).
[36] *On the Advantage of Believing* 34 (CSEL 25/1, 42; WSA I/8, 144).

to its object until they could undergo a renewing of their minds. Here what ushers the believer into the circle is faith in the message proclaimed by the Christian church, at which point understanding that message becomes a project that stretches out over time. Thus, ecclesiology is indispensable to Augustine's thinking in this work in a way it was not in *On the Teacher*.

In *On Christian Teaching*, there is once again a reciprocal interdependence between interpreting signs and having a grasp of their subject matter. This treatise applies the scheme much more thoroughly to the biblical text than any of Augustine's earlier works does, being the main focus of the whole treatise; in addition, the reader's affective orientation toward God, rather than simply one's understanding, becomes the focus of interpretive effort. On the one hand, Augustine says that "things are learned through signs" (*res per signa discuntur*):[37] to a certain extent, the reader depends on being able to access the signs, and understand them as they were intended, in order to understand the claims that the Bible makes about God. Interpreters should not interrogate biblical signs for the sake of learning about the signs themselves, for the value of the signs is precisely that they direct readers to that of which they are signs. The biblical text is a privileged resource for engaging with God, a key conveyance by which humans beings may undertake the journey of reorienting their affections.[38] It is possible, however, for a reader to arrive at an interpretive judgment about a passage that does not coincide with the author's meaning, while that reading still serves to build up their love of God and neighbor, thus fulfilling the end of interpretation without doing so by following the means toward which Augustine defers.[39] Yet readers who get into a habit of being mistaken about what the text is saying are bound, over time, to drift away from the path the text exists to keep them on, for

[37] *On Christian Teaching* 1.2 (CCSL 32, 7; OWC Green, 8).
[38] *On Christian Teaching* 1.39 (CCSL 32, 28–29; OWC Green, 26–27).
[39] *On Christian Teaching* 1.40 (CCSL 32, 29; OWC Green, 27).

they are unlikely to be able regularly to repeat the fortunate accident of being in accord with the text's overall purpose, if they are wrong about its details.[40] Biblical signs are crucial in the sense that they are reliable pointers to the *res* of the text.

On the other hand, reading those signs properly necessitates some prior acquaintance with that very *res*. In *On Christian Teaching*, what brings interpreters inside the circle and provides the required provisional grasp of the *res* is ecclesiology in the sense that the nature of the text's subject matter is spelled out via a creedal outline which centers on the incarnation as the way in which divine wisdom adapts itself to the human condition and makes God known within the material order of the world. The apostolic creed thus serves as a hermeneutical framework for reading the text by providing a compressed narrative of the life, death, resurrection, and return of Jesus Christ, together with an affirmation that he is not only the way to God, but that there is no hiatus between him and divine wisdom itself, such that he is both the way that human beings come to God and indeed God himself.[41] Readers who are in the process of purifying themselves, in the sense of divesting themselves of the affection they have for things less important than the subject of the text, and who love above all else the God who makes himself known in this way, can "perceive that light and then hold fast to it."[42]

What difference does all this make for the interpretation of Scripture? The following two sections of this chapter specify

[40] *On Christian Teaching* 1.41–42 (CCSL 32, 30–31; OWC Green, 27–28).

[41] *On Christian Teaching* 1.10–19 (CCSL 32, 12–16; OWC Green, 12–16). Note, however, with Cameron that Augustine is still a bit fuzzy on this point as of *On Christian Teaching*, as was mentioned already in Chapter 1 of the present work (*Christ Meets Me Everywhere*, 227–31, 58–81). Pollmann observes that the creed Augustine utilizes to structure his exposition in the first book was not universally recognized within the church of his time, but rather received local recognition in certain geographical contexts: "Augustine's Hermeneutics as a Universal Discipline!?," 213–14.

[42] *On Christian Teaching* 1.10 (CCSL 32, 12; OWC Green, 12).

concretely how being inside the circle of understanding and love makes a difference for reading in *On Christian Teaching*: in brief, the hermeneutical framework indicates the aim of interpretation and influences the methods by which interpreters pursue that goal.

## *Scientia, Sapientia,* and the Aim of Reading

There is an important section of *On Christian Teaching* that spells out the aim of reading, or the results to be expected from it, and also the spiritual-theological dynamics of the process of meditative reflection on the content of the text as the reader reaches out toward descrying the ultimate divine *res* of Scripture. This passage deals with reading in the relatively narrow sense of absorbing biblical data and gaining an awareness of the basic content of the text. The dynamics of the ascent, though, characterize reading in a broader sense: through this whole process, the reader assumes a deferential posture toward the text, assimilates the words of the text in a relatively raw form, and reflects on the subject matter about which the text speaks, seeking to understand the theological claims the Bible is making and how these claims press for a response on the part of the reader. Brian Stock nicely characterizes this as contemplative reading, the reader's effort to engage with the divine through a textually structured angle of vision: it is "a psychological state that is initiated with one's acquaintance with biblical texts but that is progressively detached from the sensory aspects of the reading process."[43] Put as simply as possible, interpretation occurs for the sake of this engagement with the subject matter.

The passage that details this occurs in the second book of *On Christian Teaching*, in which the Bible is at the center of the believer's ascent. This is not a physical movement, but an increase

[43] Stock, *Augustine the Reader*, 198.

in knowledge of the truth and, even more importantly, an increasing affective attachment to it, together with a corresponding divestment of misdirected affections and habits of mind that draw one away from God.[44] This ascent passage serves as a lens through which the entire discussion of interpretation in the rest of *On Christian Teaching* is framed. It thus sets the overall direction for all consideration of the "how" of reading, and it deserves close attention for that reason.

Scholars sometimes take the passage as indicating that the practice of reading Scripture is isolated to, or is almost entirely comprised by, a single stage among the seven steps of the upward movement, namely, *scientia*,[45] yet this is misleading. *Scientia* refers to sense knowledge or a sensory acquaintance, whether visual or aural, with the text, together with a construal of its meaning. By itself, step three yields results that are both positive and negative: readers know God's will, that is, that they are to love God first of all and others equally with themselves; but they see that they have not

[44] For a synthetic, developmental account of how the ascent's content and structure change as Augustine's thinking matures over the course of his career, see Lewis Ayres, *Augustine and the Trinity* (Cambridge: Cambridge University Press, 2010), 93–173. For a discussion focused around the antecedents to *On Christian Teaching*'s view of the ascent within non-Christian sources, to which Augustine offers his own response, see Frederick Van Fleteren, "St. Augustine, Neoplatonism, and the Liberal Arts: The Background to De doctrina christiana," in *De doctrina christiana: A Classic of Western Culture*, ed. Duane W. H. Arnold and Pamela Bright, Christianity and Judaism in Antiquity (Notre Dame: University of Notre Dame Press, 1995), 14–24.

[45] Kolbet, *Augustine and the Cure of Souls*, 282n27; Edward Morgan, *The Incarnation of the Word: The Theology of Language of Augustine of Hippo*, T. & T. Clark Theology (London: T. & T. Clark, 2010), 66; Pollmann, "Augustine's Hermeneutics as a Universal Discipline!?," 229. There is detailed discussion of this stage, without any assertion that the work of the treatise pertains only to it, in J. Patout Burns, "Delighting the Spirit: Augustine's Practice of Figurative Interpretation," in *De doctrina christiana: A Classic of Western Culture*, ed. Duane W. H. Arnold and Pamela Bright, Christianity and Judaism in Antiquity (Notre Dame: University of Notre Dame Press, 1995), 186–88.

fulfilled this standard.[46] The discussion of the central books of the treatise is not set up simply by what Augustine says about this single stage of the ascent. The principles for reading that books 2 and 3 lay out do not just show how to read the Bible so as to understand the double love command and how one falls short of it. Augustine does say, with reference to step three, "This is the area in which every student of the divine scriptures exerts himself,"[47] yet readers put forth this effort with a view toward progressing on to later stages by means of the knowledge they gain in the third step. As the next section of this chapter argues, the principles take readers beyond the point of seeing themselves as falling short by breaking down the barriers to having a fitting love, and by fostering that love in various different ways.[48] Even the stages that follow after the third are definitely important for reading in the wider sense of the theological reflection that is funded by input readers receive from Scripture. The steps following *scientia* inform how interpretation ought to occur in that they point out the end toward which readers should channel the knowledge the text provides, or how it should be understood with respect to God. These steps also offer a compressed outline of what is happening in readers' minds and hearts as they undertake this process. Thus, all the stages have a bearing on reading in the broad sense, and there are ways in which even reading in the narrow sense connected with stage three is a practice marked by being situated within the ascent.

All of the steps of the ascent form part of a progressive and cumulative sequence: the middle stages presuppose the earlier ones

[46] *On Christian Teaching* 2.10 (CCSL 32, 37; OWC Green, 34).

[47] Ibid.

[48] In this connection, see *On Christian Teaching* 2.10, 12 (CCSL 32, 37–39; OWC Green, 34, 35). In the latter passage, saying that he is returning to the third stage, Augustine discusses how to go about assimilating textual data, and which versions of the text deserve attentive study. There is a focus on *scientia* at this point, but when the discussion broadens out as the book proceeds, the dynamics associated with the higher stages of the ascent come into play.

and build toward the later ones where they climax. Because *scientia* is precisely a single step in a progressive sequence, its importance derives from what it contributes toward reaching the overall goal of the entire ascent. Augustine draws the name for each step from the gifts of the Spirit that are attributed to the messianic king mentioned in Isaiah 11. Yet in the prophetic text, the terms are simply a serial list; they do not build on one another and constitute a logical progression, as they do in Augustine's appropriation of them in *On Christian Teaching.* The same gifts of the Spirit appear in an earlier text of Augustine, *On the Lord's Sermon on the Mount,* which portrays the ascent in similar terms to its depiction in his treatise on reading the Bible. In the exposition on the sermon, Augustine correlates each of the gifts of the Spirit with one of the beatitudes in Jesus' Sermon on the Mount.[49] The beatitudes form a constitution for the new order that Jesus came to establish. "As the founder of this new kingdom, Jesus already represents the messianic king prophesied in Isaiah; by linking the prophecy with the Beatitudes, Augustine makes it valid for every Christian taught by Jesus, who came to fulfill the Old Testament (Matthew 5:17)."[50] That is to say, the wisdom, for instance, that the king was to have is not only embodied by Jesus himself, but is also accessible to those who follow him and who become like him by understanding and imitating him. In *On Christian Teaching,* the steps that lead up to knowledge, and those that follow after it, are important for the sake of what they contribute to the human person acquiring wisdom, the product of contemplating God, which is the essence of the human person's telos. The very nature of the purpose of a process is that it is that for the sake of which everything else within the process occurs. It is that toward which all the steps within it are directed.

[49] *On the Lord's Sermon on the Mount* 1.3–4 (CCSL 35, 7–13; FOC 11, 24–30).

[50] Pollmann, "Augustine's Hermeneutics as a Universal Discipline!?," 227.

As has been suggested, the goal of reading broadly understood, and the end toward which *scientia* of the Bible should be put, is to move the reader toward attaining *sapientia* or wisdom. While *scientia* refers to knowledge concerning the external world, for instance the Bible, as it is perceived by the senses, *sapientia* denotes a direct contemplation of eternal truths unmediated by any external forms. Study of the Bible itself cannot in principle confer *sapientia* on a person, because what is gleaned from the Bible is a mediated, indirect form of engagement with the truth. If Scripture cannot deliver this, how can readers put interpretation of the Bible toward the end of reaching out for *sapientia*? If a reader has *scientia*, how can she move toward *sapientia*?

Ultimately *sapientia* refers to a divine-human agent, the eternal God entering into the temporal order in order to give human beings knowledge of himself.[51] The incarnation is the giving of the eternal within the realm of the temporal, and thus secures access to the eternal for human beings. Jesus Christ as the self-revelation of the triune God is the one that human beings are to contemplate; he is the thing to which the Bible is a sign, but who is himself a sign of no other thing. The biblical text is, thus, the "primary derivative of Christ,"[52] and the truths of faith that it contains concern the incarnation above all else. Readers should read the text with this in mind, holding these truths about Christ in their minds, delighting in them, contemplating them, and living in light of them. The transition between the *scientia* the biblical text makes available and the *sapientia* that constitutes the telos of humanity runs through Christ. He is the end of reading: just as the humanity of Christ mediates his deity, the verbal text of the Bible is subordinate in the course of the economy of salvation to the person of Jesus Christ by virtue of signifying him and directing the attention of the reader to him. The Bible does not offer up *sapientia* to interpreters, but reading it is

[51] *On Christian Teaching* 1.11, 13 (CCSL 32, 12, 14; OWC Green, 13, 14).

[52] Williams, "Language, Reality and Desire," 141.

their point of departure for an increasingly direct engagement with him as its subject matter.

There are, of course, intermediate stages between the most directly text-oriented stage, *scientia*, and the final stage of the ascent, in which Scripture is definitely superseded, and the dynamics of this transition cut across the process of interpretation broadly construed. They characterize what is happening in readers as they deliberate over how to understand what they have read. These transitional stages, numbers four through six, mark a shift in the reader, from being crushed under the demand of a double command he has not kept, to beginning to delight in God and allowing love for him to displace prior attachment to things of inherently less value. Extricating "himself from all the fatal charms of transient things," "turning ... to the love of eternal things," purifying "his mind, which is somehow turbulent and in conflict with itself because of the impurities accumulated by its desire of what is inferior," cleansing "the eye by which God may actually be seen"[53] – all of these things are crucial if the reader is to understand textual content in light of its proper end.

An example will help illustrate how these processes play out in interpretation. When God is described as "alive," determining the sense in which this is true of him requires reflection on what it means simply to be alive, and divesting from the standard notion of life associations it carries when applied to corporeal forms, such as animals and human beings, both of which are mutable.[54] Understanding God as alive means forming a concept of life that is superior in many ways to these other instantiations of life, not least by being immutable, for applying the term to God requires understanding him not as a temporarily or derivatively living thing, but as life itself, the source of the life of all other living things that depend

[53] *On Christian Teaching* 2.10–11 (CCSL 32, 37–38; OWC Green, 34–35).

[54] *On Christian Teaching* 1.8 (CCSL 32, 11; OWC Green, 11). I am indebted to the reading of this passage found in Ayres, *Augustine and the Trinity*, 132–33.

on him. Interpreting biblical language requires going through this process of relating textual signifiers to the *res* of the text and puzzling through what this means for how they should be understood. Though Scripture exists to redress the effects of the fall, interpretation exists in a space where the process is subject to being distorted by sin's effects. Thus reading and text-based contemplation are caught within a tension between the residual effects of sin on the mind and will of the reader, on the one hand, and the direction in which transformative divine grace is leading those who interpret the text, on the other.

In connection with *On Christian Teaching*, Frances Young says that for Augustine: "The theologian is exegete; the exegete is theologian."[55] The meaning of the first thesis is easy enough to discern, and less pertinent to the present discussion as compared with the second, the idea being that theological reflection ought to grow organically out of the interpretation of Scripture. The second thesis, that the exegete is a theologian, means that exegesis requires a reader who is in the process of turning toward the *res* of the text in order to see how to construe the language of the text with reference to the text's subject matter. No reader can fully understand the text's material content, because its topic is the incomprehensible God. However, the act of interpreting the text in light of the triune God entails an experience on the part of readers that replicates the ascent in microcosm: it is marked by all of its key dynamics, and readers should aim to press the knowledge they gain from the Bible into the service of engaging with the text's subject matter in this way. The following section builds on the argument that the ascent passage makes this assertion, and demonstrates something of the difference that it makes for the practice of exegesis as Augustine discusses it in books 3 and 4 of *On Christian Teaching*.

[55] Young, *Biblical Exegesis*, 282.

## Exegetical Practice

If this is the aim of reading the Bible, how should people interpret the text so as to read it toward this end? What strategies for reading become fitting in light of the practice's overarching purpose? What do readers actually do with the text to fulfill the purpose of interpretation?[56] Augustine puts his own spin on the established techniques for interpreting texts that he learned in his literary education and that were a standard part of text-based education in his period. The way that Augustine contextualizes or tailors these techniques reflects both his vision of God and the nature of the reader's ascent to God, for reading falls within the compass of the ascent and is marked by the forces that govern it. Proper reading moves readers toward their end, while improper reading stalls progress, or even effects spiritual regress (or is a product of that). Techniques are not neutral, but are caught within a tension between the reader's conflicting desires. That the end of reading and the interpreter's location within the ascent affect the precise formulation of techniques is evident across the whole range of these methods, from the most rudimentary to the highest levels of engagement with the text and its subject matter.

Before exploring how Augustine adapts the standard techniques, it is necessary to survey briefly what might be considered their default form, or the form they took in the educational system which inculcated them in Augustine and others who received a literary education in this time period. The main techniques of textual

[56] Bertrand de Margerie is right that one of the ways in which Augustine's approach to the Bible makes a contribution is that he clearly interlinks what he has to say about reading strategies with the rest of his theological commitments, including the nature of the text and the purpose of interpretation. See Bertrand de Margerie, *An Introduction to the History of Exegesis*, Vol. III: Saint Augustine (Petersham: Saint Bede's, 1991), 128. Bochet also notes the connection between Scripture's use and nature (*Le firmament de l'écriture*, 51–53).

interpretation that Augustine customizes are as follows.[57] Reading would begin with establishing as accurately as possible the form of the text itself. Since manuscripts in the fourth and fifth centuries were copied by hand, there were variations in the wording of the available manuscripts of any given work. After deliberating on the words to be interpreted, the reader came to the task of inferring how these words should be read aloud. Readers encountered texts written in *scriptio continua* form, meaning that the individual words did not have spaces between them, and sentences were not structured by explicit punctuation marks. This made the task of realizing the text orally a much more active and demanding process than that of articulating a modern text. Intelligent reading also required the interpreter to decode any unfamiliar terms contained within the text, whether they were historical or literary references, words unknown to the reader, or other items. This meant acquiring sufficient background knowledge of the relevant subjects in order to illuminate what was initially obscure. It was also necessary to arrive at a sense of the overall unity of the text. What was its author seeking to accomplish in the work? Or, in other words, what was the scope of the text? The final step in interpretation was coming to a discerning judgment about the text. Literary texts in this period were read for the sake of the formation of the reader. If there were elements of the text that sent the wrong sort of moral message, these needed to be identified, specifically so that the reader did not imitate them. On a more positive side, this level of interpretation included highlighting the aspects of the text that could contribute to shaping the reader and commending those features.

Augustine's theological framework, especially because it places the reader within an ascent and has a Christological account of the

57 For general background on patristic reading strategies as adaptations of interpretive techniques conferred by ancient literary and rhetorical pedagogy, see Ayres, *Nicaea and Its Legacy*, 31–40; Young, *Biblical Exegesis*, 49–116. For some application to Augustine specifically, see Pollmann, *Doctrina christiana*, 118–21.

climactic point of this process, exercises a shaping influence at each of these levels of interpretation. It is neither possible nor necessary within the constraints of this chapter, for the sake of demonstrating the point that is ultimately important, to provide an exhaustive presentation of all the ways that interpretation's end and the reader's ascent condition the application of these techniques to the biblical text. Working through a representative set of examples from *On Christian Teaching* will suffice to establish the overall point that reading strategies serve as means toward fulfilling the end of interpretation. The discussion below begins with the most elementary techniques and continues to more advanced strategies, highlighting the contribution of Augustine's theology in each instance and as a whole to the practice of reading. The selected examples show that the standard techniques, each in their own way, bear the impress of interpretation's aim. The impression that the text has already made on Augustine, through his own acts of interpretation and through acquiring a knowledge of the text's subject matter via being embedded in the church community, thus conditions further acts of reading.

An interpretive operation that may appear to constitute a counterexample to the principle that proper reading falls within the ascent has to do with the very lowest stage of reading. According to Augustine, the higher-level operations of interpretation will proceed best if readers have loaded the data of the text into their minds, if they have simply assimilated the raw verbal content of the Bible into themselves, even if they do not know how to construe all of what they possess.[58] The assumption is that readers who are not entirely unfamiliar with the biblical books will, in the act of ingesting them, at least comprehend the general drift of the text, though they will have much work to do when it comes to understanding its challenging sections, and this knowledge will make

[58] *On Christian Teaching* 2.12 (CCSL 32, 38–39; OWC Green, 35).

them less likely to commit interpretive mistakes when they are operating at a more advanced level.[59] Why is the seemingly straightforward act of taking in scriptural information an activity that has a spiritual dimension built into it? This act is not one that is ascent-neutral, because while it is clear that any text within canonical Scripture bears authority, for Augustine some questions surround which texts belong or do not belong within the canon. For the relatively small number of texts where doubt about their status lingers, readers should defer in their judgment to the texts that are read by the preponderance of churches among all the communities, and among these they should give preference to the leading churches.[60] An element of trust in these communities is integral to establishing the de facto canon for the reader. These churches seem to deserve deference because they most closely approximate the purpose of interpretation. In this way, there is a social aspect to the ascent.[61] More importantly, however, even the basic act of absorbing the data of the text cannot be separated from theological and spiritual considerations.

The way Augustine handles another basic interpretive principle is intelligible against the background of the purpose of interpretation. When a passage from the Bible is susceptible to a plurality of possible readings, there are two ways to disambiguate it, or at least to determine if the number of interpretive options can be reduced. Readers should first make reference to the summaries of the Christian faith that are available in the more perspicuous sections of the Bible and that are affirmed by the church, ruling out readings that clash with the rule of faith as it receives articulation in both of these ways.[62] Then readers should consult the local literary context of the difficult text in order to see which of the possible readings fits

[59] Ibid.

[60] *On Christian Teaching* 2.12 (CCSL 32, 39; OWC Green, 35–36).

[61] For commentary, see Kolbet, *Augustine and the Cure of Souls*, 140–41.

[62] *On Christian Teaching* 3.2 (CCSL 32, 77–78; OWC Green, 68).

better with the flow of the text, seeking indications of the intention of the author.[63] The precept takes as its point of departure the end of reading by assigning hermeneutical utility to the rule of faith. The principle assumes a reciprocal dependence in meaning between the entirety of the text (and the community that embodies its meaning) and smaller portions of Scripture. Clearer passages spell out the rule of faith, though this is articulated in many different ways, all of which converge to an acceptable degree. This overall construal of the text, itself fluid and not entirely fixed, assists in reading challenging passages, though it is still possible that multiple options may fit the rule of faith and mesh equally well with the immediate context, in which case any may be considered viable.[64] In operating this way, Augustine adapts the standard technique of reading a text with a sense of its overall scope by understanding the scope of the text in particular material terms. This tailoring that might be described as specifically pro-Nicene because of the way the message of the whole text is seen to be congruent with the creedal statement.[65]

Readers should use essentially the same mode of dealing with ambiguity when they face questions about how to read a passage orally. Here again, fitting with the broadest possible biblical context as well as with the preceding and following words informs how the text should be interpreted. Enunciating the words of an ancient written text was not a straightforward task for the reasons mentioned above, and the ability to do so successfully reflects a non-trivial level of understanding of a text, or a reasonably developed commitment to an interpretive take on it. For instance, realizing the text orally in a certain tone of voice indicates that the text is being

[63] *On Christian Teaching* 3.2 (CCSL 32, 78; OWC Green, 68).

[64] *On Christian Teaching* 3.3–5 (CCSL 32, 78–79; OWC Green, 68–70). This delicate interdependence between whole and part is, of course, the first type of circularity mentioned earlier in this chapter.

[65] For useful further discussion of Augustine and other figures who read Scripture as having a pro-Nicene scope, see Ayres, *Nicaea and Its Legacy*, 336–39.

construed as a question, while reading it another way indicates that the reader sees the text as affirming a statement of some sort.[66] Resolving such cases of ambiguity in part by appeal to the rule of faith builds the end of reading into a stage of interpretation that falls close to its beginning. In this way the stages of interpretation interpenetrate one another. There is heuristic value in distinguishing them, but they certainly do not constitute a set of procedures that must be done in order, as if later stages do not impinge on earlier ones. Having a sense of the scope of the biblical text is important even for grasping basic semantic features of the text and the sort of speech act the text is performing.

At a later stage of interpretation, it becomes necessary for readers to draw on background knowledge to illuminate otherwise obscure parts of the biblical text, but doing so will only serve the process of ascent if readers incorporate background knowledge in such a way as to preserve Scripture's formative capacity. Interpretation of the Bible often demands knowledge the text itself does not supply; when this is the case, readers have no choice but to turn their attention to knowledge as it has been developed outside of the Christian community, and to integrate that into their process of reading texts. In this case, they are not learning these fields of knowledge for their own sake, but rather as an auxiliary for biblical study.[67] Proceeding in this way, they will find much useful material, as well as plenty of content that is not helpful, but what is crucial is that they put to a new end whatever they appropriate from non-Christian sources.[68] This process of recontextualization is important because of how signs affect the will of the human subject. As one commentator puts it, "One might say, in search of an Augustinian definition, that an intentional sign is the kind of thing which starts a motion towards what it signifies and, mediately, towards

[66] *On Christian Teaching* 3.6 (CCSL 32, 80–81; OWC Green, 70–71).
[67] *On Christian Teaching* 2.58–59 (CCSL 32, 72–73; OWC Green, 63–64).
[68] *On Christian Teaching* 2.60–62 (CCSL 32, 73–76; OWC Green, 64–66).

whomever employs it as a sign."[69] As such, intentional signs embedded in discourse with an end that is not congruent with a Christian outlook have the potential to misdirect the reader's will. It is crucial to recontextualize this isolated and borrowed material, so as to use it to illuminate the biblical text with a view toward allowing the reader to be shaped by Scripture. Augustine closes the second book of *On Christian Teaching*, in which he has discussed the use of background knowledge, with a patristic commonplace by comparing the appropriation of learning developed outside of Christian contexts to the Israelites plundering the Egyptians as they were liberated from Egypt. The Israelites took these possessions with them, but only after first taking part in the rite of Passover, and thereby collectively submitting themselves to God as a particular people.[70] Readers must not be seduced by the temptation to pride associated with the knowledge they acquire, lest pride undercut the possibility of reading with profit the book whose purpose is to teach them not to love themselves too much.

Similar spiritual-theological dynamics apply to discerning the unity of the biblical text: having a certain sort of disposition is prerequisite for properly seeing the scope of the Bible. This is especially evident in a passage where Augustine discusses the Old Testament and its interpretation. Before Jesus Christ had come in the flesh, those with a spiritual inclination participated in the cultic economy in such a way as to learn love of God from it. They did not treat it itself as ultimate, but took it as pointing beyond itself to something greater. "With the coming of Christ and his passion and resurrection the full scope of divine and

[69] Jordan, "Words and Word," 186. Kolbet makes a similar point: "By means of scripture 'so many diseases of the human will are cured' because it offers an alternative system of signification that involves one in the intention of its givers – God and the human authors' will to discover God. Since this intention is properly ordered, the more deeply one is involved in these given signs, the more one's affections begin to conform to those of the givers." See his *Augustine and the Cure of Souls*, 148.

[70] *On Christian Teaching* 2.62 (CCSL 32, 76; OWC Green, 66–67).

human *caritas* appears, so that the previous history in the light of which Christ is intelligible, and which he in turn makes newly intelligible, is seen to serve, to be 'useful', in relation to this decisively liberating event."[71] After the advent of Christ, those who had been taking the Old Testament signs as pointing to something greater were able to transition smoothly to seeing precise, literal observance of the old words and practices as no longer necessary, and the text as having Christ for its scope. Augustine is critical of Jews who do not make this transition and who continue to follow the law, but his essential critique of them is not different in kind from the way in which he castigates Gentile practices of interpretation in which *signum* and *res* are not properly related to one another: both focus unduly on temporal matters.[72] His entire treatment of how to handle the signs that constitute the biblical text in books 2 and 3 of *On Christian Teaching* is based on the assumption that all readers, Christians included, need to see properly relating signs and things as the central problem of biblical hermeneutics. Arriving at an accurate assessment of the scope of the text is a crucial part of this endeavor.

When it comes to even higher stages of interpretation, theological considerations continue to be operative. The proclivity of human beings to love themselves more than they should has the potential to warp how readers infer moral lessons from the biblical text, especially when the specific texts in question refer to radically

[71] Williams, "Language, Reality and Desire," 146.

[72] *On Christian Teaching* 3.10–11 (CCSL 32, 83–85; OWC Green, 72–73). See Williams, "Language, Reality and Desire," 146–47. Cf. also Ayres, *Nicaea and Its Legacy*, 328, who says with reference to a text by Ambrose: "Amid the polemic in this text we see a distinctively pro-Nicene linking of appropriate spiritual progress and growth in correct doctrinal belief." The parallel with the present discussion is that here Augustine is linking spiritual progress and fitting interpretation of the biblical text: in both cases, polemic is a function of positioning theological reflection within the ascent structure.

different cultural mores than the reader's own. Human beings are inclined to love themselves more than God and their neighbors, though of course they should love God most of all and their neighbors equally with themselves. This distortion of affections drives a propensity for readers to assume that their own cultural moment contains within itself the arbiter of what is ultimately good and bad, when in fact a reader is simply accustomed to a particular cultural arrangement that in and of itself contains many arbitrary elements.[73] This tendency works itself out by nudging interpreters to construe whatever is part of the biblical text, but is out of sync with their culture, as figurative in the sense of not being literally binding on them.[74] If readers see themselves as having an excessive love of self, they can be more alert to their own tendency to lighten the obligations that the biblical text puts on them; they may be tempted to lighten their obligations by reading the parts of its message that do not conform to their own cultural standards as mere illustrations of some general principles, rather than as admonitions pressing them to do things they would really rather not do. Starting out (at least partially) inside the circle of understanding does mean that readers need to have at least a minimal sense of what the Bible is all about, but it does not mean that they should build all of their particular culture-specific beliefs and practices into this normative summary of the Christian faith.

Just as they should not see their own cultural moment as the point of view from which to judge all others, readers ought to remind themselves that *no* particular cultural arrangement has this level of ultimacy. What the biblical text really commends is the enjoyment of God and the use of all else for his sake, not any particular set of actions that may manifest that love.[75] The desire to love God and others works itself out in radically different ways in

[73] *On Christian Teaching* 3.15, 18 (CCSL 32, 86–87, 88–89; OWC Green, 76, 77–78).

[74] *On Christian Teaching* 3.15 (CCSL 32, 86–87; OWC Green, 76).

[75] *On Christian Teaching* 3.15–16 (CCSL 32, 86–88; OWC Green, 76).

varying historical and geographical situations. It is a mistake to think that many practices related to marriage, diet, dress, and various other matters are, in and of themselves, either binding on Christians or not. The underlying desire behind any practice is the criterion by which it should be judged.[76] Keeping in mind the relativity of many such practices should spur readers to think about any given passage, and what its lessons may be, with an eye toward the nature of the desire that motivates the visible actions, which can provide either literal or figurative moral lessons. In this way, and in many others, Augustine's theology serves to structure his approach to reading.[77]

[76] Ibid.

[77] I have concentrated in the section above on reading strategies in the sense of ways in which Augustine interrogates the biblical text so as to perceive its sense(s). In the final book of *On Christian Teaching*, he also provides discussion of how his theological understanding shapes quite deeply the way in which he presents the results of his reading to others in the context of preaching. Augustine develops a theological aesthetics of biblical language, and he uses specifically Christian criteria to winnow rhetorical techniques that may serve as ways to bring about a response in an audience. As Carol Harrison says, "It is therefore essential for Augustine that Scripture be shown to be beautiful, be made delightful, if its true end is to be attained. This is not a concession to its refined, cultured critics, or to his own sensibilities, but is, rather, the keystone of a 'Christian aesthetic' which recognizes that God has chosen to motivate man's fallen will to the true and good through the delight occasioned by His beautiful revelation of Himself – and this includes, centrally, Scripture and preaching." See *Augustine: Christian Truth and Fractured Humanity*, Christian Theology in Context (Oxford: Oxford University Press, 2000), 76. Another outstanding account of how the theological framework of the earlier books shapes Augustine's handling of rhetoric is John C. Cavadini, "The Sweetness of the Word: Salvation and Rhetoric in Augustine's De doctrina christiana," in *De doctrina christiana: A Classic of Western Culture*, ed. Duane W. H. Arnold and Pamela Bright (Notre Dame: University of Notre Dame Press, 1995), 164–72. In this connection, it is worth noting the way James Andrews has helpfully characterized *On Christian Teaching* in its entirety as an expanded hermeneutic, one that includes a turn to delivery as the proper completion of the process of understanding: *Hermeneutics and the Church: In Dialogue with Augustine*, Reading the Scriptures (Notre Dame: University of Notre Dame Press, 2012), 24–25.

## Conclusion

The overall view of reading that is present within *On Christian Teaching* is substantive in the sense that what constitutes any given reading as proper is that the interpretations align with a theological view of reality. A fitting reading of the Bible is one that yields correct views, or gives appropriate results. This does not mean that the reader knows precisely what any given passage will say prior to doing any interpretive work on it, such that putting effort into interpretation is essentially pointless, though this is sometimes how critics portray the matter. James O'Donnell phrases this criticism especially sharply in connection with *On Christian Teaching*: "Augustine knows what Scripture will say before he begins to read it. An extrapolated core of biblical message forms the 'normative horizon' for all Augustine's attempts to read the Bible. Any reading of a given passage is predetermined by the extrapolated core."[78] Yet the relationship between theological doctrine and the trajectory of reading is more subtle than this, and reading is not the imperious imposition O'Donnell claims that it is.

The way in which Augustine understands God shapes the hermeneutical framework that sets the parameters in which the reader is to glean the meaning of texts. This happens in three major ways. Ecclesiology ushers readers into the circle of understanding: they gain a basic understanding of the triune God by learning theological teaching in a creedal outline, which establishes in them a level of prior understanding of reality, in light of which they can relate the signs that constitute the text to their referent. Theology also

[78] James J. O'Donnell, "Doctrina Christiana, De," in *Augustine through the Ages: An Encyclopedia*, ed. Allan Fitzgerald et al. (Grand Rapids: Eerdmans, 1999), 280. O'Donnell is drawing on Pollmann, *Doctrina christiana*, 121–47, though her tone is analytical, while his is more caustic. For an objection similar to O'Donnell's, see Tzvetan Todorov, *Théories du symbole*, Collection poétique (Paris: Seuil, 1977), 91–124. Brian Stock also expresses doubt that, from Augustine's point of view, readers have much to gain from reading texts in general: *Augustine the Reader*, 125, 278.

conditions the end toward which readers should put what they learn from reading the Bible: interpreters proceed with a view toward their own formation, that is, so that they love God above all else and their fellow human beings equally with themselves. This aim, in turn, puts a certain twist on the exegetical practices that had currency in Augustine's time, from the most basic levels of interpretation all the way through to the formational goal of reading. Substantive commitments factor into interpretation in all these capacities.

Part II of this book begins with a consideration of the resources that Augustine might contribute to the contemporary discussion of theological reading of the Bible. It thus faces, in connection with Augustine, the same question that Henri de Lubac posed about Origen at the conclusion of his study of biblical interpretation in Augustine's Alexandrian predecessor: "What remains of this vast doctrine, which emerges again before our eyes like a dream palace through the mist of the distant past? Depending on our perspective in approaching it, we would respond: Not much, or, on the contrary: Everything essential."[79] Paradoxical though it may sound, de Lubac's verdict is deeply discerning and provides a guide for Part II's use of Augustine, as the pages that follow explain.

[79] Lubac, *History and Spirit*, 427.

# Part II | A Constructive Proposal

But "do not lift up your eyes to this mountain in such a way that you think you must set your hope on a man." "The mountains receive only what they pass on to us; it is to the place from which they themselves receive it that we are to direct our hope (*unde et montes accipiunt, ibi spes nostra ponenda est*)."

... From the mountains that we see with our eyes we should mount up higher and higher to the invisible One who has made the visible mountains, just as John as a recipient of the divine gift was one of the highest mountains because he rose up above everything created, above all heavens and angels, to the uncreated Word that was in the beginning. And for our hearts to be able to do this [to receive the message from John], they need cleansing – for they are carnal – they need the catharsis, the purifying of continence. To us these are alien notes. But they cannot be totally or finally alien.

We are perhaps not guilty of too great misrepresentation if we go on to say that the continence that Augustine commends consists concretely of opposing to the subjective presuppositions with which, to the hurt of our understanding, we constantly approach scripture, the equally subjective but sincere and earnest desire to read and expound the Gospels, not as teachers but as students, not as those who know but as those who do not know, as those who let ourselves be told what the Gospel, and through it the divine wisdom, is seeking to tell us, holding ourselves free for it as for a message that we have never heard before.

Karl Barth, with reference to Augustine's first Tractate on John's Gospel[1]

## Transition to Part II

Augustine's works are certainly much more than "a piece of vaguely significant debris from another culture that has washed up on the shore."[2] Part II seeks to follow the overall shape of his view, which is precisely what Part I sought to outline. The structure of the position that emerges from Augustine's *On Christian Teaching* – that theological language describes the reader and the text in addition to generating a direction for interpretation – remains compelling and is worth retrieving.[3] That is, theological notions of the reader and the text should be utterly central to efforts to appropriate Augustine. Taking seriously a theological construal of the reader and the text requires not just taking up these ideas in isolation from one another, but following the implications that they have, when taken together, for the overall direction of interpretation. This aim for reading sets the parameters within which questions about interpretive strategies should be answered, though today's interpretive strategies will not be identical with Augustine's. If theological reading is to mean anything today, it should refer to attempts to connect a theological description of reality with how interpreters read the

[1] Karl Barth, *Witness to the Word: A Commentary on John 1* (Eugene: Wipf and Stock, 2003), 2, 8–9.

[2] James J. O'Donnell, "The Authority of Augustine," *Augustinian Studies* 22 (1991): 23.

[3] See Carol Harrison's helpful reminder to those exploring analogies between our own situation and Augustine's texts that they must reckon with the link between his understanding of the nature and content of Christian doctrine, on the one hand, and how Scripture should be read on the other: "De doctrina christiana," *New Blackfriars* 87 (2006): 125.

Bible. In the most general terms, then, the constructive proposal that follows is Augustinian in the sense that it insists that what is the case with regard to the reader and the text should determine how the Bible is read.[4]

It is worth spelling out a bit more specifically in what respects Part II draws on Augustine. The constructive chapters of this book utilize him as a model in the following ways. The notion of the reader advanced in Chapter 4 is one for which hermeneutical rationality is substantive, not merely procedural in nature (this repositions the discussion of substantive rationality from Part I's Chapter 2 on interpretation to Part II's Chapter 4 on the reader). Theologically specific content enters into the interpretive framework by which the reader makes sense of texts, rather than being only that which receives analysis. Chapter 5 frames its view of the text of Scripture as a collection of signs directing the reader to the triune God, just as Augustine develops an account of semiotics to apply to the Bible in *On Christian Teaching*. Chapter 6 divides up the task of interpretation differently than Augustine does, especially because of its attempt to give modern historical consciousness a role within theological reading, but it follows him in allowing theology to shape each aspect of the interpretive process. What holds together the three ways in which Part II draws on Augustine is that in each case it preserves the way in which the hermeneutical situation is marked by a certain view of transcendence. This is the

[4] I have learned from the following thoughtful appropriations of Augustine. Cyril O'Regan sees *On Christian Teaching* as a text with the potential to contribute positively to recent debates about hermeneutics by mediating between approaches associated with Yale and Chicago. See "De doctrina christiana and Modern Hermeneutics," in *De doctrina christiana: A Classic of Western Culture*, ed. Duane W. H. Arnold and Pamela Bright, Christianity and Judaism in Antiquity (Notre Dame: University of Notre Dame Press, 1995), 217–37. Frances M. Young stresses the need to keep clearly in view the differences between Augustine and contemporary reflection on language: "Augustine's Hermeneutics and Postmodern Criticism," *Interpretation* 58 (2004): 42–55.

notion of relative rather than absolute transcendence.[5] If absolute transcendence, or Transcendence with a capital "T," refers to the reality of God in his capacity as one who is beyond, as well as different from and greater than, the immanent realm, relative transcendence is about how the created world is reconceived in light of its relationship to God himself. Part II draws on Augustine's thinking so as to allow a Christian conception of God to shape how the realities involved in reading and the process itself are understood.

Drawing on Augustine to develop an approach operating out of the fourth position in the Introduction's typology allows this book to make a distinctive contribution to the present discussion of theological reading. Of course one will not find theology depicting the realities involved in reading in approaches that ask theology to be merely passive, what is described by interpretive operations, rather than something that shapes reading in a positive way. Nor will one find theology playing this role in those who quite closely follow Gadamer and consider doctrine to be one thing that determines the preconceptions with which readers operate – the expectations they have which shape interpretive questions by virtue of the text's historical influence over the culture the reader inhabits – while the text and reader are themselves accounted for in terms of more general hermeneutical theory. Nor will one find theology doing all that it might do in the most significant account of theological interpretation that has emerged from a perspective influenced by postliberalism and pragmatic semiotics, in which theology is active, but in the capacity of entering into exegetical arguments and not at a more basic level. The present debate about theological interpretation is not entirely without reflection on

[5] Ingolf Dalferth, "The Idea of Transcendence," in *The Axial Age and Its Consequences*, ed. Robert Neelly Bellah and Hans Joas (Cambridge, MA: Belknap Press of Harvard University Press, 2012), 155.

Scripture that could be considered an embodiment of type four,[6] but the discussion does not feature any book-length accounts of theological interpretation that allow theology to play this crucial role. Commenting on the link between ontology and proper conduct in general prior to modernity, Rémi Brague rightly says: "This presentation of the way the world was imagined in Late Antiquity and the Middle Ages is not merely a description of things as they were. It also has an inseparable ethical significance."[7] In the context of biblical interpretation, if this organic link between the situation of a reader before the text and how reading ought to unfold has not been eliminated, it surely has been challenged (at least for descriptions of the reader and text that deploy specifically theological categories). Premodern interpretive paradigms do not provide ready-made answers to current questions, but it is crucial for present-day interpreters to remain in conversation with their forebears and to establish continuity with them in this respect.[8] This book thus aims for connection to rather than identity with

[6] See, for instance, Matthew Levering, *Scripture and Metaphysics: Aquinas and the Renewal of Trinitarian Theology*, Challenges in Contemporary Theology (Malden, MA: Blackwell, 2004); Kevin J. Vanhoozer, *The Drama of Doctrine: A Canonical-Linguistic Approach to Christian Theology* (Louisville: Westminster John Knox, 2005). For my own critical questions about a specific way of following Barth on these issues, see Darren Sarisky, "The Ontology of Scripture and the Ethics of Interpretation in the Theology of John Webster," *International Journal of Systematic Theology* (Forthcoming).

[7] Rémi Brague, *The Wisdom of the World: The Human Experience of the Universe in Western Thought* (Chicago: University of Chicago Press, 2003), 106.

[8] In this connection, note that the works of both Levering and Vanhoozer that are cited two footnotes above stand in significant continuity with premodern theology, Levering working out of the Thomistic tradition and Vanhoozer drawing upon the Reformers. For its part, the present work sets its rationale for turning back to Augustine alongside justifications for retrieving hermeneutical insights from the premodern Christian tradition that are in many ways companionable: Brian E. Daley, "Is Patristic Exegesis Still Usable?," *Communio* 29 (2002): 212–16; Steinmetz, "The Superiority of Pre-Critical Exegesis," 12–14; Frances M. Young, "The 'Mind' of Scripture: Theological Readings of the Bible in the Fathers," *International Journal of Systematic Theology* 7 (2005): 138–40.

premodern reflection on biblical interpretation. Because of the value of what this book draws from a major premodern source, the turn to Augustine is worth undertaking, even though Part II does not retain every detail of his account. Though an interruption of the present conversation by Augustine is disruptive, it is worth listening to his voice.

While Part II seeks to articulate a view of biblical interpretation that has the same structure as the texts of Augustine that were in focus in Part I, it does not follow him slavishly. The approach here is to retrieve insights from Augustine with a view toward enriching a present discussion, yet Part II does not seek to do so guided by the premise that maximal conformity, in every matter of detail, to a commanding figure from the Christian tradition guarantees good hermeneutical thinking now. One reason this is so is that the versions of the biblical text Augustine read are not the same as those used by most readers in our own time, and therefore the same interpretive techniques are not needed to handle those texts. The entire repertoire of reading techniques that were taught in ancient schools, and that Augustine used while giving them a distinctively Christian spin, were dependent on the state of texts at that time, which is different in many ways from the conditions of the biblical texts present-day readers seek to interpret. Most reading of the Bible now is not based on the same set of Latin translations Augustine consulted. Nor do today's readers access background information about the text in the same manner Augustine did. Another reason that simple conformity will not work is that Augustine does not by himself provide an obvious way to deal with developments that happened only after his time. Those who appropriate Augustine today must at least grapple with aspects of the historical-critical tradition; the entire modern tradition of interpretation cannot simply be dodged altogether. Part II aims to integrate insights from modern approaches to the Bible into the constructive case it advances. Augustine does not provide a model for how to do that, and so reflection on that issue cannot takes its cue from him, at least not at the level of detail. Part II seeks to follow the structure of Augustine's view, as indicated above, rather than the material content in all of its culture-specific detail. The chapters of Part II thus concur with Augustine's biographer: "It would be inappropriate, absolutely pointless and even absurd to try to imagine how, having by some impossible means returned to this world, he would adapt his 'message' to our culture. . . . Let us turn the question around and ask ourselves rather what lesson *we* may draw from his life."[9]

In considering what makes biblical interpretation theological, this book thus thinks *with* and *beyond* Augustine.[10] Thinking with him means exploring his works, becoming familiar with his views, and understanding the principles that guide him. Reflecting by means of his work builds on a grasp of Augustine's thought, but the purpose is to take up his ideas as tools with which to think about the Bible, not as objects of interest in their own right. Reading a text in this way assumes that one shares "intellectually the world of discourse you are studying, that it becomes the text of which you are a part in understanding it, no matter how you apply it and to what extent you may live in another language domain in other respects."[11] The main aim of this work is, therefore, to think with rather than about Augustine.

[9] Serge Lancel, *Saint Augustine* (London: SCM Press, 2002), xviii. Emphasis added. For the sake of clarity, it is worth noting that Lancel himself qualifies the sort of lessons that he thinks modern readers should learn from Augustine by suggesting that they may not have a religious focus.

[10] This is to adapt the title of John W. de Gruchy, "With Bonhoeffer, Beyond Bonhoeffer: Transmitting Bonhoeffer's Legacy," in *Dietrich Bonhoeffers Theologie heute: Ein Weg zwischen Fundamentalismus und Säkularismus? = Dietrich Bonhoeffer's Theology Today: A Way between Fundamentalism and Secularism*, ed. John W. de Gruchy, Stephen Plant, and Christiane Tietz (Gütersloh: Gütersloher, 2009), 403–04. For my account of thinking with and beyond as key elements of retrieval, see Darren Sarisky, "Tradition II: Thinking with Historical Texts – Reflections on Theologies of Retrieval," in *Theologies of Retrieval: An Exploration and Appraisal*, ed. Darren Sarisky (London: T. & T. Clark, 2017), 193–209.

[11] Frei, *Types of Christian Theology*, 117.

Is it only Augustine who might serve as a useful interlocutor for this project? Is he the sole theologian who can serve as a useful stimulus to thinking about theological reading?[12] Augustine is not the only thinker who offers what this work draws from him, for other theologians also think of doctrine as depicting reality and having implications for action, including the human action of interpreting the Bible. However, Augustine sets out these issues in a breadth and with a depth that are arguably unsurpassed by any other figure within the Christian tradition, so he is highly suitable and indeed compelling as a dialogue partner. It is better to study him closely than to attempt an impossibly broad survey of all the figures who share the key features he contributes to this project.

Part II takes a second step by not restricting itself to Augustine and his direct concerns, but engaging with a broad range of modern thinking on the topic of biblical interpretation: in this way, it goes *beyond* him. Augustine was himself always in process as a thinker, and was loath to settle on any fixed set of formulae for handling theological problems. This book does not arrest this movement by treating a specific phase of Augustine's thinking as absolutely determinative for all future reflection, though it finds *On Christian Teaching* quite instructive for the main query of this book. Part II follows his trajectory of thinking, extending it out, and altering it in order to address pressing issues in our own context. Part II faces a distinctively modern query, and it works through modern challenges too, because here and now theological reading is an issue that confronts us. It is especially important to consider the question of what role modern historical consciousness should have within theological interpretation, and Chapter 3 takes the first step in

[12] Lieven Boeve rightly charges that certain contemporary appropriations of Augustine, such as Radical Orthodox theologies, give insufficient justification for turning to him specifically as a way out of nihilism. See "Retrieving Augustine Today: Between Neo-Augustinianist Essentialism and Radical Hermeneutics," in *Augustine and Postmodern Thought: A New Alliance against Modernity?*, ed. Lieven Boeve, Mathijs Lamberigts, and Maarten Wisse (Leuven: Peeters, 2009), 7.

doing so. By the end of Chapter 3, it begins to emerge how historical consciousness will be important for each of the topics treated in Part II. Because Part II genuinely does go beyond Augustine in the ways just mentioned, the proposal the following chapters put forward is not an example of what Charles Mathewes calls Pottery Barn theology,[13] something that genuinely is new but is made to look old so as to increase its appeal. Part II does not ask its readers to accept its conclusion simply because of the authority associated with Augustine in the Western theological tradition. Insofar as the argument goes beyond him, it proceeds on other grounds, and that aspect of the argument should be judged as such. Even in going beyond Augustine, however, there is a real sense in which we can only catch up with him, at least in one crucial respect. His insights about what theology does in relation to biblical interpretation are ones from which today's readers can and should still learn. They are worth our attention precisely because, despite their date of genesis, they outstrip many of the ideas that are currently available, in that they allow doctrine to operate in a whole different capacity than it often does within the current discussion.

[13] I owe this to a comment from Mathewes which he made at a Ford Home Seminar in Cambridge.

# 3 | In Contradistinction to Naturalism

This chapter contributes to developing an account of theological reading by spelling out what it is not, or that with which it fundamentally contrasts. What lies behind this aim is the reality that theological exegesis is one type of interpretation, though it is not the only one that exists. Inquiring into how theological reading stands in contradistinction to other modes or styles of reading can illuminate theological reading itself.[1] The chapter does not intend to explicate for its own sake or in a comprehensive manner that which theological reading is not. However, the clarifying project of this chapter contributes to the overall goal of the book, and will be fruitful to the extent that there is, at the very outset, an accurate discernment of what the nature of the contrast actually is between theological reading and something that is genuinely its negation. Though theological reading, or something very much like it, is often set over against historical or literary readings of a text, this way of framing the issue is ultimately unhelpful. What really is in contradistinction to theological reading is an interpretation of the Bible that assumes metaphysical naturalism. For the sake of understanding theological reading better, this chapter explores a historically important example of a naturalistically driven account.

Though the main goal of this chapter is to establish that to which theological reading exists in contradistinction, there is a secondary goal here as well. That aim is to highlight historical consciousness,

[1] I draw the notion of contradistinction from John C. Poirier, "'Theological Interpretation' and Its Contradistinctions," *Tyndale Bulletin* 61 (2010): 105–18.

in the sense that understanding language requires grasping how it is conditioned by its historical setting. This becomes a principle that Part II incorporates into its exposition of theological reading. The focus on naturalism inevitably raises the issue of historical consciousness, yet rejecting naturalism need not and should not mean spurning historical consciousness altogether. Thus, the two goals of this chapter relate in a subtle way. The agenda of the chapter is a complex mixture of rejecting one thing and appropriating something closely linked to it. Tracking this sifting process will doubtless require close attention from the reader, but the only alternative to putting forth a case with a level of nuance is to make a sweeping, simplistic judgment that fails to acknowledge the value of historical consciousness for theological reading. That is a trade-off which is by no means worth making. The bulk of the chapter is dedicated to outlining naturalism and how it shapes an approach to reading; the conclusion gives the most explicit discussion of historical consciousness and indicates the role it will have in Part II.

## Theological Interpretation and Its Contradistinctions

There exists a common threefold distinction between a literary reading of the Bible, a historical reading of the text, and a determinedly religious mode of engagement with the text, [2] but this does

[2] See, for instance, Robert Alter, *The Art of Biblical Narrative*, Rev. ed. (New York: Basic Books, 2011), 13–14, 17; Angela Lou Harvey, *Spiritual Reading: A Study of the Christian Practice of Reading Scripture* (Eugene: Cascade Books, 2015), 25–44; Morgan and Barton, *Biblical Interpretation*, 167–202. Similarly, Harvey Cox distinguishes between narrative, historical, and spiritual reading and correlates the three styles with stages of his biography, though he does not entirely leave behind the early stages of interpretation as his development progresses, but rather incorporates them into a multifaceted engagement with the Bible: *How to Read the Bible* (New York: HarperOne, 2015), 1–8. Jean-Luc Marion adds a fourth mode, prophetic reading, to the standard three: *God without Being*, 145–52. Krister Stendahl argues that there is only the most artificial distinction between the Bible as literary classic and the Bible as Scripture: "The Bible as

not provide a good way of saying what theological reading is not. What is meant by each of the three elements of this distinction? In general terms, a literary reading would study biblical texts with a view toward understanding features such as their genre, structure, and rhetoric, together with any arguments they contain.[3] What the poet W. H. Auden calls "read[ing] the Bible for its prose"[4] would qualify as literary reading. A historical reading, on the other hand, can take a number of different forms: focusing on the text as a set of clues to reconstruct the history of the period from which it emerged, using historical background to elucidate features of the text itself, or even studying the history of the transmission of the text.[5] Finally, a reading of the text as Scripture – the closest of these three categories to theological exegesis – would attend to how the text functions within the life of a religious community whose sacred text it is.[6] What is important here is to examine the dynamics set into play by making this particular threefold distinction. Assuming that theological reading and reading as scripture are sufficiently close to one another, why is this not a useful set of reference points for clarifying theological reading? Depending on precisely how it is articulated, the threefold distinction either creates a misleading impression about how autonomous each mode is or ends up noting

Classic and the Bible as Holy Scripture," in *Presidential Voices: The Society of Biblical Literature in the Twentieth Century*, ed. Harold W. Attridge and James C. VanderKam (Atlanta: Society of Biblical Literature, 2006), 209–15. These different approaches to reading should, of course, be understood as capacious categories containing within themselves many mutually exclusive and competing readings.

3 Kelsey, *Eccentric Existence*, 1: 135.

4 W. H. Auden, *Collected Poems* (New York: Vintage International, 1991), 339.

5 Kelsey, *Eccentric Existence*, 1: 135.

6 Ibid., 1: 136. Quite similar to Kelsey's distinction between a historical reading and reading the text as Scripture is François Dreyfus's contrast between reading in the Sorbonne and reading in the church, though the latter operates in a Roman Catholic register. See François Dreyfus, "Exégèse en Sorbonne, exégèse en église," *Revue biblique* (1975): 321–69.

so much imbrication that it does not clearly demarcate that to which theological reading is opposed.

Consider the following two examples of ways to flesh out the distinction. First, literary critic Northrop Frye makes this triplex distinction, beginning by distinguishing historical reading from reading the text as Scripture, in the course of introducing his classic book on the Bible's influence on Western literature and culture: "There have always been two directions in Biblical scholarship, the critical and the traditional, though often they have merged. The critical approach establishes the text and studies the historical and cultural background; the traditional interprets it in accordance with what a consensus of theological and ecclesiastical authorities have declared the meaning to be."[7] Frye continues by setting out yet a third mode of interpretation, how a poet might read the Bible, in order to say that he has not found historical-critical studies of much use for understanding how literary figures use the Bible.[8] The rationale Frye gives for setting historical-critical interpretation to the side in his project is that the impulse to relate discrete biblical texts to their circumstances of historical origin ends up dissolving the literary integrity of the Bible. He comments, "Instead of emerging from lower criticism, or textual study, most of it [historical-critical study] dug itself into a still lower, or sub-basement, criticism in which disintegrating the text became an end in itself."[9] This is, to be sure, a sweeping and harshly dismissive judgment of historical reading, which Frye characterizes as engaging in a "good deal of straw thrashing"[10] after having made a few initial breakthroughs early in its history as a discipline. There are many problems with what Frye says here: blithely scorning the hard-won gains of historical reading; failing to see how ecclesial dogma

[7] Northrop Frye, *The Great Code: The Bible and Literature*, Collected Works of Northrop Frye (Toronto: University of Toronto Press, 2006), 19: 11.

[8] Ibid., 19: 11.

[9] Ibid., 19: 11.

[10] Ibid., 19: 11.

emerges organically from the Bible, rather than simply being imposed on it; and – worst of all for present purposes – risking a misleading polarization of interpretive options by suggesting that theological reading, as a distinctive approach to the Bible, is ahistorical or nearly so. To claim that the results of historical investigation have not informed theological reading is a mistake, for it should be an uncontroversial point of consensus that biblical texts have a contingent origin, a knowledge of which has illuminated and can shed further light on the text. This stark differentiation between theological and historical modes of reading thus has little value as an analytical tool.

Second, neither does Kelsey's version of this distinction provide the point of contradistinction that is needed for this project, though there is certainly insight in what Kelsey says. Kelsey does not set out his framework of interpretive modes with the same polemical edge as Frye does; rather than relating the modes as antagonistic competitors, Kelsey notes ways in which the three categories overlap and reinforce one another. Though literary and historical readings of the Bible specify distinctive interpretive interests, they are also coinciding categories insofar as scholars with these two aims can borrow insights from one another, and ideas from both (overlapping) areas can feed into theological reading.[11] As Kelsey says:

> They [historical and literary reading] discipline study governed by theological interests by making unavoidably clear the concrete particularity of each of the texts on the canonical list, how they differ from one another in their literary genres and rhetoric, their cultural assumptions, their theological assumptions and affirmations, their concrete historical occasions, and the particular situations to which they were addressed.[12]

[11] Kelsey, *Eccentric Existence*, 1: 136.

[12] Ibid., 1: 151. This comment comes in Kelsey's section on "canonical holy Scripture," not simply Scripture. Some of the nuances of Kelsey's discussion, which he delineates with exquisite care, cannot be preserved in this brief treatment.

It is certainly true that theological reading can learn from the findings of these other approaches to the Bible. The point has value precisely in that it demonstrates what is problematic in conflictual portrayals of the different modes.[13] However, the degree to which the categories shade into one another and have congruent aims makes the distinction complex and fuzzy. What Kelsey's way of handling the distinction does is show how reading the Bible as Scripture is not isolated from historical and literary reading. What the distinction does not do is set out as clearly as it might what theological reading is *not*, insofar as it features three reading interests without absolute differences from each other and with a set of convergent trajectories.[14] The messiness of the distinction does not present a serious problem for Kelsey, whose project is different than the present one. Yet more clarity on the contradistinction point will prove useful for this book on theological reading. For the purpose of this work, something more is needed – something other than false

[13] Cf. the healthy skepticism about the existence of a genuinely binary relationship between theological/religious reading and historical interpretation in Talal Asad, *Formations of the Secular: Christianity, Islam, Modernity*, Cultural Memory in the Present (Stanford: Stanford University Press, 2003), 37–45; Francis Watson, "Does Historical Criticism Exist? A Contribution to Debate on the Theological Interpretation of Scripture," in *Theological Theology: Essays in Honour of John Webster*, ed. R. David Nelson, Darren Sarisky, and Justin Stratis (London: Bloomsbury T. & T. Clark, 2015), 307–18.

[14] Another possible point of contrast for theological interpretation would be what Dietrich Bonhoeffer calls "religious interpretation." This mode of appropriating Scripture relates theological concepts within the text to an isolated, private, personal or "religious" zone of a believer's life, and thus fails to respect the full scope of the Bible's message. To his credit, Bonhoeffer articulates a forceful critique of liberal Protestantism's tendency to foreshorten the substance of Scripture, and he calls for an alternative approach to reading that does not proceed on the basis of such a strong disjunction between secular and sacred, and the presumption that Scripture speaks only to the latter. Because Bonhoeffer himself did not have the opportunity to develop his own positive suggestions, this book will not deal extensively with theological as opposed to religious reading. See his *Letters and Papers from Prison*, ed. Christian Gremmels et al., Dietrich Bonhoeffer Works (Minneapolis: Fortress, 2010), 8: 372–73, 455–57.

contrasts and distinctions that fail to locate the most fundamental fault line. Theological and historical readings are not inherently opposed (contra Frye), but if they overlap and cooperate (à la Kelsey), what is it that actually stands in genuine contrast to theological reading?

What stands in the clearest contradistinction to theological reading, as a view of interpretation based on a theological ontology of the text and reader, is an approach that defines the reader and the text naturalistically, without any reference to a transcendent God, who is taken not to exist. A clear and historically important example of this comes from Benedict de Spinoza. A scholar comments on Spinoza's basic contribution to the study of the Bible: "By making biblical assumptions (especially its religious ones) part of the historical data rather than the norm of his inquiry, he achieved the critical breakthrough for the study of both the Bible and religion: theology, rather than being part of the *explanation* or religion, now became part of its *data*."[15] Theology becomes, in Spinoza's hands, what is explained instead of what possesses explanatory power: it therefore plays no role in saying who the reader is or what the text is. Theological reading, as in the example of Augustine and the position set out in Part II of this book,[16] stands in clear contrast to an approach built on a commitment to a naturalistic ontology. It is worth outlining Spinoza's view, beginning with what he says about the reader and proceeding to the text, in order to establish a clear point of contrast.[17]

[15] James S. Preus, *Spinoza and the Irrelevance of Biblical Authority* (Cambridge: Cambridge University Press, 2001), ix–x.

[16] For comparisons between Augustine and Spinoza on biblical interpretation, many of which are telling, see Maarten Wisse, "Hermeneutics," in *The Oxford Guide to the Historical Reception of Augustine*, ed. Karla Pollmann and Willemien Otten (Oxford: Oxford University Press, 2013), 2: 1131–32.

[17] Following on the insistence above that historical and naturalistic reading are different, it should be noted that Spinoza is not the founder of historical criticism, but is rather an early radical voice within that developing mode of inquiry. Many other scholars of

In selecting Spinoza as a dialogue partner, have I chosen an easy target for criticism, an older view from the early modern period, one that lacks some of the nuances and refinements that later treatments of biblical interpretation subsequently developed? Am I picking on an author who wrote at a time before much additional progress was made? This question allows me to clarify the precise purpose of engaging with Spinoza. Of course his writing on the Bible is not recent, for it was composed in the seventeenth century. Yet his *Theological-Political Treatise* is a masterly, classic work that continues to have influence even today by giving some readers of the Bible fundamental assumptions according to which they interpret the text (a few of these interpreters receive mention later in the chapter). As a classic text, it is one of the clearest statements in the entire history of biblical hermeneutics of a position based on naturalism. It is because this view is presented by Spinoza with such clarity, depth of insight, and verve that he is a fitting subject for study in a work aiming to explicate what theological reading is and is not. This chapter does not rebut Spinoza. It is not an argument against him as much as it is an explication of his working

his period were asking historical and philological questions about the Bible, and were inquiring into the sources of canonical literature, without the commitment to naturalism that drove Spinoza's way of handling all those issues. See Noel Malcolm, "Hobbes, Ezra, and the Bible: The History of a Subversive Idea," in *Aspects of Hobbes* (Oxford: Clarendon Press, 2002), 428–31. See also the further discussion of how Spinoza was more radical than many of his contemporaries in Jonathan Israel, "How Did Spinoza Declare War on Theology and Theologians?," in *Scriptural Authority and Biblical Criticism in the Dutch Golden Age*, ed. Dirk van Miert et al. (Oxford: Oxford University Press, 2017), 197–216. Though James Kugel claims that Spinoza's approach came to constitute "the marching orders of biblical scholars for the next three centuries," Kugel highlights only very broad features of Spinoza's program, and does not list a commitment to naturalism in his summary of how later moderns followed Spinoza: *How to Read the Bible*, 31–32. Further details on the broad ways in which later critics followed Spinoza can be found in Jon D. Levenson, "Theological Consensus or Historicist Evasion? Jews and Christians in Biblical Studies," in *The Hebrew Bible, the Old Testament, and Historical Criticism: Jews and Christians in Biblical Studies* (Louisville: Westminster John Knox, 1993), 96, 99.

assumptions, which, having been seen for what they are, show themselves to be different than those operative in the constructive proposal that this book is developing.

It is especially important to note that theological interpretation stands over against a naturalistic approach to reading, rather than to a historical approach, because the label *theological reading* has come to be associated with a polemically motivated devaluation of history within the practice of interpretation.[18] This denigration is problematic, and part of the appropriate response is to clarify that to which theological reading really stands in contrast. After making clear what it means to have a naturalistic account of interpretation, Part II develops views of the reader and text that seek to bring theological categories together with those that have a more immanent orientation, in so doing assuming that *historical* need not mean *naturalistic*. For a view of theological reading, it is crucial to insist that the text originates from a past context, and that this conditions how it ought to be read, without understanding such a past context in a naturalistic light.[19] This is to anticipate, however. Outlining a naturalistic view first will mean it is easier to make such points at a later stage in the overall argument.

[18] See Fowl, *Engaging Scripture*, 13–21; R. R. Reno, "Biblical Theology and Theological Exegesis," in *Out of Egypt: Biblical Theology and Biblical Interpretation*, ed. Craig G. Bartholomew et al., Scripture and Hermeneutics Series (Grand Rapids: Zondervan, 2004), 385–408. For an insightful and appropriately critical account of the trend toward demoting history in recent discussions of theological reading, see Michael C. Legaspi, "Scripture: Three Modes of Retrieval," in *Theologies of Retrieval: An Exploration and Appraisal*, ed. Darren Sarisky (London: Bloomsbury T. & T. Clark, 2017), 162–63. Francis Watson rightly says that "renouncing the tools of critical scholarship for fear of secular contamination is perhaps the least promising" way to go about theological reading. See his *The Fourfold Gospel: A Theological Reading of the New Testament Portraits of Jesus* (Grand Rapids: Baker, 2016), vii. My only emendation, in the context of the discussion above, would be to drop the word *perhaps*.

[19] This would be to have a different view of history than one finds in Harvey, *Historian and the Believer*.

## Inwardness and the Naturalized Reader

### *Descartes*

The aim of this section is to bring out an important point about Spinoza's view of human rationality, and it is useful to approach this issue by examining a similar pattern in René Descartes.[20] In autobiographical reflections in his *Discourse on Method*, Descartes reports that from his childhood he had the benefit of a literary education, in which learning took the form of a deferential, though not entirely uncritical, reading of major authors across a whole range of subjects, from theology and philosophy to the sciences. Education involved posing questions and seeking answers to them within the framework of thought provided by texts which represented the high-water mark of knowledge in each field of inquiry. This form of education was essentially a respectful dialogue between the student and major authors: learning was "like having a conversation with the most distinguished men of past ages."[21] Though he came to question text-centered pedagogy, Descartes continued to see some value in it, as reading, at a minimum, allowed students to absorb ideas from history's best minds, to ruminate on them, and to inhabit the frameworks of thought that had proven themselves to be the most fruitful.[22]

[20] Brian Stock overstates the similarity between Descartes and Augustine in concluding that both reject "bookish education." Descartes does this, but the case that Augustine does so as well rests only on the citation of a few texts and an assertion that Augustine's debt to Platonism means that what really matters for him is tapping into knowledge which is already present in the mind. See Brian Stock, *After Augustine: The Meditative Reader and the Text*, Material Texts (Philadelphia: University of Pennsylvania Press, 2001), 72–73. Charles Taylor deals with issues in a much broader perspective, but also overemphasizes the continuity between Augustine and a Cartesian trust in inwardness: *Sources of the Self*, 127–42.

[21] René Descartes, "Discourse on Method," in *Descartes: Selected Philosophical Writings* (Cambridge: Cambridge University Press, 2008), 22.

[22] Ibid., 22.

The problems Descartes came to see with this approach ultimately prompted him to replace it with something radically different. As he saw it, the difficulty with an education built around reading was that it did not allow the student fully to cultivate his own rational powers. For him, the utility of reading was not mainly to decenter the self,[23] and to expose the mind to ideas which would enrich it, though there was some worth in this. In the first instance, the purpose of engaging with texts was to provide a point of contrast by which to see one's own views more clearly.[24] Realizing the shortcomings of the education he had been given, Descartes abandoned his literary studies, divested himself of many of the ideas he had previously accepted, sought out firsthand experience of the world, and turned within himself to ascertain that on which he could rely, saying that he once "stayed all day shut up alone in a stove-heated room, where I was completely free to converse with myself about my own thoughts."[25] The way forward was to follow a set of procedures that one can carry out inwardly. "I learned not to believe too firmly anything of which I had been persuaded only by example and custom. Thus I gradually freed myself from many errors which may obscure our natural light and make us less capable of heeding reason."[26] He decided to doubt all his beliefs, except those that presented themselves to him clearly and distinctly.[27] Only the beliefs that presented themselves to him with the clarity and distinctness he experienced in mathematical reasoning remained with him, and would come to constitute a new starting point for his thinking.[28] Building on the firm base of beliefs

23 See Williams, *Why Study the Past?*, 110.

24 Descartes, "Discourse on Method," 22–23.

25 Ibid., 25.

26 Ibid., 24–25.

27 Ibid., 29.

28 There is useful exposition of this point, and the entire *Discourse on Method*, in Gerald L. Bruns, "A Grammarian's Guide to the Discourse on Method," in *Inventions: Writing, Textuality, and Understanding in Literary History* (New Haven: Yale University Press, 1982), 73.

that presented themselves with absolute certainty, and proceeding carefully from that foundation, leads to an entirely new framework of beliefs, in the totality of which one can place confidence. "Community, tradition, authority: these have all started to give way to the individual, his inwardness, his autonomy."[29]

In sum, Descartes displays a procedural, rather than substantive, view of rationality. A procedural approach is structured around the subjective state of the rational mind, not the commitments to which one adheres. Within a procedural framework, "The rationality of an agent or his thought is judged by how he thinks, not in the first instance by whether the outcome is substantively correct. Good thinking is defined procedurally. . . . Correct thinking is not *defined* by substantial truth,"[30] because the whole point of Descartes' exercise is to throw all, or nearly all,[31] of his beliefs into doubt. Truth may be the *result* of following the correct procedure, but it is not built into the process so as to define rationality as such from the beginning. What constitutes the framework of thought as rational is not the correctness of the content with which it commences, but that a foundation has been laid according to the right sort of process. Foundational beliefs must meet a certain standard – they have to present themselves as utterly certain – yet doing so does not mean that they qualify by aligning with a material standard, but that doubting them is impossible. Because internal process is so crucial to a procedural view, inwardness comes to have a greater value than it could possibly have in a system built on trust in texts. (By contrast, recall from the previous chapter that Augustine takes a substantive approach to rational reflection. For Augustine, it is impossible to be rational and simultaneously think that the best

[29] Jeffrey Stout, *The Flight from Authority: Religion, Morality, and the Quest for Autonomy* (Notre Dame: University of Notre Dame Press, 1981), 50.

[30] Taylor, *Sources of the Self*, 86.

[31] As the subsection below on Spinoza explains, Descartes sought to retain his religious beliefs.

life consists in maximal fulfillment of sensual desire. This sort of commitment sends one's thinking off in the wrong direction.)

## *Spinoza*

Descartes exempts religion from his nearly global commitment to hyperbolic doubt, and maintains his faith intact,[32] but Spinoza develops what might be called a procedural approach to the interpretation of the Bible, thus applying some of Descartes' key ideas to the sphere of religion.[33] A crucial element of this is Spinoza's commitment to naturalism. Naturalism refers to an ontology in which what exists is a single substance. As Jonathan Israel explains, this entails "conflating body and mind into one, reducing God and nature to the same thing, excluding all miracles and spirits separate from bodies, and invoking reason as the sole guide in human life, jettisoning tradition."[34] Spinoza continues to use the term God – in fact, it occurs very frequently in both of his major works, *Ethics* and *Theological-Political Treatise*, the second of which directly addresses biblical interpretation – yet it takes on a new sense in his usage. God is not a reality separate from the world: he does not have any existence apart from physical, material reality. As such,

[32] Descartes, "Discourse on Method," 31.

[33] For comments on the broad similarities between Spinoza and Descartes, especially in being dubious about certain inherited traditions, see Richard H. Popkin, *The History of Scepticism: From Savonarola to Bayle*, Rev. ed. (Oxford: Oxford University Press, 2003), 242, 245.

[34] Jonathan I. Israel, *A Revolution of the Mind: Radical Enlightenment and the Intellectual Origins of Modern Democracy* (Princeton: Princeton University Press, 2010), 19. Israel probably exaggerates the influence of Spinoza within the Enlightenment, making him utterly central to ushering in the modern order. However, Spinoza's influence on the history of biblical interpretation is widely recognized, though he represents one particular radical approach. For more details on how the one-substance metaphysic applies to biblical interpretation, see Jonathan I. Israel, "Introduction," in *Theological-Political Treatise*, Cambridge Texts in the History of Philosophy (Cambridge: Cambridge University Press, 2007), xii, xv.

God is not transcendent in relation to the world, nor does the world depend on him for its existence. Neither can God be spoken of in personal terms, as one who has a purpose for the world and directs it in any way. Spinoza terms the totality of what exists *Deus sive Natura*,[35] God or Nature, by which he intends to say that the two nouns are alternative glosses naming a single entity, a physical world unified by a chain of causes and effects, which cannot be interrupted by miraculous occurrences.[36] Because of the way he redefines what he means by God, his philosophy can be summarized without reference to God in the traditional sense. It is naturalistic even though it uses the term God often.

Such naturalism shapes a construal of the human person, and hence how Spinoza views readers and what makes their thinking rational. Under naturalism, the Christian tradition's established doctrinal language, presupposing as it does a transcendent God, no longer describes human beings: the reader is not an embodied soul whose origin and end are in God. Rather, mind and body are one, forming a single psychosomatic unity – mind and body are conflated into one, as Israel says – and this single reality is autonomous in the sense that it is not contingent on divinity. That the

35 Steven M. Nadler notes that this provocative phrase appears in the Latin version of his posthumously published works, but its equivalent does not appear in the more accessible Dutch text: *Spinoza's Ethics: An Introduction*, Cambridge Introductions to Key Philosophical Texts (Cambridge: Cambridge University Press, 2006), 53.

36 There are complex debates among Spinoza scholars about whether he should be considered a pantheist and, if so, in what sense exactly. For a careful and clear argument that even in *Theological-Political Treatise*, Spinoza at least suggests pantheism, see Yitzhak Y. Melamed, "The Metaphysics of the Theological-Political Treatise," in *Spinoza's 'Theological-Political Treatise': A Critical Guide*, ed. Yitzhak Y. Melamed and Michael A. Rosenthal (Cambridge: Cambridge University Press, 2010), 133–37. That Spinoza is a pantheist in some sense is the majority position. However, for an argument that *atheist* is a better label for Spinoza, see Nadler, *Spinoza's Ethics: An Introduction*, 117–21. For the purpose of this chapter, only a modest level of precision on this issue is necessary: it is enough to be clear that Spinoza denies the existence of a transcendent God and identifies God and nature with one another.

reality of God is not part of what makes human beings who they are gives them a certain sort of independence. Their independence in this way connects up with the final point that Israel mentions in his definition of a single-substance ontology, that is, the jettisoning of tradition. Human beings have within themselves everything they need to live morally, and therefore they do not need the extrinsic guidance of an authoritative tradition. Humans can stand on their own, both rationally and morally, without the aid of tradition. Spinoza says that human beings often come under the sway of their emotions and fail to allow reason to guide them toward an ethical life, but following reason is a matter of trusting one's internal resources, which are sufficient as guides to knowing and living.[37]

The reader of the Bible is *this* human being, a self-determining textual analyst, whose tasks do not require anything other than the standard cognitive equipment that all human beings possess.[38] As Spinoza says, after summarizing what his approach to interpreting Scripture requires, "I do not doubt that everyone now sees that this method requires no other light than that of natural reason."[39] Divine illumination is not necessary, nor is it even possible for Spinoza to see what role that notion plays in the commentaries

[37] Benedictus de Spinoza, *Theological-Political Treatise*, Cambridge Texts in the History of Philosophy (Cambridge: Cambridge University Press, 2007), 45. Throughout this book, when citing passages from the translation of the *Theological-Political Treatise*, I have used this rendering from Michael Silverthorne and Jonathan Israel. Unfortunately, the splendid new translation from Edwin Curley (Benedictus de Spinoza, *The Collected Works of Spinoza. Volume II* [Princeton: Princeton University Press, 2016]) came into print too late for me to use it.

[38] The naturalistic metaphysics that is set out fully in his *Ethics* is quietly present in *Theological-Political Treatise*. The latter text clearly grows out of a naturalistic outlook, though Spinoza holds back some of the details of his system, and regularly uses traditional theological language, which he redefines. Leo Strauss makes an overstated claim to the effect that *Theological-Political Treatise* is written in a secret code which only the canniest are able to decipher: "How to Study Spinoza's Theologico-Political Treatise," in *Persecution and the Art of Writing* (Chicago: University of Chicago Press, 1988), 142–202.

[39] Spinoza, *Theological-Political Treatise*, 111.

written by those who claim that it is doctrinally crucial, or to determine what exactly this notion is supposed to mean in the first place.[40] To apply a point made above, neither is tradition necessary for good reading. More than that, it is actually harmful if readers feel pressured to align the results of their study of Scripture with a tradition that prescribes what their conclusions should be about the meaning of the texts they are interpreting.[41] Readers do not depend on a transcendent God to open their eyes to the subject matter of the text or on a human tradition to orient them in their work on the text. Reading is not dependent on these factors that have currency within Christian theology.

Rather, undertaking a historical reading of the text calls for skills which are, in principle, universally accessible. The fundamental mandate before interpreters is that they read the Bible in a way that is informed by the history of the text. This includes becoming acquainted with the words of the text in their original languages; discerning the author's original intention in each passage, and carefully synthesizing what various passages teach, without prejudicing one's findings with the assumption that the whole Bible is harmonious, or that its teachings will seem reasonable to modern readers; and inquiring into the situations from which the texts came and into which they were sent originally as well as how they were subsequently transmitted.[42] In addition, readers should bring together what the various texts agree on (the character of the virtuous life) and what the texts treat in widely divergent ways (matters Spinoza refers to as philosophy).[43]

What skills do these tasks require? Performing these tasks necessitates a working knowledge of the specific languages in which the texts of the Bible were written. In addition, readers need skills in

[40] Ibid., 112.
[41] Ibid., 113–15.
[42] Ibid., 99–102.
[43] Ibid., 102–05.

analytical thought in order to ascertain the authorial intent of the passages that they are studying, together with the ability to synthesize the Bible's teaching on various topics, and to see where different authors are or are not at odds with each other. Readers also need to be able to distance themselves from their own assumptions enough to spot where a biblical author is, as is often the case, employing an outlook that they as readers do not share. That is, readers need to be able to perceive the intellectual-cultural distance that exists between themselves and the biblical documents. Further, readers need to develop sufficiently honed historical skills that they can situate the biblical texts in their precise milieu or origin, discerning how they reflect their author's personalities, the concrete circumstances that prompted their authors to write, and the situations to which the writings were directed. Finally, the faculty of reason is necessary to determine whether a specific teaching in the Bible is actually true or not.[44] Reason is an analytical tool here, though reason in the sense of a body of rational beliefs plays no role in ascertaining the text's meaning.[45] These are the things that readers must do, and anyone can do these things (assuming one has received a certain level of education). None of this requires a theologically informed self-understanding or participation in a religious tradition.

Reading the Bible is about having skills to *do* certain things, not about being committed to received (theological) beliefs as starting points, which then come to be operative within the practice of exegesis. The significance of this stress on doing – that the enterprise of interpretation is delineated according to normative procedures, in sharp opposition to the reader having to affirm certain

[44] Ibid., 100, 110–11. There is a qualification to add, which is that reason is not competent to judge in some cases where the alleged truth is utterly fantastical.

[45] I owe this distinction to Steven M. Nadler, *A Book Forged in Hell: Spinoza's Scandalous Treatise and the Birth of the Secular Age* (Princeton: Princeton University Press, 2011), 134–35.

accepted beliefs as given assumptions – is that hermeneutical obligation is essentially procedural, not substantive. The sense in which this is true requires careful specification. Reading is about doing certain things, not following *received* views, especially ones that are part of a theological tradition that countenances the centrality of a transcendent God. As Spinoza sees it, naturalism does structure how the reader should engage with the Bible; the reader's obligations are defined against a naturalistic backdrop. In this way, naturalism is a presupposition of the whole approach to interpretation. However, naturalism is not a received view in the sense that an intelligent person could not see its truth by herself.[46] Interpretation is procedural in that it eliminates all beliefs that the reader could not generate inwardly. It does not operate on the basis of any substantive commitments apart from those that can arise from within oneself. As has already been stressed, belief that what the Bible says is true and that its various passages cohere is not to be presupposed by readers, nor should the long history of interpretation be assumed to be a reliable guide, just as the contemporary church's most prominent teachers should not receive deference in interpretation. Instead, the reader can and must operate solely on the basis of his own internal resources, once he possesses the historical and linguistic information he requires through studying the background of the Bible. "Ordinary people who can read or hear the Scriptures do not need theologians or other religious officials to identify the fundamental doctrines on which their salvation depends, and to some extent they can resolve interpretative problems by using their ordinary capacity for reasoning."[47] (It is necessary to say "to some extent" here because lack of knowledge about

[46] See Benedictus de Spinoza, *Ethics*, Oxford Philosophical Texts (Oxford: Oxford University Press, 2000).

[47] Susan James, *Spinoza on Philosophy, Religion, and Politics: The Theologico-Political Treatise* (Oxford: Oxford University Press, 2012), 160.

the language and the background of the Bible means that not all passages can be understood.)

Both Spinoza and Descartes present an essentially procedural conception of human rationality, Descartes developing his view in quite broad terms, and Spinoza applying something similar to the interpretation of the Bible. Procedural notions of human rationality as strategies for displacing theological ideas from the way in which readers reflect on theological texts have had a significant afterlife in our own context. Van Harvey's *The Historian and the Believer* provides an illustration. As he sees it, the Christian tradition and modern academic research follow what he calls contrary ethical systems: a traditional Christian believer is obligated to believe the essential tenets of the Christian faith, while researchers such as historians inquiring into foundational texts of the Christian faith are forbidden from taking for granted the truth of this (or any) religious system, lest their adherence to that system misdirect their research. Researchers put forth arguments, which their colleagues have an obligation to test critically.

> And when these claims are challenged one is able to produce some appropriate justification for them. Whether any specific claim is to be regarded as a valid one can only be judged on its merits which . . . are functions of the argument and the evidence brought forward on its behalf. Without such merits, the assertion can only be considered as a belief or an opinion.[48]

In other words, substantive theological beliefs cannot factor into justificatory arguments for conclusions that one may properly hold. Such conclusions gain whatever warrant they have by means of conforming to procedures (what Harvey calls "standards" or "canons")[49] into which theology is in no way built.

[48] Harvey, *Historian and the Believer*, 44.

[49] Ibid., 44.

It is worth flagging here a point to which I return at the conclusion of this chapter. The issue relates to the specific procedures Spinoza recommends, rather than to the whole procedural notion of rationality. A naturalistic ontology is one of the major commitments standing behind these procedures and providing a rationale for them. First, biblical texts should be studied in their original language because the subsequent religious traditions of interpretation, both Jewish and Christian, do not deserve the interpreter's deference. These traditions involve indulging in prejudice more than anything else. Second, texts should be read individually, and it cannot be assumed that all of the texts in the biblical canon cohere with one another. The canonical collection contains contradictions and tensions, despite the way in which readers from the Jewish and Christian traditions are in the habit of trying to read the text as an integral unity which points to a transcendent God. No such God actually exists. Finally, the proper context for studying scriptural texts is their setting of genesis: the meaning they had for their original audiences is their only real meaning. The notions of illumination, inspiration, ecclesial context, and the rest, on which later Christian readings depend, are not creditable, and similarly incisive objections can be made to the presuppositions of Jewish interpretive practice.

Yet appropriating the valuable aspects of these procedures does not automatically invoke a naturalistic metaphysic. There are other ways to ground the need to study the original languages of the Bible than to say that the interpretive traditions which pass on understandings of the texts are in grave error about the most important matters. Many religious readers have their own rationale for reading the texts in the languages in which they were composed. What is even more important for our purposes – and this is the point to which this chapter recurs – is that there is real value in some of Spinoza's principles (assuming that they can be supplemented with other procedures), even on the assumption that a transcendent God does exist. Moreover, this same valuable contribution is not to be found in Augustine's approach or in many other premodern religious systems of reading. While Augustine insists that some texts require close historical study,[50] he does not call for *all* biblical texts to receive such study in the way that Spinoza asks readers systematically to inquire into the historical circumstances behind each and every text. Naturalism is one way to underline the value of historical consciousness, but it is by no means the only way. If the meaning of an utterance is a function of its use, and this use refers to employment in a specific context, which cannot be assumed to be identical to use in other circumstances, then there is every reason for readers to pay close attention to the context from which a given speech-act first emerged. The historical relativity of language can be discerned without naturalism, but a different ontology would also ground a process of going beyond the text's original context and seeing how it speaks into the present. I return to these issues at the close of the chapter as well as later in the book.

## The Bible Naturalized

### *Meaning and Truth*

A major point where Spinoza's *Theological-Political Treatise* is original, and where it has had a significant impact on the subsequent history of the study of the Bible, lies in the firm distinction he draws between the actual meaning of a given passage and the truth of fact. Speaking of biblical texts, Spinoza says, "For we are concerned here only with their meaning, not with their truth" (*De solo enim sensu orationum, non autem de earum veritate laboramus*).[51] Spinoza sees the two as distinguishable, not inextricably enmeshed

[50] *On Christian Teaching* 2.42–43 (CCSL 32, 62–63; OWC Green, 55–56).

[51] Spinoza, *Theological-Political Treatise*, 100, cf. 13–14; Carl Gebhardt, ed. *Spinoza Opera* (Heidelberg: Carl Winters, 1925), 3: 100.

with one another, and he commends reconstructing meaning as the focus for the biblical interpreter's energy, specifying as a separate task reason's work of inquiring into what is true.[52]

It is worth expounding the sense of each of the two key terms in this distinction and what it means for them to differ from one another. First, meaning is the semantic value of a small, isolated textual unit – say a single verse from the Bible – and that string of words is construed as a past act of communication, that is, language that is rightly read only against the background of its context of origin. Second, truth of fact refers exclusively to whether reality as it can be known matches up with the assertion made by the modest-sized textual unit, which for the purpose of testing its truth cannot be integrally connected with and a key source of the reader's larger worldview or network of beliefs, lest such a text automatically pass the truth test. Truth is thus the veracity of a discrete textual unit. Preserving the integrity of the distinction, and not collapsing the two elements together, entails that meaning is not a function of a commitment that the reader has to the claim under investigation turning out to be true, that is, that it fits as an element within his framework of beliefs. The exclusivity of historical context is a product of a commitment to a certain truth, namely, metaphysical naturalism. That commitment to truth does hang in the background of the treatise; it is not as if interpretation happens on the basis of no commitments to truth whatsoever.[53] However, readers

[52] One of Spinoza's contemporaries distinguishes textual meaning and truth of fact, only to identify them in the special case of the Bible. For historical background, see Preus, *Spinoza and the Irrelevance of Biblical Authority*, 52–53; Nadler, *Book Forged in Hell*, 122–26. Spinoza's contribution to the history of the study of the Bible consists in his dogged insistence that readers not only make an analytical distinction between the two categories, but that they not blur the categories in practice by assuming that the Bible should be treated differently than other literature.

[53] Paul Ricoeur is certainly right in making the general point that notions of meaning are always lodged in larger theories: "Esquisse de conclusion," in *Exégèse et herméneutique*, ed. Roland Barthes et al. (Paris: Seuil, 1971), 285.

cannot presuppose the truth of the individual passages they are reading.[54] The meaning of a biblical text is what the author of the text intended to communicate, as this can be reconstructed by a study of the language he used and from knowledge of the historical context from which his writing emerged – and not other factors.

An example Spinoza provides illustrates how the distinction works. When faced with the question of how to interpret the biblical claim that God is fire, he asks whether it is to be understood literally or metaphorically.[55] Whether the divine literally is a physical flame or whether the words should be taken to mean that he is jealous, as Spinoza concludes, must be answered by testing each interpretation against the immediate biblical context of the remark, not by fitting it into the theological framework of the interpreter. There is not a clear logical link between a given reader believing that God is either jealous or (more exotically from the point of view of the Christian theological tradition) that he is a physical flame, and deciding on the sense that the text bears. A lazy interpreter might merge his beliefs on God and the meaning of the text, but such an interpretive move would be completely fallacious as Spinoza sees things.

One of the overriding concerns that prompts Spinoza to formulate this distinction is that many religious readers in his own time are, in a facile way, aligning their interpretation of the Bible with their own pre-understanding of what is true, and in the process skewing their reading. From Spinoza's point of view, they are therefore ideologically driven. Readers, both those in positions of

[54] On Spinoza's opponents assuming, rather than proving, that the Bible conveys the truth, see *Theological-Political Treatise*, 8. Hans Frei argues that Spinoza and other figures in this period fit the Bible into a more determinative picture of reality than the biblical narrative itself provides. Frei locates Spinoza at the very beginning of what he terms the "great reversal," prior to which interpreters more often located their understanding of the world within the vision of reality provided by the Bible itself. See *The Eclipse of Biblical Narrative*, 42–43, 130.

[55] Spinoza, *Theological-Political Treatise*, 100–01.

authority and those who follow society's leaders, often project their beliefs onto the Bible in order to confer sanctity and authority on their views, thus enhancing their power over others.[56] The effect of the distinction, when it is applied to any given short passage of the Bible, is to disengage what the text says from the reader's assumptions, thus forcing the interpreter to face the thoughts and assumptions of the text on their own terms – and thus genuinely to become an interpreter, a bona fide reader who encounters what is actually present in the text itself, and whose encounter is not occluded by what Spinoza considers to be mere prejudices. At least as Spinoza presents it, initially suspending the question of the text's veracity is a hermeneutical stipulation designed to force the reader to encounter the text in its alterity and strangeness.

Though this distinction is central to Spinoza's hermeneutic and its influence within the subsequent history of interpretation, it does sometimes at least seem as if he himself does not observe it. For example, the entirety of one of the chapters of his *Theological-Political Treatise* appropriates political principles from the organization of the ancient Hebrew state, as this is presented in the biblical text.[57] The state of Israel thus functions as a biblical example in support of the modern political arrangements that Spinoza writes to champion. This move certainly appears to assume that scriptural texts contain truths about the ideal configuration of a state, not simply a meaning that is a function solely of factors that shaped the text's context of origin, and that may well be limited in its pertinence to the situation out of which the text arose. What prompts Spinoza to treat certain political principles he finds in the Bible as

[56] See, for example, his none-too-complimentary comments on both the masses and theological experts in Spinoza, *Theological-Political Treatise*, 97: "We see them [i.e., the common people] advancing false notions of their own as the word of God and seeking to use the influence of religion to compel other people to agree with them. As for theologians, we see that for the most part they have sought to extract their own thoughts and opinions from the Bible and thereby endow them with divine authority."

[57] Spinoza, *Theological-Political Treatise*, 230–38.

truths of abiding interest, not just points that are context-relative? In instances where truth and meaning begin to shade into one another, Spinoza is employing a rhetorical strategy of offering to his audience the kind of rationale that would be most persuasive to them – that is, a biblical one.[58] It remains the case that the truth of a given passage is not an integral commitment of the method for discovering the meaning of that same biblical text. In addition, while he does employ the texts as if they demonstrate or at least illustrate truths he wants to commend, he does not *need* the biblical texts in order to learn the truths in question, for they can be arrived at on other grounds, namely, by means of independent rational reflection. In this way, the distinction remains intact, its two elements continuing to be differentiable from one another. Texts can be used illustratively when their truth is determined by means of reason, so long as such determination of their truth plays no role in the original discernment of their meaning.

Applying this truth/meaning distinction, which Spinoza formulated, to the Bible retains an intuitive appeal, even a self-evident correctness, to many in our own context. For instance, biblical critic John Barton insists that readers abide by what he calls a two-stage

[58] See Preus, *Spinoza and the Irrelevance of Biblical Authority*, 199–201; exceptions to do with Solomon and Paul, where Spinoza blurs their teaching into his, and which nevertheless prove the general rule, are discussed in Sylvain Zac, *Spinoza et l'interprétation de l'écriture*, Bibliothèque de philosophie contemporaine. Histoire de la philosophie et philosophie générale (Paris: Presses universitaires de France, 1965), 167–74. For his part, Brad Gregory presses the case that Spinoza is deeply inconsistent in his hermeneutic, prohibiting philosophy in principle from influencing biblical interpretation, while at the same time shaping his own approach to the Bible around his philosophical system: "Introduction," in *Tractatus Theologico-Politicus (Gebhardt Edition, 1925)* (Leiden: Brill, 1989), 40–42. However, see the response in Preus, *Spinoza and the Irrelevance of Biblical Authority*, 199n47, who argues convincingly that Spinoza manages not to conflate the biblical text and non-biblical ideas, even as he constructs his hermeneutical framework out of non-biblical resources. Preus's point, however, underscores that Spinoza's approach to the Bible, even though it includes a differentiation between discerning the meaning of a particular passage and considering that passage to be true, does rest on commitment to certain other truths.

approach to reading the text: "One must establish what it means; one may then ask whether what it means is true."[59] The two steps, discerning meaning and assessing truth, must proceed independently of one another, the results of assessing the text not bleeding back into the initial step of determining meaning. Barton seems incredulous that anyone would demur from this: "The bracketing out of the question of truth while one tries to make sense of the text is not the result of some kind of skepticism or unwillingness to believe that the text is right; it is simply a procedure without which we have no meaning whose truth value we can even begin to assess."[60] What Barton is calling for is a neutral starting point for interpreters, a stance which assumes neither that what the Bible communicates is true nor that it is false. Apart from the possibility that one might read without a settled conviction about the text's meaning – this should serve at least as an ideal toward which the reader should strive, though it cannot be attained fully in actual practice – it is impossible for Barton to imagine how readers can ascertain a meaning in the text that is not already mingled together in a problematic way with their own beliefs, such that the reader's beliefs can easily become conflated with the sense of the text.

### *Metaphysical Naturalism*

Though Barton's reasons for adhering to this distinction are different,[61] Spinoza must install a strict meaning/truth distinction because, when his opponents assume the truth of a given text, they interpret it against the background of a theological worldview, one

[59] Barton, *The Nature of Biblical Criticism*, 171. Barton credits this principle directly to Spinoza: *The Nature of Biblical Criticism*, 144n11. Tellingly, Spinoza's meaning/truth distinction stands right at the heart of Barton's inaugural lecture: *The Future of Old Testament Study: An Inaugural Lecture Delivered before the University of Oxford on 12 November 1992* (Oxford: Clarendon Press, 1993), 9.

[60] Barton, *The Nature of Biblical Criticism*, 171.

[61] See this book's Conclusion.

that runs counter to his own metaphysical naturalism.[62] From this naturalistic point of view, he gives an account of the Bible that serves as an alternative to traditional Jewish and Christian views of their sacred text. His alternative includes a naturalistic view of the Bible's reception, its context of origin, and the end toward which it should be read.

First, he dismisses the history of religiously committed interpretation of the Bible, portraying it not as a careful and honest seeking out of the text's meaning in humble deference to ultimate truth, but simply as a game of power politics. As Spinoza says in his critique of those who begin their interpretation of the Bible with theological beliefs about it in place, the text "has no need of human fabrications."[63] For Spinoza, "Religion as we know it . . . is nothing more than organized superstition. Power-hungry ecclesiastics prey on the naïveté of citizens, taking advantage of their hopes and fears in the face of the vicissitudes of nature and the unpredictability of fortune to gain control over their beliefs and their daily lives."[64] On his account, the common people do not understand the nexus of cause and effect that governs the world; they are gripped by fears about what the future holds, they yearn for a source of comfort, and so they put their trust in religious authorities who claim to offer understanding and reassurance. These religious authorities are elite

[62] Richard H. Popkin's assessment is that Spinoza's major contribution to history is his development of a fully naturalistic ontology, which he applied to the Bible. See "Spinoza and Bible Scholarship," in *The Cambridge Companion to Spinoza*, ed. Don Garrett (Cambridge: Cambridge University Press, 1996), 404. One scholar questions whether this characterization does justice to the way Spinoza preserves a sense in which the Bible is indeed sacred: Nancy Levene, *Spinoza's Revelation: Religion, Democracy, and Reason* (Cambridge: Cambridge University Press, 2004), 84. Levene's point is not entirely baseless, but neither does it amount to very much, for the Bible's sacredness consists, even on her reading of Spinoza, in nothing more than the sacredness any given thing can have. In this sense, the Bible is sacred in same way as are Shakespeare or one's family (*Spinoza's Revelation*, 130).

[63] Spinoza, *Theological-Political Treatise*, 8.

[64] Nadler, *Book Forged in Hell*, 31.

interpreters, who can manipulate the behavior of the credulous masses by the readings they offer. However, from a naturalistic point of view, that the Bible has its source in the revelation of a God who is the ultimate cause of the world and its transcendent end is flatly untrue, though this false view invests the text with the credibility it has with many people.

Second, Spinoza has a naturalistic view not only of the history of the interpretation of the Bible, but also of the Bible itself. The way to break free of the regnant prejudice which characterizes religious reading of the Bible is through attending to its circumstances of origin, which Spinoza construes in the light of naturalism. In an important statement, Spinoza likens study of the Bible to an empirical study of nature:

> The [correct] method of interpreting nature consists above all in constructing a natural history, from which we derive the definitions of natural things, as from certain data. Likewise, to interpret Scripture, we need to assemble a genuine history of it and to deduce the thinking of the Bible's authors by valid inferences from this history, as from certain data and principles.[65]

When Spinoza says that a scientist constructs a "natural history" when studying phenomena in the natural world, he means that the scientist does careful, controlled experiments to gain a comprehensive awareness of the pertinent facts.[66] Scientists look at nature, and their work is not structured by a set of substantive first principles they must accept a priori. The "definitions" they arrive at are the essences or natures of the things they are studying. The equivalent

[65] Spinoza, *Theological-Political Treatise*, 98.

[66] For Spinoza's debt here to Francis Bacon, see Zac, *Spinoza et l'interprétation de l'écriture*, 29–32; Nadler, *Book Forged in Hell*, 132–33. On this point, Spinoza is not Cartesian, for Descartes preserves a place for first principles that are theological-metaphysical. Jean-Luc Marion makes much hay about this aspect of Descartes in such works as *On Descartes' Metaphysical Prism: The Constitution and the Limits of Onto-Theo-Logy in Cartesian Thought* (Chicago: University of Chicago Press, 1999).

object of attention in the case of biblical study is the text together with its history, quite apart from any theological convictions that the reader may have about the text. In accord with a strict subject/object distinction, no such factors belong within the scope of the method: theological construal is a matter of the reader's view, not the reality of the object being understood. What the reader can glean, if she follows this process strictly, is the "thinking of the Bible's authors," that is, their communicative intentions, the analogue to the essences or natures that the scientist finds. Theological categories are not needed to understand the text, for it is ultimately only the work of human hands, and indeed one whose subject matter differs substantially from the common understandings of Jews and Christians.

Spinoza's insistence on interpreting the text against the background of its origin and his naturalistic view of those circumstances puts a distinctive spin on what he means when he charges readers not to accept a teaching as biblical unless they can see precisely how it derives from the Bible.[67] Spinoza sounds reminiscent of the Protestant Reformers in his distrust of interpretive tradition, and his corresponding call for rigorous demonstration that "biblical teachings" do indeed originate from the biblical text, as opposed to other sources. This dual emphasis, both positive and negative, is captured in the slogan *sola scriptura* (by Scripture alone), one of the rallying cries of Reformed Protestants. Steven Nadler provides a lucid explanatory gloss on Spinoza's version of this hermeneutical principle:

> Spinoza has a rather extended understanding of *sola Scriptura*. The proper approach to the Bible will require examining not only the text itself and the language in which it was written but also factors such as the social and political circumstances of its composition and the biographies of its authors. Examining Scripture "from Scripture alone" apparently means studying it from exclusively, but *all*,

[67] Spinoza, *Theological-Political Treatise*, 97.

> relevant scriptural considerations. It is as if to say that by "Bible" is meant the *world* of the Bible.[68]

This is what being biblical means because of what the Bible is assumed to be. The Bible is a set of texts with an origin in the history of religious communities. The texts played certain roles in the dynamics of those communities; traditional theological terminology, such as inspiration or witness to revelation, provide no purchase on what the text is and are not part of its ontology. The backdrop of the Bible's origin is marked by factors that can be analyzed in horizontal terms, using social and political categories.

Third, specifically theological language is not necessary to describe accurately the Bible's purpose, just as it is dispensable in considering the text's genesis. It is not built into the concept of what the Bible is that it should be read as a privileged sacred text, one that provides a window onto transcendence in a way that other texts do not. Alasdair MacIntyre explains that some things are defined in terms of the purpose or function that they are typically expected to serve.[69] When they fail to serve their purpose, they are considered defective. For instance, "From such factual premises as 'This watch is grossly inaccurate and irregular in time-keeping' and 'This watch is too heavy to carry about comfortably,' the evaluative conclusion validly follows that 'This is a bad watch.'"[70] The Bible does not have serving

[68] Nadler, *Book Forged in Hell*, 134.

[69] MacIntyre, *After Virtue*, 58.

[70] Ibid., 58. Spinoza's overall position on the category of purpose is nuanced: he does not reject it categorically. Spinoza makes some striking statements seemingly to the effect that nothing can be explained by reference to its acting for a purpose. He is sometimes read in just this way, as he is by Jonathan Bennett, *A Study of Spinoza's Ethics* (Indianapolis: Hackett, 1984). However, for generally persuasive counterargument to granting no scope at all in Spinoza's thought for teleology, see E. M. Curley, "On Bennett's Spinoza: The Issue of Teleology," in *Spinoza: Issues and Directions*, ed. E. M. Curley and Pierre-François Moreau, Brill's Studies in Intellectual History (Leiden: Brill, 1990), 39–52; Don Garrett, "Teleology in Spinoza and Early Modern Rationalism," in *New Essays on the Rationalists*, ed. Rocco J. Gennaro and Charles Huenemann (Oxford: Oxford University Press, 1999), 310–35.

as a distinctively sacred text as part of its purpose, such that it fails to fulfill its proper function when it is not read as revealing God and his will for human creatures. The text is sacred precisely as long as it moves people toward devotion – and no longer. "Should it [i.e., the Bible] become completely neglected, however, as it once was by the Jews, it is thereby rendered nothing but ink and paper and becomes absolutely devoid of sanctity and subject to corruption."[71] There is no basis for deeming improper a failure to attend to the Bible in this way, because it lacks a determinedly theological end.

The Bible does have a purpose, in the sense of a role that it should play, but spelling that out does not require recourse to theological language. Spinoza gives a concise, emphatic, and sharply focused summary of the text's function: "The sole aim of Scripture is to teach obedience [to the moral law]. This no one can contest. Who does not see that both testaments are nothing but a training in such obedience? And that both testaments teach men this one single thing, to obey in all sincerity?"[72] The claim here is that the text does one thing: it presents a simple ethical code and encourages readers to follow it. This is the text's purpose in the sense that this is something that the text actually does effectively. The Bible is mired in contradictions on other subjects, but a basic moral message runs through each of the Bible's constituent texts. Readers should avail themselves of the resources it provides – or at least they may as well. Yet people who have a sufficiently well-developed capacity to reason can arrive on their own, via reflection which proceeds without the guidance of any text, at the conclusion that the ethical teachings that happen to be in the Bible are in fact binding on them.[73] The Bible's stories help the uneducated to understand and

[71] Spinoza, *Theological-Political Treatise*, 166.

[72] Ibid., 179.

[73] His *Ethics* is not a historical and exegetical work, as *Theological-Political Treatise* is, but rather an abstract philosophical argument intended for those with advanced training.

follow true moral principles.[74] So the Bible has a purpose in the sense that it offers teaching that is of value. However, people with sufficiently developed ability to reason on their own do not require the Bible to learn the only thing it teaches. Thus, at least for the educated, the Bible has a purpose, but not a unique purpose in the sense of something it confers on readers that they could not find elsewhere. Depicting this modest sense of purpose does not necessitate mention of a transcendent God. Therefore, theological language is, once more, dispensable.

The upshot of Spinoza's view of Scripture, underpinned as it is by a commitment to a metaphysical naturalism that has implications for every aspect of his account of the Bible – from how its history of interpretation is viewed to the nature of its origin and end – is that the text becomes something to *look at* rather than to *look through*.[75] It is more something to examine and analyze than that through which a reader understands and navigates the world. True, one *may* look through it, so to speak, in order to understand a moral code of conduct. However, one can learn these moral lessons by turning within oneself, provided that one has the intellectual skills that sustained, abstract reflection on morality requires. And one may use it to illustrate certain points for a constituency which values the text highly, yet this rhetorical employment of the text is different from looking to it as something from which one needs to learn. Spinoza's stance on closely related matters prompts the following probing questions from Louis Dupré: "If Christian doctrine is to fulfill more than an educational heuristic function for the sole purpose of reaching practical conclusions that reason could have reached by itself, does revelation not become superfluous once the mind attains the level of reason? ... Spinoza neither draws this

[74] Spinoza, *Theological-Political Treatise*, 76–80.

[75] The phrasing of this conclusion is indebted to Michael C. Legaspi, *The Death of Scripture and the Rise of Biblical Studies*, Oxford Studies in Historical Theology (Oxford: Oxford University Press, 2010), 26.

conclusion nor explains how he can avoid it."[76] Does reading the Bible not become superfluous here? Is there any reason that even the most dedicated follower of Christ should not simply put it to the side?

## Conclusion

Though a critique of Spinoza's position which is worth pursuing has emerged, the above does not intend to refute his approach to the Bible: that is not the purpose of this chapter. The point, instead, is simply to lay out his position as a clear example of what theological reading is *not*. Theological exegesis is a hermeneutical framework standing in contrast to a metaphysically naturalistic outlook. Theological reading is not based on a naturalistic understanding of the reader and the text, but rather on a theological view of each, together with the entailments they together generate for interpretation. Without an outline of how naturalism impacts biblical hermeneutics, it is more difficult to challenge the presumption that a commitment to theological reading means discounting the importance of history. If history and naturalism are conflated with one another, applying theological categories will seem to have a dismissal of history built into it right from the beginning. It is important to make it clear at the outset of this part of the book, lest misunderstanding arise, that theological reading can and should build on a historical engagement

[76] Louis K. Dupré, *The Enlightenment and the Intellectual Foundations of Modern Culture* (New Haven: Yale University Press, 2004), 235. There is a modest exception to this general point, which is that readers need the Bible to see that it is sufficient for salvation or happiness to follow the injunctions of Scripture, even if one does not understand them for the eternal truths they are. The moral principles can be grasped by unaided reason, but only the Bible explains that a person can follow them without understanding them and still be happy. See Spinoza, *Theological-Political Treatise*, 189, 194, 271. That said, this is hardly the sort of material content that would provide a reader with a basis to make regular recourse to the Bible.

with the Bible. It is better to resist conceptions of history that either collapse God into the world order (as Spinoza does) or picture him as having withdrawn to a supernatural sphere from which he can act only remotely on the world (as many others do[77]), than it is to accept a fundamentally ahistorical form of interpretation. This account of theological interpretation seeks to eschew a "separated theology," one that promotes "a growing remoteness of the inner realities of faith from the ordinary – 'worldly' – concerns of daily life."[78] An important part of the agenda for Part II's Chapter 5, and indeed for the constructive proposal as a whole, thus becomes avoiding a history/theology dualism.

How does Part II intend to be theological without thereby becoming ahistorical? It is far too ambitious a task for the chapters that follow to try and integrate theology and history in general and in all their various aspects. Part II takes a more focused tack. Because of the intimate connection between naturalism and a complete or absolute distinction between meaning and truth, the view Part II unfolds does not accept an absolutized version of this distinction. The assumption is very much *not* that interpreters are obliged to construe passages of the Bible exclusively against their context of origin, divorcing every aspect of the interpretive process from a theological worldview. Rather, the constructive proposal works with a relativized differentiation between how a biblical passage should be read and a commitment to the truth of said passage, or the truth of that passage taken in the context of the canon.[79] These two things are related, insofar as interpretation does rest on some theological presuppositions, but they are nevertheless

[77] For a survey of this as a trend in modern culture, see especially Dupré, *Passage to Modernity*, 15–90.

[78] David L. Schindler, Introduction to *The Mystery of the Supernatural*, by Henri de Lubac (New York: Crossroad, 1998), xvi.

[79] For more on the difference between absolute and relative distinctions, see Hilary Putnam, *The Collapse of the Fact/Value Dichotomy and Other Essays* (Cambridge, MA: Harvard University Press, 2002), 9–13, 28–45.

not identical, which is to say that the stock of theological presuppositions should not dominate or dictate the reading of a given passage, as if the content of the assumptions can simply be equated to the passage's sense. Operating with a relativized distinction does not mean bracketing out all theological commitment, but working initially with a modest core of theological belief, as I explain further in the chapters that follow. Readers should undertake historical analysis of biblical passages[80] – *all* passages, not only some[81] – but doing so need not mean detaching history itself entirely from theology, that being a de facto capitulation to naturalism. There is worth in historical analysis of biblical language because the semantic value of terms changes over time, and historical work highlights precisely this: meaning is use, and such use varies across different historical contexts.[82] Readers ought to do historical analysis while

[80] For a major example of a retrieval of patristic perspectives that by no means spurns historical consciousness, but sees it as something that can be integrated with theology, see Lubac, *History and Spirit*, 429; Henri de Lubac, *At the Service of the Church: Henri de Lubac Reflects on the Circumstances That Occasioned His Writings* (San Francisco: Ignatius Press, 1993), 311–14. For a clear exposition of this position, see Rudolf Voderholzer, "Dogma and History: Henri de Lubac and the Retrieval of Historicity as a Key to Theological Renewal," *Communio* 28 (2001), 648–68.

[81] On historical distance in authors such as Augustine, see Ayres, *Nicaea and Its Legacy*, 33n74. Ayres helpfully comments, "Ancient readers do recognize a certain sort of historical 'gap': for instance, a recognition that the text *may* contain references and terminology whose meaning may not now be clear. This historical sense may enable multiple interpretations even though the text is still read as speaking immediately to one's 'imaginative universe'" (emphasis added). Augustine certainly does think that, for readers without the requisite historical knowledge, *some* biblical texts are rendered obscure: see, for instance, *On Christian Teaching* 2.42–43 (CCSL 32, 62–63; OWC Green, 55–56). The point I am making in Part II, however, is that an ideal reading would include historical inquiry into *all* biblical texts. As I also argue, this need not prevent a text from speaking to a reader who can identify in a strong sense with its original recipients.

[82] See the point about the necessity of retrieval projects coming to terms with modern advances: Gerhard Ebeling, "The Significance of the Critical Historical Method for Church and Theology in Protestantism," in *Word and Faith* (London: SCM Press, 1963), 18.

holding in balance with this a basic set of theological commitments, allowing them to have their rightful role in theological reading, while at the same time preventing them from overwhelming the practice of exegesis.

The chapters constituting Part II develop all of this in more detail. The proof can only be in the pudding. However, it is worth giving a preview here of the basic way in which the desideratum just indicated plays out in each of the following chapters of the book. Chapter 4 begins the constructive case proper with a theological treatment of the reader: it asks how the sort of distance between the reader and the text that a theological account acknowledges can remain compatible with reading the biblical text receptively, as a work that engages today's readers and speaks to them. In addition, Chapter 5 stews on how the text's origin in the past should factor into its capacity to signify a transcendent God. Finally, Chapter 6 explores the sense in which there ought to be a moment within theological interpretation that steps back, to some degree, from questions of the application of the text, or from reflective analysis of its contents – though these phases are crucial for a complete reading – and seeks to begin interpretation on a prior level. Thus, each of the three loci within the constructive account of interpretation is shaped by a concern to distinguish historical work from theological thinking without separating the two entirely. The proposal aims to be historically conscious while remaining acutely theologically conscious. It intends to interrelate the two sets of considerations, rather than casting one or the other to the side so as to dispense with it completely. Historical consciousness should not be spurned just because of its association with naturalism in Spinoza and others, but should be turned to good ends in the account of theological reading.

In this way, Part II takes forward a major overarching point from its (critical) discussion of Spinoza. It implements a modified version of the distinction between meaning and truth, altering the unqualified version to bring it into accord with the primary priority that emerged from the engagement with Augustine in Part I. The constructive case aims to combine a qualified version of the meaning/truth distinction with Augustine's insight that reading should involve thinking theologically about the reader and the text and being true to what they each ultimately are. We now turn to the first step in this process.

# 4 | Faith and the Ecclesial Community

In the phrase *theological reading*, the adjective precedes the noun so as to specify, not that theological readers simply possess a special interest in the theological aspects of the biblical text,[1] but that theologically specific content is a constitutive element of the hermeneutical framework by which the text is read. That the reader observes theological aspects of the text, while holding it off at a distance, does not suffice for a view of the reader to count as theological according to the notion of theology developed in the Introduction. What is necessary is that theology shapes the reader's interpretation of the text in the sense that the reader looks *through* it, rather than simply *at* it. Merely to look *at* the text would be to "place ourselves outside a certain space of meanings while examining the things of this domain."[2] The importance of looking through the Bible is that readers understand themselves in a theological light, and theological resources enter into their interpretive reflection as hermeneutical first principles. There are, therefore, differences in the way they look at the text as a result of how they look through it at themselves as interpreters. In this way, readers utilize a substantive notion of hermeneutical rationality, as Augustine does. The hermeneutic proposed here assumes that it is neither actually possible nor genuinely desirable for readers "to strip off all our particularities – particularities of gender, race, nationality, religion,

[1] For an example of a work in which the reader's aim is primary, rather than derivative of something else, see Morgan and Barton, *Biblical Interpretation*, 94, 273.

[2] Taylor, *A Secular Age*, 284.

social class, age – and enter [upon proper inquiry] purely as normal adult human beings."[3] The overall similarity between this constructive proposal and Augustine's thinking lies in the notion of rationality being substantive: in this way, he serves as an example that this chapter follows.

What difference does it make when hermeneutical first principles are shaped by theology? Putting oneself within the space of theological meaning – having a view of oneself as a reader that is the result of perceiving the self theologically, thereby thinking about oneself from a biblical point of view, even while interpreting the Bible – entails several things. The most basic difference that a substantive approach to rationality makes for a notion of the reader is, as this chapter contends, that the reader becomes *receptive* to the text's claims because a theological reader has the capacity to exercise faith in the God who discloses himself through the text. It likewise influences how one sees readers participating together with other interpreters in synchronic and diachronic communities: the way in which readers are shaped by membership in an ecclesial community is part of what makes them who they are. Finally, the application of theological categories puts an inflection on how the nature of the distance between a present-day reader and the various contexts from which biblical texts emerged is understood. Theology has an impact in all of these ways. Spelling out in more detail how this works is the primary job of this chapter. The chapter closes with a brief assessment of some alternative views of the reader, according to which the interpreter is portrayed as being active rather than mainly receptive. However, first it is necessary to expand on the brief rationale that was given initially in this book's

[3] Nicholas Wolterstorff, "The Travail of Theology in the Modern Academy," in *The Future of Theology: Essays in Honor of Jürgen Moltmann*, ed. Miroslav Volf, Carmen Krieg, and Thomas Dörken-Kucharz (Grand Rapids: Eerdmans, 1996), 38. Wolterstorff's analysis of why learning is not really a generically human affair and, accordingly, why universities have opened up research and teaching, especially in the humanities, to a range of particularist approaches is brief but compelling (ibid., 44).

Introduction for including the reader within an account of theological interpretation. To this preliminary task I now turn.

## The Reader as a Necessary Locus

I claimed in this book's Introduction that the existing literature on theological reading neglects the reader: this is not to say that the reader is never mentioned at all (that is not the case), but that the interpreting subject does not receive the same level of attention, within formal accounts, as the interpreted object, that is, the text.[4] The current literature treats the reader in passing while paying greater attention to the text as what is key to making an approach to reading specifically theological.[5] Therefore, this literature provides helpful building blocks for the more explicit treatment this chapter offers, though what is present in the literature does not suffice by itself. A more extended explication of the reader is

[4] On the low profile of the reader in accounts of theological reading, see the literature cited in footnote 110 of the Introduction. It is worth noting additional doctrinal literature, apart from works attempting to say what theological reading is, that makes some headway in thinking about the reader's importance in interpretation: Willie James Jennings, "Baptizing a Social Reading: Theology, Hermeneutics, and Postmodernity," in *Disciplining Hermeneutics: Interpretation in Christian Perspective*, ed. Roger Lundin (Grand Rapids: Eerdmans, 1997), 117–27; Eugene F. Rogers, "How the Virtues of an Interpreter Presuppose and Perfect Hermeneutics: The Case of Thomas Aquinas," *Journal of Religion* 76 (1996): 64–81; Daniel J. Treier, *Virtue and the Voice of God: Toward Theology as Wisdom* (Grand Rapids: Eerdmans, 2006); Kevin J. Vanhoozer, "The Spirit of Understanding: Special Revelation and General Hermeneutics," in *First Theology: God, Scripture & Hermeneutics* (Downers Grove: InterVarsity Press, 2002), 207–35; John Webster, "Hermeneutics in Modern Theology: Some Doctrinal Reflections," in *Word and Church: Essays in Christian Dogmatics* (Edinburgh: T. & T. Clark, 2001), 76–86; Rowan Williams, "The Discipline of Scripture," in *On Christian Theology* (Oxford: Blackwell, 2000), 44–59. Perhaps the most substantial treatment is the chapter on the reader in the economy of grace in Webster, *Holy Scripture*, 68–106.

[5] This literature is also listed in note 110 of the Introduction.

necessary. Why is this?[6] Even granting that there is a gap in existing work on this issue, why does this gap deserve to be filled? The reader should receive explicit attention within any account of theological reading that operates according to a substantive paradigm of hermeneutical rationality, as this one does. This section seeks to demonstrate this by arguing that, where a theological view of the reader is thought to be genuinely dispensable, its lack of importance is a function of a commitment to disengaged reason and a procedural conception of reflective activity.

Disengaged reason was mentioned briefly in the introduction's typology of positions on the function of theology in relation to biblical interpretation. To expand on what was said there, this conception of rationality stresses that a human being's social and historical location, status as an embodied agent, or religious allegiances (if any) should *not* factor into how she reflects rationally about issues of concern to her.[7] For the purpose of this discussion, it is of course theological issues that are of the greatest import: for an approach to biblical interpretation to operate according to

[6] The purpose of stressing the reader is not to portray the interpreter as somehow more important than the text, as if in an account of reading the "concern is less with the thoughts and expressions of the ancient text, and more what people have done with those texts." See Elliot, *The Heart of Biblical Theology*, 35. Pursued in the wrong way, an interest in readers can serve to portray interpreters as active creators of meaning, not as those seeking to engage with something beyond themselves that has the power to transform them. Discussions of the reader need not take place in this way, and the one in this chapter aims to avoid this problem.

[7] Taylor, *A Secular Age*, 283–88. That this work does not operate within the confines of disengaged reason means that the viewpoint being advanced does not exclude the notion of race from the set of factors that determine the reader's identity and condition interpretive reflection. Though this book mentions race only very briefly, the type of position being presented here is not the sort that puts forward a view of rationality claiming universality, only to be revealed as covertly bearing the particularity of whiteness. Cf. footnote 29 in the Introduction on the potential for further dialogue between those involved in the current discussion of theological reading and a more diverse constituency than usually takes part. The commitments regarding rationality here mean that this broadening is very much a possibility.

disengaged rationality with respect to theology is for it to insist that readers bracket their theological beliefs when interpreting the Bible. It means that one has to disengage one's self-understanding as a rational agent from "tradition and social authority, and the whole domain of what is experienced in common. We can't take the truths we have learned on trust, we have to generate them, each for ourselves, in a process of certain reasoning from clear and distinct ideas."[8] Such beliefs cannot constitute starting points for a hermeneutic of the Bible. Theological belief is by no means deemed categorically false here, but it is held at a distance from the process of generating an understanding of what it means to be a human being who asks questions and seeks answers to them in a rationally acceptable way.

What difference does this make for interpretation? Within this paradigm, for a reader of the Bible, "to fulfill his service of critical reflection, he must start the inquiry without an assumption either for or against the meaning, meaningfulness, and truth of the symbol or doctrine under analysis."[9] This means one cannot assume what the semantic value of any doctrine is, or whether it is useful as a tool with which to think (or, for that matter, whether it is adequate to experience, though this is less pertinent to the current discussion); therefore, the theological reader cannot build specifically Christian theological material into his self-understanding. The reader can think about theology to be sure, and can even confess some theological beliefs, but these beliefs cannot become definitive for her self-conception as a rational agent. They thus do not structure reasoned reflection on the text.[10] In that sense, they are not tools

[8] Taylor, *A Secular Age*, 285. On disengaged reason with special reference to Descartes, see Taylor, *Sources of the Self*, 143–58.

[9] Tracy, *Blessed Rage for Order*, 239. While I differ from Tracy here, his views on biblical interpretation are worth pondering and deserve far more attention than the very recent discussion of theological reading usually affords them.

[10] While Tracy wants to exclude theology from the reader's self-understanding, especially in his later work his vision of hermeneutics as absolutely central to theology

that aid the reader's reflection. Theology does not, for instance, portray readers as those who interpret with the eyes of faith, nor does it relativize readers' distance from the world of the Bible by situating them in the economy of salvation, nor does it locate readers in a community of fellow believers who share similar reading strategies. All of this is excluded from hermeneutical consideration. The human subject's self-understanding as an interpreter must acknowledge their location within history and the shaping influence of the epoch-making changes that have created modern life – the scientific revolution, the Enlightenment, the industrial revolution, and the growth of historical consciousness, and so on – but theology does not factor in at the basic level of self-understanding.[11] Because theological beliefs do not enter into her most fundamental self-conception and how she sees her obligations as an interpreter, their force is not felt in the deepest reaches of the account of interpretation.

Notions of interpretation operating within the framework of disengaged reason tend toward procedural rather than substantively oriented notions of hermeneutical rationality. David Tracy's ideal for the modern theologian, one whose approach to rationality is not built on any theological commitments, serves as a convenient illustration:

> He recognizes that such a commitment [to a purely procedural model of rational reflection] imposes the ethical duty to provide the proper kind of evidence for whatever claim he advances. He

makes it clear that he insists quite strongly on including many other factors within the interpreter's process of reflection, not least one's historical location: *The Analogical Imagination: Christian Theology and the Culture of Pluralism* (New York: Crossroad, 1981); *Plurality and Ambiguity*. Thus, it might be possible to say that there is embedded in Tracy's thinking a conception of human rationality that is disengaged from theology, but not from the historical determinants of the reader's life. He uses a notion of reason that is disengaged in one respect but not in another.

[11] Tracy, *Plurality and Ambiguity*, 8.

> recognizes further that the announcement of his own tradition's beliefs does not and cannot constitute such evidence for his fellow community of historical or philosophical inquirers – *or even for himself* as one committed to the morality of autonomous critical inquiry implicit in the canons and methods of the discipline in question.[12]

Members of a theological tradition may well hold to theological beliefs, but such are absent from the outlooks that determine how they engage in rational reflection, including reflection on how to interpret biblical texts. What commands the ultimate loyalty of such a theologian is neither any theologically specific content nor even God himself – though this is "monumentally inauspicious as a stance for a Christian theologian"[13] – but procedures of study that are field-relative and, at least in an ideal case from this point of view, bereft of any tradition-specific content.[14] Biblical hermeneutics thus becomes a local application of an entirely general scheme, without that application involving any substantial modification to fit the specific textual content under consideration.[15] This sort of theory is procedural, not in the sense that it is fixated on questions of method, but in that it does not assume commitment to a particular set of substantive (theological) beliefs.[16] Theologians

[12] Tracy, *Blessed Rage for Order*, 6. At this point, Tracy is inspired by Harvey, *Historian and the Believer.*

[13] Alvin Plantinga, "Advice to Christian Philosophers," *Faith and Philosophy* 1 (1984): 264.

[14] Tracy, *Blessed Rage for Order*, 6.

[15] See the application of general hermeneutical theory to the Bible in Tracy, *Blessed Rage for Order*, 72–81; Grant and Tracy, *A Short History*, 167–74.

[16] It is not that a basically procedural approach precludes belief across the board, for as Tracy says, "Sometimes the theologian will approach a full conversation with the biblical text with the response of faith" (Grant and Tracy, *A Short History*, 169). However, as he sees it, interpreters who enter into conversation with the text about its subject matter have to put their faith at risk; their theological beliefs must be under threat to such an extent that they cannot enter into the reader's essential self-understanding as a firm part of it.

can employ this sort of theory only if they are willing to set their theological convictions aside.

The focus in this section has been on disengaged reason as a force that isolates theology, prohibiting it from influencing conceptions of hermeneutical rationality. There are reasons not to base an account of theological reading on disengaged reason. The guiding assumption of this project is that theological language has a part to play in understanding the rational subject, and there is also, reinforcing this, the whole postmodern critique of universal reason, which challenges reasoners to acknowledge how their claims depend on standards which are at some level customary.[17] The purpose of focusing on disengaged reason here, however, has not been to mount a case against it, but to highlight an important implication it has for the structure of accounts of theological reading. From within this perspective, it is relatively unimportant to discuss the place of the reader in a view of interpretation, since the operative conception of the reader is less specific by one major factor (i.e., tradition-specific theological belief), which would otherwise shape it. The greater one's commitment to disengaged reason as a principle applicable to theology, the more one has a corresponding

[17] See, for instance, Paul A. Bové, *Intellectuals in Power: A Genealogy of Critical Humanism* (New York: Columbia University Press, 1986); Paul A. Bové, *Mastering Discourse: The Politics of Intellectual Culture* (Durham: Duke University Press, 1992); Jean-François Lyotard, *The Postmodern Condition: A Report on Knowledge*, Theory and History of Literature (Minneapolis: University of Minnesota Press, 1984). In a new preface, written a couple of decades after he originally authored *Blessed Rage for Order*, Tracy concedes that he had not yet taken onboard the most useful insights of postmodernity when he wrote his first constructive book (*Blessed Rage for Order*, xiv–xv). In his later phase, he retains his commitment to a public theology that is accessible in principle to "all intelligent, reasonable, responsible persons," though appropriating postmodern ideas complicates this undertaking considerably, because they do a great deal to undermine all unitary notions of rationality (*Blessed Rage for Order*, xiii). To be clear, it is the view of theology's relationship to biblical interpretation outlined in this book's Introduction that grounds the stress here on the particularities of the reader's identity. That is not rooted mainly in postmodern criticism, but is merely reinforced by its best insights.

basis not to discuss the reader, because a specific factor is elided from the overall picture of who the reader is, thus being unavailable to explain what sets theological reading apart from other approaches.[18] Because the present project is not wedded to disengaged reason, and works instead with a substantive notion of rationality, it has a very definite basis for discussing the reader as a locus in the overall account. The reader should be discussed because the specifics of the interpreter's identity shape the whole approach to reading: the reader is stressed for the sake of emphasizing the interpreter's theological identity. Against the widespread trend to bracket out theology, a dedicated treatment of the reader is necessary to underscore that theology matters in reading and to begin to show how that is so. That is why this chapter must be present in this book.

Does insisting on a theological view of the reader entail that only those with faith can read the Bible? Put even more bluntly, the question is whether I am arguing that only Christians can interpret the text. To do so would obviously limit the appeal of my constructive proposal, for, as Schleiermacher correctly says, alluding to 2 Thessalonians 3:2, "From time immemorial faith has not been everyone's affair."[19] In response to this question, it is necessary to distinguish between what *this account* of theological reading needs, on the one hand, and what a given *embodied practice* of reading requires, on the other. The first category refers to a theory of interpretation, the second to the actual practice of making sense of biblical passages. There are all sorts of embodied practices of interpretation that are

[18] This assumes, of course, that theological reading is indeed a distinctive hermeneutical mode of engaging with the Bible. If it is, rather, simply the application of an utterly general theory to a specific text, without adapting the theory to fit the particularities of the text in question, then the goal of an account of theological reading would not be to characterize it as distinctive, but to show how the general scheme applies to the Bible.

[19] Friedrich Schleiermacher, *On Religion: Speeches to Its Cultured Despisers*, 2nd ed., Cambridge Texts in the History of Philosophy (Cambridge: Cambridge University Press, 1996), 3.

applied to the Bible, and many of these do not require that a reader has any investment in the system of beliefs that the biblical text itself projects.[20] Any implementation of the position designated as type one in this book's introduction would qualify as an example here, and there are innumerable others as well. The constructive proposal being developed in Part II deliberately heads off in a different direction, of course, but the result is not to limit interpretation only to the baptized. Rather, the effect is that part of the rationale for this particular mode of reading is constituted by a specifically theological account of the reader. That is, to read in the particular way spelled out in Chapter 6, which deals with the locus of interpretation, does indeed depend on the reader either having faith or at least being willing to experiment with this posture in reading. However, that does not preclude others from following alternative hermeneutical options that have their own integrity. Nor does it forbid others from seeing, as if from the inside, how this version of a specifically Christian hermeneutic operates (as I say in the preface, this proposal is offered in the hope that it will facilitate the understanding of Christian reading by others). The section below outlines the theology of the reader that is needed in the sense just specified.[21]

[20] For this reason, I concur entirely with Francis Watson when he says that not all interpretation even needs to address the questions related to Christian doctrine that the biblical texts raises. As Watson says, "The text raises many questions that are tangential to Christian faith yet still significant in themselves." See *The Fourfold Gospel*, vii. (To read in this way *consistently*, however, would be not to treat the text as a set of signs pointing the reader toward God. Of course, this is not a commitment that underpins every style of reading, but it is a view for which I argue in the next chapter.)

[21] Take a variant of the question above: is it an implication of this position that only those with a faith commitment can read the Bible *as a coherent whole*? Is it only Christian doctrine that can keep the centrifugal force of associating individual texts with their diverse historical settings from pulling the collection of canonical documents apart? Jenson's position is close to this. He writes, "What Christians call the Bible, or Scripture, exists as a single entity because – and only because – the church gathered these documents for her specific purpose: to aid in preserving her peculiar message, to aid in maintaining across time, from the apostles to the End, the

## A Theological Anthropology of the Reader

### *Belief and the Reader*

The way in which readers reach interpretive judgments about biblical texts is a function of the capacities for readerly deliberations that are part of the operative anthropology of the reader. Whether or not such an anthropology makes use of theological categories makes all the difference here. The main focus of this section is to develop a theological anthropology, but consider a naturalistic picture briefly by way of comparison. Here a hermeneutic is

self-identity of her message that the God of Israel has raised his servant Jesus from the dead. . . . Outside the community with this purpose, there is no reason to treat all and only these documents as making any kind of whole or to read them as a part of a whole." See Robert W. Jenson, "Scripture's Authority in the Church," in *The Art of Reading Scripture,* ed. Ellen F. Davis and Richard B. Hays (Grand Rapids: Eerdmans, 2003), 27–28. Jenson makes a rather swashbuckling move in claiming that the Bible has no intrinsic reason to hold together outside of the church. It is certainly the case that literary approaches, even ones that are essentially secular in their inspiration, are applied to the Bible and manage to read biblical texts in relation to one another, treating the entire Bible as a single unit for study. See, for example, Frye, *The Great Code.* Jenson does not comment at all on this objection, simply passing right by it. Perhaps literary approaches take it for granted that the Bible is unified, while it would not exist as such apart from the church's work of assembling it as written testimony to its faith. Of course, the latter claim is historical, rather than doctrinal, in nature – though it is not an implausible one at that. Richard B. Hays contends that figural reading, which knits together the two testaments, only makes good sense if the God of Israel is the same one who was crucified and raised in the person of Jesus Christ: *Reading Backwards: Figural Christology and the Fourfold Gospel Witness* (Waco: Baylor University Press, 2014), 108–09. Hays makes a strong case that reading in this way is an inevitable practice assuming the truth of that cardinal Christian doctrine, which is a key aspect of the doctrine of the Trinity, though certainly not the whole of it. Thus, figural reading or something like it holds the canonical collection together, and this interpretive practice is tied up with a doctrine of God that includes Jesus Christ within it. Assuming that Hays is correct, reading the Bible as a whole goes hand in hand with doctrinal material that one may either subscribe to oneself or that has influenced a reader's cultural situation to the point that the reader defaults to thinking along the lines it suggests.

constructed on the assumption that the reasoning faculties that people have qua human beings are the only abilities that should operate within biblical interpretation, à la Spinoza's view of the reader, which was outlined in Chapter 3. For Spinoza, readers employ the following rational capacities: they perceive the textual data that they must then come to understand; they engage in deductive or probabilistic reasoning when working through possible readings of a text, so as to determine which interpretation is, on balance, the most compelling option; they defer to the testimony of others, as they must in order to understand the original languages in which the Bible was written, for they have to trust the traditions that convey the lexical value of terms, even though they may not trust the religious tradition as a whole; and in all of this, they discern the thoughts and feelings of the people who expressed themselves in authoring the biblical texts.[22] In reading the Bible, interpreters may use all these rational capacities, but capabilities that would be operative in a theological account cannot play a role in interpretation. As Spinoza himself says, "And as the highest authority to interpret Scripture rests with each individual, the rule of interpretation must be nothing other than the natural light of reason which is common to all men, and not some light above nature or any external authority."[23] Spinoza's dictum rules out the possibility that such things as the illuminating work of the Holy Spirit or guidance provided by a religious tradition that seeks to be faithful to a transcendent God may influence the interpretive acts readers undertake. These factors find no place within his naturalistic depiction of the interpreter.

By contrast, for a theological view of the reader, exercising faith in God and being part of a community of faith become crucial

[22] I am indebted here to explanation from Plantinga, "Two (or More) Kinds of Scripture Scholarship," 274. On the need to trust the Jewish tradition at least on the meaning of the words in the Hebrew language, see Spinoza, *Theological-Political Treatise*, 105.

[23] Spinoza, *Theological-Political Treatise*, 116–17.

within the scope of interpretation.[24] This section deals first with faith, leaving the communal location of the reader until later in the chapter. Faith is treated first in order to put the immediate focus on God, who is the object of faith as well as the one who confers it on human subjects as a gift of grace. It is of course true to say, "Faith is social,"[25] as a section later in the chapter comes to explain. That is, one's faith is not only one's own: it is not one's exclusive possession, for it is the lifeblood of the community of faith, which instructs its members in the articles of belief together with how to live in light of them. While there is certainly a social dimension to faith, its essence is that of being a response to the God who transcends the life of the community, and therefore it is fitting to explicate this aspect first.[26]

What then is faith? Faith is not credulity, a willingness to believe something (or nearly anything!) one is told by a member of a religious hierarchy, which shuts down one's own inquiry and cancels out one's own process of reflection, but that still has an appeal because it promises to calm anxieties about matters that are themselves inherently uncertain.[27] In other words, faith is not a baseless trust driven by one's passions, which comes to function as prejudice, providing a firm conclusion in the absence of proper

[24] Cf. Hays, "Reading the Bible with Eyes of Faith," 5–7.

[25] Martin, *Biblical Truths*, 45.

[26] Saying in these general terms that the reader of the Bible is one who responds in faith to the divine self-disclosure the text mediates is not ultimately irreconcilable with the reality that each specific biblical text has a slightly different view of its implied reader. Certainly the implied reader of Proverbs is not identical in every respect with the implied reader of the Fourth Gospel. The differences could be spelled out, and the point of underscoring faith is not to deny that they exist. The reason for highlighting faith here with respect to all the texts, when they are taken together as Scripture, is that faith is the disposition on the part of the reader that is necessary for these texts to have their intended effect. They want, as it were, what they say about God to be believed. The account of the reader above does not aim to say absolutely *everything* that is true of the interpreter of the Bible, but only to draw attention to what is the case for the theological reader as such. Having faith is a key distinctive of theological readers qua theological readers and is compatible with many other things also being true of them.

[27] Spinoza, *Theological-Political Treatise*, 3–5, 7–8.

investigation. While there is surely something right in decrying blind conformity to external statutes, such obedience is by no means the essence of faith. Nor is proper faith what Immanuel Kant refers to as faith that is "pure" (as opposed to "historical" or "ecclesiastical"), a rearticulation of tradition-specific material in a more general idiom that preserves only the aspects of the original content that constitute the necessary background assumptions supporting the categorical imperative. This faith, having been rigorously stripped of all signs of historical contingency, coincides with conclusions that all rational people could reach independently, without the aid of a revelation that entered history at a particular time and place. Since the biblical text in all its detail should not, then, "have any influence whatever on the reception of moral maxims but is rather given to this [ecclesiastical] faith only for the vivid presentation of its true object (virtue striving toward holiness), it should at all times be taught and expounded in the interest of morality."[28] These two ways of understanding faith will have some plausibility for those looking at communities of faith with a view toward transposing their language into an explanatory framework that rejects the basic premises of the tradition itself, or that transforms the discourse of faith into something putatively universal in its appeal. Yet this work is operating in an essentially different mode: it seeks to grasp what faith is on its own terms, rather than trying to explain it away, or to convert it to something more manageable within another frame of reference.

For the reader of Scripture, two senses of faith are important, and it is worth distinguishing them from one another. As Augustine says, "What is believed is one thing, the faith it is believed with is another."[29] The difference here is between the objective material

[28] Immanuel Kant, "Religion within the Bounds of Mere Reason," in *Religion and Rational Theology*, ed. Allen W. Wood and George Di Giovanni (Cambridge: Cambridge University Press, 1996), 160.

[29] *The Trinity* 13.1 (CCSL 50A, 386; WSA I/5, 346).

content of faith (*fides quae creditur*), or the confession about God that the believer makes, and the deeply personal trusting assent by which the believer invests himself in this content (*fides qua creditur*). Both senses are crucial for the purpose of this chapter, and I begin with the second, subjective sense (meaning, of course, *oriented to the human subject*, rather than *arbitrary and uncontrolled*).

First, then, what makes faith as the capacity for belief in God relevant here is that it is the (not simply *a*) way in which a human being can perceive God.[30] To perceive God is to engage with something fundamentally different than a discrete physical object. As Augustine writes, "Neither is God bread nor is God water, nor is God this light, nor is God clothing, nor is God a house. For all these are visible things and are individual."[31] God is not a finite physical object but the transcendent ground of the existence of the world. Yet was not Jesus Christ divine as well as an object of this sort, both visible and individual? As a man, Jesus was indeed physically perceptible in an entirely ordinary way. However, his intimate connection with God, and his status as Son of God, were something different. As Jesus says to Peter in Matthew's Gospel when Peter recognizes Jesus as the "Son of the living God," "Blessed are you, Simon son of Jonah! For flesh and blood has not revealed this to you, but my Father in heaven" (16:17). God is not a physical object; he is rather an immaterial spirit. Because God is spiritual in nature, he can be perceived only by a human being's capacity for spiritual perception. If God can be seen, so to speak, it is not with the

[30] I do not intend to deny that there is a sense in which God remains greater than and beyond all creaturely knowledge of him, but this is not the place to pursue that discussion any further.

[31] *Tractates on the Gospel of John* 13.5 (CCSL 36, 133; FOC 79, 49). I owe this quotation to Matthew R. Lootens, "Augustine," in *The Spiritual Senses: Perceiving God in Western Christianity*, ed. Paul L. Gavrilyuk and Sarah Coakley (Cambridge: Cambridge University Press, 2014), 63, which provides a helpful overview of the spiritual senses in Augustine.

physical eyes but with the "eyes of faith." Faith is not about making up for a lack of the requisite empirical data; instead, it is the way to perceive things of a spiritual, non-empirical sort. This is important because engaging with God as the subject matter of the biblical text is the reader's desideratum. The reader aims for something more than simply reading "the text on the basis of itself"; the goal of interpretation is not "the simple encounter of the text by its reader."[32] Faith is indispensable because reading the Bible is about perceiving God through it.

Though faith is a capacity to perceive God that human beings can exercise, it is not an inherent ability, but one they receive as a gift. Søren Kierkegaard's thought project contrasting Socratic questioning and Christian faith is instructive here. In his dialogues, Socrates asks his interlocutors questions designed to prompt them to realize things they already know inchoately. "Thus the ignorant person merely needs to be reminded in order to know, by himself, to call to mind what he knows. The truth is not introduced into him but was in him."[33] All that must happen is that latent knowledge must come to one's conscious awareness and be clarified. Because the questions with which Socrates plies his dialogue partners are designed to draw out of them knowledge they already have, Socrates' task is merely to serve as a midwife, to participate in a delivery, rather than to confer knowledge on those with whom he speaks.[34] The ability spiritually to perceive God is fundamentally different however. Readers do not summon up faith from within themselves by means of their own power or ability. It is received as a gift of divine grace and is conferred by the power of the Spirit. Faith thus means receiving "theoretical or practical direction coming from a

32 Marion, *God without Being*, 145.

33 Søren Kierkegaard, *Philosophical Fragments*, Kierkegaard's Writings (Princeton: Princeton University Press, 1985), 9.

34 Ibid., 10.

source other than the mind itself."[35] The capacity to discern God might best be termed an eccentric capacity, as it is something that a human being gains the ability to do, yet this ability rests on conditions that are not internal to the human subject. This important qualification notwithstanding, Spinoza's naturalistic framework and the theological one being proposed here assume different anthropologies in that they presuppose different conceptions of which factors should influence how the reader reads, the naturalistic account placing exclusive emphasis on capacities internal to the reader as a person, and the theological view including the capacity of belief as well.

Seeing with the eyes of faith is genuinely possible for human beings as they receive faith as a gift, yet the vision that faith involves is a penultimate and mediated mode of sight. The faith that human beings have in the current stage of the economy of salvation is penultimate in that it falls short of being the direct vision of God, which becomes possible only in the *eschaton*. In this sense, there is a distinction between faith and sight proper (when the "eyes of faith" are spoken of, and there is the suggestion that faith is a form of seeing, the idea is that faith is a mode of perception). This sight of the face of God would be overwhelming for human beings now, for as Augustine says, "Authority is there for those who are incapable of gazing on the truth, so that they may become fit to do so by allowing themselves to be purified."[36] Or again, "Faith nourishes us with milk, so to speak, while we are babies in the cradle of this temporal life."[37] Thus, faith is precisely a transitional arrangement that prepares human beings for the ultimate form of engaging with God, seeing him face to face, rather than through a glass darkly. It acclimates them to what they will eventually experience in the *eschaton* – at which time there ceases to be any point either to faith

[35] Dupré, *Religion and the Rise of Modern Culture*, 117.
[36] *On the Advantage of Believing* 16.34 (CSEL 25/1, 43; WSA I/8, 145).
[37] *On Christian Teaching* 2.17 (CCSL 32, 43; OWC Green, 39).

or the Bible, for they will both be otiose when a direct encounter with God is possible. That faith is seeing through creaturely media highlights that it is a mediated form of perceiving God fit for the present. The biblical text is a form of words through which people perceive and understand God. That in which the believer invests faith is not so much the Bible itself as it is the God of whom the text speaks. The text's role for now is to mediate content about God to the reader who responds in faith to the message it offers.

This brings the discussion to the second sense of faith, its substantive content, or that which is believed. It is, of course, God in his being and saving action who is the subject matter of faith. More specifically, it is the triune God whom the reader perceives in reading the biblical text with the eyes of faith: "There is the Father and the Son and the Holy Spirit – each one of these is God, and all of them together are one God; each of these is a full substance and all together are one substance."[38] The triune God is the one around whom the biblical story revolves: it is this God who brings the world into existence and sustains it in being, confronts human defection, and sends Jesus Christ into the world to redeem it from the fall. As has already been suggested earlier in this section, the reader of the Bible ought to engage with the subject matter of the text when reading, and the subject matter should be understood thus. And, as the members of the Scripture Project say in their first thesis on Interpretation, "Scripture truthfully tells the story of God's action of creating, judging, and saving the world."[39] It follows that readers should read the text of the Bible with receptiveness to this message about the triune God. They should believe what it says about him. It is worth issuing the qualification that, of course, the reader's reception of the Bible is an active acceptance: because *they* are to receive the message of the text, readers must perform acts of making sense in relation to the Bible, and they must use their own techniques and

[38] *On Christian Teaching* 1.4 (CCSL 32, 8; OWC Green, 10).

[39] Scripture Project, "Nine Theses on the Interpretation of Scripture," 1.

concepts in the process of doing so. The chapter on interpretation is the most natural point in this book to expand the active aspect of interpretation, but it needs to be underlined briefly here to ward off the impression that reception is an entirely one-sided affair in which the reader plays no active role whatsoever. That is not the case.

That theological belief is a receptive response to what the text signifies means not just that readers give their assent to content derived from beyond their own internal reflection, but that they integrate this new material into their outlook and begin to engage with reality by means of it. What is crucial is that the reader not only thinks *about* the biblical text – though an awareness of what the text says is a necessary preliminary to what is most important – but that the reader ultimately comes to think *with* and *under* its guidance.[40] Reading receptively in this sense means not only interpreting the text itself, but also reading the world in light of it. Receptive interpretation is an exercise of faith in that it makes operative within a reader's perspective material content obtained from the biblical text as it discloses God. Since it is God who is the object of the reader's faith, what the reader is receptive to is precisely the Bible as a sign of divinity. This means that, while such reception may be assisted by the process of historical reconstruction, historical inquiry is not the essence of the matter: what is to be received is not essentially knowledge about the past, even about how a passage from Scripture would have been understood by its first readers. Rather, that which is received is – to state the point once more – the self-disclosure of God that is facilitated by means of textual signifiers.[41] Chapter 5 says much more about what it

[40] Cf. Webster, *Holy Scripture*, 103.

[41] Martin characterizes his entire work *Biblical Truths* as one in which he "thinks with" Scripture: see *Biblical Truths*, 5, 31. His language of *thinking with* is similar to my own, yet he means something fundamentally different by it. He risks inflating the productive dimension of interpretation to the point that the text's potential to form readers is severely impaired. For Martin, thinking with is associated with the agency of

means to construe the Bible as a sign; it is not possible to provide a proper exposition of this theme here. However, it is worth filling out this point about receptive reading a bit more with an example.

As an example of thinking with the Bible, consider how, for the disciples of Jesus walking on the Emmaus Road, scriptural texts became a "hermeneutical matrix"[42] on the basis of which they were able to understand events of which they could otherwise not make

readers in interpretation: "If we pay attention to how we and others read texts and interpret them, we can see, even through everyday examples, that the texts themselves don't control or constrain our interpretation of them. Texts do not in fact speak to us or impart their contents. We have to read them, and our reading of them is a product of our human agency and activity. Readers make meaning when they read texts" (96). On this view, thinking with also implies creativity on the part of the reader: Martin says that he practices "creative anachronism" (31), that is, his readings may well be informed by historical-critical research, but they are not ultimately determined by it. The interpretations are also guided by substantive criteria, such as the parameters of theological orthodoxy and a certain vision of what ethical life entails (70). Such substantive criteria are, however, not specified in a great deal of detail: they are only minimally unpacked. Whatever the total package of criteria is, the criteria do not, even as a whole set, mandate what a reading should be. Thus, "thinking with" is about readerly creativity and meaning-making à la a jazz musician improvising within a performance, in which there are some givens, but also a great deal of flexibility and room for self-expression (see Martin, *Pedagogy of the Bible*, 86–87).

By contrast, what I mean by "thinking with" takes for granted that the text makes definite claims when it is read with reference to God. For me, thinking with entails that the reader should see reality from the point of view that the text provides. The reader's subjectivity will no doubt be involved in perceiving how the text signifies God, and how to navigate reality in its light. However, the stress here is on the text functioning as a source of guidance, or as a work that forms the reader's perspective, which inevitably curtails readerly agency per se. The whole purpose of theological reading is that there does indeed exist a formative pressure upon the reader from the text. My reading of Martin owes a debt to an excellent assessment of his work by Susannah Ticciati, though our critiques are by no means identical. See her "Review of Dale B. Martin's *Biblical Truths: The Meaning of Scripture in the Twenty-First Century*" (paper presented at the annual meeting for the Society of Biblical Literature, Boston, MA, November 19, 2017).

42 Richard B. Hays, "Reading Scripture in Light of the Resurrection," in *The Art of Reading Scripture*, ed. Ellen F. Davis and Richard B. Hays (Grand Rapids: Eerdmans, 2003), 230.

sense (Luke 24). The disciples had already heard reports from members of their company that the tomb where Jesus had been buried after his crucifixion was unoccupied (24:22–23). They had also heard reports of angels being present at the tomb proclaiming that Jesus was alive (24:23). However, the initial reports of an empty tomb, even once they were confirmed by further witnesses (24:24), seemed like nonsense to them (24:11), for they could not put their observations together in a coherent way. The reports with which the disciples were presented were unintelligible because the disciples lacked the appropriate categories by which to understand the significance of the events that had unfolded. That Jesus initially rebuked the disciples for their failure to believe how the prophets spoke of him (24:25), and that he then explained to them "what was said in all the Scriptures concerning himself" (24:27) makes clear that the view of Jesus that the disciples needed was indeed there to be received from Moses and the prophets. What they needed to do was to mobilize scriptural concepts so as to understand the resurrection of Jesus and the implications this had for his true identity (24:27). What had not happened, up until a key moment of recognition (24:30–32), was a matter of grasping how to think with these texts about Jesus and this crucial moment in his career.[43] Relating

[43] My reading of this passage owes a debt to Marion, "'They Recognized Him; and He Became Invisible to Them'," 145–52. There are some incisive critical questions about Marion's essay in Shane Mackinlay, "Eyes Wide Shut: A Response to Jean-Luc Marion's Account of the Journey to Emmaus," *Modern Theology* 20 (2004): 447–56. Some of these pertain to Marion's phenomenology and are beyond the scope of the present discussion. For our purposes, the most important question Mackinlay poses is whether the biblical material Jesus reviewed with the disciples actually played into their eventual recognition of him. It is true, as Mackinlay notes, that the disciples did not grasp that it was Jesus who was with them until after the discussion of Scripture on the road to Emmaus; it was only with the breaking of the bread that "their eyes were opened" (24:31): see "Eyes Wide Shut," 451. Yet there are, within the passage, a set of indications that the recognition was the joint product of seeing a familiar gesture during the meal (cf. 22:18) and things the disciples gleaned from the text. In the narrative, Jesus rebuked his interlocutors for not seeing what is in a real sense present

the texts to Jesus, and seeing them as a sign pointing to him, meant reading them figurally. "As Jesus cannot be understood apart from Jewish scripture, Jewish scripture cannot be understood apart from Jesus; what is needed is an interpretation which relates the two."[44] This passage can function as a paradigm for what it means, in more general terms, to read receptively, as it serves as an example of what it means to think with the guidance of the text.

Thinking with and under the guidance of biblical texts entails divesting oneself of patterns of reflection that conflict with the vision of reality that the text projects. That the knowledge of God which the text communicates is not the natural possession of human beings means that readers have the inclination to form alternative frameworks of thinking, ones that do not mesh easily with the contents of the text. Given this tendency toward conflict between the beliefs the reader has apart from interpreting the Bible, and the outlooks that a receptive reading of the Bible will introduce, it is only by the former giving way to the latter that a receptive reading becomes possible. Luke 24 illustrates how assumptions must sometimes be given up to open the way for a new vision. As the disciples relinquish their assumption that Jesus simply could not have been raised to new life, and as they mobilize the Old Testament texts he worked through with them, they experience an epiphany: "Then their eyes were opened, and they recognized him" (24:31). The sort of divestment that is necessary here is a purging from oneself those elements of one's worldview that stand in the

within the prophetic texts (24:25). This does not, of course, mean that the disciples were able to recognize Jesus because of this textual content, but that what they needed was there for them to find, at least as Jesus portrayed it. Jesus then explained to them how the texts testify to him (24:27). Later, after they recognized Jesus, the disciples reported that their hearts were burning within them even while they were still on the road as Jesus was "opening the scriptures" (24:32). This suggests that something was happening within them that prepared them for the final epiphany, which took place shortly afterwards.

[44] Moberly, *The Bible, Theology, and Faith*, 51.

way of allowing the text and Jesus Christ to enter into a mutually interpreting relationship.[45] In this way, it involves an epistemic transformation of the interpreter, a revision of one's perceptual categories and view of what is ultimately real.[46] This sort of reading thereby fundamentally changes who the reader is.

The present section has unpacked a notion of faith and briefly outlined a view of receptive reading that follows from it. Does saying all of this about faith and its influence on reading risk creating a rigid framework that utterly controls and determines interpretation? To what extent can theological readers reconsider their own views as they do further reading if the commitments that have just been expounded must be present in order for reading to qualify as theological in the first place? Readers may of course be in error about the details of their theological thinking, or about issues on a much larger scale, and they must undertake the hard effort of rethinking when they discover they have made mistakes. Augustine's view that there is no unmediated access to ultimate truth in this world should remind contemporary readers that they must see their views as having no more than a provisional status. His famous restlessness as a thinker, his determination to continue to grow and

[45] What is being recommended here is different from the more generic notion of divestment that is embedded in Wesley Kort's notion of centripetal reading, in which "the coherences and identities of the reader and the reader's situation are dissolved, and biblical coherences and identities, rather than be appropriated, are followed as indicators of an exit and then bypassed on the way to it" (*Take, Read*, 128). Here biblical passages function as symbols of a generic and total self-divestment, one that urges readers to leave the old behind without specifying what ought to fill the gap left after the dissolution of the prior self. The correlative moment of centrifugal reading is a matter of reconstituting the self where all moments of reconstitution become "departure points from which journeys to exits are constantly launched" (*Take, Read*, 131). For this journey, no destination is ever specified. A theological reader, by contrast, sloughs off what she must for the sake of coming to reflect on Jesus Christ from the perspective of the text, leaving elements of her thinking behind as a function of a basic commitment to this sort of receptivity.

[46] Hays, "Reading Scripture in Light of the Resurrection," 235.

learn, and his refusal to rest content with any given level of comprehension,[47] should discourage readers today from complacent satisfaction with the present disposition of their beliefs.

Yet there is a limit to the extent to which theological readers as such can reconsider their views. Revision and reformulation are indeed possible. If, however, they come to believe that *all* of their theological beliefs are incorrect, they are de facto no longer theological readers, but naturalists. If a certain modest core of doctrinal belief – a form of the trinitarian affirmation that marks out the Christian confession of God as such – cannot be operative within interpretation, then all that readers have left is an approach grounded in historical relativity. As Robert Jenson writes, "Indeed, guide your reading by church doctrine. For if, say, the doctrine of Trinity and Matthew's construal of the passion do not fit each other, then the church lost its diachronic self in the early fourth century at the latest."[48] While readers can reconsider each of their theological beliefs, theological reading becomes something else if the entire theological framework is surrendered. Hence, pressure from the text certainly can prompt revision to a reader's faith, but there are restrictions to this if the reformed faith commitment is to be in recognizable continuity with what is specifically Christian.

### *Readers' Social Contexts*

As readers engage with the text so as to receive its message, they interpret it together with others who are linked up with them in social settings, rather than as isolated and solitary individuals cut

[47] There is a lucid and penetrating discussion of how his understanding of faith and the nature of Scripture demand nothing less than this in Carol Harrison, "De Profundis: Augustine's Reading of Orthodoxy," in *Orthodox Readings of Augustine*, ed. George E. Demacopoulos and Aristotle Papanikolaou (Crestwood: St. Vladimir's Seminary Press, 2008), 253–61. See also Williams, "Language, Reality and Desire," 138–50.

[48] Jenson, "Scripture's Authority in the Church," 29.

off from their fellow interpreters.[49] All reflective activity is marked by the social and institutional dynamics in which it occurs. Summarizing a historical narrative, Alasdair MacIntyre rightly says that for all the major forms it takes, intellectual inquiry "was or is part of the elaboration of a mode of social and moral life of which the intellectual enquiry itself was an integral part," and "the forms of that life were embodied with greater or lesser degrees of imperfection in social and political institutions which also draw their life from other sources."[50] While this is a point of broad pertinence, the wider social sphere is especially relevant for theological reading because receptive reading is not about connecting with an innate knowledge of the text's subject matter that a given reader already has; it is not about simply getting in touch with resources one already possesses following the "moral and intellectual ideal of spontaneous subjectivity."[51] Instead, readers' thinking needs to be shaped if it is to align with the perspective the text projects, and participating in community life is part of what forms one's practices of interpretation. Since whatever reading practices the interpreter is inclined to apply to the text are intertwined with the various commitments he has – adverse as they are, to a certain degree, to the material content of the text – such practices need to be shaped so that interpretation can be genuinely receptive.[52] Communal life

49 It is worth noting that in Part I the discussion of interpretation's social dimension fell more within analysis of the text and interpretation than of the reader. For this constructive proposal, I have relocated discussion of the social aspect of reading to this chapter for strategic reasons, in order to forestall the objection that the account assumes an individualistic view of the interpreter.

50 Alasdair C. MacIntyre, *Whose Justice? Which Rationality?* (Notre Dame: University of Notre Dame Press, 1988), 349.

51 Webster, "Hermeneutics in Modern Theology," 55.

52 There is quite a strong emphasis on the reader needing formation in Hauerwas, *Unleashing the Scripture*; Fowl and Jones, *Reading in Communion*. Paul Griffiths deals with closely related issues from the point of view of epistemology, highlighting how religious reading depends not only on the native cognitive equipment of the reader, but also upon the interpreter existing in the larger context of a tradition that forms

helps to break down the resistance to the text's message that all readers have in some measure. For this basic reason, the reader's social context plays a crucial role in the formation of the theological reader.

How, more specifically, is social context important? Participation in ecclesial community forms readers in two ways, both indirectly and directly. First, ecclesial life has its indirect influence by building into the reader a certain prior understanding of the text's subject matter.[53] Reading is not the only way in which the reader can find herself ushered into the world of the text. There are other practices too that are fundamentally congruent with it insofar as they facilitate the process by which readers begin to see the world of the text as the real world. Such practices assist with receptivity by forming a perspective that resonates with the biblical text. "To interpret God's discourse more reliably, we must come to know God better. . . . Engaging in the practice of interpreting texts so as to discern God's discourse requires engaging simultaneously in whatever practices might yield a better knowledge of God. Those practices will be

one's thinking: *Religious Reading*, 72–76. I stand in broad agreement with these authors, over against those who work with a more individualistic anthropology, though there are some differences on the details. For instance, as Hauerwas makes the point about the necessity of formation for reading, he says, "You cannot rightly read the Sermon on the Mount unless you are a pacifist" (*Unleashing the Scripture*, 64). He does not, however, do equally well at stressing that Scripture forms the practices which in turn exert an influence on the reader and allow for proper interpretation.

53 In saying that it is in the ecclesial community where readers pick up a prior understanding of the text's subject matter, I am not intending to claim that it is essentially ecclesiology, to the exclusion of all other doctrines, which allows Scripture to function as a living voice. That Scripture speaks to readers in the present cannot ultimately be secured without an appropriately theological view of the text. There are also important considerations mentioned below in the section of this chapter entitled "Historical Distance and Receptiveness." The task ecclesiology is doing here is providing further density to the depiction of the reader by describing a key context in which the reader performs interpretive work, and it details how the communal context shapes the way readers access the text.

practices of the heart as well as the head, of devotion as well as reflection."[54] Examples of such practices include catechesis, liturgical worship, and many other ecclesial activities, all of which are undertaken together with other people who are either members of the community or its appointed leaders. Though the influence these practices have on readers and interpretation is indirect, as this is not about learning specific forms of reading per se, the whole matter of prior understanding is nevertheless significant, as it specifies the point of view from which they frame interpretive questions and begin their engagement with Scripture. That the church is a communal context in which a fitting prior understanding develops is possible only because the account of faith's material content given above aligns with how the Christian tradition has understood God. The working assumption is that, while the Christian community constantly strives to refine its understanding of God, and is fully aware that no human conception will ever be fully adequate, the tradition is not fundamentally off base in its basic commitment.

The importance for biblical interpretation that practices of devotion occurring within such a context have shines through in the final verses of Luke's Gospel – a passage that becomes important once more for this chapter. The followers of Jesus, already having been given oral instruction in how to interpret scriptural passages so as to understand the events surrounding Jesus' death from a scriptural point of view, finally understood that it was Jesus who was standing before them when he broke bread with them (24:30). Jesus had promised his disciples that he would not celebrate the Passover again before the advent of his kingdom (22:15–19), and his followers were aided in their recognition of him when he performed this symbolic action in their presence (24:31). Taking part in this act together with Jesus allowed the disciples to see that there was a sense in which his kingdom had indeed come, that Jesus was not confined

[54] Wolterstorff, *Divine Discourse*, 239.

to the grave, and that they needed to take a whole new perspective on the world.[55] This recognition gave great significance to the practices of textual interpretation they had just learned: those ways of reading would help them to understand more deeply the one whose identity came home to them in the breaking of bread. Just as breaking bread with Jesus sparked insight into who he was, so also a whole range of ecclesial practices contribute to the understanding of God with which readers in the church approach the text.

Second, the ecclesial context exerts an influence on readers more directly by training them how to utilize certain reading strategies. It is the church that brought together the constituent documents of the biblical canon, and it is the church that gathers together to read the canonical text in its regular services of corporate worship. An ecclesial reading of the Bible is a receptive one, and so the interpretive moves made within this setting, and the principles that hold these readings together and give them warrant as legitimate textual practices, are a major source from which readers can learn to read the Bible so as to think with and under its guidance. It is not that interpretive practices common within the church have authority simply by virtue of being established,[56] but rather that the church is a community of readers which subscribes to something like the concepts of the reader and the biblical text that form the wider rationale for the practice of theological reading. Therefore learning the relevant patterns of textual interpretation in this particular setting makes sense. Theological reading presupposes an existing community of interpretive practice, and in addition the way in which new readers learn to interpret strengthens the bonds between community members. As Augustine writes, the ecclesial

[55] See the comments, in connection with Luke 24, on how "a Christian understanding is inseparable from a certain kind of 'eucharistic' lifestyle and practice" in Moberly, *The Bible, Theology, and Faith*, 66.

[56] Cf. MacIntyre, *Whose Justice? Which Rationality?*, 359, where he notes that a point merely being established in the context of a tradition is the weakest form of justifying it.

community is knit together in love when those who constitute it learn things from one another, including how to interpret the Bible.[57] Chapter 6 of this book offers an embodiment of the direct version of the ecclesial community's importance for theological reading by picking up from within the Christian tradition, and adapting for this project, a set of concepts that can guide the practice of interpretation. Thus Chapter 6 provides a worked example of the present point.[58]

As important as the ecclesial context is in these two ways, it does not exhaust the social contexts readers should inhabit in order to be skilled theological readers of Scripture. Interpreters can expect to glean useful reading skills by indwelling multiple social contexts, all of which can contribute to their formation. Readers may, for instance, pick up skills in literary or historical analysis of the Bible within academic contexts that are not specifically dedicated to cultivating theological readers, though the skills that these institutions develop may be directed toward the end of thinking with and under the framework of the biblical text.[59] Literary and historical skills can be recontextualized so as to serve the goal of reading

[57] *On Christian Teaching* Prooemium 4–9 (CCSL 32, 2–6; OWC Green, 4–7).

[58] It is worth noting that, for the purpose of this section, there are not and need not be utterly sharp boundaries around the ecclesial community. The church has over the course of Western history influenced the broader culture, and therefore it would be hard to locate a context, at least in the West, where the community's prior conceptions about God are entirely absent, and perhaps the same goes for the techniques of reading that it has developed and sustained over the centuries. For this reason, it is not important to insist on a set of firm binary options for the location of readers, as if they are definitely either inside or outside the church or a specific ecclesial community. The thrust of this treatment of ecclesiology is that full participation in an ecclesial setting affords readers a chance to learn things that have a salutary influence on reading.

[59] Robert Morgan rightly says, "The non-religious assumptions of Western culture now shape most contemporary scholarship, including Christian biblical scholarship." See his "Liberal Theological Hermeneutics," *Journal of Theological Studies* 68 (2017): 212–13. Whether or not this is actually true, the situation need not be entirely determinative for the theological reader, who should adapt and reshape these interpretive techniques as needed.

the biblical text receptively, regardless of the framework within which such skills were originally embedded. In addition, Christian theological readers stand to gain by participating in social contexts in which scriptural texts are read receptively by religious others. For instance, Jewish readers operate with a different canon of texts, and even the texts they share with Christians are treated as having a different hermeneutical center. Yet Christian Scripture itself urges Christians to remain engaged with Jews, without assuming an attitude of superiority toward them (Rom. 11:18). By reading together with Jews and Muslims as well, Christians can, at a minimum, expect to gain a greater appreciation of the textual and hermeneutical differences they have with those with whom they share the Abrahamic heritage. This will help them better to understand, and perhaps even to refine, their own approach to interpretation. The practice of Scriptural Reasoning, which was mentioned in this book's Introduction, is one fruitful form this discussion may take. In two ways, then, "Christians need to read the Bible in dialogue with diverse others outside the church."[60]

## *Historical Distance and Receptiveness*

The depiction of readers that this chapter has advanced so far is theological in that it makes recourse to God in two ways, both by including faith in God as a readerly capacity (when received as a gift of grace), and by taking account of the formation readers experience within the ecclesial community, at the center of whose life is the worship of God. The conclusion to the previous chapter already indicated, though, that the constructive proposal being put forward in Part II requires readers to perform historical research on biblical texts in an effort to evade an all-too-common dualism between faith and history. That readers are to respond in faith to divine

[60] Scripture Project, "Nine Theses on the Interpretation of Scripture," 4.

self-disclosure as mediated by the text connects them with it; however, that interpreters also have an obligation to look into the historical background of texts seems to distance them from it. How do these two emphases fit together? What should a theological conception of the reader make of the notion of historical distance? If there is room within a theological view of the interpreter for historical distance (in some sense), then what happens to the concept of a receptive reading of the Bible that this chapter has stressed? In addressing these questions, this section seeks to avoid the false dilemmas that a dualistic perspective creates. On the one hand, the readers to whom theological categories are applied are also properly depicted through variables that consider them from a more mundane point of view, situating them in times and places that differ from those in which the text originally emerged. Yet, on the other hand, the theological factors in play create a unity between text and reader that means receptive reading does remain genuinely possible.[61]

In order to elaborate this response, it is necessary, first, to achieve some clarity on what historical distance might mean. Historical distance refers to the way in which the Bible's circumstances of origin and the situation of present-day readers differ in time and place, and, relatedly, that the language in which the text had its first life differs in many ways from the language of those who read it today.[62] Readers of the Bible can often gain knowledge of at least

[61] Cf. George Steiner, who considers theological texts and other literary works, and asks whether thinking in terms of distance means of necessity that an interpreter is no longer reading a text receptively, which he terms being a *critic* instead of a *reader*. He wonders if there is an "essential distinction between the judicial authority of the critic, his normative placement of the text or art object at and from an argued distance, and the 'dynamic passivity' or sufferance of the 'reader' who is, where 'reading' achieves its plentitude, the 'one being read'" ("Critic/Reader," in *George Steiner: A Reader* [Oxford: Oxford University Press, 1984], 83–84). He responds that creating a dichotomy between the two categories of reader and critic is a "fiction of contrastive absolutes," for "in the ordinary run of things 'criticism' and 'reading' interpenetrate and overlap" (ibid., 96).

[62] That the language is different is obviously the case for those who read the text in translation. However, even those who are native speaks of, say, modern Hebrew must

some of the text's historical and geographical background and the dynamics of the language of its earliest strata. Sometimes research into such issues can reach greater certainty than in other cases on specific questions, and sometimes there will be more gaps in the reader's knowledge than at other times.[63] This, in the briefest of terms, is what this section means by historical distance.

Historical distance throws up two obstacles to receptive reading. What initially separates the reader from the text, and prevents her from being able to understand it, are aspects of its historical or geographical backdrop or language that the reader does not understand: call these instances of textual *obscurity*. However, suppose that the interpreter comes to understand these things well, gaining a high degree of confidence in her conclusions and having few gaps in her knowledge. In an ideal case, instances of obscurity can be resolved with sufficient background knowledge.

Yet just when these things are understood well, the problem associated with distance morphs into a seemingly more permanent hindrance to receptive understanding: this is the *alterity* of the text's message. Once the reader comprehends the text, she understands that it pertains to people who differ in significant respects from herself, for they lived in a different place and time and conversed in another tongue. The more precisely the text is understood, the more elusive it becomes; as its language and background are grasped in detail, it seems to slip through one's fingers, showing itself to be a text that was written to *someone else*.[64] This second problem

be aware that the version of that language that they know is not precisely the same as the version in which Old Testament texts were written.

63 Cf. Spinoza's discussion of all of the forms of knowledge, both historical and linguistic, that readers of the Bible needed but did not have in their own time: *Theological-Political Treatise*, 106–11.

64 The famous conclusion to Albert Schweitzer's study of the historical Jesus thus points to a much more general issue, not simply one that pertains only to historical work on Jesus: "The study of the Life of Jesus has had a curious history. It set out in quest of the historical Jesus, believing that when it had found Him it could bring Him straight

associated with distance does not mean that the reader cannot comprehend the text, but rather – apart from ways to identify with the text's original readers – that it does not directly address her and speak to concerns she actually has, for these concerns are tied tightly to issues of history, geography, and language. G. W. F. Hegel comments insightfully on how a perception of biblical doctrines as utterly foreign, in the sense that they are not credible now, drives a hermeneutic that stresses historical distance in this second sense:

> The most important sign that these positive dogmas have lost much of their importance is that in the main these doctrines are treated *historically*. As far as this historical procedure is concerned, it deals with thoughts and representations that were had, introduced, and fought over by others, with convictions that belong to others, with histories that do not take place within our spirit, do not engage the needs of our spirit. What is of interest is rather how these things have come about in the case of others, the contingent way in which they were formed. The absolute way in which these doctrines were formed – out of the depths of spirit – is forgotten, and so their necessity and truth is forgotten, too, and the question what one holds as one's own conviction meets with astonishment.[65]

Without a way to address this issue of alterity, the text ends up functioning exclusively as a past act of communication, a

into our time as a Teacher and Saviour. It loosed the bands by which He had been riveted for centuries to the stony rocks of ecclesiastical doctrine, and rejoiced to see life and movement coming into the figure once more, and the historical Jesus advancing, as it seemed, to meet it. But He does not stay; He passes by our time and returns to His own. What surprised and dismayed the theology of the last forty years was that, despite all forced and arbitrary interpretations, it could not keep Him in our time, but had to let Him go. He returned to His own time, not owing to the application of any historical ingenuity, but by the same inevitable necessity by which the liberated pendulum returns to its original position." See *The Quest of the Historical Jesus* (Mineola: Dover, 2005), 600–01.

[65] G. W. F. Hegel, *Lectures on the Philosophy of Religion: The Lectures of 1827* (Oxford: Clarendon Press, 2006), 84–85.

communicative exchange to which present-day readers are not party. It is not a living voice or a work addressing concerns they themselves have and must have.[66]

A concrete example of textual alterity will help illustrate what is at stake here. New Testament scholar Richard Hays relates a story about how the pastor of a Christian church in Kansas reacted to his exposition of Paul's epistle to the Romans during a three-day continuing education class. Hays had presented the main teaching of Romans not to concern personal salvation – though it is often understood this way – but actually to focus around the relations of Jews and Gentiles in God's plan of salvation, and the promise of the Gospel not ultimately voiding God's faithfulness to the people of Israel.[67] The exegesis Hays provided proved compelling to this pastor, but for that very reason it was also deeply unsettling to him. The minister explained why in a lament to his teacher: "Professor Hays, you've convinced me that you're right about Romans, but now I don't see how I can preach from it anymore. Where I serve out in western Kansas, Israel's fate isn't a burning issue for my people, and there's not a Jew within a hundred miles of my church."[68] This pastor felt he had understood Paul's epistle much more securely than he had previously: prior misconceptions had been displaced by what he took to be well-grounded exegetical understanding. However, so understood, the epistle no longer spoke

[66] To read for the original sense of the text might be characterized as reading with an archaeological rather than a teleological concern, or as having a primarily retrospective rather than prospective interest. See André LaCocque and Paul Ricoeur, *Thinking Biblically: Exegetical and Hermeneutical Studies* (Chicago: University of Chicago Press, 1998), x. The co-authors make this distinction precisely to deny that the biblical scholar (LaCocque) focuses only on the first, while the hermeneutical philosopher (Ricoeur) deals just with the second: each one cares in some measure about both.

[67] Richard B. Hays, *The Moral Vision of the New Testament: Community, Cross, New Creation; a Contemporary Introduction to New Testament Ethics* (New York: HarperCollins, 1996), 5–6.

[68] Ibid., 6.

to the concerns of an audience that he, as a pastor, was bound to address, and that he presumed the epistle should engage, given that it is a piece of Christian Scripture which should be read and expounded to congregations today – despite differences in time, place, and language. Comprehension led to the discernment of alterity and seemed to stymie receptive reading.

If theological readers are to be receptive, and historical distance puts obstacles in the way of receptive reading, theological readers need to decide what their stance on historical distance ought to be. Partly because of problems like the one just explained and illustrated, some of those who have an interest in theological exegesis assign a vanishingly small role to historical distance. They aim to dispense with it. Doing so makes it seem simple to claim that the text can indeed be read as a living voice, with this mode of interpretation not dependent on the reader having done a prior reading in a more historically engaged mode, or even having the knowledge that such reading would require. For R. R. Reno, there is technically temporal distance between the reader and the text, but such distance is relatively inconsequential for the dynamics of communication. As he says, "History does not necessarily or inevitably distance us from the word of God."[69] In the cases where history creates a barrier to communication, the barrier is but a small one, which is easily overcome. The issue that really governs interpretation is the spiritual state of the reader; that is what ultimately determines whether or not the reader grasps the message of the text.[70] For readers who submit themselves to spiritual discipline, and who follow practices of interpretation that find their rationale in a spiritual-theological framework,[71] whatever gap there is between the text and the reader can be overcome fairly easily, thus

[69] R. R. Reno, "'You Who Once Were Far Off Have Been Brought Near': Reflections in the Aid of Theological Exegesis," *Ex auditu* 16 (2000): 174.

[70] Ibid., 179–81.

[71] Ibid., 175–77.

enabling communication to occur successfully. In this way, the reader's spiritual state determines whether any existing distance can be crossed. Acquiring historical knowledge does not create a bridge with the text, and so it does not have a necessary place in enabling the reader to understand the text. Readers can omit "the hard work of travelling back in time"; they do not need to use "theoretical aides, schemes of reconstruction," and "ambitious expeditions of textual archeology."[72]

Yet if spiritual proximity to the text's content neutralizes the (quite modest) alienating potential of historical distance, then no part of the original problem is a lack of historical knowledge rendering the text obscure at certain points. There really is no fundamental problem of obscurity. This makes the necessary affirmation that the text emerged from a set of past contingent circumstances seem hollow, for it does not matter to how it should be read. Reno appeals often to patristic figures to provide warrant for his approach,[73] but even Augustine insists that some textual obscurities need to be illuminated by the acquisition of historical knowledge.[74] Assessments of a hiatus between reader and text

[72] Ibid., 170.

[73] Ibid., 175, 179–81.

[74] *On Christian Teaching* 2.42–43 (CCSL 32, 62–63; OWC Green, 55–56). In a later publication, Reno assigns what seems to be an even lower profile to historical consciousness, denying that Christian readers should perceive the biblical text's original meaning in a neutral sphere without the mobilization of theological categories. Any perception of the text's meaning thus takes place through the eyes of faith. Readers should see in the text, right from the beginning, a doctrinal message which comports with the later Christian tradition, because there simply is no earlier stage to interpretive operations, in which a reader checks how well the text's original sense matches up with its subsequent reception in ecclesial communities. For this view, differences of time, place, and language are immaterial to how the reader ascertains what the text actually says, for the reader operates with doctrinal lenses at all times, and these doctrinal categories do not need to prove their validity with reference to the text's language or time and location of origin. In Chapter 6 of the present work, which focuses on interpretation, there is a counterproposal to this view, in which theology is active at an early stage of interpretation in a modest way, while

should not be made on the basis of theological criteria alone, apart from immanent ones, as if the immanent categories have no significance, or as if acknowledging them at all means that only a historical reading of the text is possible. Arriving at a proper view of historical distance requires further reflection on what a theological anthropology of the reading subject involves, for estimates of the extent of the distance between the reader and the text depend crucially on prior judgments about human identity. Such judgments should take into account the full range of factors. These decisions shape determinations about the significance of historical, geographical, and linguistic particularities – the basic reality of which ought to be taken for granted.

One way of describing what Reno is ultimately reacting against (or, more accurately, overreacting to) is a view of disengaged reason that frequently underlies assessments of historical distance. Estimates of the extent of the gap between the biblical text and the present day grow in direct proportion to a commitment to disengaged reason. From a point of view that excludes faith commitment from rational reflection, variables such as a person's place in time, his geographical location, and the language he speaks – all immanent considerations – become much more definitive of human identity than they could possibly be if theological categories serve further to specify who human beings are.[75] If theological categories

still allowing for a degree of separation between original sense and later reception. For Reno's more recent views, see especially "Theology and Biblical Interpretation," in *Sharper Than a Two-Edged Sword: Preaching, Teaching, and Living the Bible*, ed. Michael Root and James J. Buckley (Grand Rapids: Eerdmans, 2008), 2–3. Cf. the critique of Childs's interest in the discrete voice of the Old Testament within Christian interpretation in Reno, "Biblical Theology and Theological Exegesis," 397–98.

[75] David Tracy's comments on the reasons that modern readers feel alienated from their classic texts are telling. For him, the key to the identity of present-day Western readers is that they are a product of events such as the scientific revolution, the Enlightenment, the industrial revolution, the wars of the twentieth century, technological revolutions, and looming global crises. "We find ourselves unable to proceed as if all that had not happened, is not happening, or could not happen. We find

are also present, they recontextualize the mundane factors, thus rendering them other than absolutely and finally determinative.[76] If, however, human identity is not seen in light of God and the biblical narrative of God's historical interaction with humankind, "it becomes harder to take over the story [of how one's life is to be understood] ready-made from the canonical models and archetypes. The story [of one's life] has to be drawn from the particular events and circumstances of this life."[77] Thinking of immanent variables as the essence of who human beings are, and where they stand in relation to the text, leads to stark conclusions such as this: "We are no longer as we were. No longer are we sustained within a biblical matrix; or at least not solely so, and not without an acute awareness of competing claims on our spiritual and cognitive integrity. The labor of many centuries has expelled us from this edenic womb and its wellsprings of life and knowledge."[78] A strong commitment to a view of reason as disengaged from theology inevitably delivers this type of conclusion.

However, this implication is blocked since the view of the reader to which this chapter is dedicated is by no means bound by disengaged reason. As explained above, that the reader responds to the text's disclosure of God is part of what makes readers who they are: belief is key to their identity qua theological readers. They confess it to be true that God created, has judged, and is saving the world. If this is genuinely true, then it is true for today's readers, just as it is

ourselves culturally distanced from the classics of our traditions" (*Plurality and Ambiguity*, 8). While Tracy allows that readers can bridge such distance by application of hermeneutical ingenuity, it is noteworthy that theological categories are absent from this initial assessment of the nature and extent of the distance between readers and classic texts.

[76] See Troeltsch's contrast between the historical and dogmatic methods as depending on different views of history, with only the latter making recourse to the history of salvation: "On the Historical and Dogmatic Methods in Theology," 20–21.

[77] Taylor, *Sources of the Self*, 289.

[78] Michael A. Fishbane, *The Garments of Torah: Essays in Biblical Hermeneutics*, Indiana Studies in Biblical Literature (Bloomington: Indiana University Press, 1989), 121.

true as a description of the first readers of the whole range of biblical texts. There is a single economy of salvation in which all of these interpreters are situated, despite the differences that mark them with respect to immanent determinants of identity. If the latter factors were the exclusive markers of identity, then it would be very difficult indeed for today's readers of the Bible to identify with the initial audiences of scriptural texts. They may share a so-called common humanity, but at the level of specifics, their humanity is very different, for it is shaped and conditioned by the details of time, place, and language (not to mention class, race, gender, and so on). Something more is needed to produce a commonality of sufficient strength to facilitate identification. The suggestion here is that identification across differences based on time, place, and language is genuinely possible by virtue of all readers being united together within the one economy of salvation. Thus the past recipients of biblical texts, or the original audiences for whom the texts were composed, are people with whom today's readers can identify. Today's readers are not identical to them, but they can still identify with them. The reason for this is that all are subject to the fall and God's judgment, and salvation is available to all in Christ.

This way of holding differences together in a context of significant similarity means that reading will involve a process of analogical reasoning. What is revealed by studying a text's communicative function in its situation of origin is just how thoroughly embedded the communication was in the dynamics of that particular situation. This is true in a relatively obvious way for epistles, which were written for a specific target audience, but it is also true for narrative accounts and other genres as well. Exactly the same communicative exchange cannot be duplicated in later situations, for it is impossible to repeat the original correlation between circumstance and message. Yet an analogous communication is possible. If the original writing has entered into the canon, it is somewhere between nearly identical and substantially similar to the piece of writing that was first read, though it has been recontextualized into whole scriptural collection. As for later readers, they can identify with the original readers by virtue of being included together with them in the same economy of salvation. Thus, the later text and readers are not precisely the *same* as the earlier ones, but they are *like* them in nontrivial ways – assuming only that these theological conceptualizations of the two have become operative, as they are in this account. This means that readers should expect to see analogies, or similarities across lines of difference, between the way that the text they read communicates to them and the way that the text the first readers read spoke to them. Theological reading involves interpreting the Bible with an alertness to see such analogies and a willingness to make judgments about where telling similarities do indeed obtain.[79] This requires the reader to perform a comparative analysis of contexts, where theological considerations arc relevant once again: "in such acts of imaginative integration, the church has historically recognized the work of the Holy Spirit. Where faithful interpreters listen patiently to the Word of God in Scripture and discern fresh imaginative links between the biblical story and our time, we confess – always with reverent caution – that the Spirit is inspiring such readings."[80]

Let us consider how this would work in the case of the Kansas pastor and Romans. There will be divergences between how the original audience engaged with the text they read and how the later Christian community accesses the text subsequently, these differences being a product of the variables that this section has referenced repeatedly – history, geography, and language. Modern Christian readers in western Kansas will surely not connect as deeply and immediately with what Paul says to the Romans about relationships between Jews and Gentiles as the Roman readers themselves did,

[79] In addition, theological reading necessitates forming greater analogies in cases where contemporary communities of faith have failed to conform themselves to models they encounter in Scripture.

[80] Hays, *The Moral Vision of the New Testament*, 299.

though surely even the aspects of Paul's message that initially seem foreign to Midwestern Americans can stir them to think about their status as branches that have been grafted into the olive tree (Rom. 11:24), and what this should say to them about any proclivities toward anti-Semitism that may exist in their community. Despite real variations, the contemporary reading will, at the same time, stand in continuity with the first-century reading because of the location of both sets of readers in the economy of salvation, in which God is redeeming the world through Christ. Just as it was pride and self-satisfaction that made it hard for Jews and Gentiles in ancient Rome to welcome one another (Rom. 15:7), so also that same tendency toward arrogant complacency exists in the hearts of Christians who read the text now.[81] And they are likewise challenged by Paul's letter to repent and accept the divine grace that their transformation requires, for the human condition to which the text speaks is the same when this condition is seen in the light of faith. Modern readers in Kansas will, no doubt, grasp the text's challenge to them via their own interpretive categories, which means that even the aspects of its message that are pertinent to them will be understood in a manner that is distinctively their own. Overall, what makes the notion of analogy applicable here is that, for all of the differences in readers, and even in the texts (by virtue of the later version being included in the canon), the communicative engagements have the same function and operate in parallel with one another: they both work to push readers forward toward the goal of their salvation.

Analogies necessarily involve similarities and differences, but the relative balance between continuity and discontinuity in readings depends on two sets of factors. First, it is a function of the particular text in question and just how similar the present reader's situation is to that of the original readers. Texts such as Romans (understood in the way Hays reads it) make the problem of alterity clear because of

[81] I owe this point to Bryan, *Listening to the Bible*, 93.

the vast differences between the social contexts of first-century Rome and western Kansas in the twentieth and twenty-first centuries.

Second, there is also a more general factor that governs all interpretations, even of texts where the balance appears initially to tilt heavily toward the side of difference between contexts when the two are compared according to their details. This issue has already been mentioned implicitly, but it is worth spelling it out more clearly. What secures the fundamental similarity between readers is not a likeness of human nature when that is construed in solely immanent or mundane terms (focusing exclusively on those qualities frustrates identification because they spell out the differences between individuals), nor is it a faith held in common (it is not what people think but what is true of them that is important here), but rather their location within one and the same saving economy. Only if this economy is genuinely unified by the action of the triune God, who is gathering a people to himself, does the sort of similarity exist in light of which it makes good sense to read with an expectation of analogies that contain strong links. If it is problematic to think of human beings situating themselves inside the world of the Bible, that means there is only a relatively weak unity between past and present readers.[82] On a weak view of unity, estimates regarding continuity/discontinuity will tend to put less stress on continuity, and the more mundane aspects that determine identity will begin to loom larger as a result, thus making the reading less receptive to precisely the degree that discontinuity is stressed. That reading is

[82] For questions about conceiving of Scripture as a unified world, see Rowan Williams, "The Judgment of the World," in *On Christian Theology* (Oxford: Blackwell, 2000), 29–30, and for an argument that the unity of the Bible is one that is external to the text itself, being located in the set of responses to it, see Rowan Williams, "The Unity of the Bible and the Unity of the Church," *Internationale Kirchliche Zeitschrift* 91 (2001): 5–21. On the operation of analogies in light of those commitments, see Williams, "The Discipline of Scripture," 51–53, 56–59. My own reading and critique of Williams can be found in Sarisky, *Scriptural Interpretation*, 159–83. There is an even stronger emphasis on the difference in all analogies within Tracy, *The Analogical Imagination*, 446–55.

receptive necessitates a significant degree of continuity, which is secured by the sense that the economy is a unified whole, albeit one that unfolds over the course of time. Worries about premature closure need not forestall conceiving of the text as projecting a relatively unified world, which includes a variety of readers, for the text does not present itself as closed in a rigid way, or as offering a narrative whose conclusion is so clearly specified that it remains in no way elusive.[83]

It needs to be acknowledged that the similarity of readers, and the consequent possibility for identification, is definitely more complex with respect to the Old Testament than it is for the New. Christians rightly read Old Testament texts through the lens provided by the revelation of Jesus Christ, as this is conveyed by the New Testament. The canon of Christian Scripture is not a single unit without any internal differentiation. That Jesus Christ is the incarnation of God and has acted for the salvation of the world means that the signifying function of all biblical texts is transformed, so that it relates in some way to him and his work on the part of humanity. This fact – that Christians read the Old Testament in light of Christ – does not mean that they cannot identify with those who first received the texts that came to be the Old Testament. They *can* identify with them to the extent that they are responding to the same God, the one who would eventually become incarnate in the person of Jesus Christ. Yet this identification is not straightforward, precisely because of the hermeneutical significance that the life, death, and resurrection of Jesus have for Christian communities. While they can identify with those who first responded to the God of Israel, what they hear thereby is taken into a new perspective and transformed as it comes in relation to Christ. What Christians hear as they identify with these early

[83] See Richard Bauckham's account of Scripture as a "nonmodern metanarrative": "Reading Scripture as a Coherent Story," in *The Art of Reading Scripture*, ed. Ellen F. Davis and Richard B. Hays (Grand Rapids: Eerdmans, 2003), 47–53.

readers becomes, of necessity, a rich store of figures foreshadowing Christ and allowing for an enriched understanding of the significance of his person and work.

For theological reading, then, historical distance is neither nothing (à la Reno) nor everything (as those committed to disengaged reason would claim), but something – though not something that disables receptive reading. Readers should perform a level of historical investigation on the biblical text to clarify matters that would remain obscure were this research not done at all. Such historical study will inevitably reveal the alterity of the text by showing the intimate connection between it and the circumstances of its original composition and reception. However, the text's alterity, so understood, should not prevent today's readers from engaging with its substance; Scripture is not ultimately prevented from speaking to modern readers and addressing them. The text's alterity is superseded in an appropriative reading when today's readers identify themselves with the original readers and interpret the text as speaking to them in a way that is analogically related to its communicative operation in its initial setting. Such is the unitive force of contemporary interpreters inhabiting the same economy of salvation as the original readers: they can identify with them strongly enough to feel themselves addressed and gripped by the message that the text speaks forth to them (note, again, the caveat regarding the Old Testament). Thereby, the text functions as a genuine word for today.[84] Readers now can indeed identify strongly enough with past readers so as to experience the text's address directly, not just indirectly and secondarily, as if the text were really intended for others instead of them. They are at one with the original readers in

[84] That this is the case does not mean that the actual readings sponsored by this view would, in effect, be identical with those that Reno would favor. Readings produced according to the view articulated here would be different. They would have greater texture than those that pass right by the stage of historical inquiry because of the association with the original context that is established by the analogical structure.

a real way. Historical distance, in this form, having been relativized by the application of theological categories, does not block receptive reading. Readers today can indeed listen to the text.

## An Active Reader?

This chapter opened by arguing that it is necessary to develop a theological anthropology of the reader within an account of theological interpretation, and the most fundamental result of creating space for this locus has been to underscore that the reader ought to be essentially or basically receptive to the way in which the text serves as a pointer to God. (As I pointed out above, even a reader whose overriding orientation toward the text is one of receptivity will be active in a real way: Chapter 6 has more to say about the sense in which receptivity requires a certain sort of activity.[85]) Because of the aspect of the reader that this chapter has highlighted (i.e., the capacity to express faith in that to which the text points), its treatment of the reader has roughly the opposite effect that an emphasis on readers and interpretive communities often has within much of the literature on hermeneutics. On the basis of the view that has been spelled out above, it is now possible to venture some judgments about a sampling of contemporary material in which the

[85] See especially the section on *mediatio*. The ultimate doctrinal ground according to which passivity and activity do not form a contradiction is creation *ex nihilo*. On the one hand, the reader is passive before the divine self-disclosure the text mediates: there is a basic obligation to receive it. On the other hand, interpreters undertake readerly operations on the text to engage with its material content and come to understand it. These two ideas fit together because there is a fundamentally noncompetitive relationship between divine and human activity: God is not a single, discrete item in the universe in the way that a human agent is; he is, rather, that upon which each finite reality is contingent. The two do not clash with one another because they exist on different levels. Cf. Brad East, "The Hermeneutics of Theological Interpretation: Holy Scripture, Biblical Scholarship and Historical Criticism," *International Journal of Systematic Theology* 19 (2017): 44.

upshot of discussing the reader is to play up the reader's activity in relation to the text of Scripture.

For instance, in her article "Scripture as Popular Text," Kathryn Tanner argues for conceptualizing the Bible not as a piece of high literary art, though it is sometimes understood this way, but as a work which is universally accessible: "it seems able to speak to everyone, whatever their circumstances."[86] Why does the Bible speak to all people, rather than only a select few? It addresses all readers neither because its message floats above any particular set of circumstances (the text is historically conditioned)[87] nor because the message is able to adapt itself for every audience (this falsely assumes that texts are unified wholes, even as the unified meaning is not static)[88] but because of the many lacunae within the text that need filling.[89] It falls to the reader to plug these gaps, and this task gives readers a quite active role in interpretation. Tanner explains what is lacking in the Bible itself with a simile: "[The Bible's] refusal of detailed description is like that found in television situation comedies where no narrator voice-over provides any comprehensive overview and viewers are left to infer a depth of motivation and feeling from nothing more than a character's raised eye-brows, or tone of voice; fan gossip like biblical commentary fills in what is missing."[90] Because interpreters must attend to such gaps and aporiae, biblical texts "depend in a strong sense on their readers for any production of a definite sense."[91] As Tanner sees it, absent such readerly activity, the texts themselves do not make any specific claims. Yet it is necessary to point out that while readers may have a

[86] Kathryn Tanner, "Scripture as Popular Text," *Modern Theology* 14 (1998): 291. In just this connection, she takes note of Augustine, who noticed the Bible's "low" style when he first attempted to read it.

[87] Ibid., 280–83.

[88] Ibid., 284–86.

[89] Ibid., 291–92.

[90] Ibid., 291.

[91] Ibid., 293.

fair amount of work to do in order to understand the Bible, that is not incompatible with the text saying something to them, and for this reason exercising a formative influence on them. Having to wrestle with a hard text fits with reading it receptively so long as all of the textual signifiers can be related to its *res*, which is not a collaborative creation of readers and the text, but rather that about which readers learn, even in the midst of coming to understand a challenging passage.

Consider another example. In Mary McClintock Fulkerson's essay on the priority of interpretive communities, a key early move is to repudiate what she terms "textual formalism": "the notion that meaning is a feature of abstract relations in language apart from use."[92] Against anything smacking of formalism, she aims to radicalize the idea that interpretation is communally situated, doing so by asserting that the text has no reality of its own apart from the application of reading strategies to it.[93] Meaning cannot possibly be a property of the text apart from use if no such text really exists. Inevitably, therefore, ecclesiology becomes the center of gravity for her treatment of biblical interpretation, for it is the interpretive conventions of the ecclesial community that give rise to whatever meaning the text is taken to possess. In making her case, McClintock Fulkerson makes some use of recent literary theory, including the work of the critic Stanley Fish, but she ultimately grounds her position theologically, noting that a "non-idolatrous posture toward worldly entities such as knowledge"[94] requires acknowledging that all claims to understand the text are contingent on the resources of the community making those claims. In one way, McClintock Fulkerson's view fits well with the perspective this chapter has advanced in

92 Mary McClintock Fulkerson, "'Is There a (Non-Sexist) Bible in This Church?' A Feminist Case for the Priority of Interpretive Communities," *Modern Theology* 14 (1998): 227.

93 Ibid., 226.

94 Ibid., 232.

that both operate at some distance from any notion of disengaged rationality, seeing all hermeneutical reflection as tied up with tradition-specific theological considerations. At the same time, because she goes to the point of "'disappear[ing]' the interpreter-text distinction into interpretive communities,"[95] communities of interpreters are thrown back on their own resources as the basis on which to navigate the Christian life, since the text has nothing to say to them apart from their activity in co-constituting its sense. This evinces a species of self-trust that is fundamentally at odds with faith's orientation to what is *extra nos*. The anthropology this chapter has offered is different in that it assumes an orientation to without, to something that transcends the community of interpreting subjects.

As noted above, McClintock Fulkerson's appeal to the literary theory of Stanley Fish is part of the way she articulates her position. While some of his main contentions shine through in her work, it is worth commenting specifically on his viewpoint and some closely related theories about readers. Fish's reader-response theory accentuates the response of readers to written texts, as opposed to any stable internal features texts might have which would determine how they should be understood.[96] That is, for Fish, readers must take an active

[95] Ibid., 227.

[96] See, for example, Stanley E. Fish, *Is There a Text in This Class? The Authority of Interpretive Communities* (Cambridge, MA: Harvard University Press, 1980). For an outline of what it would look like to apply reader-response criticism to the Bible, see The Bible and Culture Collective, *The Postmodern Bible* (New Haven: Yale University Press, 1995), 20–69. An application to a Gospel text is Robert M. Fowler, *Let the Reader Understand: Reader-Response Criticism and the Gospel of Mark* (Minneapolis: Fortress, 1991). For a critique of reader-oriented approaches and strong counterproposals from within literary studies, see E. D. Hirsch, *Validity in Interpretation* (New Haven: Yale University Press, 1967); William K. Wimsatt and Monroe C. Beardsley, "The Affective Fallacy," in *The Verbal Icon: Studies in the Meaning of Poetry*, ed. William K. Wimsatt (Lexington: University of Kentucky Press, 1954), 21–40. For a theological critique, see Kevin J. Vanhoozer, *Is There a Meaning in This Text? The Bible, the Reader, and the Morality of Literary Knowledge* (Grand Rapids: Zondervan, 1998).

role in reading and render interpretive judgments in the face of textual indeterminacy. He makes the broad point that the reading strategies interpreters employ are a function of their community affiliation: it is this claim that McClintock Fulkerson particularizes and applies to the church as the primary interpretive community engaging the Bible. Reading strategies *constitute*, rather than uncover or find, the text's sense, which has no definite existence apart from readerly activity. Thus, reading is barely distinguishable from writing: the interpreter quite literally makes sense of the text.

The position set out in this chapter is *toto caelo* different from reader-response theory, though in their own ways both views foreground the place of the reader. Beyond this vague level of resemblance, there are crucial differences. First, while Fish stresses the reader's contribution to the practice of interpretation in order to unsettle a view of the text as having a definite communicative intention, my position draws attention to the reader for a different reason: because the reader is granted the capacity to respond in faith to divine self-disclosure, interpreters should be essentially receptive to the text's work in this regard. Second, an additional contrast relates to the stances toward theology within these two outlooks. Some forms of literary criticism that expand the role of the reader do so with the intent of undermining textual authority, especially any theological authority that a sacred text might bear. Roland Barthes states this agenda forthrightly: "In precisely this way literature . . ., by refusing to assign a 'secret,' an ultimate meaning, to the text (and to the world as text), liberates what may be called an anti-theological activity, an activity that is truly revolutionary since to refuse to fix meaning is, in the end, to refuse God."[97] My highlighting of the reader works toward the opposite

[97] Roland Barthes, "Death of the Author," in *Image, Music, Text*, ed. Stephen Heath, Fontana Communications Series (London: Fontana, 1977), 147. See also the distinction between "readerly" and "writerly" texts in Roland Barthes, *S/Z* (Oxford: Basil Blackwell, 1975), 4–6.

end: it does not get rid of God, but displays the result for an account of theological reading of the reader interpreting with the eyes of faith. This work seeks to show how all of the elements that factor into reading must be seen from a theological point of view, and thus insists on speaking more about the reader, lest the theological aspect of the reader's identity slip from view.

By surveying a few examples of portrayals of the reader as much more active than this chapter suggests ought to be the case, this section has aimed to accomplish two things. More modestly, the literature canvassed above draws a contrast between the proposal of this chapter – that the reader be basically receptive to the biblical text – and the relative stress within the wider discussion on the activity of the reader, thus adding a bit more texture to the constructive view being advanced. More importantly, by reviewing these other positions in theological hermeneutics and literary theory, this section has reinforced one of the major contentions of the book as a whole. Tanner, McClintock Fulkerson, and Fish all assume a more active reader, thereby showing in their own way that whatever view of the reader is operative in an account of interpretation shapes it fundamentally. For them, the reader is competent and obligated to redress lacunae in the text, and this becomes one of the fundamental tasks of reading, a basic condition for making sense of the text. This section thus aims to complement the argument at the beginning of this chapter on the reader as a necessary locus within the account of theological reading. However the reader is seen, the working conception of the reader makes a major difference to an overall view of interpretation.

## Conclusion

This chapter took as its point of departure that the contemporary discussion of theological exegesis puts too much stress on what is distinctive about the text and, correlatively, too little on the reader, both of which are important. The assumption behind elaborating a theological account of the reading subject is that a more satisfactory understanding of theological reading should bring a notion of the reader into sharper focus, rather than leaving claims about interpreters implicit and scattered amidst discussion of other topics, by combining the most important points together. A theological view of the reader makes operative within the practice of reading the capacity of the reading subject to express faith in the *res* of whom the text speaks. In addition, readers interpret the text in a way that is conditioned by their location in a range of social contexts, not the least important of which is the ecclesial tradition, immersion in which inculcates and further develops skills of reading receptively. The stress on receptivity is incompatible with absolutizing historical distance, but a balanced view of distance, one that is compatible with reading for the sake of appropriating its content, emerges from applying to the reader categories that are both theological, on the one hand, and historical as well as geographical on the other. That the reader should take a receptive stance toward the text is the most fundamental change that results from viewing the interpreter theologically, which is to say as one who has capacities that are part of a theological anthropology. This chapter has thus put in place the first element of the positive view of theological reading. Chapter 5 develops the second point.

# 5 | The Bible and Theological Semiotics

The second element of a constructive account of theological reading is a theological view of the biblical text, for the text is the other of the two realities necessarily involved in reading. This chapter follows Augustine in using the category of *signs* as a way to think about the biblical text. It also draws on figures from our own context who employ the notion to think theologically about the Bible and its interpretation.[1] As became clear in Chapter 1, construing the text of Scripture in semiotic terms means treating it as an icon, so to speak, an object that directs attention away from itself and to something else; as a set of signs, the Bible draws the focus of the interpreting subject in order to redirect the subject's gaze to something more significant than the text. An important feature that makes the present treatment of the Bible as a collection of signs distinctive, over against the precedent found in Augustine, is that it takes up and wrestles with the challenge of modern historical consciousness. In this connection, the key issue is how knowledge of the text's history factors into the text's work as a sign pointing to a transcendent *res*. The chapter seeks to frame a notion of signs such that it takes more seriously than do some in the discussion of

[1] See Marion, *God without Being*, 146–49; Thomas F. Torrance, *Divine Meaning: Studies in Patristic Hermeneutics* (Edinburgh: T. & T. Clark, 1995), 235; Karl Barth, *Church Dogmatics I.2: The Doctrine of the Word of God, § 19–21*, Study ed. (London: T. & T. Clark, 2010), 500, 513, 581, 583, 587. It is true that sign is not Barth's lead concept – witness is more important for him – but he still does make significant use of the former category. Further on signs, see also Daley, "'In Many and Various Ways,'" 611–13; Webster, "The Domain of the Word," 10.

theological reading biblical texts' circumstances of origin in various concrete past historical situations.

The concept of sign has an advantage over another way to relate the text, with its contingent origin, to its ultimate subject matter. Thinking of the text as *testimony* – an alternative category that boasts strong roots in the Christian tradition – also relates text and subject matter without equating the two. It is a useful notion in that it ties the text to God while keeping the interpreted object and the subject of which it speaks distinct from one another. This chapter leavens its proposal with insights from this concept. However, testimony has the disadvantage that it can suggest, depending on precisely how it is deployed, that there is something of an arbitrary relationship between the creaturely text and the God to whom it testifies. This is especially so when the text's inherent lack of fitness to act in this capacity is stressed quite strongly.[2] In addition, there can also be within the notion of testimony the suggestion that divine use of the text as such is occasional, rather than an enduring state that makes the text what it is, "an act from above which arrests and overwhelms the creaturely reality, employs it, and then puts it to one side."[3] While these problems may not necessarily be inherent in testimony as a term, it can easily be unpacked in such a way as to trigger them, and some theologians have explicated it without being able to avoid them entirely. Yet this project bases itself in an ontology of Scripture, and this means that the lead category for depicting the text needs to portray what the text as such is, on an ongoing basis, without of course in the process denying that it is what it is as a function of its contingency on God. For this reason, sign is to be preferred as the primary way of construing Scripture within this project.

It should be clear that to refer to the Bible as a set of signs is not to make a claim about what the Bible does as opposed to what it is.

[2] Webster, *Holy Scripture*, 23–24.

[3] Ibid., 26.

It is to say that the text is a work which has the quality of pointing its readers to the triune God. Of course, terms such as sign do speak to what the text does: it signifies something to its readers. That the term immediately suggests how the text functions recommends it for this project, since it makes unavoidable and obvious connections with interpretation. It serves the overall purpose of this book's constructive proposal, which is to claim that the dynamics of interpretation are a function of commitments regarding the nature of the text and the reader taken in tandem (by itself, of course, the notion of sign focuses only on the first item in this pair). Though this depiction of the text has clear implications for how it is read, the view of the text developed in this chapter is worth differentiating from a primarily functional view of the text. On a functional view, to say "that a text is a part of either scripture or a sacred canon is not to ascribe a property to the text: in neither case is it to make an informative remark about the character of the text itself. It is rather to say something about the way the text functions in the religious community; it is to say something about the way the text is used, about what is *done with* the text."[4] A functional account of the Bible thus characterizes the operation of the Bible *rather than* its nature, or it at least marginalizes the issue of ontology, pushing it into the background and out of sight. The present chapter centers on a view of the text itself that has entailments for how readers engage with it: Scripture can be read in this way *by virtue of* its nature.[5] Whereas a functional view of the text leaves questions about the nature of the text to the side, concentrating instead on

[4] Kathryn Tanner, "Theology and the Plain Sense," in *Scriptural Authority and Narrative Interpretation*, ed. Garrett Green (Philadelphia: Fortress, 1987), 62. Tanner is describing the view of David Kelsey, on which she herself is building.

[5] Undergirding this view of the text as a collection of signs is the text's status as the word of God: it signifies as such. I make the term *sign* central to this chapter because the links between it and issues of interpretation are more immediate than for *word of God*. However, for an argument that the text's status as divine discourse does have implication for hermeneutics, see Wolterstorff, *Divine Discourse*, 202–22.

how the text operates in an interpretive community, this ontology of the Bible depicts function as a product of nature. The text does what it does because it is what it is.

## Boundary Conditions for a View of Scripture

For the purpose of this project, a successful view of Scripture must fittingly relate two things: the written form of the biblical text and the subject matter it addresses. Frank Kermode introduces a helpful distinction when he says, "We are so habituated to the myth of transparency that we continue . . . to ignore *what is written* in favor of *what it is written about*."[6] Kermode makes this observation in order to overturn what he takes to be the customary prioritization of subject matter. He aims to reverse this polarity, prioritizing *what is written* to the neglect of *what it is written about*, and associating this interpretive stance with Spinoza.[7] It would be more accurate to say, not that Spinoza neglects what the Bible is about, but that he has a different assessment of what its central theme is (that is, ethics) than either the Jewish or the Christian traditions do. It is true, however, as Chapter 3 of this book concluded, that for Spinoza the Bible is more a book to look at and analyze than one to look through and think with, for its ethical content is discoverable by unaided reflection: reading the text is not ultimately necessary to learn what it has to teach. Though Spinoza does not exactly ignore one of the poles of the interpretive dialectic, the best way to relate them is as follows: *what is written* is a sign of *what it is written about*. The one is a means of access to the other. Even where the text's subject matter seems expressible in absolutely no other way than in the precise manner that the literary form actually conveys it,

[6] Frank Kermode, *The Genesis of Secrecy: On the Interpretation of Narrative* (Cambridge, MA: Harvard University Press, 1979), 118–19.

[7] Ibid., 119.

so tight is the relationship between form and content, the semiotic point still obtains, for what is textually mediated is the subject matter. The text serves its subject matter and ought to be read in light of it.[8] When that does not happen, the reader is enjoying the biblical text in the sense of which Augustine rightly disapproves: it is not that readers should not like interpreting the Bible, but because it is a sign, they should access its subject matter through it.

The present section explores a boundary condition for a theological view of the Bible by examining a key criterion for such a view to succeed. For a theological ontology of Scripture to work, it must predicate something theological of the Bible, and crucially it must apply that predicate to the actual text of Scripture, in its full determinacy. The texts that constitute the Christian Bible originate in a range of ancient historical contexts. As such, the texts, even as they are presently read, have historical features or marks of their circumstances of origin. For instance, the nuances in meaning for many words found in the Bible will not be apparent without an understanding of the semantic force of those words in their historical context. To apply the category of sign to the biblical text is to say that a text *with these qualities* bespeaks a certain theological subject matter. More strongly, the historical features condition how what is written communicates what it is written about. These qualities affect the way in which the text says what it says, and readers cannot ignore or downplay the relevance of these features without blurring out aspects of what the Bible really is.

To fail to honor the way the text's constitutive historical features factor into it having a certain theological meaning is dualistic. The essence of dualism is that it creates a disjunction between history and theology: it insists that readers engage with the text as *either*

[8] In this connection, see Francis Watson's companionable claim that "theological interpretation must be oriented towards the extratextual truth mediated through the biblical texts": *Text and Truth: Redefining Biblical Theology* (Edinburgh: T. & T. Clark, 1997), 12.

one *or* the other, rather than as a text which has within it signs of its origin which themselves point toward God.[9] The reader should rather give heed to the "basic pattern of meaning that is perceived when the interpreter not only looks at the written words but looks through them at the objective center of reference."[10] A construal of the Bible does not qualify as dualistic merely by saying that a historical description of the text is one valid way of depicting it. History is indeed one factor that goes into giving an account of the text, but it is not the only one. A reading is dualistic either if it excludes historical considerations entirely in its search for theological meaning, or if it is governed by the assumption that attending to a text's historical features is the only valid way of engaging with the text, since these features do not themselves open up a window onto transcendence. In a world of highly specialized scholarship, some readers will focus more on history, others more on theology. However, it is an indication of dualism if a historical focus and a theological focus come to be seen as in an inherent tension, such that the two paths diverge from one another, and they in principle cannot be integrated.

As has been suggested, there are two ways to be dualistic. Call the first tendency ahistorical dualism. This means failing to insist that the text's historical features are part of the way it serves as a set of signs, and thus considering knowledge of these aspects unnecessary for a theological engagement. This pattern manifests itself in certain contemporary works of theological interpretation and more widely. For instance, Katherine Sonderegger says, speaking with reference to canonical criticism:

> To see in the book of Numbers a "priestly redaction," a sacerdotal ordering that preserves the people of Israel from defilement by the

[9] These reflections on dualism are inspired by Torrance, *The Christian Doctrine of God*, 35–37.

[10] Torrance, *Divine Meaning*, 235.

> profane, is to describe, however vividly, an archeological site, a past literary sediment. Just this act, however devout – and there can be no doubt that Childs offered his work with deep piety and devotion! – can only deliver a living tradition into the storehouse of the past, where a book sits upon a shelf, open to the gaze of any eye that falls upon it. But theology breathes another air.[11]

Yet seeing that this part of the Pentateuch is funded by a priestly source simply does not, in and of itself, relegate the text to the past. Far better is saying that, qua text with a particular past history, which may be known via understanding its various sources, this biblical text continues to speak now.[12] What often drives ahistorical dualism is overcorrecting in response to the likes of Spinoza and his naturalistic approach to the Bible. That Spinoza secures the exclusive legitimacy of historical context by means of naturalism does not, however, mean that later efforts to read the text theologically ought to deny the reality or importance of the text's contingent history. Instead, Erasmus is right to say, "It happens that not a little light is thrown on the understanding of the sense of Scripture if we weigh up not only what is said, but also by whom it is said, to whom it is said, in what words it is said, at what time, and on what occasion; what proceeds, and what follows."[13] The text speaks beyond its original milieu, and indeed it presents a theological message to later readers, but the way in which it does so relates intimately to how these questions receive answers.

[11] Katherine Sonderegger, *Systematic Theology*, Vol. 1: The Doctrine of God (Minneapolis: Fortress, 2015), 511.

[12] Sonderegger's position is not entirely without any nuance or subtlety. Giving a measure of balance to her quote above, she says, "The Eternal seizes the past and its texts, and brings them out of their graves" (ibid., 512). Yet this comment serves as something of a qualification to the main thrust of her presentation, the drift of which falls clearly on the side of minimizing the import of historical background for theological reading.

[13] Quoted in Barton, *The Nature of Biblical Criticism*, 128.

The alternative form of dualism is a product of going to the opposite extreme, and focusing exclusively on the text's mundane qualities, so as to give minimal attention to how they point beyond themselves toward the triune God. Call this a dualism of the immanent frame. It could be considered a form of protest against this form of dualism when Karl Barth complains that his theological education had not prepared him to preach on the text's subject matter: "I myself know what it means year in year out to mount the steps of the pulpit, conscious of the responsibility to understand and to interpret, and longing to fulfil it; and yet, utterly incapable, because at the University I had never been brought beyond that well-known 'Awe in the presence of History.'"[14] Interest in history can take the form of seeking to reconstruct the world behind the text, the sequence of events of which the Bible speaks. Or it can amount to using historical background knowledge to ascertain what the text meant as a past act of communication, rather than as a text that speaks into the present. However, when this form of reading is the *only* mode that is considered legitimate, rather than a contribution to a full range of forms of engagement, this approach is arrested by the phenomenal level of Scripture, asking what sense it appeared to have to people in the past but not now. If it is considered wrong in principle to press through that level to find the Word in the words, or the Word as it relates to a present audience, then a dualism of the immanent frame is operative.

The purpose of the two subsections below is *not* to provide a survey of views on the Bible and its historical background which is comprehensive in scope, even for the recent discussion. There are works that offer something approaching that, but this is not one of them.[15] As was indicated in this chapter's introduction, the aim of this chapter is to outline a constructive view of the biblical text as a set of signs. The subsections that follow serve that overall goal; they

[14] Karl Barth, *The Epistle to the Romans* (Oxford: Oxford University Press, 1968), 9.

[15] Klink and Lockett, *Understanding Biblical Theology*.

consider examples of each mode of dualism precisely and only for the sake of illustrating key problems that can arise in framing a view of the Bible. Each subsection focuses on one major figure, and there are a few additional references in the notes. These parts of this chapter demonstrate the importance of the issues that shape how the constructive position is framed, showing how the view of Scripture this project requires must avoid both versions of dualism. That is, boundary conditions for an understanding of the text as a collection of signs emerge from considering the two views that follow. The telos of the chapter is the section on signs, and there is interaction there with mediating views on which I build. The preceding material is included only for the sake of setting up the constructive content.[16] There already exist some significant works with an explicitly anti-dualistic thrust that insightfully address how biblical interpretation might extricate itself from this problem.[17] Yet in none of these valuable works does one find an effort to articulate a view of Scripture in a nondualistic fashion as part of an extended

[16] Cf. Kathryn Tanner, who briefly expounds some non-Christian views of the world for the sake of elucidating her own doctrine of creation, cautioning her readers to have appropriate expectations given what her declared purpose actually is: "Since my description of Hellenistic cosmologies is a means for elucidating the rule-governed character of Christian discourse, the primary concern here is not for the integrity of non-Christian ways of speaking. The reader should expect such descriptions to have only the general sort of schematic accuracy sufficient to make points about Christian discourse." See her *God and Creation in Christian Theology*, 39.

[17] For an excellent work considering a wide range of doctrines that should be involved in this repair, see Murray Rae, *History and Hermeneutics* (London: T. & T. Clark, 2005). In addition, a valuable monograph seeking to reestablish a participatory-sacramental view of reality after the breakdown of this sensibility in the late medieval period is Matthew Levering, *Participatory Biblical Exegesis: A Theology of Biblical Interpretation*, Reading the Scriptures (Notre Dame: University of Notre Dame Press, 2008). Many of the essays within a recent collection wrestle with the interrelationship between theology and history and are rightly loath to dismiss the importance of either side: Craig G. Bartholomew et al., eds., *"Behind" the Text: History and Biblical Interpretation*, Scripture and Hermeneutics Series (Grand Rapids: Zondervan, 2003).

exposition of the nature of theological interpretation of the Bible. That is the precise intention here.

### *Ahistorical Dualism*

The way some theological commentary series are framed risks establishing an ahistorically dualistic view of the Bible. This is especially true for the Brazos Theological Commentary on the Bible, the series preface for which establishes a more polemical stance toward historical criticism than the statements of purpose from any of the other theological commentary series. Within the Brazos series, postbiblical doctrinal language, and especially the trinitarian theological framework set out in the Nicene Creed, exercises a broad hermeneutical utility. According to the general editor's charter in the series preface, "This series of biblical commentaries was born out of the conviction that *dogma clarifies rather than obscures.* The Brazos Theological Commentary on the Bible advances on the assumption that the Nicene tradition . . . provides the proper basis for the interpretation of the Bible as Christian Scripture."[18] Individual commentators contributing to the series are allowed to work out for themselves exactly how doctrine will function in their commentary. However, in order to establish a doctrinally shaped reading of the text, the series preface distances itself from historical criticism.[19] If commentators are to fulfill the

[18] R. R. Reno, "Series Preface," in *Acts*, by Jaroslav Pelikan, Brazos Theological Commentary on the Bible (Grand Rapids: Brazos, 2005), xiii–xiv. Emphasis added. For an expanded version of Reno's account of theological exegesis, see Reno, "Biblical Theology and Theological Exegesis," 385–408.

[19] Reno's statement connects with a longer history of debate over the merits of historical criticism from the point of view of Christian theology. This discussion exists even in German-speaking contexts, where the prestige of historical methods runs quite high. See the radical critique by Gerhard Maier, *Das Ende der historisch-kritischen Methode*, 2nd ed., Abcteam 901: Glauben und Denken (Wuppertal: R. Brockhaus, 1975); a more moderate view is found in Peter Stuhlmacher, "Historische Kritik und theologische Schriftauslegung," in *Schriftauslegung auf dem Wege zur biblischen Theologie*

stated goal of the series, they will have to shake themselves free from an idea that is engrained in the historical-critical tradition, namely, that interpreters should limit themselves to expounding the categories that are present in the Bible itself (albeit in their own terms), and that categories arising later, in the postbiblical doctrinal tradition, cannot be assumed to be effective expository tools, as they often impose foreign forms of thought on the text.[20] Friedrich

(Gœttingen: Vandenhoeck & Ruprecht, 1975), 59–127. For Stuhlmacher's critique of Maier, see "Historische Kritik und theologische Schriftauslegung," 103–07.

A number of distinguished biblical scholars have warned that spurning historical criticism inevitably results in a specifically theological error, namely, a docetic view of the Bible, according to which it only *seems* to be historical, but is not treated as such: James Barr, "Historical Reading and the Theological Interpretation of Scripture," in *Bible and Interpretation: The Collected Essays of James Barr*, ed. John Barton (Oxford: Oxford University Press, 2013), 38; Stuhlmacher, "Historische Kritik Und Theologische Schriftauslegung," 101–02; Ernst Käsemann, "Thoughts on the Present Controversy About Scriptural Interpretation," in *New Testament Questions of Today*, The New Testament Library (London: SCM Press, 1969), 277. There is good analysis of Käsemann to be found in A. K. M. Adam, "Docetism, Käsemann, and Christology: Why Historical Criticism Can't Protect Christological Orthodoxy," *Scottish Journal of Theology* 49 (1996): 391–410. Adam perceptively observes the polyvalence of the term *docetism* in this discussion (and also astutely observes some of the limits of conventional historical research in relation to reaching theological conclusions). Making the following assessment involves a slight extension of the meaning of docetism beyond the precise sense it has for Käsemann, for whom it means harmonizing passages, viewing the Bible as inerrant, and so on. Yet it is genuinely problematic, in a broadly docetic way, to think that reading the Bible properly need not involve the process of interpreting the text in its context of historical origin. It is docetic simply to skip that step entirely, spurning it to rush straight to hearing the text speak more directly to oneself. Unfortunately, this point has been ignored by some today who are interested in theological reading.

On the other hand, Eleonore Stump argues that to claim divine revelation is accessible *only* via historical research is broadly deistic: "Revelation and Biblical Exegesis: Augustine, Aquinas, and Swinburne," in *Reason and the Christian Religion: Essays in Honour of Richard Swinburne*, ed. Richard Swinburne and Alan G. Padgett (Oxford: Clarendon Press, 1994), 166–70. There are, thus, opportunities to make theological mistakes either by neglecting history or by stressing it to the neglect of the point that the Bible continues to speak to readers beyond its circumstances of origin.

20 Reno, "Series Preface," xii.

Schleiermacher is an influential early witness to this general historical-critical principle:

> To the extent, therefore, that one wants to understand completely one should free oneself from the relation of what is to be explicated to one's own thoughts, because this relationship precisely does not at all have the intention of understanding, but instead of using as a means that which in the thought of the other relates to one's own thoughts. Everything must be understood and explicated via his [the original author's] thoughts.[21]

The move away from this sensibility in the charter to the Brazos series is not dualistic in and of itself, though the point is made with gusto and with few safeguards, so there a real risk attendant to it. Perhaps it springs from optimism that categories with a later genesis can, if properly handled, explicate the flow of biblical texts.[22]

What is more troubling is that a disjunction is instituted between, on the one hand, skill in lexical analysis and knowledge of the historical backdrop of the biblical documents and, on the other hand, an understanding of the Christian doctrinal tradition. The series editor writes that commentators were selected *not* "because of their historical and philological expertise," *but instead* "because of their knowledge and expertise in using the Christian doctrinal tradition."[23] It seems that the latter is valued at the expense of the former. If doctrine is to be integral to the project of commenting, it must serve in some way to explicate the words of the text, which cannot be divorced entirely from their historical background. The

[21] Schleiermacher, *Hermeneutics and Criticism*, 135. It is worth noting here that biblical studies is a diverse and pluralistic enterprise today. Practitioners with a special interest in reception history are typically less likely to see later categories as problematic. Something of the same applies to critics with a strong interest in the unity of the biblical canon.

[22] For Schleiermacher, one cannot assume continuity between text and tradition: *Hermeneutics and Criticism*, 139.

[23] Reno, "Series Preface," xiv.

overall stance sustained in the preface toward historical study seems to be that it is optional or perhaps dispensable – some commentators may employ it, others may not[24] – rather than necessary. It is certainly not sufficient for a theological reading. Those who do elect to employ it must do so with great care, without committing themselves to the presupposition that the postbiblical doctrinal tradition is discontinuous with Scripture itself. The difficulty the Brazos series has in articulating its distinctive mission is not simply that it fails in setting up a collegial relationship between systematic theologians and biblical scholars but that there are dualistic tendencies in its statement of purpose. The preface envisions the interpretive endeavor in problematic terms, though some volumes manage to negotiate this issue well, despite how the series preface frames matters.[25] The point here is not to produce a tally of how widespread this record of success actually is; rather, it is to examine

[24] Ibid., xvi.

[25] Though the series preface makes some dangerous claims, some of the commentators writing for Brazos navigate this issue with skill, producing commentaries that are *both* informed by historical research *and* guided by the doctrinal tradition. See, among others, Joseph L. Mangina, *Revelation*, Brazos Theological Commentary on the Bible (Grand Rapids: Brazos, 2010).

It is also fortunate that other theological commentary series, even ones in which it is theologians who serve as commentators, orient themselves differently toward historical study and discuss historical criticism in a more positive tone. The Belief series presents historical-critical reading as, in rough terms, necessary, but not sufficient, as the first step toward a theological reading that is useful for the church today, though not as constitutive of or identical with a theological exegesis that brings the church forward in the life of discipleship. See William C. Placher and Amy Plantinga Pauw, "Series Introduction," in *Mark*, by William C. Placher, Belief: A Theological Commentary (Louisville: Westminster John Knox, 2010), ix. Placher's own volume on Mark does fairly well on this count.

Another work that identifies itself as undertaking a theological reading, and that achieves some success in bringing together history and doctrine is Joseph Ratzinger, *Jesus of Nazareth: From the Baptism in the Jordan to the Transfiguration* (New York: Doubleday, 2007). However, there are still questions about how well Ratzinger deals with history in Richard B. Hays, "Benedict and the Biblical Jesus," *First Things* 175 (2007): 49–53.

a problematic tendency precisely for the sake of articulating a criterion for a nondualistic theological view of the biblical text.

A more detailed analysis of one particular commentary will be useful toward that end. One of the first volumes to be published in the Brazos series is disappointing in its failure to establish an intimate link between historical analysis and doctrine. That this difficulty is on clear display makes the volume especially instructive regarding the role of history in a theological reading of the Bible: this commentary can serve as a case study in the sort of integration that is the ideal, even though it does not achieve this goal itself – or precisely because it shows clearly what ought *not* be the case. The commentary in question is Stanley Hauerwas's *Matthew*. Despite this problem, the volume has many positive features: it has met with some commercial success; as is the case for many of Hauerwas's works, it is accessible, readable, and even gripping at times; and it rightly presents the life of Christian discipleship as one that puts serious demands on those who would follow Jesus Christ and be members of the community of his followers.

Hauerwas's commentary on the first canonical Gospel contains interpretation occurring at three different levels: explication of the sense that words and phrases in the text bear (exegesis in the narrow sense), theological reflection on the language of the text, and especially application of the text to contemporary concerns (exegesis in the broader sense would include all three of these levels). For the commentary to succeed as theological exegesis, these levels must be integrated with one another. The later stages should emerge organically from the first stage,[26] being based on it but not

[26] This is not to say that interpretation has a foundationalist character. For a useful warning against foundationalism as it affects interpretation, see William J. Abraham, *Canon and Criterion in Christian Theology: From the Fathers to Feminism* (Oxford: Oxford University Press, 1998), 137. Basing later stages on earlier ones is not a foundationalist move when theology is integrated within the earlier stages. For an explanation of this point in relation to my constructive position, see the section on *explicatio* in Chapter 6 of the present work.

reducible to it. It is precisely here where the commentary falls short. Of course, the later stages should also influence the earliest stage: there is a reciprocity of influence between them, or a non-viciously circular relationship among them, rather than a straightforwardly one-directional movement from the earlier to the later. What must not be the case, however, is that the later stages seem to have almost no link whatsoever to a basic explication of the text. They should not appear suddenly and without preparation, as if they are properly independent from anything prior, existing almost on their own. Yet this is what we find.

The overall goal of this commentary is to depict Jesus Christ as the divine Lord and to inscribe the community of his followers into the story that begins with and centers on him.[27] In the introduction to his commentary, Hauerwas explains the form that his work takes: "As the reader will discover, I believe Matthew wrote to make us disciples of Christ. I have tried to show the 'how' of that project in how I have written, that is, by retelling the story Matthew tells."[28] As Hauerwas narrates the story of Matthew, he is only very rarely in dialogue with historical-critical commentators. He repeatedly and forcefully makes the point that an understanding of who Jesus is requires the transformation of the human subject: coming to grips with the identity of Jesus requires divesting oneself of certain patterns of thought and action.[29] Hauerwas seems to fear that entering into a more sustained dialogue with historians would not simply be unhelpful; on his view, it would actually undermine the whole purpose of his work, for the picture of Jesus that emerges from historical-critical work depends on the acquisition and dispassionate interpretation of historical information, not on the moral transformation that his commentary presupposes and seeks

[27] Hauerwas, *Matthew*, 18.

[28] Ibid., 19.

[29] Ibid., 127–28, 247–49.

to effect in its readers.[30] For the sake of advancing a theological view of Jesus, with all its attendant demands, Hauerwas judges historical criticism to be an active impediment. For him, Matthew's Gospel is to be understood less against the backdrop of its history of origin than by means of the *circumstantia litterarum*, the way the words of the text run, that is, their forming a coherent literary whole, and how the ecclesial community applies reading strategies to the biblical text in order to make sense of it.[31]

Given this overall orientation, it is not surprising that readers of Hauerwas's *Matthew* find in it some doctrinal reflection, and a special concern with Jesus as well as the community that gathers around him. The doctrinal material in the commentary appears in two different forms: first, concise but unambiguous affirmations of a high Christology, together with more developed discussions of the sort of community that must exist in order to recognize and (what is the same on Hauerwas's account) follow Jesus as Lord. For instance, when commenting on Peter's confession of Jesus as the Christ in Matthew 16, Hauerwas concentrates on the sort of transformation of Peter's perspective that his discernment of Jesus' divine identity requires, and on how Peter serves as an icon for the moral formation that present-day members of the church must undergo.[32] Peter must come to see Jesus' status as messiah to include, and not to exempt him from, suffering – the same sort of suffering in which Peter and the Christian community after him must take part. Hauerwas's way of allowing the biblical text to absorb the world is to cast a vision of the lordship of Jesus that

[30] Stanley Hauerwas, *The Peaceable Kingdom: A Primer in Christian Ethics* (Notre Dame: University of Notre Dame Press, 1983), 72–74. In his introduction to the commentary, Hauerwas confesses that he has little interest in the world behind the text: *Matthew*, 20–21.

[31] Hauerwas, *Matthew*, 25.

[32] Ibid., 149–53.

vitiates the world's understanding of how status operates, and to call the ecclesial community to conform to the paradigm of Peter.[33]

However, the commentary usually passes quickly by historical questions over which the standard historical-critical commentaries pause, while the historical matters it does treat are handled in a desultory manner. Such historical matters include dealing with semantic questions, issues connected with historicity, and the analysis of genre. Consider how Hauerwas handles these matters in Matthew 16, referred to above, and more broadly in the commentary. Sustained lexical analysis is exceedingly rare. Joseph Mangina provides a modest defense of Hauerwas's handling of the very words of Matthew, noting that he sometimes exploits linguistic detail to good effect.[34] Yet, as Mangina also observes, such cases are truly the exceptions that prove the rule: individual words or phrases from Matthew are seldom singled out for close attention regarding their meaning. In addition, Hauerwas's symbolic construal of characters from the Gospel depends only very tenuously

[33] There is incisive analysis of Hauerwas's commentary in Nicholas M. Healy, *Hauerwas: A (Very) Critical Introduction*, Interventions (Grand Rapids: Eerdmans, 2014), 69–71. Healy concludes that Hauerwas's commentary is not a work of traditional theological interpretation because the operative understanding of doctrine is ecclesiocentric, not theocentric. That is to say, the doctrinal language in the commentary does not so much address who Jesus himself is as a way of understanding the triune God; rather, the focus is on how Jesus relates to human beings and shapes a distinctive community. I am sympathetic to reading Hauerwas as being reticent to say much about who God is, and as concentrating instead on what God does via the church. See Sarisky, *Scriptural Interpretation*, 197–200. It could be the case – though it is not my intent to argue the point here – that an ecclesiocentric notion of doctrine is more likely to lead to dualism than is a traditional view of doctrine, insofar as the former is built on a notion of the church as an *alternative* community, one with a different orientation than any other social body, including the historical-critical guild. For Hauerwas's response, see Stanley Hauerwas, "Postscript: By Way of a Response to Nicholas Healy's Book, Hauerwas: A (Very) Critical Introduction," in *The Work of Theology* (Grand Rapids: Eerdmans, 2015), 270. This reply is, however, not convincing because Hauerwas cites very little evidence in his own defense.

[34] Joseph L. Mangina, "Hidden from the Wise, Revealed to Infants: Stanley Hauerwas's Commentary on Matthew," *Pro Ecclesia* 17 (2008): 17–18.

on the historical particularity of the people being referred to in the text. For instance, at the outset of chapter 16, the Sadducees and the Pharisees together simply "represent the religious establishment."[35] Their representative function, the way in which they stand for the religious status quo, is not linked closely to a historically specific description of the Sadducees or Pharisees. What Hauerwas is doing is something like what Hans Frei calls figural reading, though figural interpretation is a more historically shaped procedure, in that it extends a detailed and historically rooted understanding of biblical characters, weaving that into a common narrative that extends into the present.[36] In Hauerwas's hands, how the Sadducees and Pharisees function as symbols of vice depends mainly just on them being empowered groups.[37] Finally, Hauerwas evinces no more care when inquiring into the genre of Matthew's Gospel. He sees the genre as apocalyptic, due to its subject matter being Jesus Christ.[38] Apocalyptic is a category that scholars more often apply to Mark's Gospel, which of course also focuses on the person of Jesus, as do all the Gospel accounts. How the specific literary shaping of Matthew, and not simply its subject matter, factors into the determination of the text's genre is a question Hauerwas fails to pursue.[39]

Overall, readers of the commentary certainly find some doctrine, and they can even locate a few historical judgments, albeit usually ones that are not rigorously argued and are often rightly challenged, but the general pattern is that doctrine is not tied tightly to a close,

[35] Hauerwas, *Matthew*, 146.

[36] Frei, *The Eclipse of Biblical Narrative*, 2–3, 28.

[37] Cf. the worry about spiritualization in Markus Bockmuehl, "Ruminative Overlay: Matthew's Hauerwas," *Pro Ecclesia* 17 (2008): 23.

[38] Hauerwas, *Matthew*, 24.

[39] There are many other ways in which Hauerwas's treatment of historical matters is inadequate. For a litany of additional issues, and a passionate overall indictment of Hauerwas's commentary, see Bockmuehl, "Ruminative Overlay: Matthew's Hauerwas," 20–28; Luke Timothy Johnson, "Matthew or Stanley? Pick One," *Pro Ecclesia* 17 (2008): 29–34.

historically informed reading of the text.[40] The strength of the commentary lies primarily in application,[41] and secondarily in

[40] Hauerwas so seldom deploys theological categories as a way to pursue a sequential reading of the text, and his application tends to float free on his exposition, that it becomes dubious even to call Hauerwas's *Matthew* a commentary. For a written text to qualify as a commentary, it must not only contain signs of the presence of another work by means of quotation, paraphrase, and summary, but attending to these signs must constitute the driving force of the work as a whole, giving the "metawork" (a work about another work) both its content and structure. See Griffiths, *Religious Reading*, 80–85. Hauerwas does give a loose reiteration of Matthew's Gospel, but his own theological preoccupations often obtrude into the text where they seem only tangentially related to its focal concern. He often selects and recombines units of the original in response to his own agenda. Whatever shape it takes, the commentary genre imposes a basic requirement that must be met, but is not actually met by Hauerwas: "A commentary must first be nothing more than an aid to understanding the language of the Bible, a simple tool that serves the text." See Karlfried Froehlich, "Bibelkommentare – Zur Krise einer Gattung," *Zietschrfit für Theologie und Kirche* 84 (1987): 491.

There is only a small body of literature on what qualifies a commentary as a commentary. For helpful insights, in addition to the literature just cited, see Bernhard W. Anderson, "The Problem and Promise of Commentary," *Interpretation* 36 (1982): 341–55; René Kieffer, "Wass heißt das, einen Text zu kommentieren?," *Biblische Zeitschrift* 20 (1976): 212–16; Andrew T. Lincoln, "From Writing to Reception: Reflections on Commentating on the Fourth Gospel," *Journal for the Study of the New Testament* 29 (2007): 353–72, together with the six responses to Lincoln's commentary published in the same issue, to which Lincoln issues a rejoinder; Eckhard J. Schnabel, "On Commentary Writing," in *On the Writing of New Testament Commentaries: Festschrift for Grant R. Osborne on the Occasion of His 70th Birthday*, ed. Stanley E. Porter and Eckhard J. Schnabel, Texts and Editions for New Testament Study (Leiden: Brill, 2013), 3–31.

[41] Bruce McCormack contends that Barth's commentary on the epistle to the Romans provides only the final stage of interpretation, application, not the preceding stages. See his "Historical Criticism and Dogmatic Interest in Karl Barth's Theological Exegesis of the New Testament," in *Biblical Hermeneutics in Historical Perspective*, ed. Mark S. Burrows and Paul Rorem (Grand Rapids: Eerdmans, 1991), 329. McCormack rightly points out that offering the early stages as well would only have increased the length of Barth's book and thereby risked making the entire presentation utterly unwieldly. This is a plausible reading of the commentary, and the practicalities of book production cannot be entirely dismissed. However, this exclusive focus on application is surely a major reason that there is still a running debate about whether Barth's *Romans* is really an exercise in the commentary genre at all. Offering more in the way

theological reflection; the most obvious weakness is in "simple explication of the text."[42] The essence of the overall difficulty is that application and theological reflection do not arise out of explication. The text *itself* is not seen as a pointer to the transcendent reality of God; it therefore does not operate as a sign or testimony to the divine.[43] What is necessary to shake free from dualism is not spurning historical analysis; rather, what is required is "a delicate balance between the commentator's philological and historical and critical awareness and his or her understanding of, and commitment to, the tradition of faith in which the text is

of exposition, or at least making a stronger in-principle statement about the importance of application emerging from exposition, even if this commentary does not major on that, would have gone some distance toward guarding against the specter of dualism.

[42] Mangina, "Hidden from the Wise, Revealed to Infants," 17.

[43] This is true, mutatis mutandis, of the conception of the biblical text in Martin's *Biblical Truths*. Throughout the book, he argues the persuasive point that a historical-critical reading of the Bible will not ultimately deliver an orthodox Christian theology. See, for instance, *Biblical Truths*, 29, 85, 169. Trying to force this set of reading strategies to deliver orthodoxy as a conclusion pressures interpreters to engage in tendentious readings, thereby making them bad historians. Yet he himself wants to hold on to theological orthodoxy. His solution is to refuse to allow historical criticism to serve as an arbiter of acceptable interpretation: "It will be my contention in this chapter [on Christ], however, that we need not become bad historians in order to be good theologians. Even if the New Testament authors were not familiar with the doctrine of the trinity as it became defined in the great councils and creeds, we may take the liberty of reading the New Testament *theologically* (rather than *historically*) as teaching trinitarian theology." See *Biblical Truths*, 172. While it is surely true that there is a caesura between standard historical-critical reading practices and orthodox theology, what Martin uses to close the gap is readerly creativity and interpretive agency, that is, input from the interpreting subject rather than a way of following out a line of argument that is present within the text. This risks conveying the impression that orthodoxy is something made rather than found, not something that is *in* the text in any strong sense. My tack in handling this set of issues is to reconceive the text as a sign directing the reader to God, all the while insisting that historical knowledge is important for reading the text, though not granting to status quo historical criticism a monopoly on possessing that knowledge.

recognized as part of God's saving work."[44] Thereby doctrine might clarify rather than obscure. Theological commentary requires not the rejection of historical analysis, but its integration with doctrinal perspectives.

### *Dualism of the Immanent Frame*

Many of the works that explicitly identify themselves as examples of theological reading tend to err on the side of ahistorical dualism. The single text discussed in detail above is by no means the only instance of the problem, though it displays the nature of the fundamental issue especially clearly. Pausing to reflect on the other sort of dualism will nevertheless help clarify what a nondualistic view would look like, though this discussion can be briefer because this is not where the main corrective is needed. For an example of dualism of the immanent frame, consider James Barr's view of the Bible. Barr's perspective depends on a specific set of auxiliary disciplines that together provide knowledge of what the text is. Linguistics makes clear how the original language of the text operates, textual criticism investigates what the wording of the text actually is, literary studies provides a window onto how the authors of biblical literature shaped their material according to various genres, history supplies an understanding of the events occurring while the biblical books were composed, and knowledge of surrounding cultures provides further useful points of reference.[45] These branches of knowledge affect the meaning the text has, yet "many of these elements of the text are of a nature over which theology as such cannot pronounce."[46] These disciplines offer readers an understanding of the text because the biblical text has linguistic, literary, historical, and cultural features that are genuine

[44] Daley, "The Acts and Christian Confession," 25.
[45] Barr, "Exegesis as a Theological Discipline Reconsidered," 132.
[46] Ibid., 132.

properties of the text. Such properties are together *constitutive* of what the text is; they are not merely *instrumental* to understanding it, with any other perspective, such as theology, adding to the multifaceted picture of what the text is.[47] "All of these [approved disciplinary perspectives] are not instruments which must (perhaps painfully and regretfully) be learned up and thereafter used: they are part of the fabric of Scripture and part of its own means of conveying its own meaning to us."[48]

From this list of features, as has already been suggested, theology is notably absent. It does not provide the reader with an understanding of what the text actually is (and therefore how it ought to be interpreted). Its complete exclusion is an implication of, first, none of the valid disciplinary perspectives being conditioned by a connection to theology, and, second, the features of the text deemed real being constitutive of rather than instrumental to obtaining its theological meaning: "They are part of Scripture itself, they evidence the subtheological structure without which it would not have any meaning at all and would be uninterpretable."[49]

Because theology is not integral to an account of the text, the text is simply a set of written documents to be considered exclusively according to its immanent features. The Bible is just a "natural or 'horizontal' field, peopled by texts and intentional authors

[47] Ibid., 135–36.

[48] Ibid., 136.

[49] Ibid., 136. For a helpful account of how key auxiliary disciplines such as history, philology, and literary aesthetics reconfigured themselves over time without reference to theology, see Jonathan Sheehan, *The Enlightenment Bible: Translation, Scholarship, Culture* (Princeton: Princeton University Press, 2005), 93–221. Barr is by no means entirely unfamiliar with these basic issues, though they are not fully faced in his defense of a mode of biblical interpretation indebted to "an enlightenment that was itself theological": "Biblical Criticism as Theological Enlightenment," in *Bible and Interpretation: The Collected Essays of James Barr*, ed. John Barton. Vol. I: Interpretation and Theology (Oxford: Oxford University Press, 2013), 168. Working to reconnect these disciplines with theology is an ongoing challenge for theological reading.

considered *per se*."[50] These features are objects of interest in their own right because they are the only features of the text that are genuinely real. They are not pointers to something else that is more important than they themselves are. The Bible is a set of speech acts performed in the circumstances that gave rise to the text, or a past act of communication. As Barr says, "'What it meant' in [Krister] Stendhal's terms is its *only* meaning."[51] Barr refers here to Stendahl's famous distinction between what the Bible *meant* in its context of genesis and its initial reception, and what it *means* in the present, for instance in contemporary preaching. To say that what the text meant is its sole sense is to demote what the text "means" to being something less than an actual sense of the text; what the text "means" is really an intermeshing of the text's meaning with later, different concerns, which combination risks blurring the line between the text and the reader, who may well be influenced by later ideas that he attributes to the text without being aware of their true origin elsewhere. Any reading of the Bible – if it is to count as a genuine reading that responds to the text, rather than being driven by other factors – must therefore treat the text exclusively in terms of what it meant.[52]

That this is what the text *is* means that reading it any other way comes in for criticism, the purpose of which is to track the influence of any "subjectivity" in interpretation. If they so choose, readers can take the text in hand and attempt to tease out its "own inner intentions"[53] by thinking with and beyond it about the realities it

[50] This line comes from a description of differences between Barr and T. F. Torrance in John Webster, "T. F. Torrance on Scripture," *Scottish Journal of Theology* 65 (2012): 52.

[51] Barr, *The Concept of Biblical Theology*, 203.

[52] However, see the qualification of this in Barr's modestly positive evaluation of readings done from within a canonical context, which produce different layers of meaning: "Historical Reading and the Theological Interpretation of Scripture," 40–41. The Conclusion of this book returns to the distinction between what a text meant and what it means.

[53] Barr, "The Bible as a Document of Believing Communities," 61.

addresses, and pondering questions that "press for consideration under the more deliberate, more disciplined, more conscious and perhaps even more abstract process that is theology."[54] However, the text itself does not impel readers to do this, and doing so inevitably creates discontinuities and tensions with the original speech act, because subsequent reflection introduces new conceptual idioms that have their own distinctive force and network of associations, although they may allow readers to engage with the same reality with which the original utterance was concerned. Even when similarities at the level of reality are significant, what must be stressed is verbal differences, because what the subsequent reflection is or is not in continuity with is the original speech act, not the reality about which the text and subsequent reflection both concern themselves. To so stress differences at the verbal and conceptual level, without considering similarities at the level of substance to represent at least a countervailing factor, demonstrates that the focus of hermeneutical effort is precisely on what might be called the surface features of the text, rather than its depth. That is, a reader is to look at the words so as to determine their sense, *as opposed to* peering at reality through the perspective that the verbal and conceptual instruments provide. Text and subject matter subtly diverge.

Such reflection, which takes the text as its point of departure and explores questions about the reality of which it speaks, is what Barr refers to as theological exegesis,[55] yet because of how the text is viewed, this counts as *reading* only in a heavily attenuated sense. It is more accurate, from his point of view, to refer to this use of the text as a series of reciprocal engagements between the Bible and the external discipline of systematic theology.[56] Influence from the latter counts as something the reader brings to the process.

[54] Ibid., 61.

[55] Barr, "Exegesis as a Theological Discipline Reconsidered," 133, 135, 137.

[56] Ibid., 133, 135, 137.

Theological exegesis, in this sense, is an interaction between the biblical text and "other texts and with pre-existing theological tradition,"[57] with these so-called extrinsic variables often serving as the driving force within the process. Here theological exegesis is less genuinely exegetical, or less an interpretive response which is sensitive to the text for what it really is, because the text is conceived within a solely horizontal perspective. That Barr views the text this way means that what should be stressed regarding the relationship between the New Testament and, for instance, the later theological tradition of reflection on the status of Son and the Father – a topic Barr rightly says is a key theological issue that the text prompts readers to consider – is the verbal differences between the text and later Christian thought. "How completely . . . does the Jesus of the Gospels fail to present himself *in terms* that fit with the classical trinitarian/incarnational doctrine!"[58] The emphatic stressing of such dissimilarities cannot but come across as ironic for anyone who, with the mainstream of the Christian tradition, takes the two sets of locutions to refer to the same agent.

In sum, Barr views the literary, historical, and linguistic aspects of the Bible as features that generate textual meaning, which ought to be the object of attention in its own right. Insofar as he sees these as facets of the text that do not of themselves open up to and speak of a higher reality, Barr's view counts as dualistic in an immanent mode. It would perhaps be appropriate to call this a soft dualism, as

[57] Ibid., 138.

[58] Barr, "The Bible as a Document of Believing Communities," 55. Emphasis added. Barr's skepticism about the possibility that topical preaching might be genuinely biblical is intelligible against the same background. Topical preaching is homiletical practice based on a synthetic reading of a range of canonical documents, and it aims to draw together what various pertinent texts say about a defined topic. If it is to be biblical, it must correspond closely with the original communicative intent of the text and adhere tightly to the thread of the text itself, following the flow of the writing, rather than becoming focused on the subject matter or elements of that, but it is necessarily difficult for a topical approach to do those things. See "The Bible as a Document of Believing Communities," 55–56.

it is not exactly true that the Bible absolutely *cannot* be brought into connection with the *res* of which the Christian tradition has taken it to be a sign, but rather that all engagements with the substance of the text become an optional undertaking, one whose very distance from the text itself must be constantly underscored. The influence within such engagements from non-biblical factors has to be highlighted studiously.[59] The text itself does not constitute a way of seeing divine reality; it is not a *signum* that directs the reader's attention to God. Therefore readers have to choose between paying attention to the text itself and undertaking theological reflection. They must do either one or the other.

Ahistorical dualism and dualism of the immanent frame are both driven by the perception of a tension existing between the text's immanent qualities and origin in a natural history and, on the other hand, the possibility that it might serve as a sign to divine reality. Just as Hauerwas refuses to make reading contingent on historical knowledge, lest the reader assumes the wrong sort of stance toward the Bible, Barr stresses how theological reflection depends on many factors other than the text of the Bible itself, which readers should understand through historical and literary analysis. In neither case does the text's function as a collection of signs directing the reader to God clearly supervene on its historical features, so that differences in any two given texts' historical qualities affect how they serve differently as signifiers of God. By contrast, a successful theological view of the Bible requires seeing the text in such a way that these differences make a difference. One might claim that Hauerwas's view is an outlier in the larger discussion of theological reading (and perhaps the same is true for Reno), and that

[59] In this connection, see John Barton's summing up of what stands at the heart of Barr's interpretive work, distinguishing what is of the Bible and what is not: "James Barr as Critic and Theologian," in *Language, Theology, and the Bible: Essays in Honour of James Barr*, ed. Samuel E. Balentine and John Barton (Oxford: Clarendon Press, 1994), 24–25.

allowances need to be made for his tendency toward an unbalanced presentation, which is the natural and unavoidable outworking of his forcefully polemical rhetoric. It is no doubt true that Hauerwas's view on this topic exists at one end of a spectrum; however, the basic problem that afflicts his position, ahistorical dualism, is indeed a larger trend within this debate, the mapping of which is not the primary objective here (to repeat once more this same point from earlier in the chapter).[60] It is especially easy to discern this

[60] See the footnotes to Martin (43) and McCormack (41) earlier in this section for other illustrations, though of course Martin and Barth, on whom McCormack is commenting, are much less extreme than is Hauerwas. For his part, Fowl frames the relationship between historical study and theological interpretation as essentially a competitive one. That he sees a basically agonistic interaction between the two is evident even from the headings he uses in discussing these topics. In his recent textbook, there is a chapter called "Theological Interpretation and Its Relation to Various Other Concerns," and history is one of those other issues. It is something else, an other, in relation to theological reading. See Fowl, *Theological Interpretation of Scripture*, 15–24. In his earlier monograph, there is a similar heading, "Theological Interpretation rather than Biblical Theology," in which he discusses how theological convictions are systematically excluded by the invocation of historical frames of reference (*Engaging Scripture*, 13–21). His main point is that over the course of the past few centuries, the rise of historical criticism has marginalized the theological convictions that need to operate *within* interpretation, if interpretation is going to count as theological and prove useful toward specifically Christian ends. Fowl's is not a ferociously ahistorical perspective insofar as he grants that historical study can indeed have "ad hoc usefulness" (*Engaging Scripture*, 21). Yet the predominant idiom for depicting the relationship between history and theology is still clearly competitive: as Fowl sees things, history was in the dominant position for several centuries, yet "if there is to be a revival of theological interpretation of Scripture among scholars and students, we must relearn how to grant theological concerns *priority over* other concerns," including those of history (*Theological Interpretation of Scripture*, 23, emphasis added). It would be better to balance the adversarial language with discussion of how history can in principle have a positive role, if the brief note about ad hoc usefulness is to serve as more than a qualification issued in passing. Fowl writes in a different tone about historical criticism in a very recent essay: "Theological Interpretation of Scripture and Its Future," *Anglican Theological Review* 99 (2017): 678–80, which contains a brief section called "Theological Interpretation and Historical Criticism: No Need for War." It will be interesting to see where this modified posture will lead in Fowl's future work.

problem in Hauerwas, which is why he is a useful interlocutor for a section that sets up a constructive proposal. The purpose of this section is merely to point up a conceptual problem that the constructive position of the following section addresses.

Strong reactions against historical methodologies on the part of Hauerwas and similar figures are understandable, if not compelling. Historians often present historical research as a totalizing intellectual agenda. For instance, Troeltsch says, "All these necessities were entailed by the historical method itself, which, once admitted at any point, necessarily draws everything into its train and weaves together all events in one great web of correlated effects and changes."[61] Therefore, "Give the historical method an inch and it will take a mile. From a strictly orthodox standpoint, therefore, it seems to bear a certain similarity to the devil."[62] If historical research marginalizes theology, then the most effective strategic countermove against it may appear to be outright rejection, an exorcising of the devil from the subject that has been possessed. Many involved in the theological interpretation discussion perceive their approaches as ones that are emerging, developing, and getting established in the face of a hostile status quo. Given that self-understanding, it should not come as an absolute shock that the discussion of theological reading contains some polemical engagement with opponents and a propensity to develop lopsided views to

There are upbeat comments to be found among literature that explicitly identifies itself as theological reading of Scripture. For instance, Joel B. Green contends that theological reading should see itself as dependent on historical research when history is understood as study of the concrete situations in which biblical texts were generated and of the communicative conventions that the texts themselves presuppose, even as other understandings of history require critique. See his *Practicing Theological Interpretation: Engaging Biblical Texts for Faith and Formation*, Theological Explorations for the Church Catholic (Grand Rapids: Baker, 2011), 44–45.

[61] Troeltsch, "On the Historical and Dogmatic Methods in Theology," 15. See also Ernst Troeltsch, "Historiography," in *Encyclopedia of Religion and Ethics*, ed. James Hastings and John Alexander Selbie (Edinburgh: T. & T. Clark, 1913), VI: 716–23.

[62] Troeltsch, "On the Historical and Dogmatic Methods in Theology," 16.

counter them. Perhaps it is simply a case of a set of new voices feeling the need to shout a bit to receive initial recognition. This background is entirely worth registering. Yet the following section works on the assumption that these dynamics have generated an overreaction against history, and that it is wiser to contextualize an emphasis on history within a theological view of the Bible than to continue along an ahistorical trajectory.[63] Better than repudiating history is seeing it as having an "intrinsic openness to something greater."[64] "It is necessary to keep in mind that any human utterance of a certain weight contains more than the author may have been immediately aware of at the time. When a word transcends the moment in which it is spoken, it carries with itself a 'deeper value.'"[65] It is this sensibility that informs the constructive position below.

## The Bible and Theological Semiotics

In line with the criteria that emerged from the section above, this section seeks to frame a theological ontology of Scripture so as to avoid both types of dualism. And, once more, the Bible is a written work with a contingent history marked by key moments – including composition, redaction, initial reception, and subsequent transmission – but whose mundane features point readers beyond the immanent realm. In this way, the text is a set of signs pointing to God.

[63] There is a certain resemblance between what I am suggesting above and Augustine's insistence on plundering the Egyptians in his own discussion of the usefulness of historical knowledge for biblical interpretation. Of course, this process will require hard critical and theological thinking, but the point here is to articulate an ideal of theological reading.

[64] Ratzinger, *Jesus of Nazareth*, xxiii.

[65] Ibid., xix–xx.

To claim that the Bible is a collection of signs means that readers should engage with it for the sake of engaging with what it is about. As was mentioned at the outset of the chapter, signification is the key middle term that links up *what is written* in the text and *what the text is written about*. What is written mediates knowledge of what the text is written about, and the text therefore ought to be read from that point of view. When the text is viewed in this way, readers must, of course, attend to the details of the text itself; indeed, they should do so with an intensely focused attention. However, for those who take the text as a collection of signs, their ultimate obligation is not to look *at* the text per se but to attend to it as a vehicle, or as something to look *through*, contemplating the reality to which it points, even though that reality defies their full comprehension and all attempts at mastery (the eyes of faith are crucial to this semiotic conception of Scripture because of this focus on what is seen via the text). Readers should think with and along the line established by the text. Augustine's distinction between using and enjoying the Bible is a bit confusing, but his purpose in framing it is a sound one, namely, to highlight that the text is finally less important than that to which it grants the reader access. As a set of signs, the text points the reader to God.

That the text is a set of signs does not mean that reference to God arises only where there are aporiae within the text, where readers think they have found "marks of excess and of intra-textual strain that might have to do not only with immediate ideological context but with God."[66] This links up text and subject matter too loosely. Yet neither does the text being a sign mean that the written work and God are nearly equated with one another, or resolved into each other. There must indeed be "a subjectivity outside language"[67] in order to underscore that God transcends the sign itself. The sign

[66] Williams, "Historical Criticism and Sacred Text," 225.

[67] Davies, *The Creativity of God*, 93. Davies elaborates a sophisticated theological semiotics predicated on denying this very difference.

conveys the Word to the reader, while at the same time there is more to the Word than what the sign delivers. To refer again to Augustine, who plays on biblical language about mountains and help that may come from them:

> So let us lift up our eyes to the mountains from where help will come to us; and yet not in those mountains is our hope to be placed; the mountains, in fact, receive what they pass on to us. So then, our hope is to be placed in the one from whom the mountains receive. When we lift up our eyes to the scriptures, because the scriptures have been provided by human beings, we are lifting up our eyes to the mountains from where help will come to us.[68]

The biblical text is thus a set of signs, or, more precisely, it is a *privileged* set of signs (recall the use of this same terminology in the discussion of Augustine in Chapter 1). While its subject matter is more important than the text itself, that the text is a privileged set of signs means that readers have no better access to the subject matter than via interpreting this text. There are other collections of signs that pertain to the same subject matter as the Bible. For instance, there are other texts that concern themselves with God, such as the Nicene Creed or Augustine's *On the Trinity*. In addition, there are sets of signs that are non-textual, for instance, the created world as a whole: even without the assistance of words, the world directs human beings to the God who is its creator when it is seen with the eyes of faith. The semiotic function of these other signifiers should be acknowledged, but Scripture remains privileged in relation to them. It is privileged over and above other textual corpora that deal with the same subject matter because non-biblical texts derive their teaching from it, whether in obvious or less obvious ways. Both the text of Nicaea and Augustine's great work on the Trinity present themselves as being expansive glosses on Scripture

[68] *Tractates on the Gospel of John* 1.6 (CCSL 36, 3; WSA I/12, 43).

that utilize and transform philosophical categories in their exposition. Scripture is privileged in connection with the created order since the world as a whole reveals God when read with the assistance of scriptural narratives and categories. This special status for Scripture is liturgically marked: the text is elevated in assemblies of worship, it is read aloud to those gathered, and it is the subject of preaching. Biblical texts exist in conjunction with other signs, and are not isolated from them, but they nevertheless have a special status in that their signifying work is the benchmark and basis of the semiotic function of other signs.[69]

The text of the Bible directs the attention of readers specifically to the incarnation as the locus of revelatory divine presence. Achieving knowledge of God is not a possibility for human beings if they rely on their own cognitive capacities. Apart from God's work to reveal himself, the path to knowing God stands blocked. However, God has, in fact, revealed himself in the person of Jesus Christ. "And the Word became flesh and lived among us, and we have seen his glory, the glory as of a father's only son" (John 1:14). Theological readers engage with the text to trace the way in which the words signify the Word, for, though human beings would remain ignorant of God apart from his active revealing of himself, "It is God the only Son, who is close to the Father's heart, who has made him known" (John 1:18). Theological exegetes should ultimately attend, by means of the text, to the way in which the Son makes known the one whose essence he shares. The route to knowledge of God thus runs this way: from the text to the humanity of Jesus Christ and in his humanity – not apart or separate from his manhood – to his divinity and perfect representation of the Father in his very being. The drive to move beyond the text to the *res* to which it refers is built into the construal of the Bible as a *signum*, and thus the text is instrumentalized from the beginning, rather than serving as the

[69] On this topic, I appreciate comments from one of the anonymous reviewers commissioned by Cambridge University Press.

cynosure on the part of the interpreter. "The theologian must go beyond the text to the Word, interpreting it from the point of view of the Word."[70]

The Christian God is triune, and there is an ineluctably trinitarian dynamic to the way in which he reveals himself, which includes the action of the Holy Spirit working together with the other persons. The Spirit's action is tied to the reception of the Father's gracious self-manifestation in the person of the incarnate Son. As the apostle Paul writes, understanding the divine is impossible apart from the Spirit: "'What no eye has seen, nor ear heard, nor the human heart conceived, what God has prepared for those who love him' – these things God has revealed to us through the Spirit; for the Spirit searches everything, even the depths of God" (1 Corinthians 2:9–10). The Spirit effects understanding as he indwells human beings: "Now we have received not the spirit of the world, but the Spirit that is from God, so that we may understand the gifts bestowed on us by God" (1 Corinthians 2:12). In this way, the Spirit completes the action of revelation by facilitating its reception and appropriation. The human response that corresponds to and answers God's initiative to disclose himself in this way is faith, which is itself a gift the Spirit gives, not simply a human achievement. Faith is trust in the proclamation of Jesus as the revelation of God in the power of the Spirit, to whom the words of Scripture attest, and on whom human beings are invited to rely as they interpret the written words of the text. This is the way in which God reveals himself.

Two important passages that feed into trinitarian theology have just received brief comment, yet it is by no means from them alone – but only from Scripture in its totality – that the doctrine emerges.

[70] Marion, *God without Being*, 149. For probing critical questions about the larger context of Marion's view of the text and its relation to revelation, see Tamsin Jones, *A Genealogy of Marion's Philosophy of Religion: Apparent Darkness*, Indiana Series in the Philosophy of Religion (Bloomington: Indiana University Press, 2011), 116–29.

Thus, it is the Bible *as a whole* which is a (privileged) set of signs pointing to the triune God. To speak of the Bible signifying God most certainly does not mean that readers should seek to squeeze a doctrine of the Trinity out of each and every verse of the text when such verses are taken singly and in isolation. Rather, the Bible directs the reader's attention to the triune God when it is read as an interconnected unity. It is not the purpose of this chapter to array all of this evidence and contend that a doctrine of the Trinity fits the full range of biblical data. Of course that is not possible here, nor is it needed.[71] The aim of this section is to detail a semiotic conceptualization of Scripture, with the present point being that this conceptualization is of the entire canonical collection rather than smaller units of texts taken individually.

Taking the whole canonical collection as a set of signs requires, first, reading the New Testament against the background of the Scripture of Israel, or what Christians are accustomed to calling the Old Testament. For instance, a more illuminating reading of the Last Supper text in Luke 22:7–38 is possible when that text is related to the Passover pericope of Exodus 12:1–13:16. Passover prefigures the Last Supper, and yet the original figure's contribution to the canon remains, even after its fulfillment has occurred. "The New Testament's insistence that the divine deliverance is a spiritual transformation does not abrogate the Old Testament's witness that the physical is involved as well. In spite of its ambiguity, the political overtones of Israel's deliverance are part of the whole biblical message."[72] Second, it is also necessary to read the Old Testament in light of the New: concerns about anachronism will not forestall this move so long as these texts are seen not only as

[71] For excellent readings of several biblical corpora as offering testimony to the Trinity, see the essays in part I of Gilles Emery and Matthew Levering, eds., *The Oxford Handbook of the Trinity*, Oxford Handbooks in Religion and Theology (Oxford: Oxford University Press, 2014), 15–90.

[72] See Brevard S. Childs, *The Book of Exodus: A Critical, Theological Commentary*, The Old Testament Library (Louisville: Westminster John Knox, 1974), 214.

past acts of communion, but as pointing beyond themselves to the being and saving act of the triune God. When such texts are understood as part of a complex network of signs, they take on new senses in addition to those they would have had for their first audience.[73] To take another example, a book such as Song of Songs is "about more than what the surface of its text says. That more is always and necessarily the triune Lord and, necessarily, that Lord's incarnation as Jesus Christ."[74] A poem about erotic love between a man and a woman represents not only that of which it more obviously speaks, but also the relationship of Christ and the church.[75] The human figures thereby illuminate the divine mystery without even mentioning it in so many words. Seeing the two testaments in reciprocal interpretative dependency is thus an important aspect of what it means to construe the entire canonical collection as a set of signs.[76]

[73] I use the phrase "in addition" advisedly here: reading against historical background is necessary but not sufficient for an interpretation of these texts.

[74] Paul J. Griffiths, *Song of Songs*, Brazos Theological Commentary on the Bible (Grand Rapids: Brazos, 2011), lvi–lvii

[75] Richard Swinburne is entirely right when he says that the Song of Songs demands to be read figurally. "For someone who longs to interpret the Bible in terms of the 'original meaning' of its books, there is always one acid test of whether this is a reasonable construal of the Bible as canonized and promulgated as a Christian book by the Church of early centuries: how do you interpret the Song of Songs? It is ludicrous to suppose that any Church Father, even the most 'literal-minded' one, would have supposed that its meaning was its meaning as a book on its own. On its own it is an erotic love poem. They would all have said that its meaning was to be understood in terms of its place in a Christian Bible." See *Revelation: From Metaphor to Analogy* (Oxford: Clarendon Press, 1992), 207–08.

[76] Christopher Bryan makes a point that helpfully qualifies this insistence on the integral wholeness of the Bible: "We cannot avoid perceiving that, while they [various biblical texts] indeed witness to parts of a single story, they do not all say the same things about that story or take the same attitudes" (*Listening to the Bible*, 77). There is development within the canon, and there are tensions between different texts, to be sure. What the above requires is that, even though the canon consists of a plurality of voices, a shared subject matter emerges from them, to which each voice is responding in its own way.

To read the text of the Bible as a *signum*, seeing it as a privileged indicator of the Trinity when it is read as a cohesive corpus of texts, it is logically necessary to operate with an incipient understanding of God which precedes reading the particular text in question (there will be a blurry line here between operating with this understanding because of personal faith and doing so as a function of existing within a culture that has been impacted and shaped historically by the Christian tradition). Taking the text as a sign pointing to God means that the reader needs to have a background conception of God as triune in order to inquire into how this text points to him. In the words of Jean-Luc Marion, one "must have an anticipated understanding of the referent, for lack of which he will not be able to spot its effects of meaning in the text."[77] Without a doctrine of God in place, this question would never arise as a comprehensible and indeed pressing query. This recalls the hermeneutical circle, which was discussed in connection with Augustine in Chapter 2, for this view of the text assumes that the subject matter of which the text speaks is not entirely unknown to the reader. The reader has some acquaintance with the material content of the text prior to any given instance of interpretation, though this inchoate understanding is provisional and detailed textual study provides the opportunity for understanding to mature, be refined, and even to receive revision.[78] The requirement of a proleptic understanding of the text's subject matter does not imply that a reader must have

[77] Marion, *God without Being*, 155. There is a nearly identical point made in Robert W. Jenson, "Hermeneutics and the Life of the Church," in *Reclaiming the Bible for the Church*, ed. Carl E. Braaten and Robert W. Jenson (Grand Rapids: Eerdmans, 1995), 99.

[78] This chapter's designation of the Trinity as the subject matter of the text also builds on the previous chapter's treatment of ecclesiology as a key social context for interpretation. Readers gain the prior knowledge that they need via a whole range of ecclesial practices, including previous readings of the Bible as well as participating in the liturgy, undergoing catechesis, and so on. Thus, this semiotics of the biblical text builds in ecclesiology at the most basic level, for the conception of the text assumes into itself the formation of readers within the community of the church.

comprehensive knowledge of the divine *res* – in any case this would be impossible to attain. Because the interpreter's understanding of God is always and necessarily incomplete, the process of reading can be expected to be an informative one, shedding new light on an inexhaustibly rich topic. What the reader needs is sufficient knowledge to begin to engage in a dialogue with the text, to be able to pose questions about how it says something about *this* God.

This provides a basis for responding to a relevant variant of the following incisive question from James Barr: "Even if the text is seen as a witness beyond itself, how do we know what it is witnessing to? We have to know what the theology of the text is before we can tell what aspect of 'the divine purpose of God' it is saying something about."[79] The same question might be rephrased as an objection against the present view of the text as a collection of signs that prompt the reader to engage with the triune God. Barr is certainly right in that readers do need to pay close attention to the details of the text in order to see what it is saying about God. However, coming to the text with a view toward asking theological questions presupposes having in place a framework in which those questions can and should be asked, and in which they are shaped in a particular (trinitarian) way. Viewing the text as signs builds in pre-understanding in this way, by foregrounding the angle from which interpretive queries are posed. In this way, the terminology of signs is not a hermeneutically feckless notion, as he suggests the notion of witness can be for many who subscribe to it in principle as a key concept in their theology of the Bible.[80]

[79] See Barr, *The Concept of Biblical Theology*, 195.

[80] By way of clarification, of course it is possible to interpret the Bible according to other hermeneutical modes, quite apart from any background knowledge of God or faith commitment on the part of the reader. Theological background beliefs are not absolutely necessary for any engagement with the Bible; they are instead conditionally necessary, required for interpretations based on this theological view of the text. The difference is between pre-understanding being required because it is built into what it means to read the text as a set of signs signifying the triune God, and it being

Yet the pre-understanding on the part of the reader, the need for which is an essential part of reading the text according to the model being proposed, is not fundamentally a matter of human subjectivity being given scope to operate within the practice of interpretation. It is not that "the *I* always determines the phenomenon through anticipation"; it is wrong to say that "the phenomenon will be known to the *I*, since the *I* will organize its entire possible intuition according to the concept or signification that it will have assigned to it *in advance*."[81] Crucially, it is not a matter of granting leeway within reading to an entirely *unformed* subjectivity. At one level, it is unavoidably the reader who gives input into the process, insofar as it is precisely pre-understanding that this semiotic view of the text necessitates. However, this pre-understanding is shaped authoritatively by other canonical texts (and is reinforced by ecclesial practices). It is other constituent documents from a complex, differentiated Scripture that form the subjectivity of the reader and orient the reader to God as the subject matter of the text as a whole. The focal text on which the reader concentrates thus signifies in conjunction with other writings from the canon. For this reason, "An exposition is trustworthy to the extent that it not only expounds the text in front of it, but implicitly at least expounds all other texts, to the extent that it at any rate clears the way for the exposition of all other texts."[82]

Because the reader's pre-understanding is shaped by a range of canonical documents, the way in which a focal text is read as a collection of signs is shaped by (preliminary) judgments about the truth of other texts, and by the intention to relate the text to its subject matter. Putting in place a theological ontology of the text

ineradicable though it must be marginalized as much as possible for interpretations that seek the text's original communicative impact.

81 Jean-Luc Marion, *Givenness and Revelation* (Oxford: Oxford University Press, 2016), 52.

82 Barth, *Church Dogmatics I.2*, § 19–21, 485.

means that there cannot be here an unqualified distinction between meaning and truth. Taking the text as this sort of *signum* does not, of course, depend on a naturalistic background, as is the case with Spinoza, but on a deferential reading of other canonical texts. In this way, a construal of a discrete text's communicative force is tied up with, or entangled in, conclusions about the truth about the God to whom the rest of the biblical text attests. Proper reading and questions of truth are interrelated or interdependent issues. They are not linked in the sense that conclusions from prior readings are simply projected onto other texts. Rather, prior conclusions generate the sort of interpretive questions that are put to a given text: readers put trinitarian questions to biblical texts because of the pressure exerted on them by prior readings of a range of canonical texts, as will be explained in Chapter 6. A further point that is unpacked there is that there are conditions under which the wider literary context can be used to disambiguate texts that are, on other grounds, open to several different possible readings. However, this is to anticipate.

In addition to calling up this pre-understanding, a full appreciation for the signs that constitute the Bible requires grappling with the text's relativity and limitations, which are a function of the temporal and geographical location in which the text originated as well as of other factors that condition the author's perspective and compositional goals. Inquiring into these matters means delving into precisely how this text offers a determinate communication. What Barth says of the author of the Fourth Gospel can also be said of all other biblical authors: "He is *only* a man. He has not said it as it *is* but as he could."[83] The need to investigate the particularity of any given biblical text is thus a product of acknowledging the humanity of the textual signs. Historical knowledge is, thus, a means toward reading a focal text, and its tacit background, as a

[83] Barth, *Witness to the Word*, 6.

collection of signs at whose center is Jesus Christ. An awareness of history is instrumentally important, but its importance is limited to serving as a means toward what is of ultimate significance. As Barth says: "As a medium what is historical, the human word of the witness to revelation, demands our total, concentrated, and serious attention. But only as a medium, not for its own sake and not to be understood in terms of itself, but as witness which itself needs witness and expects witness – the witness that its subject matter must give."[84] To transpose Barth's point into the idiom of this chapter, it is necessary to concentrate on the historical features of the biblical signs, yet precisely because they are signs, the purpose of studying them from the angle of history is to see more clearly how the final form of the text renders exact, determinate signification of God.[85]

There is something of a tension that arises from understanding biblical texts in relation to two different types of context, both literary and historical.[86] Interpretive deliberations on any given passage must relate the words of the focal passage to other words within the canonical texts as well as to patterns of usage from the text's immediate historical backdrop. There is no guarantee that these two contexts will turn out to mesh easily, and in fact there are often divergences between the two. There is no general way to be rid entirely of this tension, as it is an implication of the conception of signs that has been outlined to this point. Part of what it means for the text to be a set of signs is evoking the global scriptural context, which provides the background for asking particular types of interpretive questions; another aspect of what it means is resolutely

[84] Ibid., 7.

[85] Brevard Childs rightly says that the decisive reason for reading the final form of the text is theological in nature: "It is the final text, the composite narrative, in its present shape which the church, following the lead of the synagogue, accepted as canonical and thus the vehicle of revelation and instruction." See *The Book of Exodus*, xv.

[86] There is lucid description of this tension in Levenson, *The Hebrew Bible, the Old Testament, and Historical Criticism*, xiii–xiv.

focusing on the details of the passage in question and puzzling through these textual features with their circumstances of origin in view, something which is key in order to honor the distinctive contribution of this specific text to the canon. If the latter does not occur, the overarching pre-understanding may well run roughshod over the communicative force of the text in question. What is crucial is to attain an equilibrium or reciprocal balance between the two factors. The way in which the two contexts tug in different directions is only inherently problematic if readers feel an obligation to give complete and unqualified loyalty to only one of the two types of context.[87] Viewing the tension as finally problematic is unnecessary, though, for both contexts are integral to the text serving as a set of signs. The text is genuinely human – with all the implications this carries for the particularity of its angle of vision and therefore its limitations – and also a work whose pointing beyond itself and its setting of origin can be seen when commitments from prior readings of other passages begin to exert their influence in the way it is read.

All reading of the Bible as signs involves reaching out to relate appropriately to its subject matter, but there is a limitation to how far this process can proceed. Interpreting the Bible requires connecting to one another *what is written* and *what it is written about*, neither considering *what is written* for its own sake nor contemplating *what it is written about* apart from textual mediation – as if readers could have direct and immediate knowledge of the *res*. The restriction is that while readers reach out to the subject matter on the basis of textual direction, readers as such will never achieve the sort of unmediated intercourse with God that would render reading dispensable. At this point in the economy of salvation, readers continually stretch forward to connect with one whom they cannot

[87] For an example of attempting to hold these contexts together, see the comments from Richard B. Hays on the overall aim of his seminal work on intertextuality in Paul: *Echoes of Scripture in the Letters of Paul* (New Haven: Yale University Press, 1989), xi–xii.

discern directly, reading with the eyes of faith as long as faith is a relevant capacity, so long as human beings do not find themselves in the immediate presence of God. By contrast, consider how Augustine imagines the condition of the angels vis-à-vis God: "They have no need to look up to this firmament [i.e., the Bible] and to read so as to know your word. They ever 'see your face' (Matt. 18:10) and there, without syllables requiring time to pronounce, they read what your eternal will intends."[88] Reading is an ongoing process of striving to understand, which will continue as long as human life in this world does, without readers ever achieving final comprehension of what they seek to know.

Viewing the text as a set of signs rules out one way of thinking about historical distance, but at the same time it invokes another, which fits with the treatment of historical distance developed in Chapter 4. If Scripture does in fact speak of God for today's readers, there cannot be the sort of separation between the Bible as a whole, or each of the various biblical texts individually, and present-day readers that means the text simply does not communicate to them at all. It has often been claimed that just this kind of distance needs to be admitted as real and indeed consequential. Robert Jenson rightly says,

> It has been supposed that in the case of Scripture the historical distance kept open is between the story Scripture tells and us, or to put it another way, between the community of Israel and the primal church on the one hand and us on the other. On this supposition we of course must have the same problem relating to Scripture as [Bill] Clinton has relating to [Julius] Caesar.[89]

This is to say that they operate in fundamentally different worlds, and so a modern American president cannot learn how to handle current problems from the Roman general. Thinking of distance as obtaining between the reader and the world of the Bible pulls the

[88] *Confessions* 13.18 (CCSL 27, 251; OWC Chadwick, 283).
[89] Jenson, "Hermeneutics and the Life of the Church," 103.

reader out of the sphere of divine self-disclosure, and so fundamentally undercuts a conception of the text as *signum*. However, because the Bible is an internally differentiated human text, one which originates from a wide range of contingent circumstances, it is worth acknowledging the historical distance that exists between different strands of the Bible.[90] The texts form a unity as they reach out to include the experience of present-day readers. Yet biblical texts do not all signify in the same way or from the same angle, and it does an injustice to the internal variety of the Bible to construe it as a tightly unified monolith. The reality the text indicates is so profound, its richness impossible to exhaust, that a variety of points of view together offer a more fully adequate picture of the text's subject matter, and not all of these points of view are strictly simultaneous with one another.[91]

Does the Bible being a collection of signs imply that every individual text within it must be interpreted as what philosopher of language John Searle calls a referring occurrence? To be a referring occurrence, a sentence must unambiguously identify a particular object, which actually exists, and it must say or ask something about that object.[92] For example, the following sentence is a referring occurrence: the book you are now reading addresses the topic of biblical interpretation. Referring is one of many things that a sentence can do; it is one of many speech acts that a speaker or writer of a sentence can perform. Other examples include promising, issuing a command, and warning someone.[93] Construing the

[90] Ibid., 104.

[91] Cf. the way in which accounts of theological reading which are more heavily indebted to phenomenological hermeneutics relativize the distinction between reading subject and interpreted object, declining to portray the two as entirely independent of one another: Schneiders, *The Revelatory Text*, 159–60.

[92] For a detailed account, with all the refinements which the constraints of space do not allow here, see John R. Searle, *Speech Acts: An Essay in the Philosophy of Language* (London: Cambridge University Press, 1969), 81–85.

[93] Ibid., 22–26.

entire Bible in semiotic terms does not rule out that the text can and does perform the full range of speech acts, such as those just mentioned as well as many more beside. What the notion of signs has in common with a single, albeit prominent, type of speech act is that both are centrally concerned with an object outside the text and indeed presuppose, as a condition of the text being a sign or the success of an act of reference, the existence of some relevant object. However, it is not true that the only way in which signs relate to their subject matter is by stating something about it. Just as a stop sign can command drivers of automobiles to stop in a certain spot, construing the Bible as a collection of signs is compatible with the text performing a variety of speech acts. The notion of signs creates a connection with the text's subject matter, but the types of connection vary greatly and should not all be homogenized into a single unifying category.[94] Using speech-act philosophy in connection with the Bible stresses the variety of things that the text does in relationship to its readers, but each of these things contains at least an implicit connection between the text and its subject, which is the same effect that the notion of signs has.

## Conclusion

To view the text of the Bible theologically means to think of it as a text with a contingent origin that serves as a set of signs to the triune God. It is therefore neither a work whose historical origin is

[94] There is a substantial literature now, coming from biblical studies, systematic theology, and philosophy of religion, which seeks to apply the insights of speech-act theory to biblical interpretation. Major works include Anthony C. Thiselton, *Thiselton on Hermeneutics: The Collected Works and New Essays of Anthony Thiselton*, Ashgate Contemporary Thinkers on Religion (Aldershot: Ashgate, 2006), 51–149; Vanhoozer, *Is There a Meaning in This Text?*; Wolterstorff, *Divine Discourse*. The notion of signs developed in this chapter is not incompatible with the vantage point of these works. I am grateful to Hans Burger for conversation about this topic.

immaterial to the way in which it addresses its subject matter, nor is it a text which should be read only as having spoken rather than continuing to say something about its subject matter to those who read it now. A full reading grows out of inquiry into the history of the text and goes beyond this starting point. Yet such a reading must indeed take seriously the text's historical origin by insisting that any perception of the text's subject matter through the medium of the text is contingent on a responsible handing of information regarding the Bible's history. In this way, seeing the text as a set of signs intends to avoid both dualism of the immanent frame and ahistorical dualism.

If this is indeed what the text of Scripture is, and if readers engage it without setting aside their basic theological commitments, then it follows that they should read the text in certain ways, which deserve to be referred to as theological interpretation, because this mode of handling the text springs from having in place theological views of both the interpreting subject and the interpreted object. Theology is thus the key to the entire structure of the hermeneutic, rather than simply the reader's focusing interest. How a theological view of the whole interchange between reader and text makes a difference for interpretation is the subject of the following chapter. Thinking theologically by no means determines all the details of how readers read, for the perspective is too high-level to have those sorts of implications, but it does create a set of parameters within which interpreters must make judgments about which reading strategies are fitting to apply to the Bible.

# 6 | Exegetical Ends and Means

The final element of the constructive account of theological interpretation is a treatment of reading that makes sense against the background of the preceding views of the reader and text. The central terms for this chapter, *reading* or *interpretation*, can mean a number of different things.[1] First, and most obviously, reading the Bible can mean seeking the sense of the text, attempting to understand the speech act it is performing. Without grappling with the text in this way, and indeed meeting with some success, it is impossible to move on to higher-level interpretive acts. At a second stage, reading the Bible means understanding what the text is saying within a set of analytical categories that is privileged in that the reader calls on them to explain the subject matter of the text. For readers inclined to accept the claims they encounter in the Bible, understanding them entails absorbing them into a framework of belief and allowing them to find their place within a larger structure that constitutes the reader's worldview. (By contrast, for those who see scriptural discourse largely as a matter of false consciousness, interpretation as understanding requires the "reduction of the illusions and lies of consciousness."[2]) Finally,

[1] John Webster elects to use the term *reading* rather than *interpretation*, because he wants to distance his own account from the way in which the latter has come to be understood in discussions of theological hermeneutics since Schleiermacher as stressing the activity of the interpreting subject in relation to the text. See his *Holy Scripture*, 86. Though I also aim to emphasize receptivity, I use the two terms interchangeably, on the assumption that *interpretation* as a term has not been so spoiled that it cannot be redeemed by a clear specification of the meaning it carries in this discussion.

[2] Ricoeur, *Freud and Philosophy*, 32.

reading the Bible can mean using the text or applying it to oneself.[3] When the Bible is understood positively, as in Christian communities, and brought within a reader's framework of beliefs, its imperatives must also be enacted. "Its crystallization in the reader's inwardness results from a paradox of 'dynamic passivity,' from the suspension of self which we experience when we pay utter attention to something, when we make acceptance and apprehension strenuous. This condition can produce a tensed openness which allows, which invites the text to 'read us' as much as we read it."[4] Thus, reading or interpretation can refer to three levels of engagement with the biblical text: acquisition of the text's sense, attempts to comprehend that meaning, and embodiments of it – all of which blend together in practice.

There are some tasks falling under the broad rubric of interpretation on which theological belief seems to impinge less. These are what we might call "small matters": the most elementary reading acts that feed into and precede what was referred to above as the first phase of interpretation. Karl Barth provides the example of assembling a concordance as an activity in which it is possible to achieve "exact scientific knowledge."[5] For instance, a reader of Paul's epistle to the Romans can know for certain how many times the Greek word *pistis* (faith/faithfulness) occurs in a given manuscript of the letter, and where each of these instances is to be found. If the manuscript to be studied is stipulated, then questions of theology do not arise when counting and locating terms within it. There may, however, be controversy surrounding which textual manuscripts are to be preferred, and these questions are not best seen as theology-neutral, for advocacy of a version of the text to be read is often a function, at least in part, of

3 Some think it is in the service of clarity not to include application underneath the broader heading of interpretation or reading. See, for instance, the objections in Barton, *The Nature of Biblical Criticism*, 176–77. However, there is certainly precedent for categorizing application under reading, as this chapter does. See Hays, *The Moral Vision of the New Testament*, 3–7.

4 Steiner, "Critic/Reader," 91.

5 Barth, *The Epistle to the Romans*, 6.

one's confessional location. Thus even the wording of the text is caught up, to some degree, in wider questions. Furthermore, readers of Romans are most often exercised about the lowest-level questions for the sake of arriving at secure answers to broader queries. Theological readers most often ultimately want to know what Paul is saying about faith/faithfulness, how it fits in the wider scope of his theology, and how that bears on the whole question of humanity's relation to God. What stands in the text must be established, but readers usually make this determination with a view toward investigating larger issues. On such issues, theology has a more obvious and significant bearing.[6] There are, thus, some reading acts that precede the determination of the sense of a passage, and that may appear to be isolated from questions about the reader's beliefs, but even for these issues, theological queries still hang in the background.

One of the main theses for which Chapter 2 argued is that Augustine allows his interpretive aim to influence each of the steps in the approach he employs in coming to understand the biblical text, and the present chapter follows Augustine in significant ways. First, it follows him structurally by having an aim that is generated by a theological understanding of the realities involved in interpretation. Second, it follows him materially in seeing that aim as engaging with the triune God. Third, it follows him by exploring how theology affects each aspect of interpretation. And fourth, it follows him by stressing the need to understand the subject matter of the text, though it does this in a different way than Augustine

[6] It is worth noting that a philosopher of religion has ventured that theology becomes pertinent to academic issues to the degree that such issues relate to understanding human nature or understanding things in general, as opposed to establishing control over the world. This is to generalize Alvin Plantinga's comment about natural science: "Methodological Naturalism?," in *Facets of Faith and Science*, ed. J. Van der Meer, Vol. 1: Historiography and Modes of Interaction (Lanham: University Press of America, 1996), 178. Cf. the similar comments by James Barr on the irrelevance of theology to the lowest levels of interpretive activity: "Does Biblical Study Still Belong to Theology?," 15.

himself does – one that assumes the division of interpretation into the three stages just outlined. There are thus strong continuities between this chapter and Part I, but there is also some discontinuity. This presentation draws inspiration from Augustine; however, there is no intention here of imitating him down to the last detail. "It is useless to wonder what exactly one of the ancients would do if he were suddenly transported among us."[7] What this chapter aims to do overall, as it relates to Part I, lines up with what de Lubac recommends, "If we aspire to find something of what was the spiritual interpretation of Scripture in the early centuries of the Church, it is important to look at things both in greater depth and with greater freedom. Without either a return to archaic forms or servile mimicry, often by totally different methods, it is a spiritual movement that we must reproduce above all."[8] It is this movement of attending to God via the text that I have termed the goal of interpretation. That drives the whole approach to reading here.

The viewpoint advanced in this chapter is a way of responding to a set of insightful diagnostic questions from historian George Marsden: "Scholars do not operate in a vacuum, but rather within the frameworks of their communities, traditions, commitments, and beliefs. Their scholarship, even when specialized, develops within a larger picture of reality. So we must ask: What is that larger picture? Is there a place for God? If so, does God's presence make any difference to the rest of the picture?"[9] The task of the locus of reading within an account of theological interpretation of Scripture is to spell out the difference theology makes. Theology exerts an influence on interpretation in each of the three phases discussed above, shaping how readers grasp the sense of a biblical text, how they understand its claims, and whether and in what way they apply what the text says.

[7] Lubac, *History and Spirit*, 429.

[8] Ibid., 450.

[9] George M. Marsden, *The Outrageous Idea of Christian Scholarship* (Oxford: Oxford University Press, 1997), 83.

This chapter connects back to the previous two by opening with a discussion of the aim of interpretation that builds on the analyses of the reader and the text laid out in Chapters 4 and 5. This leads to the main task of the chapter, expanding the three-phase interpretive scheme with which the chapter opens, and showing how it constitutes a set of strategies that can fulfill the aim of reading.

## The Aim of Theological Interpretation

This determination of the aim of interpretation begins with a doctrine of God in place from the outset: a doctrine of the Trinity is operative; faith in God is not written off as mere prejudice that infects and distorts the practice of reading.[10] Faith constitutes the reader's proper response to divine self-disclosure by means of the biblical text. Interpreters who read in faith are fundamentally receptive to the text of Scripture, recognizing their distance from the contexts in which biblical texts originated, but also discerning their participation in the economy of salvation of which the text speaks, and reading together with others who have developed and passed on to them hermeneutical strategies that are responsive to the text. The text is a collection of signs at whose center is Jesus Christ, a written work that points to him as the revelation of the triune God. The texts bear the imprint of their circumstances of genesis, yet they are caught up in the work of signifying divine things.

[10] Nicholas Lash draws attention to the specifically affective dimension of faith in the way that Augustine expounds it: *Believing Three Ways in One God: A Reading of the Apostles' Creed*, 2nd ed. (London: SCM, 2002), 20. While I have not stressed that point a great deal in explicit terms, it is implicitly present in the emphasis on the aim of reading. The claim that the reader has the overarching purpose of engaging with God in reading is one that could well have been spelled out with more openly affective language, for it deals essentially with what the reader wants to do as an interpreter, or what one desires to see happen via reading.

It follows, therefore, that readers ought to interpret the text with a view toward grasping its subject matter; that is, they should read for the sake of engaging with Jesus Christ. Receptivity to textual content means reading for an understating of God in Christ, as this God relates to the interpreter. Interpretation is thus governed by "existential interests in God's way of relating to humankind, in who the God is that relates in those ways, in how to understand all other realities as God-related, and in responding appropriately to the ways in which God relates to all else."[11] The end of interpretation is, in a real sense, identical with its beginning. The goal of interpretation follows from views of the reader and text that themselves make reference to God, and the aim that this procedure leads to is that interpreters ought to strive to engage more and more fully with the triune God via a practice of reading that unfolds and bears fruit over time.

Laying out some contrasting positions will highlight the formal structure of this treatment of interpretation. For instance, Kelsey's view of interpretation does not give the same prominence to a notion of the reader that the present proposal does.[12] His view of interpretation is similar, though, in that the rest of its focal topics are the same as the ones animating this book: aims in interpretation, a perspective on the text, and reading strategies that correspond to and fulfill the interpreter's aim. There are, naturally enough, logical connections between these topics in Kelsey's account: interpreters have aims or interests which generate a particular sort of construal of the biblical text. That is, the interpretive aims take the text to be a particular sort of thing. In turn, this construal makes it appropriate to read the text according to certain reading strategies, or what he calls disciplined modes of study.[13] Such modes of study serve to fulfill the reader's interpretive aim because they deliver what the reader seeks; they may be too loose in many cases to be considered methods, but

[11] Kelsey, *Eccentric Existence*, 1: 141.

[12] Ibid., 1: 132–56.

[13] See, for instance, ibid., 1: 133.

they are modes of interpretation that are responsive to the reader's construal of the text.

The crucial difference to highlight is that the topics in Kelsey's view interconnect according to a fundamentally different logic than in my account of theological interpretation. For Kelsey, interpreters come to interpretation with certain aims or interests that then govern the practice of reading. For me, the reader's aim is also crucial to the practice insofar as it prompts the selection of appropriate reading strategies, but this aim itself *derives* from the nature of the realities involved in reading. The realities operative in reading exert pressure for interpretation to follow a certain course rather than others. The text asks, as it were, to be read in a certain way (this is correlative with acknowledging its status as sign), and the reader is impelled to respond to the text in faith (for faith is a readerly capacity rather than prejudice with a pious gloss), and both of these together prompt theological reading. The basic difference in logic is that Kelsey's proposal runs from interests to construal to reading strategies, while mine starts with the nature of the text and reader and only then proceeds to interpretive aim and finally to strategies.[14] Only in the latter case does a theological account of reality constitute the starting point for the hermeneutical framework.

Neither is ontology governing the entire approach of Fowl, and this for two reasons. On his view, the ecclesial community's theological beliefs and practices become marginalized if generic theories of meaning entirely determine how biblical texts should be read. Instead of allowing theology to be squeezed out of interpretive

[14] My concern with Kelsey here is at the formal level, concentrating on his analysis of various views of the Bible rather than on his actual exegesis. For a perceptive and wide-ranging commentary on his readings of Scripture, which challenges him to integrate a fuller range of canonical texts into his constructive proposal, see David F. Ford, "Humanity before God; Thinking through Scripture: Theological Anthropology and the Bible," in *The Theological Anthropology of David Kelsey: Responses to Eccentric Existence*, ed. Gene Outka (Grand Rapids: Eerdmans, 2016), 31–52.

deliberations, Fowl insists that such convictions, habits, and so on should enter fully into considerations of how to read biblical passages. That is, these factors should shape reading. This is one aspect of what he calls underdetermined interpretation. Though the obverse side of underdetermined interpretation is that the matrix of theological affirmations and embodied ecclesial existence that shapes reading should in turn be shaped by it,[15] the rectitude of these beliefs and practices is generally taken for granted. There is no full-dress argument for taking them to be justified and therefore as having a salutary rather than malign influence on interpretation.[16] Fowl seems loath to venture global judgments on these beliefs and practices of the church for fear of having to assume a stance outside of the ecclesial community itself as a perch from which to issue a verdict on its principles and praxis.[17] Yet, in my proposal, ontology governs practices while such an ontology is specifically theological rather than generic. In his recent textbook on theological reading, there is some role for ontology – at least for an ontology of Scripture. It becomes clear here that a view of what the Bible is, and not merely a possible construal of it generated by a set of readerly interests (cf. Kelsey), is one of the parameters that factors into decisions on how to read it.[18] Nevertheless, the main investment in ontology is in that of the object being read rather than also that of the interpreting subject. The scope of the investment in ontology, even in this most recent evolution of Fowl's view, is

[15] Both sides of the dialectic are evident in Fowl, *Engaging Scripture*, 60, 62.

[16] While it is clear that doctrines and practices determine interpretation (a theory of textual meaning alone does not suffice), it is much less clear what determines these doctrines and practices. Granted, interpretation is said to *shape* them: Fowl, *Engaging Scripture*, 60. However, the whole perspective unravels unless the reader can trust such thought and practice to do what no theory of meaning alone can, to mobilize different interests with the result that readers have clear goals in mind when working through texts. Ecclesiology rather than ontology functions as the starting point.

[17] I owe this idea to personal conversation with Stephen Fowl at the 2006 Society of Biblical Literature Annual Conference in Washington, DC.

[18] Fowl, *Theological Interpretation of Scripture*, 1–12.

narrower than that of the present book. This is one way in which the influence of ontology is more limited in Fowl's work.

There is also a second way in which the sway of ontology is less significant on Fowl's view than it is in my proposal: it is not the case for Fowl, as it is here, that an interpretive aim generated by a theological ontology guides the selection of any definite reading strategies (the following section of the chapter details the strategies being recommended). As firmly as Fowl maintains that there should be interactions between theology and interpretations of given biblical passages, he declines to indicate what form those interactions should take, preferring to leave things more flexible. He says, "What I cannot do is provide a method for specifying in advance how these interactions will work,"[19] allowing his position to be filled out by a set of worked examples, rather than a regimen of rules or guidelines. His view is, therefore, clearer *that* theology and Christian practices belong together with interpretation than on *how* that relationship should be characterized in general terms. As with Fowl's work, this chapter does not provide rules for reading in the sense of procedures to follow that will guarantee proper reading in every case; that is asking more than any collection of rules can successfully provide. Yet this work does offer broad strategies of reading that allow readers to move toward the goal of interpretation. This treatment of interpretation is thereby less open-ended and evinces more structure by more explicitly addressing the how of reading, instead of offering the bare affirmation that Christian doctrine and biblical interpretation do indeed belong together – as crucial as that commitment certainly is. In sum, Fowl's view does not feature an aim for interpretation as thoroughly determined by ontology as what is proposed here, nor does he provide guidelines or reading strategies that can help fulfill such an aim. In these two ways, ontology does less work within his account of interpretation.

[19] Fowl, *Engaging Scripture*, 60.

A final example of a different position reverses the relationship of reading techniques and interpretation's aim. It is wrong to assume that a set of procedures that are stipulated in advance of any consideration of reading's aim must be applied to the text in every case, thus in effect determining what sort of interpretive aim readers might pursue. For instance, as Sandra Schneiders says, in describing well a view she rightly works to discredit, if it becomes part of the training of students to insist that historical methods are the only legitimate modes of engagement with the Bible, then it will seem to those students that they can ask only historical questions of the text.[20] Answering these queries becomes the de facto aim of interpretation if only historical methods are legitimate. Teaching interpretation in this way stigmatizes other questions, such as missiological, theological, or feminist ones, for it portrays these types of queries as ones that cannot receive answers by the only proper approach to reading.[21] To begin with a set of privileged methods, and then to infer from them which aim is valid, approaches the matter from the wrong end, and does not work from an aim for interpretation that is generated by the theological construal of the reader and the text.[22] For interpretation to have an aim means, rather, that methods or reading strategies function as means in relation to the end of interpretation. Methods thus become instruments or tools by means of which readers realize their goal, and what makes a method fitting as a way of reading toward this end is precisely its effectiveness in that capacity.

The goal of discussing the aim and strategies of reading here and in what follows is to indicate in broad terms the sort of tasks

[20] Schneiders, *The Revelatory Text*, 112.

[21] Ibid., 112.

[22] For other works that relativize method to something more important, or that set it in a larger context, see the following: Webster, *Holy Scripture*, 105, where the focus is on the purpose exegesis should pursue; Griffiths, *Religious Reading*, 74–75, which sees religiously engaged reading as located inside traditions of thought and practice, within which interpreters learn appropriate reading skills and the rationale for them.

methods should perform and to point out which methods can function in this way. As a systematic theological work, this project will not address the details of exegetical practice, but will reserve its focus for second-order reflection on interpretation, concentrating especially on the implications that doctrinal commitments in the domains of the reader's self-understanding and the construal of the text have on the trajectory of reading. The second-order question this section addressed is the nature of the work readers should expect whatever techniques they employ to perform. The following section discusses strategies that are appropriate as ways to fulfill this goal, and provides some illustrations of these strategies, yet it leaves detailed questions about the implementation of methods to particular texts for other contexts.

## How to Read Theologically

This section outlines a set of concepts which, as a whole, constitute strategies for theological reading. The key concepts, which structure three phases of interpretation, are *explicatio*, *meditatio*, and *applicatio*.[23] The following subsections expound each of these concepts in turn, beginning with the first. These reading strategies fulfill the aim of interpretation because these ways of relating to the text have a Christological focus, they include a moment in which the text is situated in its context of origin, but they also have subsequent moments in which interpreters allow textual content to enter into their frameworks of thought more fully, and in which they bring it to bear on their problems and concerns.

[23] The exposition is most indebted to Karl Barth's use of these concepts, though the division traces back at least to the pietistic theologian Johann Jakob Rambach. Similar schemes can also be found in other modern authors, though the larger theory in which they are placed is very different than the one here: Gadamer, *Truth and Method*, 306; Luz, "Reflections on the Appropriate Interpretation of New Testament Texts," 273.

Although these reading strategies are certainly different than those Augustine used, they echo in a modern way a pattern that runs through his whole set of interpretive techniques. There is a movement here, as in the strategies Augustine learned in his education when they are taken collectively, that begins with a detailed analysis of the text, moves toward developing a construal of it, and brings the text to bear on the readers' circumstances. Modern interpreters engage different versions of the biblical text than early Christians did, but they cannot commence their process of reading without closely and conscientiously attending to the particularity of the text. This involves historical research on its language, and I will propose below that it is more than just the occasional unfamiliar reference that should receive the illumination historical study provides. In addition, today's readers are not faced with a biblical text written in *scriptio continua* form, so they do not need to separate out each word from a continuous string of letters, and reading often goes on silently in our setting today. Yet modern readers still need to come to an understanding of the words of the text. Their more comprehensive commitment to historical engagement does not preclude what formed the final phase of reading in Augustine's context, discerning how the text exerts a formative influence upon the reader, though it does mean that this process unfolds differently than it did for Augustine. *Explicatio*, *meditatio*, and *applicatio* are not the concepts that structured Augustine's reading; however, they do some of the same work his techniques did – all with a modern spin.

Before unpacking these concepts, it is worth noting how this terminology is preferable to an alternative framework of concepts that, like the one expanded below, both values historical consciousness and allows for an appropriation of textual content. According to Paul Ricoeur's threefold account of mimesis, whatever prior understanding of the text's subject matter a reader had before engaging with the text itself is transformed by a close reading, which requires historical investigation along with other approaches. Interpretation then reaches its culmination in exploring the intersection of the world the text projects and the world the reader inhabits.[24] Crucially, though, the world that the text opens up is precisely a *possible* one for the reader to enter, not an outright claim to depict the actual world. Ricoeur explains, "For some years now I have maintained that what is interpreted in a text is the proposing of a world that I *might* inhabit and into which I *might* project my ownmost powers."[25] The view of interpretation that this chapter is in the midst of unpacking is one built on an ontology in the sense of a depiction of reality in light of God. It is this from which the purpose of interpretation derives; and it is this purpose to which reading strategies are answerable. A mere statement of what may perhaps be the case, or what a possible mode of being in the world is for a reader, does not mesh well with this tack. Because of this basic commitment to ontology,[26] what follows operates in the register of actuality and norms that follow from an account of the actual world.[27]

[24] Paul Ricoeur, *Time and Narrative* (Chicago: University of Chicago Press, 1984), 1:52–87.

[25] Ibid., 1: 81. Emphasis added.

[26] I grant that there are ontologies oriented around what can or will be, what could be, or even what is not the case. However, what I mean by ontology is not any of those things, as was indicated in the Introduction of this book. What I mean by ontology is an account of what is, and more specifically what is the case regarding the reader and the text as they are understood from a theological point of view. This book also pays attention to what should be the case, yet only as a result of what is first said about what is. That is the view of theological discourse as it relates to biblical interpretation that this work elaborates.

[27] For this reason, the whole proposal put forth in Part II of this book does not, strictly speaking, embody what Ricoeur calls the second naïveté. It fits with reading in the spirit of a second naïveté to a limited extent, as it calls for interpreting "in and through criticism": see his *The Symbolism of Evil* (Boston: Beacon, 1969), 351. The viewpoint on interpretation here refuses to view history naturalistically, but it does ask interpreters to consider the historical context of biblical passages. Yet this stress on history is only part of what Ricoeur has in mind with his well-known rubric, though it is often assumed in discussions of theological reading to be the entirety of the meaning of the second naïveté. The other main part is that particular formulations of a faith position are only *possibilities* rather than firm statements about how things really are. Ricoeur comments about faith in modern contexts, "In every way, something has been

## *Phase One:* Explicatio

The first stage of interpretation is *explicatio*, in which readers observe the sense of the written word. The aim of *explicatio* is to respond to the act of writing in an effort to secure an "inversion of the movement of thought which now addresses itself to me and makes me a subject that is spoken to."[28] *Explicatio* presupposes that the text is ultimately understandable, but that it requires some deciphering work, "the unravelling or unfolding of the scriptural word which comes to us in a, so to speak, rolled-up form, thus concealing its meaning, that is, what it has to say to us."[29] The Word presents himself in the words of the biblical text, though this self-presentation comes to readers in rolled-up form, and the duty of readers is to respond to this self-presentation, first by representing for themselves what the meaning of the focal text actually is. The work of *explicatio* is fundamentally an attempt to describe or depict intelligibly what is present in the text, and thereby to honor the subject matter of which the text speaks.

The essential drive of this phase of reading is not explanation in a reductionist sense, which intends to resolve the text into the contextual determinants of the situation from which it arose.[30] Explication rests on a keen awareness of such factors – and the deeper and more reliable a reader's understanding of these factors is, the better the resulting explication will become – but the work of *explicatio* does not reduce the text to such contextual variables,

lost, irremediably lost: immediacy of belief" (ibid., 351). For the view of theology outlined in the Introduction to this book, one which connects with classical precedent, adhering to a faith framework means making its core affirmations one's own and accepting their entailments, all the while being fully aware that faith is not equal to the knowledge that is possible in the *eschaton*, and therefore being willing to revise one's views, but nevertheless remaining invested in the framework as a fundamentally compelling outlook.

28 Ricoeur, *Freud and Philosophy*, 31.

29 Barth, *Church Dogmatics I.2, § 19–21*, 722.

30 Ricoeur, *Freud and Philosophy*, 31.

operating rather on the assumption that the text can be disengaged from them to the extent that it continues to speak to interpreters, even beyond the text's circumstances of origin.

Historical investigation of the background to the biblical text is one of the key aspects of the process of *explicatio*. This is necessary because the text's message supervenes on contingent factors that characterize its origin. The need is thus to construct, as accurately as possible, the historical backdrop to the biblical writings: this historical work will depend on a combination of inferences that can be validly drawn from the text itself as well as the picture emerging from extra-biblical source material. The reader should seek to understand the situation and events prior to the composition of the text in addition to how the situation changed after the text was composed and first read, thus situating the document in the flow of events with a view toward discerning how it spoke into those circumstances and effected changes in them. What is needed is focused investigation that centers on the circumstances surrounding the text's composition, editing, initial reception, and subsequent career. Readers should investigate questions such as the following: who authored any given text, what prompted the author to write, was the text produced by editing together preexisting works and if so how, what circumstances did the text intend to address, what assumptions did the author and his audience make about the issues being discussed, and what was the text's impact on the community which first encountered it? In asking these questions, theological readers must be alert to social, cultural, and political currents within the text's milieu of origin, but they should not proceed with a commitment to a naturalistic view of historical causation, according to which the social, cultural, and political exhaustively describe the real. This is one way in which theology makes a difference even at this stage of interpretation.

There is a second way in which theological belief conditions interpretive work in this first phase, that is, by making literary investigation an additional aspect of interpretive activity that is included in *explicatio*. Biblical texts should receive both literary and historical study; these two forms of study balance one another, literary work discerning connections among individual biblical texts (as well as within them), and historical study recognizing links between biblical texts and their various historical contexts. What ultimately authorizes literary study as a component part of *explicatio* is that all of the constituent texts of the biblical canon are signs to the triune God. "The object of the biblical texts is quite simply the name Jesus Christ."[31] They all demonstrate concern for this subject matter by saying something about it, and they can be studied in conjunction with one another, though they do not by any means all say the same thing about their subject. Part of what is involved with studying the Bible from a literary-critical angle is utilizing certain tools that have developed within the historical-critical tradition. Readers should avail themselves of insights provided by source and redaction criticism, in order to understand the literary shaping of biblical texts and what their original contributions are, over against the material that funded them. They should also understand as best they can the type of writing any given element of the Bible is by analyzing its genre. These tools can and should be accessed so as to facilitate a reading of the final form of the canonical text as a unified literary work.

Texts should thus be read in relation to one another, as all of the signs within the canon constitute a whole, and they exist in mutually interpretive relationship with each other. This point, though, works itself out differently in relationship to each testament. The texts of the Old Testament are, no less than those within the New, signs signifying the God who ultimately shows himself to be triune. Readers should first seek to understand Old Testament texts against the background of their historical context and their local literary environment. That is, they should read the final form of the text, but without immediately attempting to see how these texts chime in with elements of the New Testament. This is necessary in order to grasp as

[31] Barth, *Church Dogmatics I.2*, § 19–21, 727.

well as possible the text qua signifier. It is a matter of paying taut attention to the signifier in its own right initially. Readers should start by asking, for instance, what Exodus 12–13 says about the Passover rite. Having examined the signifier, they should at that point relate it to what it signifies, discerning that of which it is a sign. This second move obviously brings in the wider literary context of the canon. Interpreters ought at this point to consider how the Passover text shines a light on the discourse on the Last Supper found in Luke 22, and how both texts together say something about God. The first finds fulfillment in the second, but even so the first continues to add its voice to what the entire Bible says. Reading Old Testament texts thus requires accessing two types of literary context (local [OT at book level] and global [OT plus NT]) in two discrete steps, first focusing mainly on the signifier as such, and second moving on to examine how the signifier points to that which is signified as a broader set of intertextual connections is made.

How does the mutually interpretive relationship of biblical signs work for New Testament texts? Suppose that a given New Testament passage, when read in relative isolation from other books in the canon, can be interpreted in two different ways. It seems as if it could bear two possible senses when it is read in relation to its historical setting and in the context of the book in which the passage occurs. Suppose further that one of these senses fits rather poorly with the larger literary context of the canon, while the other coheres substantially better with it. If the text remains ambiguous when seen against the background of its local literary context and its historical situation, then it is legitimate to make recourse to the text's wider literary environment, the Old and New Testaments, as a way to settle on a final interpretation. Construing the whole biblical text as a collection of signs that directs the reader toward the triune God entails that biblical texts other than the single passage in question bear on the challenging text. Because of the deep resonance that biblical texts have with one another, they can serve as one of the contexts in which a difficult text should be read. When the wider literary context becomes operative in this way, the discrete voice of a given text is not drowned out by the voices of other texts, because every passage's local literary and historical contexts invest it with a significant degree of determinacy in meaning, even when the level of determinacy stops short of yielding a single definite reading for a text, which only the broader context can supply. The basis of this is not precisely that John's Gospel tells us what Paul's epistles mean (when the latter are taken fundamentally as autonomous texts), but that John's Gospel has factored into constructing a doctrine of God, and Paul's epistle is construed as a sign of that God. The construal as sign thus drives the mutually interpretive relation.

The third way theology makes its presence felt during *explicatio*, and which also ties in with the text's literary unity, is that the reader focuses in on the theological substance of the text by virtue of biblical interpretation's theological aim. Interpreters concentrate on the theology of the text in the sense that they consistently ply the text with trinitarian questions. They ask themselves while reading a given passage what it says about God, who is construed in trinitarian fashion. Readers thereby reflect how other passages from across a range of canonical documents have formed at least a minimal outline of the doctrine that specifies what is distinctive about the Christian concept of God. Given that readers have a specifically theological aim, they operate with theological presuppositions during this phase to the extent that their dialogue with the text is shaped by theological commitment, though not in the crude sense that they force biblical texts to meet an arbitrary set of expectations. "The openness of a question is not boundless. It is limited by the horizon of the question."[32] That the *res* of the text is a doctrine of the Trinity recalls Augustine's position, which sees in Scripture the same interpretive center. In this way, theological reading is not generically theological in that it has only a general

[32] Gadamer, *Truth and Method*, 357.

concern for some sort of divine entity. This is not a project in the service of a bare theism. Rather, it is a specifically Christian effort as a function of focusing the interpretive endeavor around the Christian understanding of God.

All three of the broad features of explication that have just been mentioned are on display in a recent effort to plumb the depths of Markan Christology. First, Richard Hays's chapter on Mark's Gospel in his book *Reading Backwards* derives quite a bit of interpretive leverage from situating Mark in the literary context of the canon; however, the work also uses historical background information to illuminate the text. This takes the form of assuming basic points of historical-critical consensus, such as the compositional priority of Mark in relation to Matthew, and noting other illuminating historical points as well.[33] Second, more stress falls on attending to "the poetics of allusion imbedded in Mark's intertextual narrative strategy."[34] The claim is that by tuning in to the way Mark narrates the story of Jesus, such that it resonates at many points with Israel's Scripture, "the full impact of Mark's Christology can be discerned."[35] Stated as simply and plainly as possible, the insight that drives Mark's Christology is "Jesus' identity with the one God of Israel."[36] Though this is what animates Mark's story, he actually presents less a forthright statement about Jesus than indirect indications of who he is, that is, hints and suggestions, including those that echo earlier scriptural texts. While Hays's exposition of Mark is not a comprehensive commentary on the entirety of the Gospel that works through it verse by verse, it does

[33] On the priority of Mark, see Hays, *Reading Backwards*, 17. For his overall intention to enrich rather than to overthrow historical criticism, see ibid., 131n1.

[34] Ibid., 28. Emphasis removed. I spoke above about how a New Testament passage's location within the canon can come to bear on deciding between competing readings of that text. The point here is not about disambiguating texts from Mark's Gospel but about deepening one's reading of them when the way they echo other scriptural texts is understood. These are both ways in which the widest context can be important.

[35] Hays, *Reading Backwards*, 28.

[36] Ibid., 19. Emphasis removed.

hit many of the narrative's highlights. In doing so, it aims to underscore how Mark constructs his story to both conceal and reveal who he sees Jesus to be. Because Jesus is one whose identity is disclosed most fully only at a moment of great obscurity – in a shameful death on the cross – it is fitting that the story is filled with veiled rather than overt indications of who he is. It is as if the truth is too great for a more open description. Explication should note well this strong connection between form and content.[37] Third, of course Mark is far from giving his readers a full doctrine of the Trinity, yet his Gospel makes a significant contribution to the doctrine. The Gospel depicts Jesus as divine, though not simply identical to the God of Israel: it is a story that "poses the riddles that the church's theologians later sought to solve in the Christological controversies of the fourth and fifth centuries."[38]

Though interpretation pushes beyond *explicatio*, this must always be reading's first phase, which is to say that interpretation should commence by observing the sense of the text in the closest and most exacting way possible, before moving on to the further stages, which build on the results of this stage. As Barth writes, "Interpretation as presentation is an introductory attempt to follow the sense of the words of Scripture. If interpretation cannot be exhausted by presentation . . . nevertheless it must in all circumstances begin with this attempt."[39] Interpretation must take honest and conscientious observation of the sense that Scripture bears as its point of departure, prior to assimilating the product of this initial work into the reader's

[37] As will become clear below, the synthetic drive of the second stage does not allow for preserving this entirely. I note that, as interpretation proceeds to this further stage, readers must not become obsessed with the conceptual representations which allow *them* to grasp the content of the text in their own terms. They must see these glosses as parasitic in relation to a text to which they constantly return.

[38] Hays, *Reading Backwards*, 27. Additional examples of explication can be found in Moberly, *The Bible, Theology, and Faith*, 45–130, 184–224; Watson, *The Fourfold Gospel*, 21–102.

[39] Barth, *Church Dogmatics I.2*, § 19–21, 722.

native frame of reference, and antecedent to bringing the text to bear on situations which are different in certain respects from those surrounding the text's genesis. The reason starting here is necessary is to establish a difference in principle between the givenness, determinacy, and specificity of the text's content and the conceptual means by which readers who are removed from the text's circumstances of origin may grasp it. Historical consciousness can function as a gift to theological interpretation insofar as it challenges readers to come to grips with the communicative force of each text, requiring them to ask whether ways in which they are accustomed to construing a given tract of biblical teaching match up well enough with what stands in the text. Preserving this as a defined stage, on which subsequent ones build, ensures that readers consistently confront this challenge when they engage with the Bible.

Crucially, though, as has already been stressed in this section, the deliverances of prior readings must and should still serve as deep background even for this initial level of interpretation. That the view of history built into inquiry regarding a text's historical background cannot be naturalistic, and that a text's literary environment must be accessed as a countervailing context of study, are both a function of the theological commitments shaping *explicatio*, as is the commitment to ask trinitarian interpretive questions of the text. This is, thus, not a foundationalist approach to exegesis, one that would build up from a version of *explicatio* conceived of independently from theology, one that moves toward but never from the later phases of reading. This proposal declines to ground the earliest phase of interpretation exclusively in "neutral" or generic beliefs.[40] This view of the first phase of interpretation is not issued from that

[40] For the observation that there is much to commend a theology that does not look for external verification of its own basic assumptions, see Johannes Zachhuber, *Theology as Science in Nineteenth-Century Germany: From F.C. Baur to Ernst Troeltsch*, Changing Paradigms in Historical and Systematic Theology (Oxford: Oxford University Press, 2013), 293.

utopian location, "a place to stand upon the desirability of which all reasonable people can agree."[41] Instead, theology delimits the parameters within which observation of the text's sense is made, while not dictating in advance what the substance of those observations actually turns out to be. This means that even during *explicatio* and before the later stages of reading, there is not an absolute distinction between meaning and truth in interpretation, for commitment to a set of truths hangs in the background while interpreters undertake their study of the details of the text in its historical and literary contexts. Such commitments ought not be held too tightly, thus allowing texts to challenge the reader's construal of the triune God. All such conceptions have to remain provisional and must not harden to the point that they simply deflect evidence that calls for their revision. That this account is not foundationalist means that, in principle, theological commitments do and indeed must shape each stage of reading, including this first one.

What this entails is that this view counts as a "one-step" account of interpretation, to employ John Barton's terminology, even though it includes the three phases of *explicatio*, *meditatio*, and *applicatio* – the latter two of which receive comment later in the chapter. This is a one-step view in the sense that the determination of the text's sense within *explicatio* depends on the prior assessment of other biblical texts as true. This is and must be a one-step account, for it does not want to establish any aspect of interpretation as a theology-free zone. Avoiding just that is the whole purpose of theological interpretation.[42] At the same time, this presentation acknowledges insight in two-step accounts such as Barton's, as it seeks to be modest in deploying theological commitment in this initial phase of reading.[43] The rationale for caution is

[41] Griffiths, *Religious Reading*, 183.

[42] For Barton's defense of two steps, see *The Nature of Biblical Criticism*, 159.

[43] It may be objected that it is difficult to set aside one's theological assumptions while reading. However, it is certainly possible to do so to some degree, and this account calls

that it is necessary to do justice, within the limits of this conception of theological reading, to meaning being use, and to usage changing across diverse contexts. Since meaning-as-use is relative to historical location, some historical study of the text is necessary to honor this fact. That step cannot be skipped entirely, nor can the theological commitments that shape *explicatio* be so strong that they become the sole factor driving interpretation. Yet for any exegesis that is worth deeming theological, analysis of such language cannot occur without theological background in place. The best way to bring together theological commitment and an acknowledgment of the relativity of language is to have the package of theological assumptions exercise a modest force initially. The presupposition of this proposal is that theology and history are not utterly antithetical to one another, such that bringing them together is possible, but neither are they to be equated with one another, and thus it makes sense to allow room for the historical relativity of language.

The point of this subsection has been to insist that theological readings of the Bible should start with explication of the text. This is a norm of interpretation, and therefore it can readily be converted into a criterion to adjudicate between interpretive clashes. There do, of course, exist a vast number of different and indeed conflicting readings for any given pericope within the Bible, and theological readers are bound to sort through the wild diversity of interpretations.[44] They can do that by asking several questions about how well a reading fulfills the

for a much less intense process of bracketing out commitment than does Barton's program, for instance. If what he is calling for is feasible, then what I am recommending must surely be seen to be so as well.

44 In saying that adjudication is necessary precisely because of the diversity of existing readings, am I assuming that there is a single correct explication of the text, perhaps one to be identified with the intention of an original author? This project has not foregrounded authorial intention, but has put its focus on how the biblical text signifies something about its subject matter. Readings should be true to what the text signifies, but given how rich what is signified actually is – it is the infinite triune God – this signifying work will not be completely represented by a single interpretation. As I say in what follows in the paragraph above, the determinacy of the text's subject

three requirements of *explicatio*. First, to what extent does the interpretation fit with the text's historical backdrop? Other things being equal, readings that fare better on this count are to be preferred. A further question is how well a reading accords with a passage's local and global literary context. Tensions are bound to arise between these two sets of contexts, as passages from around the canon of Scripture did not all originate in the same historical period. The two types of context need to be balanced against each other. A final query is to what extent a reading has a theological focus, seeking to determine what the passage in question says about God. Especially because of the second query's focus on local literary context, when the concept of *explicatio* is turned into a criterion for assessing readings, those that fare best will be cursive readings of the text, ones that follow the line of thought being presented, and use background information toward that end, rather than becoming fixated on such details in their own right: it will favor readings that are genuinely readings.

### *Phase Two:* Meditatio

The second stage of interpretation is *meditatio*, or reflecting on the content of the text and beginning to think within the framework of the text, as the reader grasps that content through the work done in the previous phase. This second phase is, in essence, "the moment of the transition of what is said into the thinking of the reader or hearer."[45] This level of interpretation remains text-based insofar as

matter can still be used to rule out certain readings, and hence it is not the case that absolutely anything goes.

45 Barth, *Church Dogmatics I.2, § 19–21*, 727. The term *meditatio* appears rarely in more recent discussion of theological reading. For an example, however, see Graham Ward, "How I Read the Bible," in *Theologians on Scripture*, ed. Angus Paddison (London: Bloomsbury T. & T. Clark, 2016), 189–91. Insofar as *meditatio* is text-based reflection on theological issues, the following are also relevant: Webster, "Biblical Reasoning," 733–51; and the literature on Scriptural Reasoning cited in footnote 18 of the Introduction. A worked example displaying the difference between *explicatio* and

what the reader reflects on is the verbal substance of the text itself. However, this phase is not strictly about the text per se; it is less exclusively text-oriented than the previous one in that the reader begins, at this point, to think by means of the text, to utilize it as a perspective from within which to engage the world in order to understand it and to act on this basis.[46] Or, to put the point more precisely: the text becomes an integral part of the reader's framework of beliefs, and has an impact on the totality of her thinking and activity. *Meditatio* is to "equate the understanding of meaning with a total interpretation of existence and reality in the system of Christianity."[47] Perception is a function of one's stock of operative concepts, in the sense that one cannot perceive anything apart from what the perceiver's mobilized concepts will allow, and this stage allows the categories of the text to function as means by which the reader understands and engages with the text, and through it, all of reality. Yet inasmuch as it moves beyond the text, it does so in a way that pays the ultimate compliment to it, for it privileges its point of view.

The line between understanding via the text and *explicatio* itself is quite fine. The end result of exposition is that the reader comes to understand the speech act that the text is performing, and she grasps this in linguistic categories that are what they must inevitably be: her own. This is the only way for understanding what the text says to amount to something more than simply repeating the words that stand in the text. Exegesis, even in the narrowest sense, obviously aspires to something more than verbatim repetition of the text's sequence of words. However, if the operative linguistic

*meditatio* would be Frances M. Young and David F. Ford, *Meaning and Truth in 2 Corinthians* (Grand Rapids: Eerdmans, 1988), in which the former's sections deal mainly with original meaning and the latter's with reflection on that.

[46] See the treatment of reason's role in rational reflection on the content of the Bible in Williams, *Architecture of Theology*, 17–19.

[47] Paul Ricoeur, "Preface to Bultmann," in *Essays on Biblical Interpretation* (Philadelphia: Fortress, 1980), 53. Ricoeur is most directly discussing Henri de Lubac, but the overall intent of his exposition is to describe not just a single interpreter.

categories by means of which the reader glosses and comprehends the claim of the text are slightly different in substance than those present in the text, then the reader is already beginning to appropriate the text, even during the phase of explication. Already here, to understand is to understand differently. The way the text's claim has been understood immediately enmeshes it in the worldview of the reader, however much the reader may try to minimize this. So it is both the case that "the author's experience is interpreted by his sacred texts" (in that he looks through the texts at his world) and that "his sacred texts are reinterpreted by his own experience" (in that what the reader brings to the text influences how he understands it).[48] In this way, the first stage sets up and builds momentum that impels the reader into the second stage. The key difference remains, however, for to see the text with one's own eyes is not precisely the same as seeing the world through it. Theological readers ought to take this subsequent step on the basis of the first.

That every interpreter of the Bible uses a scheme of thought in the process of reading the text becomes especially evident at this phase of interpretation. The reader ought to subordinate his own point of view to that of the text, and he must proceed circumspectly in the process of reflecting on it, seeking all the while to concentrate on the content of the text and to ruminate on it. Yet *she* must see it, which implies that subjectivity can be eliminated entirely only at the expense of rendering understanding utterly impossible. "'As we only hear with our own ears and see with our own eyes, we can apprehend by means only of our own understanding, not of that of another.' Naturally, for if we do not do so, we do not understand at all."[49] That the reader inevitably adds something to the process of interpretation – not despite his effort to receive the message of the text, but for that very reason – means that there is a genuinely

[48] Janet M. Soskice, *Metaphor and Religious Language* (Oxford: Clarendon Press, 1985), 159.

[49] Barth, *Church Dogmatics I.2*, § 19–21, 727.

dialogical element to the process of coming to understand the Bible. Any reading, in the sense of a reflective report of what the reader has gleaned from the Bible, will contain elements of the reader's self. What precisely is the nature of the reader's contribution?

The reader contributes to the dialogue in two ways. First, because *meditatio* is essentially about understanding the claim of the text, theological readers will use, as appropriate, the theological categories that have become part of their minds in their effort to grasp the subject matter of Scripture. Though theological readers will be alert to instances where no category from the postbiblical tradition fully and precisely represents the material content of the text,[50] for they have an interest in reflecting on what is genuinely present in the text, they will not eschew in principle all categories with a later genesis. However, because the purpose of reflection is to understand in a fruitful way what the biblical text is saying, reflective readers are bound to draw on categories to which they assign real explanatory power. These categories are part of their theological tradition, but this tradition is not something external to them. As readers call these concepts into service, interpreters are not only part of the tradition, but the tradition is part of them, supplying them with the tools by means of which they think and reflect on the material content of the text.

At first glance, it may seem that this could not be more different than what is happening in a hermeneutic of suspicion. For those who operate in the mode of suspicion, the intentionality of biblical authors is not seen as kerygma and does not convert into good news, but amounts rather to something sinister, for the text is judged to contain dangerous content.[51] No text, however, openly proclaims its dangerous qualities, making clear for all to see how it

[50] For instance, see E. P. Sanders's claim that the analytical categories by which post-Reformation Western Christians are most accustomed to understand Paul's theology do not match up well with it: *Paul and Palestinian Judaism: A Comparison of Patterns of Religion* (Philadelphia: Fortress, 1977), 492n57.

[51] Ricoeur, *Freud and Philosophy*, 30.

works to the disadvantage of some (and to the advantage of others). The drive of suspicion is, thus, toward a "tearing off of masks, an interpretation that reduces disguises."[52] It is a matter of exposing supposedly innocent claims for what they are seen to be within this point of view: misleading language that serves certain interests and reinforces the power of those in the ascendancy. Consider, for instance, how readers with a hermeneutic of suspicion might understand the familiar biblical story of the Golden Calf (Exod. 32; Deut. 9:8–21). In the narrative, the Golden Calf is condemned as an idol. The backcloth to the story is the existence of indigenous polytheistic religions that clash dramatically with a monotheistic system that privileges the written word of God. "Viewed from a materialist perspective," one that sets claims regarding transcendence to the side and understands what is referred to in the text via social, economic, and cultic categories, "the story of the Golden Calf thus seeks to disempower those for whom the divine is manifest in material, iconic form."[53] The biblical story aims to undercut systems that are friendlier to materialism itself than is the religion requiring final allegiance to Yahweh. Within the parameters of a materialistic outlook, understanding this story means highlighting how it operates in registers that are recognized as valid from inside this ontology, "examin[ing] the ideological aspects of symbolic (and other indexing) constructs and the ways in which they function in systems of exploitation and control."[54] If this is really all the story is doing, as this version of a hermeneutic of suspicion takes to be the case, then it is only fitting to undermine the force of its rhetoric.

At one level, this hermeneutic of suspicion is obviously different than what is being recommended here in terms of *meditatio*: the

52 Ibid., 30.

53 Francesca Stavrakopoulou, "Materialist Reading: Materialism, Materiality, and Biblical Cults of Writing," in *Biblical Interpretation and Method: Essays in Honour of John Barton*, ed. Katharine J. Dell and Paul M. Joyce (Oxford: Oxford University Press, 2013), 225.

54 Ibid., 224.

former seeks to undermine the text, while the latter aims to receive it, judging it to be a salutary word. However, at another level, what is happening within the hermeneutic of suspicion is fundamentally the same as the moment of *meditatio* within theological reading – to grasp, in a way that seems viable from within the mental framework of the interpreter, what is said in the Bible. Suspicion operates on the basis of a different judgment about which categories should be operative within an understanding of reality. The categories that any reader, whether one who sees interpretation as the recollection and actualization of meaning or as an exercise in suspicion, calls on to understand the content of the text will necessarily be those that constitute the viewpoint on reality in which that reader genuinely believes. One way or another, the text's claims need to be understood. That must occur, and this impulse to understand mobilizes the categories by which the reader engages with reality.[55] This is the first way in which readers make a contribution during this phase.

There is a second way in which they are active in *meditatio*. Readers also contribute in that the terms in which they understand the biblical text will bear the stamp of various other facets of their identity, not just their theology. Wolterstorff rightly says, "No one is *just* a Christian. He is also, say, an American, a Caucasian, a member of the middle class, a somewhat paranoid personality."[56] Reading is a practice that human beings undertake, therefore it proceeds from a

[55] Gordon Kaufman's essay on what to do with the Bible is an exercise in *meditatio* of a certain sort, in that he muses on what sense modern readers, with the secular outlook many of them have, can make of the biblical text, in which God is a ubiquitous presence. He concludes that they cannot believe its claims, though they do well to understand the effect of God within cultural memory: "So long as much of this highly ramified experience, thought, and activity of ours is thoroughly secular, it will remain doubtful whether God can or should be related to it; whether 'God' names anything we can any longer regard as independently and autonomously real" ("What Shall We Do with the Bible?," 111).

[56] Nicholas Wolterstorff, *Reason within the Bounds of Religion*, 2nd ed. (Grand Rapids: Eerdmans, 1999), 83.

limited, human point of view, not from a God's-eye perspective.[57] Nationality, race, class, personality, gender, and all the rest shape the set of operative categories by which any individual navigates the world. To take the example of class, it is not the case that readings of the Bible are simply epiphenomenal manifestations of one's position in a struggle for power between different classes of society. Nevertheless, it is still true that readers' class identities may well mark how they interpret the Bible. That part of the reader's identity will often form one coefficient within a whole range of factors that shape how the text's message is understood. Each of the nontheological categories has a definite texture to it, and reflection on the text that takes place through such categories will put a certain spin on the reading that any given interpreter produces. This is a major reason that there is a variety to the readings done by different people in one context or by people across distinct historical and cultural milieus.[58]

The process of ruminating on the biblical text constitutes a midpoint between establishing the sense of the text and discerning its appropriate use, and the value of this phase is the way in which it facilitates the transition between the two. It is thus a key part of the appropriation of Scripture. Without passing through this phase of interpretation, readers lack something significant: "the 'deposit of faith' does not really come into contact with *ourselves*."[59] It is important that the Bible be seen in connection with its context of

[57] Hilary Putnam, *Reason, Truth, and History* (Cambridge: Cambridge University Press, 1981), 49–50.

[58] For a thoughtful analysis of two case studies in Christian hermeneutics beyond the West, one from Africa and another from India, together with a proposal for how interpretive practice in these contexts gives reason to revise established assumptions in Western interpretive theory, see Joshua D. Broggi, *Diversity in the Structure of Christian Reasoning: Interpretation, Disagreement, and World Christianity*, Studies in Systematic Theology (Leiden: Brill, 2015).

[59] Rowan Williams, *Arius: Heresy and Tradition*, Rev. ed. (Grand Rapids: Eerdmans, 2002), 236. The value of being able to understand the Bible in one's own mental and verbal categories is closely linked to the Christian tradition's established commitment that the Bible be translated into the full range of vernacular languages: Lamin

origin, and readers must be willing to allow an actual engagement with the Bible to challenge their preconceptions about its meaning. However, any reader who takes up the text with the assumption that it is something other than another of the "silent relics of the past"[60] will not stop at the point of understanding what it is that the text is saying, and will proceed further to grapple with the ideas themselves, considering them as they make a claim on him, thinking about them from a point of view that is uniquely his, even as he subordinates his mind to the text. *Meditatio* often amounts to a reader reflecting in a more abstract register on the content of the biblical text. "Yet this abstraction, like all abstractions, can be enriching by producing some needed explicitness and clarity for the community's self-understanding."[61] The contribution of *meditatio*, the chance to contemplate the truth claims that the text proffers and to enter into a dialogue about the subject matter, thus grappling with the text in one's own native categories, is a significant one.[62]

It will help illustrate how *meditatio* works to discuss a sample reading. The affirmation within the Nicene Creed that Jesus Christ is *homoousios* (of the same substance) with the Father means that the two subjects are of the same divine nature. This key term,

O. Sanneh, *Translating the Message: The Missionary Impact on Culture*, 2nd ed., American Society of Missiology Series (Maryknoll: Orbis, 2009).

60 Gadamer, *Truth and Method*, 195.

61 Tracy, *The Analogical Imagination*, 294n57.

62 On the other hand, there is a risk that this process of reflection and assimilation will miss out aspects of the original biblical message because this phase of interpretation has its own specific goal and trajectory. It is important for the reader not to overestimate the enduring worth of her conceptual paraphrase of the biblical text, for the gloss does not replace the text itself, but remains subordinate to it. Success in the phase of *meditatio* means that the reader interprets *aspects* of the biblical text, not that her paraphrase is ever truly adequate, such that the reconceptualization of the text comes to replace the original, to which it is somehow now seen to be superior. See Tracy, *The Analogical Imagination*, 293n57. Readers must remind themselves that even the best reading is always partial. They will thus strive to achieve an interpretation that matches up well with the text, and will return to the text itself to seek further illumination over and above what their first reading is able to provide.

*homoousios*, does not occur anywhere in the Bible, and it is an anachronistic mistake to claim that any biblical author is operating with this category. For this reason, the Nicene creedal affirmation is not a conclusion that would follow validly simply from the exposition of any given text within the Bible – or even from a synthesis of expositions done across the whole range of canonical documents, if the act of synthesis is separated from theological reflection on textual observations. Though it is not possible to present all the details of the argument here, the substance of the creedal claim does emerge from theological reflection on exegetical observations from the Old and New Testaments when they are read as texts making up a complex but unified whole. The point is not to claim that the single term *homoousios* holds together all biblical texts, such that one piece of terminology summarizes all of what biblical revelation is about, with the result that other linguistic forms are hardly needed by way of supplementation. Instead, this term serves as one historically important example of the process of *meditatio*, which can be reaffirmed with a different spin in light of historical consciousness.

A close reading of the two testaments reveals a pattern of using the same names and titles, such as Lord, for both the God of Israel and the human person Jesus Christ, with the same basic meaning.[63] This presses the interpreter to identify the two, at least at the level of how God manifests himself within history. However, Nicaea says more than simply something about the so-called economic Trinity. The claim it makes pertains to the nature of Jesus Christ and God the Father, saying that they do not have two different natures, but rather are the same in essence. To think in terms of nature or substance is not just the habit of Greek philosophers. Within the Old Testament itself, which was binding scriptural testimony for all the authors of the New Testament texts, there is a clear and

[63] C. Kavin Rowe, "Biblical Pressure and Trinitarian Hermeneutics," *Pro Ecclesia* 11 (2002): 295–312.

repeated prohibition of worshipping any deity apart from the single, true God.[64] Though the Bible does not use the same terminology as philosophical discourse, there is, in this sense, a concern for ontology within biblical texts.[65] Early Christians could not have worshipped Jesus as they did, and simultaneously followed the prohibition of worshipping other deities, without considering Jesus, in a sense that needs to be specified precisely, to be on the same ontological level as God. "Thus . . . the two-testament canon read as one book pressures its interpreters to make ontological judgments about the trinitarian nature of the one God *ad intra* on the basis of its narration of the act and identity of the biblical God *ad extra*."[66] Again, it is not that the Bible formulates this judgment in so many words. However, its readers ought to do so if they turn over its content in their minds and see where it is all pointing and how the text taken as a whole makes it inevitable that they ought to think about God in this way.[67]

[64] Ibid., 300.

[65] Hans Frei is right to say that there is a philosophical dimension to this second phase: *Types of Christian Theology*, 92. Yet as concepts with a philosophical provenance enter into interpretation at this stage, their task is to draw out and reflect on the content of the Bible itself, and thereby to serve the text.

[66] Rowe, "Biblical Pressure and Trinitarian Hermeneutics," 308.

[67] For broadly similar arguments, all of which observe some version of a distinction between the original sense of the biblical texts and recapitulations of their subject matter in a different idiom, see Karl Barth, *Church Dogmatics I.1: The Doctrine of the Word of God, § 8–12*, Study ed. (London: T. & T. Clark, 2010), 308–15; Robert W. Jenson, "The Bible and the Trinity," *Pro Ecclesia* 11 (2002): 329–39; David S. Yeago, "The New Testament and the Nicene Dogma: A Contribution to the Recovery of Theological Exegesis," in *The Theological Interpretation of Scripture: Classical and Contemporary Essays*, ed. Stephen Fowl (Oxford: Blackwell, 1997), 87–100.

For further examples of the second phase of reading, each of which focuses more on a single text than the discussion above does, see Coakley, *God, Sexuality, and the Self*, 100–51; Marion, "'They Recognized Him; and He Became Invisible to Them'," 145–52; Kevin J. Vanhoozer, "Body-Piercing, the Natural Sense, and the Task of Theological Interpretation: A Hermeneutical Homily on John 19:34," *Ex auditu* 16 (2000): 1–29.

In summary, a way to gloss what is happening for theological readers during the phase of *meditatio* is to say that they *use*, and do not simply *mention*, the theological vocabulary and conceptual tools they find in the Bible and in the postbiblical Christian tradition.[68] To mention a theological term, in this technical sense, is to employ a linguistic form for the sake of saying something about the word itself. Mentioning a term could take the form of expounding the meaning of the word in a passage of the Bible, of detailing its history prior to its employment in Scripture, or of relating it to other terms whose meaning falls within the same general semantic domain. Using, on the other hand, refers to utilizing the word actually to do something. It does not speak about the word in question, but presses it into the service of a task. How does this distinction help explain *meditatio*? Within this phase, readers use theological vocabulary to understand the biblical text they are studying. Just about any significant study of the Bible will entail focusing on theological vocabulary in some way. However, for a theological reading operating at this level of interpretation, when this vocabulary is understood, it can be grasped within the framework of a theological outlook that is itself shaped by the Bible and the postbiblical tradition. The vocabulary of the Bible does not need to be transposed into an entirely different idiom that shears off its theological specificity and converts it into something else. For the theological reader, theological terms are deemed worthy of use. This is how theological belief makes a difference at this phase of interpretation.

Just as it was possible in the previous subsection to use the concept of *explicatio* as a standard for evaluating interpretive clashes, it is now worth outlining how *meditatio* can function in the same capacity for this second aspect of interpretation. Doing so requires asking questions about both of the things that readers are seeking to accomplish

[68] For this distinction, see Griffiths, *Religious Reading*, 184.

in *mediatio.* How well does a purported understanding of a text give the reader purchase on the actual passage? Potential readings that do not integrate at all well with the results of explication must be judged nonstarters. Conceptual paraphrases of a passage that operate at too high a level of abstraction, or that are simply inaccurate as representations of it, have to be set aside. This is the first aspect of *meditatio.* The complementary question is about the degree to which the paraphrase feels natural to the reader. Readers are supposed to be representing what they have understood a passage to say; the language in which they do so must be theirs if it is to reflect understanding that they themselves have genuinely achieved, rather than constituting a set of words they have borrowed and parroted. Familiar linguistic forms nearly always need to be adapted and transformed in order to serve well as representations of biblical content. Yet even in their adapted form they can still retain a significant degree of familiarity and naturalness for the interpreter. An understanding of a passage is not a replacement for the text being understood, and it is certainly not an improvement on the sacred text, but it is an attempt to follow what it says, and candidate readings should be judged on this basis.

### *Phase Three:* Applicatio

The final phase of interpretation is the reader's application of the content of the text to her own situation. "From *explicatio* we must pass over the bridge of *meditatio* to *applicatio.*"[69] The bridge of *meditatio* has already set up this third move by bringing the subject matter of the text within a reader's own frame of reference. Yet *applicatio* takes the further step of using the conceptual tools that readers have understood via reflection in order to solve problems

[69] Barth, *Church Dogmatics I.2, § 19–21,* 736.

that face them, and to navigate situations in which they find themselves. The text does not just enter into the worldview of the reader, but the text's language is actively mobilized by the reader to perform discrete functions within his outlook. There are two dimensions to application, namely, a cognitive or conceptual one that concerns beliefs, and also a lived or enacted dimension that pertains to how the reader lives and embodies the message of the biblical text. Both are crucial, and in practice it is hard to separate them. This twofold *applicatio* is necessary to a complete reading of Scripture, and without it the prior levels of interpretation are abortive. As Karl Barth explains:

> There is no possibility of a valid and fruitful examination of what is said to us in Scripture or reflection upon it, unless, proceeding further, it develops into appropriation of them. Without this, observation can be only a historically aesthetic survey, and reflection only idle speculation, in spite of all the supposed openness to the object in both cases. The proof of our openness to the object is that our observation and reflection on what is said leads to assimilation. . . . By "assimilation" is to be understood that what is declared to us must become our very own.[70]

In the final phase of interpretation, "the *sensus* must also show itself to be the *usus scripturae*,"[71] but the term *use* does not refer to readers' mastery of the text, but rather to the opposite of that – its mastery of them. The interpreter cannot approach the text with a pre-understanding of it that is fixed to the point of being sclerotic, nor should the reader consider the questions and interests with which he approaches the text to be entirely up to him to determine. Readers have to risk their prior construals of the text in their engagement with it, and they must ensure that their interpretive questions are actually fitting to the text they are reading. A reader

[70] Ibid., 736.
[71] Ibid.

can come to the biblical text assuming that it is fecund and presuming that it will speak in some way about the burning questions of the day.[72] However, she has to allow the text to set its own questions, and she must defer to its agenda. In the process, the text can redefine for the reader what the most pressing issues of the moment actually are. The reader may learn less about some topics than she was hoping to learn, but at the same time more about things that outstrip in importance the topics that preoccupied her at the outset of her interpretive endeavors. This is an implication of allowing the text's claims to describe reality. Subordinating one's questions to the subject matter of Scripture is a crucial part of what it means to use the text in a proper sense, that is, to allow it to use or master oneself as reader.[73]

In applying the text to themselves, readers identify themselves, to an extent, with those who first received the text. Readers identify themselves not directly, but indirectly, with the first readers of the text. A twenty-first century interpreter is not the same in every respect as a first- or second-century interpreter of a New Testament text. The modern reader lives in different historical, cultural, and geographical circumstances, and these factors make a difference to interpretation. Yet neither is today's reader entirely different from those who first took up the text with a view toward receiving its message. There is some distance between the two communities of readers, but distance is relativized by significant unifying elements in the experience of the two groups. Both read the text as a way to engage with the same God, and both do so as part of the same economy of salvation. The text is not absolutely contemporaneous with the experience of today's readers, for it bears the marks of its circumstances of origin. Yet its message is simultaneous with their

[72] Ibid., 739.

[73] See Colin E. Gunton, "Using and Being Used: Scripture and Systematic Theology," *Theology Today* 47 (1990): 248–59.

lives to the extent that their lives are unified, in the ways just mentioned, with those who first read the text.[74] Thus it genuinely speaks to them, not only to others.[75]

[74] For this reason, what I am calling application overlaps significantly with figural reading. On the latter, see especially these recent works: Griffiths, *Song of Songs*, lvi–lvii; Hays, *Reading Backwards*, 1–3, 93, 104; Ephraim Radner, *Time and the Word: Figural Reading of the Christian Scriptures* (Grand Rapids: Eerdmans, 2016). Radner's treatment is the most comprehensive in scope – providing a definition of figural interpretation as well as extensive exemplification, a history of the reading strategy, and polemic against ways of reading that fall short of it – though the exposition is sometimes hampered by a lack of clarity. Hays and Griffiths offer brief and illuminating accounts of what figural reading is, though they concentrate on implementation rather than theory. There are several aspects to figural interpretation. It is not precisely the same as application in that figural reading is something that takes place within the Bible itself, as New Testament texts take up passages from the Old Testament and see in them figures or foreshadowings of the reality of Jesus Christ. Figural reading also diverges from application in that it runs in two directions, for the original figure and that which it figures each illuminates the other. It is not just that Old Testament background sheds light on the New Testament, but when the Law, the Prophets, and the Writings are read retrospectively in light of Jesus, they take on new layers of meaning: see Hays, *Reading Backwards*, 3, 93. The key similarity lies in that just as figural reading establishes links between events whereby an earlier one represents a later one, and thereby a text can jump a temporal gap and speak into a situation other than its circumstances of origin, application operates on the recognition that a biblical text can address today's readers by virtue of construing them as identified with the original readers of the text. There is also a secondary similarity insofar as I have stressed that application operates on the basis of earlier levels of engagement with the text that takes its particularity seriously, and likewise the three authors cited above want to start with a richly textured, historically dense understanding of all figures: Griffiths, *Song of Songs*, lviiin36; Hays, *Reading Backwards*, 131n1; Radner, *Time and the Word*, 6–7, 10, 17, 25. Each of these authors aims to be "more attentive to the historicity of the figure," than one sees in ancient analogies to figural reading: Lubac, *History and Spirit*, 492. I am calling specifically for application because doing so allows me to commend the entire sequence of *explicatio*, *meditatio*, and *applicatio*, of which it is a part. The approving references to figural reading throughout the book make clear, however, that I view it in a positive light, though it is less obviously connected to the other interpretive moments I also intend to stress.

[75] Gadamer explains well how this is a different interpretive operation than that which historians take upon themselves: *Truth and Method*, 330–31.

In this way, a theological description of the reader, as one who reads with interest in the same triune God as the first readers and as one who is caught up in the same economy of salvation as them, is a significant part of the undergirding warrant for *applicatio*. Theology is part of what triggers this sort of reading; without it, a crucial part of the rationale is simply lacking, for there is an insufficient basis for thinking of present and past communities of readers as united in a sufficiently strong sense. In this way, theological belief plays a key role in the last level of interpretation by authorizing it to take place. Theological belief here amounts to more than simply a unity of interest, that is, it is not just that present-day readers and ancient readers are both interested in the subject matter of which the text speaks. Both are indeed interested in what the text says about God. However, it is also true that both are part of the world that God is reconciling to himself in Christ. For this reason, a modern-day New Yorker has a great deal in common with the Corinthians with whom the apostle Paul had correspondence.

An example of application is found in the *Barmen Declaration*. The statement was written in 1934 by representatives of the German Protestant churches as a vehement protest against a tendency on the part of some within those churches to compromise with the National Socialist movement, which sought to reinterpret Christianity as an Aryan religion free from all Jewish influence. The text of the declaration is peppered throughout with biblical texts, and the Bible is especially central to its six core articles, lending authority to each affirmation. Of course, none of these biblical passages, or any passage within the Bible, mentions specifically the threat to which *Barmen* was responding, the conflation of following Christ with being a member of the racial community with which the National Socialists identified themselves. Yet *Barmen* offers itself as a declaration of what absolutely *must* be said on biblical grounds in light of the present situation facing Protestant churches in Germany. Readers are invited to affirm the statement if and only if it is a legitimate reading of the Bible. The authors write, "If you find that we are speaking contrary to Scripture, then do not listen to us!"[76] The Bible speaks into the context of twentieth-century Germany by lifting up Jesus Christ as the only Word of God, allegiance to whom must outstrip all other loyalties that a person has. The first article cites John 14:6, "I am the way, and the truth, and the life; no one comes to the Father but by me," and on this basis categorically rejects the claim that God was somehow speaking via Aryan culture in a way that was in tension with the proclamation of Jesus Christ.[77] *Barmen* applies the Bible by calling on Christians to eschew the idolatry of race and to remain true to the terms of their own basic confession. There is both a cognitive dimension to this, insofar as the statement clarifies the implications of the confession of the exclusive lordship of Jesus Christ, as well as an enacted aspect to it in its stipulation of a non-conciliatory stance toward National Socialism.[78]

Once again, this norm can shift to become a standard of evaluation. The task of *applicatio* is to discern ways in which the text

[76] Jaroslav Pelikan and Valerie R. Hotchkiss, eds., *Creeds & Confessions of Faith in the Christian Tradition*, Vol. III, Part Five: Statements of Faith in Modern Christianity (New Haven: Yale University Press, 2003), 505.

[77] Ibid., 507.

[78] None of this is to say that *Barmen*'s application is entirely immune to any possible criticism. John W. de Gruchy takes with full seriousness the critiques that there were no minorities among the drafters of the statement, and that *Barmen* is all-too silent on the plight of the Jews. See his *Bonhoeffer and South Africa: Theology in Dialogue* (Grand Rapids: Eerdmans, 1984), 125–131. Despite its limitations, however, *Barmen* was nevertheless able to speak to those struggling against apartheid in South Africa later in the twentieth century. Just as its authors felt that what they said was the right thing to say in their context, the statement contained sparks that led to further application in another situation, and this application was not limited in the same way that *Barmen* itself was. As de Gruchy writes, "But the striking fact that testifies to the symbolic power of *Barmen* is that it has once again become significant, but this time within the context of black theological endeavor and witness" (emphasis removed) (ibid., 135). For an example of application which is keenly alert to the threat of race-based oppression, see James H. Cone, *A Black Theology of Liberation*, 40th anniversary ed. (Maryknoll: Orbis Books, 2010), 110–15.

bears on readers themselves. The key questions to press, then, are about the extent to which an application fits with the results of *explicatio* and *meditatio*, and how fully the reader is brought inside the world that the text presents (not as the first one to ever hear this message, but as one who does indeed genuinely hear it speaking to her). Readers are involved in every stage of reading, with this being most obvious in the final stage: the whole point of application is that the text is applied *to oneself*. That is an absolutely necessary condition of application; without it, there is no application. The involvement of the self in *applicatio* is not inherently problematic, but it does mean that the abiding temptation here is for application to become too self-oriented, for it to devolve into forcing the text to answer questions that the reader feels to be especially pressing, rather than allowing the text to reframe those questions as necessary. The question is which point of view is privileged, that of the text or that of the reader. Jenson is right to say, "Do not when reading Scripture try to figure out how what you are reading fits into some larger story; there *is* no larger story. Try instead to figure out how American history or scientists' predictions of the universe's future course or the travail of a family in your congregation fit into Scripture's story."[79] Putative applications of the Bible that reverse the direction of conformity should be rejected. Prefer those that show the reader how to inhabit the world in light of the God to whom the text points.

Having laid out all three interpretive moments, the final move in this chapter is to consider their interrelationship more fully. How should this final phase, application, relate to the previous two? *Applicatio* is distinguishable from *meditatio* and *explicatio*, but what should tie them together and make reading into a single unified process? In one way, the final phase is assumed into the first because explication works on the basis of theological

[79] Jenson, "Scripture's Authority in the Church," 34.

commitments that derive from prior readings of the biblical text: *explicatio* itself operates on the basis of application. Because deliverances of prior readings are built into this first phase of interpretation, the approach being proposed here does not have a foundationalist character, as has already been expounded. Though results from the final stage feed back into the first, it is also true that the second and third levels of reading should build from the first. The two stages that follow after *explicatio* must emerge organically from it. Otherwise a problematic dualism arises, in which theological reflection and the significance of the text for the lives of its readers are both cut loose from the most rudimentary level of reading, which positions texts in their situation of origin. The previous chapter's discussion of Stanley Hauerwas's commentary on Matthew's Gospel explored it as a work that demonstrates the importance of this point by being very much in breach of it. Thus, the different levels of interpretation stand in dialectical relationship with one another, the last having a bearing on the first, even as the first and second form the basis for the final one.

Current curricular arrangements create dynamics that are relevant to achieving this type of integration. The division of labor in today's theology and religious studies curricula means that what will tend to happen is that biblical scholars will concentrate mainly on *explicatio* and perhaps also *meditatio*, while the parties most concerned with *meditatio* will be systematic theologians and historians, with *applicatio* being the primary concern of practical theologians as well as systematicians with an interest in the embodiment of texts. There will be some exceptions – for instance, biblical scholars influenced by Gadamer will see themselves as involved in application – but what is indisputable is that specialization in research exerts a pressure against any single scholar attending fully and equally to all of these tasks. In light of this, the best way for theological reading to flourish is to sponsor interdisciplinary conversations where participants representing the whole range of specializations can contribute to a discussion that is to some degree unified around a shared aim. Hence, dialogue across customary disciplinary lines should serve as a necessary counterbalance to specialization, which is an absolute prerequisite of making original contributions to a particular field of knowledge. The best work in theological reading usually emerges from departments which are congenial to interdisciplinary efforts, and from conferences where this sort of discussion takes place. It is because contributions to theological exegesis are in fact made, and are probably best made, from several different disciplinary angles that this chapter has offered illustrations of each phase of interpretation separately, rather than putting forward a single sample reading that attempts to do everything all at once.[80]

## Conclusion

On this account, theological belief is not idle, either for the aim of interpretation or the means that seek to fulfill this purpose.

[80] I am sympathetic in principle with Francis Watson's call that disciplinary boundaries be collapsed to a great degree (see the case he makes in the whole of his *Text and Truth*). However, I am not convinced that this proposal can be implemented on a large scale. Watson has been able to master an immense range of material, but how many others have proven themselves capable of doing the same? There is also a virtuoso solo performance in Hays, *The Moral Vision of the New Testament*, but there are very few works indeed that successfully bring so much material together into a coherent synthesis.

That I have allowed here for contributions that undertake only part of what theological exegesis entails, and have indeed said that most efforts at implementation will attempt nothing more than this, may seem to be in tension with my critique in the previous chapter of Barth's Romans commentary for offering a final stage of interpretation that appears to come out of nowhere, rather than basing the last phase of interpretation on prior ones. See footnote 60. Recall, however, that I made the point there that Barth might at a minimum have insisted more strongly than he does in the front matter of his *Romans* that, while he has not shown all the work that stands behind his commentary, he considers what he does offer to be dependent on that effort.

Theology does not spin "in one place like the wheel of a car stuck in the snow."[81] It genuinely does something. Theology has a role in defining what the reader seeks to do with the text of Scripture and how she seeks to accomplish this. The aim of theological reading, moreover, follows from the theological ontology of the reader and the biblical text. The account of theological reading is thus theological from the ground up. It does not seek to build a hermeneutical framework on a foundation of generic, nontheological beliefs. Theology sets the overall trajectory of reading, and for each of the phases of interpretation, theology shapes how they occur, though theological belief exerts a bit less pressure on the first phase than on the latter two. Even at the very beginning of the process, though, its influence is felt in unmistakable ways.

This chapter's assertion of theology's role in interpretation, and indeed the very structure of the entirety of the whole constructive proposal, will seem to some like the polar opposite of faith being idle. In the eyes of some critics, this proposal will seem to have not a modest, healthy role for theology to play; it will seem as if faith is becoming violent and coercive, as if it is "imposing itself oppressively."[82] To these readers, the danger that lurks behind the constructive view of the nature of theological interpretation is one of overcompensation: "Wanting to overcome idleness, faith becomes coercive."[83] Is this really the case? After summarizing the whole constructive proposal, the Conclusion takes up this challenge.

[81] Miroslav Volf, *A Public Faith: How Followers of Christ Should Serve the Common Good* (Grand Rapids: Brazos, 2011), 13.

[82] Ibid., 17.

[83] Ibid., 17.

# Conclusion

What, then, is theological reading of the Bible? What difference does theological commitment make to interpretation? Doctrine's fundamental task is to depict the realities involved in reading. Theology is not just what needs accurate interpretation within the biblical text, nor is it essentially a set of preconceptions that readers bring to the text, nor does it consist of a set of ideas (and correlative practices) that contribute mainly to how particular exegetical deliberations find resolution within ecclesial communities. The center of gravity for this proposal for how theological reading should occur is *being* rather than *doing* – what is understood theologically, though implications emerge from the systematic interconnection of the notions of the reader and the text for what readers should do. Readers ought to be understood via a theological anthropology, with the result that their basic posture toward the text is responsiveness, rather than spontaneity of self-expression. When readers are so understood, they are distant from the text in space and time, but they exist in a world to which God has revealed himself, and they are situated in a social context together with others who have an interpretive stance toward the text that is similar to theirs. In addition, a genuinely theological understanding of the text avoids a dualism between history and theology by viewing the text as a *signum* to a transcendent *res*, and seeing the specifically historical features of the Bible as participating in and contributing to its function in this capacity.

All of this implies that readers ought to focus their interpretive energy around putting theological questions to the text, seeking out what it has to say about the triune God, and inquiring into how the content of the text has a bearing on themselves. As the introduction's typology showed, within the current discussion of theological reading, it is possible to find many different ways in which theological belief can play a role in interpretation, including entering quite directly into interpretive deliberations, so as to impact decisions on which interpretation is considered proper. Theology enters into the process of interpretation here too, but as an implication of its primary role; hence, readers are fundamentally receptive, or one might even say obedient, to the text and the nature of their situation *coram Deo*. Theological commitment should influence reading by altering how a passage's context is understood and what sort of interpretive questions are put to it in the first phase of interpretation, by supplying interpretive categories in the second, and by authorizing the third phase of application as well as shaping its implementation. In the words of James Kugel: "What Scripture is, and how it is to be read, cannot ultimately be separated from still larger questions, questions about our very way of thinking about God, and about ourselves in relation to Him."[1] Theological interpretation is about recognizing that reading the Bible is caught up in this field of questions. The thrust of the argument as a whole is that the hermeneutic outlined immediately above is a proper one, given that theology's primary role is to offer a theological ontology of the reader and the text, and given that the reader ought to respond in faith to the text's signifying activity.

The book's two major dialogue partners contribute to the overall project. Spinoza helps to show what theological reading is by providing a clear and forceful account of what it is not, namely, naturalistic reading (Spinoza returns once again in this concluding chapter, as we shall see). A theological account must take history seriously, and it ought to integrate historical consciousness within

[1] Kugel, *How to Read the Bible*, 46.

its scope, but it should not understand history according to a naturalistic view of the past. By contrast with Spinoza, Augustine offers something more positive by providing, from much earlier in the history of the reception of the Bible, an example of how to think theologically about interpretation, and by serving as precedent for the tack of seeking reading strategies to fulfill an aim of reading, which is generated on the basis of theological analysis. Part II follows him in operating with a notion of hermeneutical rationality unconstrained by the strictures of disengaged reason (Chapter 4); in distinguishing between the biblical text and its subject matter but relating them by construing the text as a set of signs to this subject matter (Chapter 5); and in several ways, including having theology influence every aspect of interpretation, from the earliest step through to the end (Chapter 6). Most basically, Augustine proffers a theological ontology that entails an ethics of interpretation, and the position here follows his model, not in all its details, but at a broader level in each of his position's major components. In so doing, Part II relates to Augustine's work "so as to exhibit the *effectus* monumentally, that is to say as something exemplary and worthy of imitation," thereby attending to Augustine's work, but also paying more attention to present circumstances than to the situation that precipitated Augustine's writings (their *causae*).[2] The argument of this book draws on Augustine deeply, and enters into dialogue with Spinoza as well, because they position the discussion of interpretation within an ontological register, as do other interlocutors such as Barth and Torrance.

The account of theological exegesis I have proffered in this book is of a particular sort. Even the most casual reader will have noticed the presence of a fair amount of interpretation of the contemporary discussion of theological reading, but providing that is not the essence or purpose of this book. It is not fundamentally a

[2] Nietzsche, "On the Uses and Disadvantages of History for Life," 70.

descriptive explanation of theological reading, one that would begin with a set of approaches to the Bible, all of which are provisionally accepted to count as theological reading, on the basis of which it would be possible to tease out what makes them distinctively theological. The aim of a descriptive approach would be to establish an equilibrium between the initially accepted examples and an account whose task is to characterize what they all have in common. If an example must count as theological reading, then it would have to fit with the account, and it would have to be explicated perspicuously by it; if a component part of the account seemed compelling, it could be used as a criterion to rule in some examples, while ruling out others.[3] The purpose of this book is not to analyze the current debate, though the present discussion forms the backdrop to this effort.

I apply the nomenclature *theological reading* stipulatively rather than descriptively. The purpose of a stipulative definition is not to describe accepted usage correctly, but simply to make clear and explicit how language is being used.[4] Though I assign the term this meaning by definitional fiat, it does seem fitting to refer to interpretations of the Bible that take their cue from a specifically theological construal of the reader and the text as theological reading, for theology makes all the difference in shaping these interpretations. Of course, it would be possible to call this sort of reading something else, perhaps reading the Bible as Christian Scripture. The terminology intends simply to highlight the salient features of this mode of engaging with the Bible. Yet, ultimately, the book is

[3] On the idea of bringing a group of examples into conformity with a general principle, both of which might be revised in the process of attaining what analytic philosophers call "reflective equilibrium," see John Rawls, *A Theory of Justice*, Rev. ed. (Cambridge, MA: Harvard University Press, 2003), 42–44.

[4] For a famous philosophical example of a stipulative definition, see Nelson Goodman, *Fact, Fiction, and Forecast*, 4th ed. (Cambridge, MA: Harvard University Press, 1983), 74.

not about the semantics of a particular label: the argument here can be detached from the label *theological exegesis* and evaluated independently of it.[5] Call it what you will, the book puts before its readers a case that a hermeneutic follows from viewing the realities involved in reading *sub specie divinitatis.*

Though the terminology is applied stipulatively, this book offers a constructive account of theological exegesis, because it propounds a positive proposal regarding the nature of theological reading, one which is framed against the background of the current discussion and a much longer history of debate, and one which uses the terminology in a carefully defined way reflecting the essence of the constructive argument. Probably the most significant obstacle standing in the way of this argument is the common objection, alluded to several times already, that proper reading necessarily requires interpreters to bracket out all the theological beliefs they hold, lest they interfere with the activity of reading. The final step in developing a case for theological exegesis, therefore, is facing up to this objection and demonstrating the legitimacy of theological belief playing a clearly demarcated hermeneutical role: having presented a case for why one should read a certain way, it is necessary to grapple with an objection to the effect that one should not do so.

[5] In this way, I am sympathetic to Moberly's suggestion that there may well be value in exploring alternative nomenclature, and that it is certainly not worth obsessing over the label *theological interpretation*. See Moberly, "What Is Theological Interpretation of Scripture?," 169. The rubric of theological interpretation has been used differently than I am using it here. For instance, it is not clear that my proposal would even count as theological interpretation given the way Michael Legaspi characterizes it (mainly with reference to Fowl and Reno), for he says, "Theological interpretation has no real stake in the regulation or deregulation of historical contextualization per se" ("Scripture," 163). My intent to avoid dualism means that I place a higher premium on historical background. While it is not worth squabbling over who has a right to a particular rubric, it is important to be clear – as Legaspi is and as I have tried to be – on how terminology is being used.

## The Specter of Eisegesis

### *The Objection Briefly Stated*

The major objection to theological exegesis – a variant of which is leveled at Augustine by James O'Donnell, to the effect that Augustine knows what the Bible says before he reads it, and thus conflates his views with the text[6] – is that it leads inevitably to and licenses eisegesis.[7] In other words, there is no such thing as theological *exegesis*, because an approach to reading that takes its cue from a specifically theological construal of the text and reader tacitly encourages interpreters to impose their own theological views on the text of Scripture. The idea is that theological exposition really amounts to imposition of a reader's own views: "It reads out of the text what it has put into it."[8] Now whether or not the proposal this book advances entails eisegesis depends crucially, of course, on precisely what eisegesis means. This is a matter of some complexity, but consider this first approximation. When readers approach the biblical text with firmly held theological convictions, and decline to

[6] See Chapter 2, footnote 78.

[7] For an example of the usage of this term (*Einlegen* in the original German) in a classical source, see Schleiermacher, *Hermeneutics: The Handwritten Manuscripts*, 50. For a response to a broadly similar concern, see Kelsey, *Proving Doctrine*, 170–75; cf. 14. Kelsey contends that the construals of the Bible that various theologians employ are logically prior to attention to any particular biblical text: they determine the type of thing the Bible is seen to be, and it cannot be apprehended with sufficient determinacy to be interpreted without them. This does not entail, he argues, that the Bible becomes "the weathercock in the church tower," a text whose interpretation is subject to the whims of theologians, because there are constraints on how construals are formed. The biblical text itself and ecclesial practices can both function as constraints. See also Kelsey, *Eccentric Existence*, 1: 141, in which the author argues that theological reading does not artificially foreclose the interpretive process, but rather, "It defines a field of questions; it does not close off the questions before they can even be asked." In what follows, I explore how essentially the same critique applies to my own proposal, which centers on theological ontology rather than a functionalist view of the Bible.

[8] Gadamer, *Truth and Method*, 328.

sequester them while interpreting the text, it is all too easy for them to project their views onto texts whose communicative intention is not to articulate exactly those views. Such an insensitive reading fails to perceive the actual message of the text, though it may be triggered by something in the text which roughly resembles an element of the reader's own framework of beliefs. Because such interpreters have failed to apprehend the text's true intention, their theological views are insulated against being challenged by Scripture itself.[9] It does not suffice to relativize a distinction between meaning and truth; the distinction must remain utterly absolute in the sense that the reader may not assume the veracity of the claim of the text under investigation, or of any other text or set of texts. In essence, the objection is that unless all theological commitment is put to the side, eisegesis follows as a matter of course.

That theological commitment is dictating the results of exegesis is a charge commonly leveled, and it is not hard to find examples of it. For instance, this type of criticism occurs when theologians who are resolutely opposed in principle to what is called natural theology – determining the existence or character of God apart from his reality being revealed in a special way, such as through the biblical text and what it says regarding Jesus Christ – claim to found their theological reflection on a scriptural basis, but fail to discern that the Bible itself can be read as teaching that natural theology is indeed possible. The criticism here is that an absolute antipathy to natural theology can blind readers to the Bible's effort to relativize itself, portraying itself as not the only path to knowledge of God.[10] Natural theology is a large, complex discussion, and it is not the purpose of this chapter to take sides on the question of

[9] Were this line of critique correct, theological reading could be considered an instance of "strong misreading," an interpretation which is interesting in itself but does not accurately depict the text it claims to expound: Harold Bloom, *The Anxiety of Influence: A Theory of Poetry*, 2nd ed. (Oxford: Oxford University Press, 1997), xxiii.

[10] See James Barr's treatment of natural theology in the Bible: *Biblical Faith and Natural Theology: The Gifford Lectures for 1991* (Oxford: Oxford University Press, 1993).

what the Bible really teaches on this topic. What makes this exegetical discussion pertinent is that it serves as an example – or, rather, some scholars see it as an example – of reading in that is encouraged by a refusal to bracket out all theological belief while engaging with the Bible. Does theological exegesis, as it has been outlined above, encourage a retrojection of one's own views, or the views that have currency in one's tradition, onto texts that offer them scant support? Is theological exegesis simply rationalization in the sense of "the process of giving reasons for positions already taken as distinct from the process of determining in a reasoned way whether the positions already taken are, in fact, worth taking"?[11] Is theological exegesis something like Rorschach tests, in which people report what they make of an inkblot, and the interesting thing about the process is what their reports indicate about *them* as human subjects, instead of about the objects to which they are reacting?

It would be difficult to locate a more passionate statement of this concern than one finds in *The Anti-Christ*, a late polemical work by Friedrich Nietzsche, who as a student withdrew from a university course in theology to pursue the study of philology instead. Nietzsche was not a classic nineteenth-century historicist with a supreme commitment to interpretive objectivity, but the reading habits of the theologians nevertheless caused revulsion in him:

> – Another mark of a theologian is his *incapacity for philology.* Philology should be understood here in a very general sense, as the art of reading well, – to be able to read facts *without* falsifying them through interpretation, *without* letting the desire to understand make you lose caution, patience, subtlety. Philology as *ephexis* in interpretation: whether it concerns books, newspaper articles,

[11] Schubert M. Ogden, *Faith and Freedom: Toward a Theology of Liberation* (Belfast: Christian Journals Limited, 1979), 116. Ellen Davis rightly claims that it is often the case that both liberal and conservative ecclesial communities approach the text as if they already know precisely what it says: *Wondrous Depth: Preaching the Old Testament* (Louisville: Westminster John Knox, 2005), xi.

> destinies, or facts about the weather, – not to mention "salvation of the soul" . . . The way a theologian, whether in Berlin or Rome, interprets a "verse of Scripture" or an event (a military victory by his fatherland, for instance) in the higher light of the Psalms of David is *brazen* enough to drive a philologist crazy.[12]

In Nietzsche's unsympathetic portrayal, the failure of theologians to understand is due to a lack of *ephexis*, or suspension of judgment: everything seems to have been decided beforehand, in advance of the activity of reading itself. In which case, what really is the point of reading? It seems to be an utter sham, a matter of claiming to find something one has in fact deposited in the text oneself. Such handling of a text is bold in the sense that it is fundamentally an exercise in self-assertion, rather than being a responsive or receptive procedure.[13]

Something very much like this objection is often voiced within our contemporary context in debates about theological reading of Scripture. For instance, John Barton contends that theological reading may refer to any interpretation of the Bible that attends to the theological content of the text, but if it means, instead, an "exegesis" that is controlled by a religious vision, then the meaning found in the text will necessarily be determined by prior commitments.[14] Barton renders this assessment after canvassing accounts of reading from recent advocates of theological interpretation. Though Barton issued these evaluative comments before the publication of most of the Brazos commentaries that are presently in print, his vantage

[12] Friedrich Nietzsche, *The Anti-Christ, Ecce Homo, Twilight of the Idols, and Other Writings*, Cambridge Texts in the History of Philosophy (Cambridge: Cambridge University Press, 2005), 51.

[13] For similar remarks on boldness in theological reading, see Spinoza, *Theological-Political Treatise*, 115. Cf. Kierkegaard's wrestling with the charge that reading the Bible with reference to oneself represents an excess of subjectivity and is, more specifically, a form of vanity: *For Self-Examination*, 36.

[14] Barton, *The Nature of Biblical Criticism*, 176–77.

point could provide him with a way to explain why the volume discussed in this book's fifth chapter is inadequate – granted, though, it is a different explanation than the one I myself offered there. Perhaps, as Barton would have it, giving as much scope within the process of interpretation to doctrine as the Brazos series does makes it a foregone conclusion that commentators will turn the text into a mouthpiece for their own convictions. Maybe it is simply a bad idea to think that doctrine can clarify rather than obscure what the Bible has to say.

Variations on essentially the same remonstrance have a long history. In the twentieth century, Karl Barth's commentary on Paul's epistle to the Romans provoked critics to charge that his theology had run roughshod over the message of the apostle. As Barth explained, he aimed to treat the text not simply as an ancient document that communicated a message within its context of origin alone but as a testimony even in his own day to a certain theological subject matter. "It has been asserted," Barth acknowledged, "that I mean, of course, [by the text's subject matter] my own 'system.' I know that I have laid myself open to the charge of imposing a meaning upon the text rather than extracting its meaning from it, and that my method implies this."[15] Likewise, Rudolf Bultmann's famous, concise essay "Is Exegesis without Presuppositions Possible?" sets forth his own response to the critique that his approach to the New Testament was yet another form of eisegesis, because it acknowledged its dependence on a certain way of posing interpretive questions, as a function of having an incipient understanding of the subject matter of which the text spoke.[16] Bultmann's conception of the Bible's subject matter had a more anthropological slant than did Barth's, but both of these twentieth-century theologians found

[15] Barth, *The Epistle to the Romans*, 10.

[16] Rudolf Bultmann, "Is Exegesis without Presuppositions Possible?," in *The New Testament and Mythology and Other Basic Writings*, ed. Schubert M. Ogden (Philadelphia: Fortress, 1984), 145–53.

it necessary to respond to the objection that an interpretation that was in any way informed by a prior construal of the text's subject was problematic.[17] What their critics seemed to want was for them to read any given text such that their interpretation was not contingent on theological beliefs that they may have acquired from other biblical texts, their participation in an ecclesial tradition, their own contemporary milieu, or (what actually seems most likely) any complex combination of these factors. In interpretive disputes over the Bible, contending parties have always charged their rivals with reading their own opinions into texts that provide their views with little justification. However, the specific form that the objection most often assumes in our context, that *theological* allegiance hampers a reader's attempt to discern a text's true and original sense, traces back at least to the early Enlightenment period.[18]

### *Further Exploration of the Objection*

Before probing any further into the history of this objection, however, it is necessary to unpack its meaning and the rationale for this critique as it receives articulation in a contemporary setting. On this

[17] For a parallel to this discussion from within the fields of general hermeneutical theory and literary studies, see E. D. Hirsch's critique of Hans Georg Gadamer. According to Gadamer, readers understand texts when their horizons fuse with those of the text: this involves the text's history of effects reaching out to and enclosing the reader, and the reader drawing the text's claim about its subject matter within his own framework of meaning. This view does not picture a situation of strict dualism between interpreting subject and interpreted object, nor is interpretation simply the historical reconstruction of authorial intention. See Gadamer's magnum opus: *Truth and Method*. E. D. Hirsch curtly concludes that Gadamer allows interpretation to be governed by prejudice in its standard pejorative sense, though Gadamer had tried to develop a view of the term that broke out of the Enlightenment's prejudice against prejudice: *Validity in Interpretation*, 258–64.

[18] In what follows, I am indebted to Mark Bowald's perceptive study on the contemporary discussion's propensity to abstract divine activity from the realm of human existence, though he does not deal specifically with the question of eisegesis, which is my focus. See his study *Rendering the Word in Theological Hermeneutics*.

line of thinking, the overarching goal of interpretation ought to consist of providing an objective depiction of what actually stands in the text of Scripture. "Objectivity" is a key term that has come up already in this book, but it is necessary at this juncture to explore it in more depth. It bears two linked senses here. Primarily, it means rearticulating the actual content of the Bible, not simply by repeating it, but by presenting the material in categories that allow contemporary readers to grasp the text's meaning. Secondarily, it evokes the idea that one must distance oneself from one's own preconceptions in order reliably to carry out this task, for the reader's presuppositions inevitably differ from those that are present in the text, coming as it does from a time and place quite different from the interpreter's own milieu. A proper objective description of the contents of the Bible means rendering an interpretive account of what a given passage means – whether or not one agrees with the claim made by the author of the text.[19] Reading in this way requires distanciation, distancing oneself from one's own views, apart from which readers will in all likelihood simply understand texts to say just what they expected them to say. "What makes biblical interpretation possible is radical detachment, emotional, intellectual, and political distanciation. Disinterested and dispassionate scholarship enables biblical critics to enter the minds and world of historical people, to step out of their own time and to study history on its own terms, unencumbered by contemporary questions, values, and interests."[20] Apart from a commitment to read in this way, mistakes are bound to arise.

[19] Barr, *The Concept of Biblical Theology*, 198, 205. Barr notes that the locus classicus for the "cool, descriptive" historical and objective position is Stendahl's article in the *Interpreter's Dictionary of the Bible*. See Barr, *The Concept of Biblical Theology*, 189. Stendahl himself, though, makes clear his debt to prior German-language discussion, especially the History of Religions School: "Biblical Theology, Contemporary," in *The Interpreter's Dictionary of the Bible: An Illustrated Encyclopedia*, ed. George A. Buttrick (Nashville: Abingdon, 1962), 1: 418.

[20] Elisabeth Schüssler Fiorenza, "The Ethics of Biblical Interpretation: Decentering Biblical Scholarship," *Journal of Biblical Literature* 107 (1988): 9. Schüssler Fiorenza

According to our objectors, the lurking danger that threatens to destabilize the exegetical task is that the reader may fuse her own views with the substance of Scripture itself, so the best way to secure objectivity is by establishing a firm distinction between perceiving a text's sense and evaluating its claims. This is the purpose that lies behind Krister Stendahl's simply stated and memorable distinction between what a text *means*, how it bears significance to the present community of faith whose sacred scripture it is, and what it *meant*, its sense as it was originally composed in its setting of genesis and as it was received by its first readers.[21] Giving an account of what the text originally meant is essentially a task of description, while considering what the text means in the present involves hermeneutical reflection and results in normative recommendations on how the text might shape lives now. After surveying interpreters such as Barth and Bultmann, who do not share his fundamental commitment to abiding by a strict separation between past and present, Stendahl ventures, "It thus appears that the tension between 'what it meant' and 'what it means' is of a competitive nature, and that when the biblical theologian becomes primarily concerned with the present meaning, he implicitly (Barth) or explicitly (Bultmann) loses his enthusiasm or his ultimate respect for the descriptive task."[22] John Barton does not employ the same terminology as Stendahl, but he is just as dogged in his insistence that reading should be undertaken in two discrete stages, first, the discernment of the meaning of the text and, second, an evaluation of the text according to what one already believes.[23] The more that readers insist on understanding the Bible in such a way that what

here summarizes eloquently the ethos and aim of a view she seeks to unsettle, if not to reject entirely.

21 Stendahl, "Biblical Theology, Contemporary," 1: 419. For an insightful critique of this formulation, which is nevertheless deeply sympathetic to what Stendahl is trying to achieve, see Barr, *The Concept of Biblical Theology*, 202–05.

22 Stendahl, "Biblical Theology, Contemporary," 1: 421.

23 Barton, *The Nature of Biblical Criticism*, 158–64.

they construe it to say is true, and the more they identify their theological beliefs with Scripture, the greater the pressure on them to twist the sense of the text such that it matches up with their preexisting beliefs.[24] Evaluation depends on ascertaining meaning, but ascertaining meaning does not depend on any of the beliefs according to which the text might be assessed; more than that, those beliefs will most likely trammel the process of looking into the sense of a passage. (The means/meant distinction is thus closely related to Spinoza's distinction between meaning and truth, which was covered in Chapter 3. Both distinctions aim to separate considerations of textual meaning from [theological] questions or beliefs on the part of the reader that can be deemed private.)

Recent advocates of the objection that theological reading amounts to eisegesis all concede that complete objectivity is impossible, but they continue to recommend it as reading's desideratum, and are sanguine that it is achievable, at least in large measure. Hence, interpreters should bracket out their beliefs as much as they possibly can. It becomes especially obvious that interpreters, and not just the Bible itself, are situated in a particular context when one reads expositions of the Bible that were written in a time far removed from one's own. Then alien interpretive grids shine through most clearly. As Stendahl admits, "We can smile when we see how an earlier generation of biblical scholars peddled Kantian, Hegelian, and Ritschlian ideas, all the time subjectively convinced that they were objective scholars who only stated 'facts.'"[25] Yet at the same time, "The relativity of human objectivity does not give us an excuse to excel in bias."[26] The most imposing obstacle standing in the way of objectivity is not anything inherent in the practice of reading itself, but rather a failure to pursue this goal zealously, perhaps as a result of being convinced by advocates of

[24] Barton, "James Barr as Critic and Theologian," 19.

[25] Stendahl, "Biblical Theology, Contemporary," 1: 422.

[26] Ibid.

theological reading that the ultimate objective is misplaced. It is not hard to see why those who think that the objective stance is neither completely within the interpreter's grasp nor even worth striving for as much as possible risk coming across as fanatics, for they can seem self-indulgent with regard to their own predispositions and wary to acknowledge what appears to others as a readily available hard interpretive standard.[27]

A factor that lends plausibility to this objection, and shapes its rhetoric, is an implication of there being, at present, no societywide consensus on any transcendent framework that might give meaning to human life. Our critics portray theologically shaped reading as an engagement with the Bible that is highly individualized, perhaps even idiosyncratic in its methods or results, and deeply personal – the farthest thing imaginable from reading being a function of a universally shared human rationality that works toward consensus. What makes this possible is that religious belief today seems entirely optional. By contrast, as Charles Taylor explains, "In earlier ages … when the major definition of our existential predicament was one in which we feared above all condemnation, where an unchallengeable framework made imperious demands on us, it is understandable that people saw their frameworks as enjoying the same ontological solidity as the very structure of the universe."[28] Yet things are different now: "The very fact that what was once so solid has in many cases melted into air shows that we are dealing not with something grounded in the nature of being, but rather with changeable human interpretations."[29] If theological belief really is a matter of mutable human construction, no form of which is shared widely enough to dominate the culture, then it becomes

[27] See the discussion of the overwhelming zeal of some biblical interpreters, whom Barton admonishes with these words: "One must turn down the heat in order to do the criticism." See *The Nature of Biblical Criticism*, 174.

[28] Taylor, *Sources of the Self*, 27.

[29] Ibid.

easier to see how the objectors can characterize approaches to the Bible that make some version of theological belief operative seem dependent on beliefs that, while deeply held, command assent from only a precious few. They are nothing more than one's own. The disenchanted cultural situation contributes to making it seem that this form of reading is an exercise in asserting one's own subjectivity where it does not belong.

Just as there is no societywide consensus on a transcendent framework of meaning, there is also a pervasive perception that Christian theology itself is a fractured enterprise, and this contributes to the sense that if theology were to impinge on biblical interpretation, that process would be anything but orderly. The fear is that theological exegesis treats Scripture "like a Nose of Wax, to be turn'd and bent, just as may fit the contrary Orthodoxies of different Societies. For 'tis these several Systems that to each Party are the just Standards of Truth, and the meaning of the Scripture is to be measur'd only by them."[30] That is, the theological beliefs that any one reader has may overlap with those of her religious community, but there are many Christian confessions – Protestant, Roman Catholic, and Orthodox, to name the main ones – and they are not identical in the way they portray the text, the reader, or reading.[31] There would thus be many ways in which one's

[30] John Locke, *Vindications of the Reasonableness of Christianity*, Clarendon Edition of the Works of John Locke (Oxford: Clarendon Press, 2012), 126. I owe this quotation, though it appears there in a different version, to Wolterstorff, *Divine Discourse*, 226. Wolterstorff considers this problem, judiciously concluding that reading the Bible for what he calls divine discourse requires employing the reader's own convictions about God, but adding a number of factors that can relieve a great deal of the anxiety surrounding this inevitability: *Divine Discourse*, 236–39.

[31] See Jonathan I. Israel, *Radical Enlightenment: Philosophy and the Making of Modernity 1650–1750* (Oxford: Oxford University Press, 2001), 3–22, who notes that since the early Enlightenment, the once uniform structure of authority and belief that united the various branches of Christianity, even after the divisions of the Reformation, has been riven by conflicts over how to respond to the rise of the new philosophy. For more on the multiplication of spiritual options in modernity, see Taylor, *A Secular Age*, 299–313.

theological framework might have implications for reading, but there would not be an obvious way to adjudicate among the diverse approaches. On this basis, objectors to theological reading try to portray theological reading among a multiplicity of Christian confessions as a melee of undisciplined personal convictions.[32] Any given reader's theological views could be quite idiosyncratic, and this comes to serve as a further reason to hold such convictions back from becoming involved in prescribing how to read texts. Theological belief is essentially subjective, and the influence of subjectivity on reading must be minimized.

Though the objection insists that readers with theological convictions put them to the side for the sake of an unhindered engagement with the Bible, the root motivation behind this pursuit of objectivity is not secular but religious. Ironically, faith serves itself best by silencing itself, by marginalizing its own affirmations for the sake of an uninhibited focus on "the *givenness* of linguistic structures, of the wording of texts, of the realities to which biblical writers were responding, of the presence of religious ideas in the human race."[33] People of faith are deeply motivated to find out what their sacred text actually says, and recovering and presenting what the text says is the aim of an objective-descriptive approach to the Bible. The only way for the Bible to nourish the faith of believers is if the believers can actually engage with it, such that it might, in theory, challenge the beliefs they already hold. Protestant discussions of the Bible place an especially high premium on the Bible being able to push back and speak against beliefs that have an established status in the life of a community. However, all Christians want to understand the message of the Bible when they are reading it. As Stendahl says pointedly, "For the life of the church such a consistent descriptive approach is a great and promising asset which enables the church, its preaching and teaching ministry,

[32] Barr, *The Concept of Biblical Theology*, 191.

[33] Barton, "James Barr as Critic and Theologian," 24–25.

to be exposed to the Bible in its original intention and intensity, as an ever new challenge to thought, faith, and response."[34] As the objectors would have it, the fundamental drive of theological exegesis, as this book has advocated for it, is mistaken, even granting a religious motivation to read the Bible. For religiously invested readers, and not only secular ones, it would be better to proceed otherwise.

To state the objection in summary form: if one completely segregates the task of describing what the message of a given biblical text is from the subsequent duty of assessing that message as to its applicability or truthfulness, then one will have protected reading from degenerating into eisegesis, in the sense of a reader allowing her own particular theological views to seep into the process of depicting the content of the text. To press the charge that my proposal licenses eisegesis is to say that because it explicitly builds an account of reading, and associated reading strategies, on an unashamedly theological view of the text and the reader, then the above consequences follow necessarily. According to this objection, that theological exegesis relativizes the distinction between interpretive stages undercuts a condition that is necessary to ensure that the text speaks in its own voice and says things other than what the reader already expects, because it builds the deliverances of reading (a theological anthropology and a theology of Scripture) into an account of the practice of reading. More specifically, what is supposedly problematic is that the first phase of interpretation, *explicatio*, is theologically conditioned, if only modestly, and that a reader's work of explication occurs with a view toward proceeding further to the stages of *meditatio* and *applicatio*. Furthermore, that the reading strategies the interpreter employs are responsive to an overall interpretive aim, which is marked by specifically theological

[34] Stendahl, "Biblical Theology, Contemporary," 1: 431. Cf. Barr, *The Concept of Biblical Theology*, 208; Barr, "Biblical Criticism as Theological Enlightenment," 167–68; Barton, *The Nature of Biblical Criticism*, 177–85.

content, will seem from the objectors' point of view to be an imposition. This criticism is distinct from the proposal that a given reader has *purposely* misread the Bible so as to align it with his own views or projects. In addition, the criticism outlined above is also distinguishable from the idea that the biblical text we presently have was corrupted by biased scribes who copied manuscripts they received in such a way as to favor a certain (orthodox) theological viewpoint.[35] With respect to theological exegesis, the objection that most obviously calls out for a response pertains not to the formation of the present text, or to how it is misconstrued by those with malicious motives, but to how theologically engaged readers interpret it.

## Exegesis and Ontology Revisited

Are there resources within my position on the basis of which to respond to this critique? The first point by way of reply is that where the border between exegesis and eisegesis lies is not an absolute given, one that holds constant irrespective of commitments in other areas. As a detailed account of eisegesis, the objection just elaborated itself emerges from an understanding of normative procedures for interpretation and a definite aim for interpretation, both of which rest on a definite (though often implicit) view of the text and the reader as well. It is just that the objectors have set in place a different ontology of text and reader, one that does not require theological categories to do descriptive work. George Lindbeck rightly notes that it is impossible to find entirely neutral ground on the basis of which to adjudicate between deeply different types of theology, for each type "is embedded in a

[35] Bart D. Ehrman, *The Orthodox Corruption of Scripture: The Effect of Early Christological Controversies on the Text of the New Testament*, Updated ed. (Oxford: Oxford University Press, 2011).

conceptual framework so comprehensive that it shapes its own criteria of adequacy."[36] The present point is not that ontological frameworks shape criteria by which they themselves should be judged, but rather that they determine the criteria of adequacy (or inadequacy) for interpretation. In other words, it is not the case that a single universally valid view of eisegesis can be used as a touchstone of interpretive adequacy. Rather, different norms for reading, and corresponding views of what constitutes a fallacious interpretive argument, grow out of different views of the ontology of the reader and the text.

### *Eisegesis and Naturalism*

A further exploration of the history of the objection will help clarify how an ethics of reading is, once again, contingent on ontological issues. Spinoza develops a criticism of his medieval forebear Maimonides that displays an important similarity to the objection above.[37] As Spinoza expounds his position, Maimonides is unwilling to accept that there can be an ultimate conflict between a genuine sense of a scriptural passage and the truth of the matter as reason is able to grasp it.[38] Of course, there might be prima facie conflicts – apparent clashes between two reliable sources – but these can be resolved in time with further probing of the deliverances of reason, further exegetical reflection on what the text really means, further thinking about the exact logical relationship between the two ideas that seem to stand in tension, or some combination of

36 Lindbeck, *The Nature of Doctrine*, 120.

37 For background on Spinoza and Maimonides, with a special focus on the political dimension of Spinoza's critical interactions with Maimonides, see Steven Frankel, "Spinoza's Rejection of Maimonideanism," in *Spinoza and Medieval Jewish Philosophy*, ed. Steven M. Nadler (Cambridge: Cambridge University Press, 2014), 79–95.

38 The primary source under discussion here is Moses Maimonides, *The Guide of the Perplexed* (Chicago: University of Chicago Press, 1963), 327–30.

these strategies. What bothers Spinoza most of all about the exegetical procedure that Maimonides recommends is that determining the sense of a biblical text depends, in part, on how it meshes with Maimonides's whole set of preconceptions. Spinoza complains about Maimonides's approach to the Bible: "If [a passage's] literal sense is found to conflict with reason, no matter how evident that [literal reading] may seem to be in itself, he insists that it should be construed differently."[39] For instance, if ratiocination makes it utterly clear that the world is eternal, while texts from the Bible, when read in relative isolation from an interpreter's other commitments, tend to suggest that God created the world, prior to which it did not exist, then the interpreter is obligated to find a new reading for the scriptural passages, even if that interpretation feels forced.[40] It would be better, in Spinoza's eyes, to develop an understanding of what Scripture means simply by reading it closely, and without trying to fit it into an external framework, which can easily distort the process of ascertaining the intention of the Bible.[41] Though Maimonides's theological views originate from reason, they are problematic in the same way that our modern critics think theological convictions often are when they are allowed a role in the practice of reading: they are read into texts where they do not properly belong. What Maimonides advocates leads inevitably to eisegesis.

Spinoza insists that, when it is interpreted correctly, the "sense of Scripture is established from the Bible itself."[42] What does it mean to make recourse to the Bible itself? The key feature of Maimonides's method that Spinoza finds fault with is that it includes rational reflection on the nature of God and other matters *within* its deliberation about the meaning of Scripture: we might say that reason as a

[39] Spinoza, *Theological-Political Treatise*, 113.
[40] Ibid.
[41] Ibid., 115.
[42] Ibid.

body of doctrine or a set of truths arrived at by ratiocination, and not just as a tool to puzzle through how to read the text, provides part of the context in which biblical words ought to be understood. Spinoza sharply rejects this and, as a counterproposal, conceives of a whole new way of thinking about what constitutes the proper context against which to read any given unit of biblical language. Spinoza's proposal had such influence in subsequent centuries that it became the default way many readers of the Bible came to approach the text. Yet he was the first systematically to articulate an exclusively naturalistic understanding of the Bible and the context in which it should be understood. This is Spinoza's charter: "The universal rule then for interpreting Scripture is to claim nothing as a biblical doctrine that we have not derived, by the closest possible scrutiny, from its own history (*ex ipsius historia*)."[43]

Breaking the Bible out of the grip of what Spinoza considers the prejudices and groundless preconceptions of its interpreters, and establishing this new view of context, involves three main tasks, which were mentioned already in Chapter 3.[44] First, readers should learn, as well as they possibly can, the original language of the text, and should read the text in its original form, rather than in translation. Second, readers ought to gather together what the texts claim about key subjects, and should allow tensions between various texts, or between a text and the views of the interpreter, to stand. Finally, readers should engage the Bible with a view toward understanding the communicative exchange that occurred in the text's circumstances of origin by asking what the author intended to say, who the initial recipients of the text were, how they understood its message, how the text was edited over time, and how it was brought into the collection of sacred books in which it presently resides. These historical considerations delimit the proper context for interpretation: there is no other proper context.

[43] Ibid., 99–100; Gebhardt, *Spinoza Opera*, 3: 99.

[44] Spinoza, *Theological-Political Treatise*, 100–01.

Spinoza thinks these considerations specify the appropriate reading context exhaustively because of his austere metaphysical naturalism. That is, he denies that God exists apart from the world; rather, he conflates God with the world, such that the two are numerically identical. This commitment to a naturalistic ontology means that Spinoza must explain all phenomena in terms of categories that refer to entities that actually exist, rather than ones that simply have a hallowed place in a theological worldview. As Jonathan Israel rightly says, he must "reduce all reality including the entirety of human experience, the world of tradition, spirit and belief no less than the physical, to the level of the purely empirical."[45] Spinoza contends with Maimonides not only because the medieval Jewish thinker bears some resemblance to traditional religious readers in his own context whose standing he wants to lower but also because he sees his own Jewish tradition as being fundamentally offtrack by virtue of giving credence to entities that have no existence outside of the human imagination, and as unable to interpret the Bible properly as long as readers allow those notions scope within approved strategies of textual interpretation. Spinoza aims to shear off these unhelpful notions and to proceed more "objectively."

Leo Strauss explains the essence of this objectivity:

> Spinoza's Bible science is "free from presuppositions" in the sense that it has fewer presuppositions than the Bible science which is based on the belief in revelation. It approaches Scripture as it would any other book. It places foursquare on the shoulders of the opponents the necessity of the more inclusive statement that the Bible is basically different from all other books in the world – different in principle, because of its suprahuman origin.[46]

[45] Israel, "Introduction," xv.

[46] Leo Strauss, *Spinoza's Critique of Religion* (Chicago: University of Chicago Press, 1997), 263.

Traditional religious readers, whether Jewish or Christian, need two sets of categories, both historical and theological ones, to describe what the Bible is. They will acknowledge that the texts of the Bible originated in a certain place and time but also affirm that these texts continue to speak of a divine *res* in subsequent circumstances. For his part, Spinoza concurs with only the historical part of the religious reader's double affirmation and drops the further layer of description, which depicts the text in light of a transcendent divinity.[47] In precisely this sense he lacks a presupposition that religious readers employ. Though his own naturalism is not shared by traditional Jews or Christians – it negates key elements of their worldviews – Spinoza proceeds on an assumption to which all parties subscribe, the legitimacy of historical context. He is objective in this modest way, even though his naturalism constitutes a controversial, all-embracing ontological framework that is at odds with the views of most of those who actually read the Bible in his time and who continue to do so in our own.

In our own day, the most articulate proponents of the stricture that theological reading is a disguised form of eisegesis are not metaphysical naturalists, but their objection resembles Spinoza's in ways that are more than superficial. First, both Spinoza and our objectors covet as much objectivity as possible, the former assuming that little stands in the way of full objectivity, the latter being more chastened but still seeking to take an interpretive stance

[47] It is worth adding a further nuance to the point above. It is a bit simplistic to claim that Spinoza and traditional Jews and Christians have common ground in affirming the historical context of the Bible, for they each view that history in their own way. The most basic difference is that Spinoza views history itself naturalistically, while traditional Jews or Christians see it as a field of divine action. Without this additional qualification, my account of reducing the operative categories in an account of the Bible would qualify as what Charles Taylor calls a problematic "subtraction story." Such a narrative portrays religious ideas as obscuring a substrate of beliefs on which all agree, when in fact views that emerge when religion recedes are actually "new inventions, newly constructed self-understandings and related practices, and can't be explained in terms of perennial features of human life" (*A Secular Age*, 22).

that approximates total impartiality.[48] Second, a further area of overlap between Spinoza and the later critics is that one finds in both the idea that the only alternative to moving forward objectively is religious fanaticism or something bordering on it. Spinoza makes this quite explicit, while in Barr and Barton it is suggested more subtly. For example, Barr suggests that it is impossible for different confessionally informed interpreters of the Bible to engage rationally with one another's interpretations and to adjudicate reasoned resolutions to interpretive disputes, unless they are willing to bracket their convictions and enter into dialogue with one another that is structured by the pursuit of an objectively valid interpretation. Or, to select another instance, Barton portrays advocates of theological reading to be overtaken by passion and no longer "coolly objective."[49] Third, all parties regularly express skepticism about readings of the Bible inherited from ecclesial traditions, or about interpretations arising from their contemporaries whom they consider to be theologically driven, and they seek to develop historically and linguistically astute interpretive

[48] Spinoza, *Theological-Political Treatise*, 97–99. Spinoza seeks to model the solidity of results attainable in all other fields on those one can achieve in the discipline of mathematics, though this desire is much more pronounced in Spinoza's *Ethics* than it is in his *Theological-Political Treatise*: George Steiner, "The Retreat from the Word," in *Language and Silence: Essays on Language, Literature, and the Inhuman* (New Haven: Yale University Press, 1998), 38–39. For the contemporary figures, see Barr, *The Concept of Biblical Theology*, 205; Barton, *The Nature of Biblical Criticism*, 6; Stendahl, "Biblical Theology, Contemporary," 1: 422.

[49] Spinoza, *Theological-Political Treatise*, 3–5, 97–99. According to Barr, those who advocate reading with a faith commitment intact are often so zealous and impassioned in their beliefs that they attack their opponents with an almost violent rhetoric, imperil standard pedagogical practice, and assign no value to fairness or valid argumentation: *The Concept of Biblical Theology*, 189, 191, 205; Barton's tone is less intense, but his overall worries about the danger of excessive passion mirror Barr's: *The Nature of Biblical Criticism*, 174. More generally, for lively and insistent questions about invoking a robust theological vision in any discussion that aspires to be more than parochial, see Jeffrey Stout, *Ethics after Babel: The Languages of Morals and Their Discontents* (Boston: Beacon, 1988), 222–23.

methodologies as a corrective to those excesses. These methods are not tightly structured enough to constitute algorithms, but even loosely structured methods, so the argument goes, are more reliable than deference to tradition. More concretely, all three recent figures share with Spinoza a commitment to the procedural requirement that interpreters must distinguish between what a text is saying and whether or not the text's claim is true or applicable to them.[50]

A key difference between Spinoza and those who develop the contemporary complaint about eisegesis is that while the former outrightly denies traditional religious doctrines, the latter maintain that interpreters should put them on hold for the sake of allowing reading to take place without hindrance. As a metaphysical naturalist, Spinoza rejects the whole package of traditional Christian doctrines, such as a deity that exists apart from the world, an immortal human soul that continues to exist even after the demise of the body, and Jesus Christ as the second member of the Trinity – this last belief clearly clashing with his Judaism as well as with naturalism.[51] These beliefs cannot be operative in interpretation because he sees them as false; he gives them no more credence than a modern chemist would grant to the key categories of alchemy. For contemporary critics like John Barton, it is also true that these beliefs play no role in reading – not because they are thought to be untrue but because all theological commitments must be held in abeyance while reading; the reader must undergo a process of (theological) epoché. Factoring these beliefs out of the practice of interpretation is not the same as denying them, but putting them

[50] Spinoza, *Theological-Political Treatise*, 113–14; Spinoza's distinction between textual meaning and truth of fact is followed most closely by Barton, *The Nature of Biblical Criticism*, 158–64. But the thrust of this distinction is very close in overall intention to Stendahl's differentiation between what a text meant and what it means: Stendahl, "Biblical Theology, Contemporary," 1: 419–20; this, in turn, is reformulated by Barr, *The Concept of Biblical Theology*, 202–05.

[51] The second would also clash with certain versions of Judaism.

decisively to the side is a sort of methodological naturalism,[52] insofar as it generates a model of reading that is procedurally isomorphic with that of a metaphysical naturalist. Today's critics proceed *as if* they were naturalists, in a way I spell out more fully

[52] I owe this term to the following sources: Paul R. Draper, "God, Science, and Naturalism," in *The Oxford Handbook of Philosophy of Religion*, ed. William J. Wainwright (Oxford: Oxford University Press, 2007), 279; Plantinga, "Methodological Naturalism?," 177–222. For both authors, the terminology occurs in discussions of the role of religious beliefs in natural science; I have adapted its meaning for this treatment of biblical interpretation. In using the category of naturalism, I am tacitly agreeing with Joseph Ratzinger, who says, "Scientific exegesis must recognize the philosophical element present in a great number of its ground rules." See his "Biblical Interpretation in Crisis," 21. What is important for this chapter is to discern how certain embedded fundamental principles shape the way eisegesis is conceived and distinguished from exegesis. Murray Rae's assessment that historical criticism in general is naturalistic is concerned with a broader question than is my investigation, which is focused around the objection that my approach leads to eisegesis. See his "Theological Interpretation and Historical Criticism," in *A Manifesto for Theological Interpretation*, ed. Craig G. Bartholomew and Heath A. Thomas (Grand Rapids: Baker, 2016), 94–109. Wide-ranging and searching questions about whether naturalism or metaphysical agnosticism are binding for all who study religion can be found in Michael A. Cantrell, "Must a Scholar of Religion Be Methodologically Atheistic or Agnostic?," *Journal of the American Academy of Religion* 84 (2016): 373–400.

For the parallel between, on the one hand, modes of biblical criticism that at least marginalize or even entirely rule out any substantial role for theological convictions within interpretation and, on the other hand, the exclusion of theological conviction from public political debate in early modern Europe, see Jon D. Levenson, "Historical Criticism and the Fate of the Enlightenment Project," in *The Hebrew Bible, the Old Testament, and Historical Criticism: Jews and Christians in Biblical Studies* (Louisville: Westminster John Knox, 1993), 117–18. What I am calling methodological naturalism approximates Rowan Williams' usage of *programmatic secularization* because the latter categorically eliminates any role for religion in public discussion, ceding the public square to instrumental considerations. Though at a verbal level, methodological naturalism seems very close to what he calls *procedural secularism*, the two are quite different, for procedural secularism means, as Williams says, that "religious convictions are granted a public hearing in debate; not necessarily one in which they are privileged or regarded as beyond criticism, but one in which they are attended to as representing the considered moral foundation of the choices and priorities of citizens." See *Faith in the Public Square* (London: Bloomsbury Continuum, 2012), 27.

immediately below, even though none of the contemporary biblical critics in focus in this chapter is a metaphysical naturalist.

Let methodological naturalism in the domain of biblical interpretation mean that interpreters cannot make direct appeal to God or use any of the doctrines of Christian theology when articulating reasoned exegetical arguments, or in justifying their basic interpretive aim. The basis of this exclusionary principle is that, whether the text ultimately is holy or sacred or whatever else, Christian doctrine is not necessary in order to grasp the features that give it the meaning it has: doctrine does not tell a reader what the text is insofar as its nature informs how it should be read. To employ the language of Chapter 1 of this book, for methodological naturalists, theology must remain passive in all exegetical operations: it cannot perform work in this domain, and it is a breach of protocol if this does occur. The arguments that readers offer for how to construe a given text must proceed on other grounds. These arguments must found themselves on appeal (only) to considerations that are historical, grammatical, lexicographical, literary, text-critical, and the like. To refer to this hermeneutical stricture as *methodological* naturalism does suggest that the critics in question follow an approach to the Bible that is governed by a strict set of steps. The point of referring to what they are doing as methodological naturalism is simply that whatever techniques they use, or whatever methods they commend, they cannot draw on theological language in so doing, or in offering an account of why they read as they do.[53]

[53] Brad S. Gregory contests the hegemony of naturalism in his call for "unsecularizing the academy," by arguing that its influence comes from its status as an assumed commonplace, not from its having been established by the force of compelling argument. Gregory thus rightly comments: "It [i.e., increasing openness to religious perspectives in academic work] would require all academics . . . to acknowledge their metaphysical beliefs as beliefs rather than to keep pretending that naturalist beliefs are something more or skeptical beliefs are something else." See his *The Unintended Reformation: How a Religious Revolution Secularized Society* (Cambridge, MA: Belknap Press of Harvard University Press, 2012), 386. In this connection, see also the

John Barton's well-delineated account of "biblical criticism" provides a useful illustration of a methodologically naturalistic approach to interpretation.[54] For Barton, biblical criticism is not, in the first instance, about reconstructing the world behind the text: an interest in history is not what defines it or gives purpose to it, though knowledge of historical background is instrumental toward what is primary. Criticism is essentially an exercise in semantics, determining the meaning of the words that constitute the text of the Bible, and it is necessary to know the state of the language at the time that the text was composed (thus, situating the text's composition at a point in history is a prerequisite to understanding it). In addition, establishing what a text means requires attention to matters of a larger scale: how a small unit of the text – a sentence, for example – is understood depends on the genre of the overall work of which it is a part. Doing the sort of work for which these first two criteria call means focusing on empirical, immanent features of the text and its backdrop; they mandate that a reader must know which words stand in the text, what meaning they had at the time the text was composed and first read, and what other texts existed at the same time and can be used as points of reference to decide on its genre. So far in spelling out the work that biblical criticism requires of an interpreter, or how it is to be done, there has been no mention of God or doctrinal language which considers other topics in light of God. The third and final criterion explicitly rules out anything of this sort, for it states that critical reading is only possible when a reader is not constrained by prior convictions about a text's meaning. As Barton's chapter on the Bible and

appreciation Paul Griffiths expresses for the academy welcoming debate about fundamental principles of knowledge production. "This is why," he says, "it may be possible for the academy to provide a haven for religious readers." See *Religious Reading*, 188. That research universities do not shut down debate about their underlying ideals is indeed of great value for the prospects of theological reading.

54 For a clear summary of Barton's account, see his *The Nature of Biblical Criticism*, 123–24.

religious belief makes clear,[55] it is readers who refuse to put to the side their theological beliefs who fall afoul of this final stipulation. As Barton defines biblical criticism, its aim is to ascertain textual meaning, and the way that it pursues this is via micro- and macro-semantics, conducted against the background of the best historical knowledge available. Whatever theological beliefs the biblical author is expressing are important here, but the reader's theological commitments must be sidelined; when they are not, they compromise reading, for interpretive acts appeal only to entities as if they were natural.[56] (For an approach that is not methodologically naturalistic, see the account of interpretation in Chapter 6 of this book, in which theology exercises an influence on each level of interpretation.[57])

In the vast majority of cases where our objectors mention religious beliefs on the part of a reader of the Bible, it is to make the point that readers project them onto texts where they are not actually present. However, it is also true that Stendahl, Barr, and Barton come closest to qualifying their commitment to

[55] Ibid., 137–86.

[56] Barr's overall position is quite similar. He notes that many biblical scholars are motivated by a personal faith to investigate a text that is sacred to them. Yet Barr continues: "This, however, does not prove that faith-commitments are logically or methodologically necessary for the operations which biblical theology in fact undertakes." If theology plays no role in the approach that Barr commends, it seems fair to deem it methodologically naturalistic. See *The Concept of Biblical Theology*, 191–92. Barr discusses metaphysical, but not methodological naturalism, rightly saying that the former is not influential among contemporary biblical scholars in the sense that few believe that only the natural realm exists: James Barr, "A Review of William J. Abraham, *Divine Revelation and the Limits of Historical Criticism*," in *Bible and Interpretation: The Collected Essays of James Barr*, ed. John Barton, Vol. I: Interpretation and Theology (Oxford: Oxford University Press, 2013), 392.

[57] Another example is found in Fowl, *Engaging Scripture*, 60: because "theological convictions, ecclesial practices, and communal and social concerns" shape biblical interpretation, theology is clearly not excluded from the process by which texts are understood, but is rather explicitly included within decisions about how to read passages.

methodological naturalism when they say that having empathy with the claim of a text can prove helpful in coming to understand precisely what that claim is. What keeps the commendation of empathy from being a violation of methodological naturalism is the difference between empathy, considering the claim to have value or to be potentially true, and outright commitment, having decided that the claim definitely is true.

This can be seen in each of the three main objectors. For instance, Barr observes just this distinction when he comments in his survey of biblical theology that what the discipline requires is "*interest* in theology and *empathy* with it, but not personal faith-commitment."[58] Likewise, Stendahl portrays the believing reader as having an advantage, though one with an attendant risk, over his nonbelieving counterpart reader in this respect: "The believer has the advantage of automatic empathy with the believers in the text – but his faith constantly threatens to have him modernize the material, if he does not exercise the canons of descriptive scholarship rigorously."[59] Stendahl uses the term empathy here to stress that while the believer will resonate with the claim a biblical author is making because of the Bible's status as sacred for him, his understanding of the text will in certain subtle ways also be a function of the modern categories by means of which he construes it. In acknowledging the limits of methods in interpretation, and in highlighting that something else is also necessary – "entering into the text at a deep level, recognizing the shared humanity of the author, so that *cor ad cor loquitur* (heart speaks to heart)"[60] – Barton also admits that an empathy that still underscores the alterity of the text's voice is quite important.

This brings the discussion to the point where it becomes possible to explain how the particular version of the eisegesis objection

[58] Barr, *The Concept of Biblical Theology*, 194.

[59] Stendahl, "Biblical Theology, Contemporary," 1: 422.

[60] Barton, *The Nature of Biblical Criticism*, 59.

sketched out previously is intelligible against the background of methodological naturalism. If the Bible is viewed as simply a past act of communication, and not as a set of signs pointing to the Trinity, then it makes sense to read it only as a communicative exchange that took place in a religious community many centuries ago. And if the present-day reader of the Bible is also seen in terms of naturalistic categories, as the inhabitant of a particular time and place that differs in many details from the circumstances in which the text originated, then it similarly makes good sense to claim that there is a gap or a hiatus between the time of the text and that of the reader. On the other hand, if the reader were construed also from a theological point of view, then the application of such categories provides a way to describe how the original readers of the text and its current readers form part of the same economy of salvation, which does not override the differences in contingent circumstances but does set them in a broader, unitive perspective. For theological reading, it is indeed important to observe the text's function in its context of origin, but valid interpretation is not limited to this setting. On a naturalistic account of reading, it is imperative not to allow reading to be influenced by theological categories, which *ex hypothesi* do not pertain to the interpreting subject or the object being interpreted. Anything else is eisegesis.[61]

[61] Of course, there are other ways to conceive of the Bible and our present context as connected with one another. For instance, seeing the text as a classic with a powerful history of effects, which influences readers even before they gain first-hand acquaintance with the work, is another way to do this, apart from making recourse to theology. Thus, theological reading as outlined here, on the one hand, and the common ground shared by Stendahl, Barr, and Barton on the other, do not constitute an exhaustive set of hermeneutical options. There do exist other vantage points from which to respond to the eisegesis objection. Yet the point above is that the objection grows out of methodological naturalism. The objectors press their point in terms that make this presupposition evident. In other words, one can be a naturalist even if one does not think this way about eisegesis, but one is a methodological naturalist if one thinks this way about the topic.

Yet theological readers of Scripture certainly should not construe eisegesis in a way that is indebted to naturalism, whether metaphysical or methodological. For advocates of theological reading to consider themselves guilty of interpretive malpractice if their readings constitute eisegesis, as understood according to the previous account of it, amounts to betraying their own cause right from the outset, because this understanding of eisegesis derives its strength from denying theology the role of depicting the text and reader. The operative sense of eisegesis within this objection emerges from theology itself being passive within interpretation. Giving too much credence to this sense of eisegesis amounts to what Peter Gay refers to as the "treason of the clerks,"[62] an attempt to gain credibility for ecclesial life by trading away that which is constitutive of it. The thrust of the foregoing discussion is not the bare, and by itself trite, point that everyone has presuppositions. This is easily enough established, but it does nothing to advance discussions of interpretation. It is rather that theological readers ought not consider themselves beholden or answerable to naturalistic presuppositions, which undercut their entire approach from the start. This would be to make theology a *disciplina otiosa*.[63] The whole point of theological reading is to allow doctrine to describe the key realities involved in the reading process and to follow through on those implications. In saying that theological readers should not allow themselves to be held responsible to an interpretive standard that presupposes naturalism, it is worth acknowledging that other theological interpreters, who polemicize against historical study, could be construed as sharing this broad concern,[64] but the latter receive

[62] Peter Gay, *The Enlightenment: An Interpretation*, Vol. 1: The Rise of Modern Paganism (New York: Alfred A. Knopf, 1966), 343.

[63] Michael J. Buckley, *At the Origins of Modern Atheism* (New Haven: Yale University Press, 1987), 11.

[64] It is worth noting that in these objections, the object of critique is historical study as it impacts biblical interpretation. The objection is not posed precisely against naturalism, which I have argued is the heart of the problem.

criticism in this book for overcorrecting to the point that they operate in a way that de facto rejects the reality that the Bible originated in a past context. This work has sought to walk a different path by insisting on the importance of a past context while also opposing naturalism. In this way, it offers a via media.

The argument presented in this book is that entailments for interpretation follow from a specifically theological view of the biblical text and the interpreting subject. That is, if the text and reader are viewed theologically, then hermeneutical implications follow. This chapter explores an objection to the effect that the hermeneutical directives that emerge from this twofold ontology amount to a set of misguided directives for reading. The chapter has pointed out that if this mode of reading is deemed fallacious, it is because a different ontology has been put in place, one that is naturalistic, not necessarily in a metaphysical key, but operationally or methodologically. Theological readers are by no means responsible to this ontology in the first place, hence they are not guilty of interpretive malpractice. They ought not bracket out all of their theological commitments because this violates the integrity of their system of belief. A Christian theological outlook ought to be maximally coherent: this means not only making affirmations of Christian belief but also seeing the entailments beliefs have and following through on them, which is precisely what is disallowed by the insistence that all theological commitment be put in "gnoseological suspense"[65] while a reader interprets the biblical text.

There is a place within theological reading for disallowing a theological system from *dictating* exegetical conclusions. However, the value on the basis of which this becomes an ideal is not the total elimination of theology's involvement in interpretive activity; it is

65 John Milbank, "The Conflict of the Faculties: Theology and the Economy of the Sciences," in *Faithfulness and Fortitude: In Conversation with the Theological Ethics of Stanley Hauerwas*, ed. Samuel Wells and Mark Thiessen Nation (London: T. & T. Clark, 2000), 41.

rather achieving a fitting dialectical balance between the details of a given text and the larger framework of belief that constitutes the reader's basic commitments. There is no need to see this issue in stark all-or-nothing terms; indeed, that is genuinely unhelpful. There *is* such a thing as culpably projecting one's beliefs onto the Bible. Having a relativized distinction between meaning and truth, rather than no distinction at all, entails that identifying a single text with the entirety of what one takes to be theologically true is going entirely too far. However, recognizing that such projection can in theory be a problem does not mean that theology must therefore be forbidden from having any positive relationship with the enterprise of interpretation. It can and should have a deep impact on reading by factoring crucially into the depiction of the realities involved in reading.

### *Final Reflections*

I conclude by considering two closing questions. First, what hope is there of handling clashes between this account of theological exegesis and others that rest on a different theological framework? Are there prospects that amount to something other than internecine conflict? There is, to be sure, a degree of diversity among different versions of theological reading by virtue of each receiving its shape from a particular governing framework of thought that is not entirely identical with the others.[66] Each version of theological reading has its own distinctiveness, yet the scope and implications of such discrepancies should not be exaggerated. As an astute commentator has observed, at present, relations among the main branches of the Christian tradition are on a different footing than they once were: "The traditional historical divides within Christianity – Protestant, Catholic, Orthodox – remain intact but have

[66] See the literature cited in note 30 of the Introduction.

become far less significant than they have been historically."[67] Agreement on a great deal now binds the varied strands of the Christian tradition together.[68] For this reason, the major fault lines run across the Protestant, Catholic, and Orthodox traditions, not between the three major confessions. Just as in the twentieth century the ecumenical movement created a space in which distinct traditions could meet and dialogue with one another, discussing their remaining differences in the context of substantial agreements and convergences on many cardinal doctrines, so also those who think theologically about the realities central to reading can engage with one another in fruitful conversation, despite not achieving complete consensus on all the details of the overarching theological vision to which they relate both reader and text.[69] Discussions of theological interpretation form a context in which theological commitments can come out into the open, be criticized, and be reformulated in order to become more fully adequate to the tasks they are assigned. The process by which a framework is refined does not necessitate fully establishing, or even striving for, a neutral, commitment-free space, despite claims to that effect from those who articulate the eisegesis objection. One tradition-specific framework can engage critically with another when adherents of the first learn the language of a second and find difficulties in the other framework that their own can address more successfully.[70]

67 David Tracy, foreword to *God without Being: Hors-Texte*, by Jean-Luc Marion (Chicago: University of Chicago Press, 1991), ix.

68 On the overlaps between Protestants and Roman Catholics in the context of exegetical issues, see Levering, *Participatory Biblical Exegesis*, 6.

69 Cf. Fowl, *Theological Interpretation of Scripture*, 74–75.

70 For a greatly expanded explanation of this point, and a demonstration of how a traditionally Christian perspective can mount a case against advocates of modern neutrality and postmodernism, see Alasdair C. MacIntyre, *Three Rival Versions of Moral Enquiry: Encyclopaedia, Genealogy, and Tradition* (Notre Dame: University of Notre Dame Press, 1990), 170–236.

Second, is it genuinely possible to read theologically today? Can the proposed paradigm actually be implemented?[71] It is necessary to find suitable institutional locations for this practice. Yet at the root of the challenge lies something deeper, the difficulty of actively mobilizing theological language as a way of thinking about and navigating reality. The challenge is real and amounts essentially to this:

> Despite the vogue of postmodern theories, most of us can no longer think of the world and of the human community except in radically historical terms; we cannot prescind from our knowledge of what is involved in natural and human causality, our sense of the cultural conditioning of language and thought, our assumption of the perspectival character of the perception and communication of truth.[72]

While he fully faces up to the difficulty, Daley is nevertheless rightly confident that inhabiting a theological point of view actually is possible. As has been argued in this book, theological reading does not deny the reality of the immanent features of the world or the gains that have been made by historical consciousness. What it does do, however, is to deny the ultimacy and finality of the immanent frame, construing both text and readers as situated within a flow of events which itself opens up onto transcendent reality, whose relation to text and readers fundamentally recharacterizes them. The proposal this book offers draws on resources from beyond our own context, with the hope that they can act as a stimulus, one capable

[71] For critical reflections on theological commentaries that have recently come into print, see Elliot, *The Heart of Biblical Theology*, 3–36. For his part, Brian Daley offers the following negative verdict on current commentaries: "It is still not fully clear how faithful and learned Christians ought to go about commenting theologically on the Bible today in a church that remains in lively conversation with the modern and postmodern world. Theological commentary, in a form capable of speaking to the contemporary church, is a genre yet to be formed." See "The Acts and Christian Confession," 25. These criticisms are understandable, though recently there have been some encouraging signs of improvement.

[72] Daley, "Is Patristic Exegesis Still Usable?," 212.

of "acting counter to our time and thereby acting on our time and, let us hope, for the benefit of a time to come."[73] The heart of the challenge here is that for theological reading to flourish, its practitioners will have to learn how to think about the immanent features of the world as real but as pointing beyond themselves and toward God.

Whatever the future holds for the writing of theological commentaries and the production of theological exegesis in various other forms, the aim of this book has been to give an account of both the underlying rationale for theological reading and the basic overall shape it might have.

73 Nietzsche, "History for Life," 60.

# Works Cited

I have cited Augustine's texts according to the titles used in the reference work *Augustine through the Ages: An Encyclopedia* (Allan Fitzgerald et al., eds., Grand Rapids: Eerdmans, 1999). The abbreviations for Augustine's works follow the forms set out in the front matter. The format of my references to his works should allow those who have other editions or translations than the ones I cite to locate passages being discussed. Below I cite both Augustine's original Latin texts and the English translation that I have used and occasionally modified slightly, without indicating each change individually. When I quote scholarly work from a language other than English without citing a translation, the translation is also my own.

Abraham, William J. *Canon and Criterion in Christian Theology: From the Fathers to Feminism.* Oxford: Oxford University Press, 1998.

Adam, A. K. M. "Docetism, Kasemann, and Christology: Why Historical Criticism Can't Protect Christological Orthodoxy." *Scottish Journal of Theology* 49 (1996): 391–410.

Adams, Nicholas. *Habermas and Theology.* Cambridge: Cambridge University Press, 2006.

"Making Deep Reasonings Public." *Modern Theology* 22 (2006): 385–401.

Allen, R. Michael, and Scott Swain, eds. *T. & T. Clark International Theological Commentary.* London: T. & T. Clark, 2016–.

Alter, Robert. *The Art of Biblical Narrative.* Rev. ed. New York: Basic Books, 2011.

Anderson, Bernhard W. "The Problem and Promise of Commentary." *Interpretation* 36 (1982): 341–55.

Andrews, James A. *Hermeneutics and the Church: In Dialogue with Augustine. Reading the Scriptures.* Notre Dame: University of Notre Dame Press, 2012.

Anscombe, G. E. M. "Modern Moral Philosophy." *Philosophy* 33 (1958): 1–19.

Aquinas, Thomas. *Summa Theologiae*. Vol. I: Christian Theology (Ia. I). Cambridge: Cambridge University Press, 2006.

Asad, Talal. *Formations of the Secular: Christianity, Islam, Modernity. Cultural Memory in the Present*. Stanford: Stanford University Press, 2003.

Auden, W. H. *Collected Poems*. New York: Vintage International, 1991.

Augustine. *Confessions*. CCSL 27; OWC Chadwick.

*On the Advantage of Believing*. CSEL 25/1; WSA I/8.

*On Christian Teaching*. CCSL 32; OWC Green.

*On Eighty-Three Varied Questions*. CCSL 44A; WSA I/12.

*On Faith and the Creed*. CSEL 41; WSA I/8.

*On Genesis, against the Manichees*. CSEL 91; WSA I/13.

*On the Greatness of the Soul*. CSEL 89; FOC 2.

*On the Immortality of the Soul*. CSEL 89; FOC 2.

*On the Instruction of Beginners*. CCSL 46; ACW 2.

*On the Literal Interpretation of Genesis*. CSEL 28.1; WSA I/13.

*On the Lord's Sermon on the Mount*. CCSL 35; FOC 11.

*On the Teacher*. CCSL 29; FOC 59.

*Reconsiderations*. CSEL 36; WSA I/2.

*Sermon* 22. CCSL 41; WSA III/2.

*Sermon* 339. SPM 1; WSA III/9.

*Tractates on the Gospel of John*. CCSL 36; FOC 79.

*The Trinity*. CCSL 50A; WSA I/5.

Ayres, Lewis. *Augustine and the Trinity*. Cambridge: Cambridge University Press, 2010.

*Nicaea and Its Legacy: An Approach to Fourth Century Trinitarian Theology*. Oxford: Oxford University Press, 2004.

"On the Practice and Teaching of Christian Doctrine." *Gregorianum* 80 (1999): 33–94.

"The Soul and the Reading of Scripture: A Note on Henri de Lubac." *Scottish Journal of Theology* 61 (2008): 173–90.

"The Word Answering the Word: Opening the Space of Catholic Biblical Interpretation." In *Theological Theology: Essays in Honour of John Webster*, edited by R. David Nelson, Darren Sarisky, and Justin Stratis, 37–53. London: Bloomsbury T. & T. Clark, 2015.

Balentine, Samuel E., ed. *The Oxford Encyclopedia of the Bible and Theology*. 2 vols, The Oxford Encyclopedias of the Bible. Oxford: Oxford University Press, 2015.

Barnes, Michel R. "Augustine in Contemporary Trinitarian Theology." *Theological Studies* 56 (1995): 237–50.

"Ebion at the Barricades: Moral Narrative and Post-Christian Catholic Theology." *Modern Theology* 26 (2010): 511–48.

Barr, James. "The Bible as a Document of Believing Communities." In *Bible and Interpretation: The Collected Essays of James Barr*, edited by John Barton. Vol. I: Interpretation and Theology, 46–64. Oxford: Oxford University Press, 2013.

"Biblical Criticism as Theological Enlightenment." In *Bible and Interpretation: The Collected Essays of James Barr*, edited by John Barton. Vol. I: Interpretation and Theology, 156–68. Oxford: Oxford University Press, 2013.

*Biblical Faith and Natural Theology: The Gifford Lectures for 1991*. Oxford: Oxford University Press, 1993.

"Biblical Scholarship and the Unity of the Church." In *Bible and Interpretation: The Collected Essays of James Barr*, edited by John Barton. Vol. I: Interpretation and Theology, 17–27. Oxford: Oxford University Press, 2013.

*The Concept of Biblical Theology: An Old Testament Perspective*. Minneapolis: Fortress, 1999.

"Does Biblical Study Still Belong to Theology?" In *Bible and Interpretation: The Collected Essays of James Barr*, edited by John Barton. Vol. I: Interpretation and Theology, 7–16. Oxford: Oxford University Press, 2013.

"Exegesis as a Theological Discipline Reconsidered, and the Shadow of the Jesus of History." In *Bible and Interpretation: The Collected Essays of James Barr*, edited by John Barton. Vol. I: Interpretation and Theology, 127–55. Oxford: Oxford University Press, 2013.

"Historical Reading and the Theological Interpretation of Scripture." In *Bible and Interpretation: The Collected Essays of James Barr*, edited by John Barton. Vol. I: Interpretation and Theology, 28–45. Oxford: Oxford University Press, 2013.

"A Review of William J. Abraham, *Divine Revelation and the Limits of Historical Criticism*." In *Bible and Interpretation: The Collected Essays of James Barr*, edited by John Barton. Vol. I: Interpretation and Theology, 390–94. Oxford: Oxford University Press, 2013.

*The Semantics of Biblical Language*. Oxford: Oxford University Press, 1961.

Barth, Karl. *Church Dogmatics I.1: The Doctrine of the Word of God, § 8–12*. Study ed. London: T. & T. Clark, 2010.

*Church Dogmatics I.2: The Doctrine of the Word of God, § 19–21*. Study ed. London: T. & T. Clark, 2010.

*The Epistle to the Romans*. Oxford: Oxford University Press, 1968.

*Protestant Theology in the Nineteenth Century: Its Background & History*. London: SCM Press, 1972.

*Witness to the Word: A Commentary on John 1*. Eugene: Wipf and Stock, 2003.

Barthes, Roland. "Death of the Author." In *Image, Music, Text*, edited by Stephen Heath, Fontana Communications Series, 142–48. London: Fontana, 1977.

*S/Z*. Oxford: Basil Blackwell, 1975.

Bartholomew, Craig G., C. Stephen Evans, Mary Healy, and Murray Rae, eds. *"Behind" the Text: History and Biblical Interpretation*. Scripture and Hermeneutics Series. Grand Rapids: Zondervan, 2003

Bartholomew, Craig G., and Heath A. Thomas, eds. *A Manifesto for Theological Interpretation*. Grand Rapids: Baker, 2016.

Bartholomew, Craig G., Joel Green, and Christopher R. Seitz, eds. *Studies in Theological Interpretation*. Grand Rapids: Baker, 2006-.

Barton, John. *The Future of Old Testament Study: An Inaugural Lecture Delivered before the University of Oxford on 12 November 1992*. Oxford: Clarendon Press, 1993.

"James Barr as Critic and Theologian." In *Language, Theology, and the Bible: Essays in Honour of James Barr*, edited by Samuel E. Balentine and John Barton, 16–26. Oxford: Clarendon Press, 1994.

*The Nature of Biblical Criticism*. Louisville: Westminster John Knox, 2007.

Bauckham, Richard. *James: Wisdom of James, Disciple of Jesus the Sage*. New Testament Readings. London: Routledge, 1999.

"Reading Scripture as a Coherent Story." In *The Art of Reading Scripture*, edited by Ellen F. Davis and Richard B. Hays, 38–53. Grand Rapids: Eerdmans, 2003.

Bennett, Jonathan. *A Study of Spinoza's Ethics*. Indianapolis: Hackett, 1984.

Billings, J. Todd. *The Word of God for the People of God: An Entryway to the Theological Interpretation of Scripture*. Grand Rapids: Eerdmans, 2010.

Bloom, Harold. *The Anxiety of Influence: A Theory of Poetry*. 2nd ed. Oxford: Oxford University Press, 1997.

Bochet, Isabelle. "Le cercle herméneutique." In *La doctrine chrétienne = De doctrina christiana*, edited by Madeleine Moreau, Isabelle Bochet, Goulven Madec, and Josef Martin, Bibliothèque augustinienne 11/2, 438–49. Paris: Institut d'études augustiniennes, 1997.

*Le firmament de l'écriture: l'herméneutique augustinienne*. Collection des études augustiniennes série antiquité. Paris: Institut d'études augustiniennes, 2004.

"Les signes." In *La doctrine chrétienne = De doctrina christiana*, edited by Madeleine Moreau, Isabelle Bochet, Goulven Madec, and Josef Martin, Bibliothèque augustinienne 11/2, 483–95. Paris: Institut d'études augustiniennes, 1997.

"Place de l'écriture dans l'économie du salut." In *La doctrine chrétienne = De doctrina christiana*, edited by Madeleine Moreau, Isabelle Bochet, Goulven Madec, and Joseph Martin, Bibliothèque augustinienne 11/2, 474–83. Paris: Institut d'études augustiniennes, 1997.

"Réflexions sur l'exégèse figurative d'augustin: *Christ Meets Me Everywhere: Augustine's Early Figurative Exegesis* de M. Cameron." *Augustinian Studies* 45 (2014): 281–90.

Bockmuehl, Markus. "Bible Versus Theology: Is 'Theological Interpretation' the Answer?" *Nova et Vetera* 9 (2011): 27–37.

"Introduction." In *Scripture's Doctrine and Theology's Bible: How the New Testament Shapes Christian Dogmatics*, edited by Markus Bockmuehl and Alan J. Torrance, 7–13. Grand Rapids: Baker, 2008.

"Ruminative Overlay: Matthew's Hauerwas." *Pro Ecclesia* 17 (2008): 20–28.

*Seeing the Word: Refocusing New Testament Study*. Studies in Theological Interpretation. Grand Rapids: Baker, 2006.

Boersma, Hans. *Nouvelle Théologie and Sacramental Ontology: A Return to Mystery*. Oxford: Oxford University Press, 2009.

Boeve, Lieven. "Retrieving Augustine Today: Between Neo-Augustinianist Essentialism and Radical Hermeneutics." In *Augustine and*

*Postmodern Thought: A New Alliance against Modernity?*, edited by Lieven Boeve, Mathijs Lamberigts, and Maarten Wisse, 1–17. Leuven: Peeters, 2009.

Bonhoeffer, Dietrich. *Letters and Papers from Prison*. Dietrich Bonhoeffer Works. Edited by Christian Gremmels, Eberhard Bethge, Renate Bethge, Ilse Tödt, and John W. de Gruchy. Vol. 8. Minneapolis: Fortress, 2010.

Bové, Paul A. *Intellectuals in Power: A Genealogy of Critical Humanism*. New York: Columbia University Press, 1986.

*Mastering Discourse: The Politics of Intellectual Culture*. Durham: Duke University Press, 1992.

Bowald, Mark Alan. *Rendering the Word in Theological Hermeneutics: Mapping Divine and Human Agency*. Aldershot: Ashgate, 2007.

Brague, Rémi. *The Wisdom of the World: The Human Experience of the Universe in Western Thought*. Chicago: University of Chicago Press, 2003.

Brettler, Marc Zvi, Peter Enns, and Daniel J. Harrington. *The Bible and the Believer: How to Read the Bible Critically and Religiously*. Oxford: Oxford University Press, 2012.

Broggi, Joshua D. *Diversity in the Structure of Christian Reasoning: Interpretation, Disagreement, and World Christianity*. Studies in Systematic Theology. Leiden: Brill, 2015.

Bruns, Gerald L. "A Grammarian's Guide to the *Discourse on Method*." In *Inventions: Writing, Textuality, and Understanding in Literary History*, 63–87. New Haven: Yale University Press, 1982.

Bryan, Christopher. *Listening to the Bible: The Art of Faithful Biblical Interpretation*. Oxford: Oxford University Press, 2014.

Buckley, Michael J. *At the Origins of Modern Atheism*. New Haven: Yale University Press, 1987.

Bultmann, Rudolf. "Is Exegesis without Presuppositions Possible?" In *The New Testament and Mythology and Other Basic Writings*, edited by Schubert M. Ogden, 145–53. Philadelphia: Fortress, 1984

Burns, J. Patout. "Delighting the Spirit: Augustine's Practice of Figurative Interpretation." In *De doctrina christiana: A Classic of Western Culture*, edited by Duane W. H. Arnold and Pamela Bright, Christianity and Judaism in Antiquity, 182–94. Notre Dame: University of Notre Dame Press, 1995.

Burnyeat, Myles F. "Wittgenstein and Augustine's *De Magistro*." In *The Augustinian Tradition*, edited by Gareth Matthews, 286–303. Berkeley: University of California Press, 1999.

Byassee, Jason. *Praise Seeking Understanding: Reading the Psalms with Augustine*. Radical Traditions. Grand Rapids: Eerdmans, 2007.

Cameron, Michael. *Christ Meets Me Everywhere: Augustine's Early Figurative Exegesis*. Oxford Studies in Historical Theology. New York: Oxford University Press, 2012.

Cantrell, Michael A. "Must a Scholar of Religion Be Methodologically Atheistic or Agnostic?" *Journal of the American Academy of Religion* 84 (2016): 373–400.

Carson, D. A. "Theological Interpretation of Scripture: Yes, But. . . ." In *Theological Commentary: Evangelical Perspectives*, edited by R. Michael Allen, 187–207. London: T. & T. Clark, 2011.

Cary, Phillip. *Outward Signs: The Powerlessness of External Things in Augustine's Thought*. Oxford: Oxford University Press, 2008.

Cavadini, John C. "The Darkest Enigma: Reconsidering the Self in Augustine's Thought." *Augustinian Studies* 38 (2007): 119–32.

"The Sweetness of the Word: Salvation and Rhetoric in Augustine's *De doctrina christiana*." In *De doctrina christiana: A Classic of Western Culture*, edited by Duane W. H. Arnold and Pamela Bright, 164–81. Notre Dame: University of Notre Dame Press, 1995.

Chapman, Stephen, Christine Helmer, and Christof Landmesser, eds. *Biblischer Text und theologische Theoriebildung*, Biblisch-theologishche Studien. Neukirchen-Vluyn: Neukirchener, 2001.

Childs, Brevard S. *The Book of Exodus: A Critical, Theological Commentary*. The Old Testament Library. Louisville: Westminster John Knox, 1974.

"Toward Recovering Theological Exegesis." *Ex auditu* 16 (2000): 121–29.

Coakley, Sarah. *God, Sexuality, and the Self: An Essay "On the Trinity."* Cambridge: Cambridge University Press, 2013.

Collective, The Bible and Culture. *The Postmodern Bible*. New Haven: Yale University Press, 1995.

Cone, James H. *A Black Theology of Liberation*. 40th anniversary ed. Maryknoll: Orbis Books, 2010.

Congar, Yves. *Tradition and Traditions: An Historical and a Theological Essay*. London: Burns & Oats, 1966.

Cox, Harvey. *How to Read the Bible.* New York: HarperOne, 2015.

Curley, E. M. "On Bennett's Spinoza: The Issue of Teleology." In *Spinoza: Issues and Directions,* edited by E. M. Curley and Pierre-François Moreau, Brill's Studies in Intellectual History, 39–52. Leiden: Brill, 1990.

Daley, Brian E. "The Acts and Christian Confession: Finding the Start of the Dogmatic Tradition." *Pro Ecclesia* 16 (2007): 18–25.

"'In Many and Various Ways': Towards a Theology of Theological Exegesis." *Modern Theology* 28 (2012): 597–615.

"Is Patristic Exegesis Still Usable?" *Communio* 29 (2002): 185–216.

Dalferth, Ingolf. "The Idea of Transcendence." In *The Axial Age and Its Consequences,* edited by Robert Neelly Bellah and Hans Joas, 146–88. Cambridge, MA: Belknap Press of Harvard University Press, 2012.

"Von der Vieldeutigkeit der Schrift und der Eindeutigkeit des Wortes Gottes." In *Die Zukunft des Schriftprinzips,* edited by Richard K. Ziegert, Bibel im Gesprèach, 155–73. Stuttgart: Deutsche Bibelgesellschaft, 1994.

Damgaard, Iben. "Kierkegaard's Rewriting of Biblical Narratives: The Mirror of the Text." In *Kierkegaard and the Bible,* edited by Lee C. Barrett and Jon Stewart. Vol. 1: The Old Testament, 207–30. Farnham: Ashgate, 2010.

Davidson, Donald. "Mental Events." In *Essays on Actions and Events,* 207–27. Oxford: Clarendon Press, 1980.

Davies, Oliver. *The Creativity of God: World, Eucharist, Reason.* Cambridge Studies in Christian Doctrine. Cambridge: Cambridge University Press, 2004.

Davies, Philip R. "Two Nations, One Womb." In *Whose Bible Is It Anyway?,* 17–55. London: T. & T. Clark, 2004.

Davis, Ellen F. *Wondrous Depth: Preaching the Old Testament.* Louisville: Westminster John Knox, 2005.

Dawson, David. *Christian Figural Reading and the Fashioning of Identity.* Berkeley: University of California Press, 2002.

"Sign Theory, Allegorical Reading, and the Motions of the Soul in *De doctrina christiana.*" In *De doctrina christiana: A Classic of Western Culture,* edited by Duane W. H. Arnold and Pamela Bright, Christianity and Judaism in Antiquity, 123–41. Notre Dame: University of Notre Dame Press, 1995.

Descartes, René. "Discourse on Method." In *Descartes: Selected Philosophical Writings*, 20–56. Cambridge: Cambridge University Press, 2008.

Dickens, W. T. "The Uses of the Bible in Theology." In *The New Cambridge History of the Bible*, edited by John Riches. Vol. 4: From 1750 to the Present, 184–96. Cambridge: Cambridge University Press, 2015.

Draper, Paul R. "God, Science, and Naturalism." In *The Oxford Handbook of Philosophy of Religion*, edited by William J. Wainwright, 272–303. Oxford: Oxford University Press, 2007.

Dreyfus, François. "Exégèse en Sorbonne, exégèse en église." *Revue biblique* (1975): 321–69.

Dunn, James D. G., ed. *New Testament Theology*. Cambridge: Cambridge University Press, 1991–2003.

Dupré, Louis K. *The Enlightenment and the Intellectual Foundations of Modern Culture*. New Haven: Yale University Press, 2004.

*Passage to Modernity: An Essay in the Hermeneutics of Nature and Culture*. New Haven: Yale University Press, 1993.

*Religion and the Rise of Modern Culture*. Notre Dame: University of Notre Dame Press, 2008.

East, Brad. "The Hermeneutics of Theological Interpretation: Holy Scripture, Biblical Scholarship and Historical Criticism." *International Journal of Systematic Theology* 19 (2017): 30–52.

Ebeling, Gerhard. "The Significance of the Critical Historical Method for Church and Theology in Protestantism." In *Word and Faith*, 17–61. London: SCM Press, 1963.

Eco, Umberto. *Semiotics and the Philosophy of Language*. Advances in Semiotics. Bloomington: Indiana University Press, 1984.

Eden, Kathy. *Hermeneutics and the Rhetorical Tradition: Chapters in the Ancient Legacy & Its Humanist Reception*. New Haven: Yale University Press, 1997.

Ehrman, Bart D. *The Orthodox Corruption of Scripture: The Effect of Early Christological Controversies on the Text of the New Testament*. Updated ed. Oxford: Oxford University Press, 2011.

Elliot, Mark W. *The Heart of Biblical Theology: Providence Experienced*. Surrey: Ashgate, 2012.

Ellul, Jacques. *The Technological Society*. New York: Knopf, 1964.

Elshtain, Jean Bethke. *Augustine and the Limits of Politics*. Frank M. Covey, Jr. Loyola Lectures in Political Analysis. Notre Dame: University of Notre Dame Press, 1995.

Emery, Gilles, and Matthew Levering, eds. *The Oxford Handbook of the Trinity*, Oxford Handbooks in Religion and Theology. Oxford: Oxford University Press, 2014.

Fish, Stanley E. *Is There a Text in This Class? The Authority of Interpretive Communities*. Cambridge, MA: Harvard University Press, 1980.

Fishbane, Michael A. *Biblical Interpretation in Ancient Israel*. Oxford: Clarendon Press, 1985.

*The Garments of Torah: Essays in Biblical Hermeneutics*. Indiana Studies in Biblical Literature. Bloomington: Indiana University Press, 1989.

Fitzgerald, Allan, John C. Cavadini, Marianne Djuth, James J. O'Donnell, and Frederick Van Fleteren, eds. *Augustine through the Ages: An Encyclopedia*. Grand Rapids: Eerdmans, 1999.

Ford, David F. *Christian Wisdom: Desiring God and Learning in Love*. Cambridge: Cambridge University Press, 2007.

"Humanity before God; Thinking through Scripture: Theological Anthropology and the Bible." In *The Theological Anthropology of David Kelsey: Responses to Eccentric Existence*, edited by Gene Outka, 31–52. Grand Rapids: Eerdmans, 2016.

*John's Gospel Now*. Bampton Lectures. Oxford: Bampton Trust, 2015.

Ford, David F., and C. C. Pecknold, eds. *The Promise of Scriptural Reasoning*. Oxford: Blackwell, 2006.

Foucault, Michel. "Technologies of the Self." In *Technologies of the Self: A Seminar with Michel Foucault*, edited by Huck Gutman, Patrick H. Hutton, and Luther H. Martin. Amherst: University of Massachusetts Press, 1988.

"What Is an Author?" In *Textual Strategies: Perspectives in Post-Structuralist Criticism*, edited by Josué V. Harari, 141–60. Ithaca: Cornell University Press, 1979.

Fowl, Stephen E. "Editor's Notes." *Anglican Theological Review* 99 (2017): 645–50.

*Engaging Scripture: A Model for Theological Interpretation*. Oxford: Blackwell, 1998.

———. *Ephesians: A Commentary*. The New Testament Library. Louisville: Westminster John Knox, 2012.

———. *Philippians*. The Two Horizons New Testament Commentary. Grand Rapids: Eerdmans, 2005.

———. "Scripture." In *The Oxford Handbook of Systematic Theology*, edited by John Webster, Kathryn Tanner, and Ian Torrance, 345–61. Oxford: Oxford University Press, 2007.

———. "Theological and Ideological Strategies of Biblical Interpretation." In *Scripture: An Ecumenical Introduction to the Bible and Its Interpretation*, edited by Michael J. Gorman, 162–75. Peabody: Hendrickson, 2005.

———. *Theological Interpretation of Scripture*. Cascade Companions. Eugene: Cascade, 2009.

———. "Theological Interpretation of Scripture and Its Future." *Anglican Theological Review* 99 (2017): 671–90.

Fowl, Stephen E., and L. Gregory Jones. *Reading in Communion: Scripture and Ethics in Christian Life*. Eugene: Wipf and Stock, 1991.

Fowler, Robert M. *Let the Reader Understand: Reader-Response Criticism and the Gospel of Mark*. Minneapolis: Fortress, 1991.

Frankel, Steven. "Spinoza's Rejection of Maimonideanism." In *Spinoza and Medieval Jewish Philosophy*, edited by Steven M. Nadler, 79–95. Cambridge: Cambridge University Press, 2014.

Frei, Hans W. *The Eclipse of Biblical Narrative: A Study in Eighteenth and Nineteenth Century Hermeneutics*. New Haven: Yale University Press, 1974.

———. *Types of Christian Theology*. New Haven: Yale University Press, 1992.

Froehlich, Karlfried. "Bibelkommentare – Zur Krise einer Gattung." *Zietschrfit für Theologie und Kirche* 84 (1987): 465–92.

Frye, Northrop. *The Great Code: The Bible and Literature*. Collected Works of Northrop Frye. Vol. 19. Toronto: University of Toronto Press, 2006.

Fulkerson, Mary McClintock. "'Is There a (Non-Sexist) Bible in This Church?' A Feminist Case for the Priority of Interpretive Communities." *Modern Theology* 14 (1998): 225–42.

Gadamer, Hans Georg. "Kant and the Question of God." In *Hermeneutics, Religion, and Ethics*, 1–17. New Haven: Yale University Press, 1999.

———. *Truth and Method*. 2nd ed. London: Continuum, 2004.

"Religious and Poetical Speaking." In *Myth, Symbol, and Reality*, edited by Alan M. Olson, 86–98. Notre Dame: University of Notre Dame Press, 1980.

Gamble, Harry Y. *Books and Readers in the Early Church: A History of Early Christian Texts.* New Haven: Yale University Press, 1995.

Garrett, Don. "Teleology in Spinoza and Early Modern Rationalism." In *New Essays on the Rationalists*, edited by Rocco J. Gennaro and Charles Huenemann, 310–35. Oxford: Oxford University Press, 1999.

Gay, Peter. *The Enlightenment: An Interpretation.* Vol. 1: The Rise of Modern Paganism. New York: Alfred A. Knopf, 1966.

Gebhardt, Carl, ed. *Spinoza Opera.* Vol. 3. Heidelberg: Carl Winters, 1925.

Goodman, Nelson. *Fact, Fiction, and Forecast.* 4th ed. Cambridge, MA: Harvard University Press, 1983.

Gorman, Michael J., ed. *Scripture and Its Interpretation: A Global, Ecumenical Introduction to the Bible.* Grand Rapids: Baker, 2017.

Grant, Robert M., and David Tracy. *A Short History of the Interpretation of the Bible.* 2nd ed. Minneapolis: Fortress, 1984.

Green, Joel B., and Max Turner, eds. *The Two Horizons New Testament Commentary.* Grand Rapids: Eerdmans, 2005-.

Green, Joel B. *Practicing Theological Interpretation: Engaging Biblical Texts for Faith and Formation.* Theological Explorations for the Church Catholic. Grand Rapids: Baker, 2011.

eds. *The Two Horizons New Testament Commentary.* Grand Rapids: Eerdmans, 2005.

Greggs, Tom. *Theology against Religion: Constructive Dialogues with Bonhoeffer and Barth.* London: T. & T. Clark, 2011.

Gregory, Brad S. "Introduction." In *Tractatus Theologico-Politicus (Gebhardt Edition, 1925)*, 1–44. Leiden: Brill, 1989.

*The Unintended Reformation: How a Religious Revolution Secularized Society.* Cambridge, MA: Belknap Press of Harvard University Press, 2012.

Griffiths, Paul J. Lying: *An Augustinian Theology of Duplicity.* Grand Rapids: Brazos, 2004.

*Religious Reading: The Place of Reading in the Practice of Religion.* Oxford: Oxford University Press, 1999.

*Song of Songs*. Brazos Theological Commentary on the Bible. Grand Rapids: Brazos, 2011.

"Which Are the Words of Scripture?" *Theological Studies* 72 (2011): 703–22.

Grondin, Jean. *Introduction to Philosophical Hermeneutics*. Yale Studies in Hermeneutics. New Haven: Yale University Press, 1994.

Gruchy, John W. de. *Bonhoeffer and South Africa: Theology in Dialogue*. Grand Rapids: Eerdmans, 1984.

"With Bonhoeffer, Beyond Bonhoeffer: Transmitting Bonhoeffer's Legacy." In *Dietrich Bonhoeffers Theologie heute: Ein Weg zwischen Fundamentalismus und Säkularismus? = Dietrich Bonhoeffer's Theology Today: A Way between Fundamentalism and Secularism*, edited by John W. de Gruchy, Stephen Plant, and Christiane Tietz, 403–16. Gütersloh: Gütersloher, 2009.

Gunton, Colin E. "Using and Being Used: Scripture and Systematic Theology." *Theology Today* 47 (1990): 248–59.

Hadot, Pierre. *Philosophy as a Way of Life: Spiritual Exercises from Socrates to Foucault*. Oxford: Blackwell, 1995.

Harris, William V. *Ancient Literacy*. Cambridge, MA: Harvard University Press, 1989.

Harrison, Carol. *The Art of Listening in the Early Church*. Oxford: Oxford University Press, 2013.

"Augustine." In *The New Cambridge History of the Bible*, edited by James Carleton Paget and Joachim Schaper. Vol. 1: From the Beginnings to 600, 676–96. Cambridge: Cambridge University Press, 2013.

*Augustine: Christian Truth and Fractured Humanity*. Christian Theology in Context. Oxford: Oxford University Press, 2000.

*Beauty and Revelation in the Thought of Saint Augustine*. Oxford Theological Monographs. Oxford: Clarendon Press, 1992.

"De doctrina christiana." *New Blackfriars* 87 (2006): 121–31.

"*De Profundis*: Augustine's Reading of Orthodoxy." In *Orthodox Readings of Augustine*, edited by George E. Demacopoulos and Aristotle Papanikolaou, 253–61. Crestwood: St. Vladimir's Seminary Press, 2008.

Hart, David Bentley. *The Beauty of the Infinite: The Aesthetics of Christian Truth*. Grand Rapids: Eerdmans, 2003.

*The New Testament: A Translation*. New Haven: Yale University Press, 2017.

"The Second Naiveté? Allegorical and Critical Readings of Scripture." Christian Scholars' Conference, Pepperdine University, 2011, www.youtube.com/watch?v=EOShHXaqtoM

Harvey, Angela Lou. *Spiritual Reading: A Study of the Christian Practice of Reading Scripture.* Eugene: Cascade Books, 2015.

Harvey, Van. *The Historian and the Believer: The Morality of Historical Knowledge and Christian Belief.* New York: Macmillan, 1966.

Hauerwas, Stanley. *Matthew.* Grand Rapids: Brazos, 2006.

*The Peaceable Kingdom: A Primer in Christian Ethics.* Notre Dame: University of Notre Dame Press, 1983.

"Postscript: By Way of a Response to Nicholas Healy's Book, *Hauerwas: A (Very) Critical Introduction.*" In *The Work of Theology*, 266–78. Grand Rapids: Eerdmans, 2015

*Unleashing the Scripture: Freeing the Bible from Captivity to America.* Nashville: Abingdon, 1993.

Hays, Richard B. "Benedict and the Biblical Jesus." *First Things* 175 (2007): 49–53.

*Echoes of Scripture in the Letters of Paul.* New Haven: Yale University Press, 1989.

*The Moral Vision of the New Testament: Community, Cross, New Creation; a Contemporary Introduction to New Testament Ethics.* New York: HarperCollins, 1996.

*Reading Backwards: Figural Christology and the Fourfold Gospel Witness.* Waco: Baylor University Press, 2014.

"Reading Scripture in Light of the Resurrection." In *The Art of Reading Scripture*, edited by Ellen F. Davis and Richard B. Hays, 216–38. Grand Rapids: Eerdmans, 2003

"Reading the Bible with Eyes of Faith: The Practice of Theological Exegesis." *Journal of Theological Interpretation* 1 (2007): 5–21.

Healy, Nicholas M. *Hauerwas: A (Very) Critical Introduction.* Interventions. Grand Rapids: Eerdmans, 2014.

Hegel, G. W. F. *Lectures on the Philosophy of Religion: The Lectures of 1827.* Oxford: Clarendon Press, 2006.

Heidegger, Martin. *Being and Time.* Suny Series in Contemporary Continental Philosophy. Albany: State University of New York Press, 1996.

Henderson, John B. *Scripture, Canon, and Commentary: A Comparison of Confucian and Western Exegesis*. Princeton: Princeton University Press, 1991.

Hirsch, E. D. *Validity in Interpretation*. New Haven: Yale University Press, 1967.

Huizing, Klaas. *Homo legens: Vom Ursprung der Theologie im Lesen*. Theologische Bibliothek Töpelmann. Berlin: W. de Gruyter, 1996.

Hütter, Reinhard. *Suffering Divine Things: Theology as Church Practice*. Grand Rapids: Eerdmans, 2000.

Iser, Wolfgang. *The Act of Reading: A Theory of Aesthetic Response*. Baltimore: Johns Hopkins University Press, 1978.

*The Implied Reader: Patterns of Communication in Prose Fiction from Bunyan to Beckett*. Baltimore: Johns Hopkins University Press, 1974.

*The Range of Interpretation*. The Wellek Library Lecture Series. New York: Columbia University Press, 2000.

Israel, Jonathan. "How Did Spinoza Declare War on Theology and Theologians?" In *Scriptural Authority and Biblical Criticism in the Dutch Golden Age*, edited by Dirk van Miert, Henk J. M. Nellen, Piet Steenbakkers, and Jetze Touber, 197–216. Oxford: Oxford University Press, 2017.

"Introduction." In *Theological-Political Treatise*, Cambridge Texts in the History of Philosophy, viii–xxxiv. Cambridge: Cambridge University Press, 2007.

*Radical Enlightenment: Philosophy and the Making of Modernity 1650–1750*. Oxford: Oxford University Press, 2001.

*A Revolution of the Mind: Radical Enlightenment and the Intellectual Origins of Modern Democracy*. Princeton: Princeton University Press, 2010.

Istace, Gerard. "Le livre I$^{er}$ du *De doctrina christiana* de Saint Augustin. Organisation synthétique et méthode de mise en oeuvre." *Ephémérides theologicae Lovanienses* 32 (1956): 289–330.

Jackson, B. Darrell "The Theory of Signs in St. Augustine's *De doctrina christiana*." In *Augustine: A Collection of Critical Essays*, edited by R. A. Markus, Modern Studies in Philosophy, 92–147. Garden City: Anchor Books, 1972.

Jacobs, Alan. *A Theology of Reading: The Hermeneutics of Love*. Boulder: Westview, 2001.

James, Susan. *Spinoza on Philosophy, Religion, and Politics: The Theologico-Political Treatise*. Oxford: Oxford University Press, 2012.

Jeffrey, David L. *People of the Book: Christian Identity and Literary Culture*. Grand Rapids: Eerdmans, 1996.

Jennings, Willie James. "Baptizing a Social Reading: Theology, Hermeneutics, and Postmodernity." In *Disciplining Hermeneutics: Interpretation in Christian Perspective*, edited by Roger Lundin, 117–27. Grand Rapids: Eerdmans, 1997.

Jenson, Robert W. "The Bible and the Trinity." *Pro Ecclesia* 11 (2002): 329–39.

"Hermeneutics and the Life of the Church." In *Reclaiming the Bible for the Church*, edited by Carl E. Braaten and Robert W. Jenson, 89–105. Grand Rapids: Eerdmans, 1995.

"Scripture's Authority in the Church." In *The Art of Reading Scripture*, edited by Ellen F. Davis and Richard B. Hays, 27–37. Grand Rapids: Eerdmans, 2003.

Johnson, Luke Timothy. "Matthew or Stanley? Pick One." *Pro Ecclesia* 17 (2008): 29–34.

Johnson, William A. *Readers and Reading Culture in the High Roman Empire: A Study of Elite Communities*. Classical Culture and Society. Oxford: Oxford University Press, 2010.

Johnson, William Stacy. "Reading the Scriptures Faithfully in a Postmodern Age." In *The Art of Reading Scripture*, edited by Ellen F. Davis and Richard B. Hays, 109–24. Grand Rapids: Eerdmans, 2003.

Jones, Tamsin. *A Genealogy of Marion's Philosophy of Religion: Apparent Darkness*. Indiana Series in the Philosophy of Religion. Bloomington: Indiana University Press, 2011.

Jordan, Mark D. "Words and Word: Incarnation and Signification in Augustine's *De doctrina christiana*." *Augustinian Studies* 11 (1980): 177–96.

Jüngel, Eberhard. *God as the Mystery of the World: On the Foundation of the Theology of the Crucified One in the Dispute between Theism and Atheism*. Grand Rapids: Eerdmans, 1983.

Kant, Immanuel. "Religion within the Bounds of Mere Reason." In *Religion and Rational Theology*, edited by Allen W. Wood and George Di Giovanni, 55–215. Cambridge: Cambridge University Press, 1996.

Käsemann, Ernst. "Thoughts on the Present Controversy About Scriptural Interpretation." In *New Testament Questions of Today*. The New Testament Library, 260–85. London: SCM Press, 1969.

Katho, Bungishabaku. "Idolatry and the Peril of the Nation: Reading Jeremiah 2 in an African Context." *Anglican Theological Review* 99 (2017): 713–28.

Kaufman, Gordon D. "What Shall We Do with the Bible?" *Interpretation* 25 (1971): 95–112.

Kelsey, David H. *Eccentric Existence: A Theological Anthropology*. 2 vols. Louisville: Westminster John Knox, 2009.

*Proving Doctrine: The Uses of Scripture in Modern Theology*. Harrisburg: Trinity Press International, 1999.

Kermode, Frank. *The Genesis of Secrecy: On the Interpretation of Narrative*. Cambridge, MA: Harvard University Press, 1979.

Khoury, Adel Théodore, and Ludwig Muth, eds. *Glauben durch Lesen? Für eine christliche Lesekultur*. Quaestiones Disputatae. Freiburg: Herder, 1990.

Kieffer, René. "Wass heißt das, einen Text zu kommentieren?" *Biblische Zeitschrift* 20 (1976): 212–16.

Kierkegaard, Søren. *Concluding Unscientific Postscript to Philosophical Fragments. Kierkegaard's Writings*. Princeton: Princeton University Press, 1992.

*For Self-Examination; Judge for Yourself!* Kierkegaard's Writings. Princeton: Princeton University Press, 1990.

*Philosophical Fragments*. Kierkegaard's Writings. Princeton: Princeton University Press, 1985.

Kirwan, Christopher. *Augustine*. The Arguments of the Philosophers. New York: Routledge, 1989.

Klink, Edward W., and Darian R. Lockett. *Understanding Biblical Theology: A Comparison of Theory and Practice*. Grand Rapids: Zondervan, 2012.

Kolbet, Paul R. *Augustine and the Cure of Souls: Revising a Classical Ideal*. Christianity and Judaism in Antiquity Series. Notre Dame: University of Notre Dame Press, 2010.

Kort, Wesley A. *Take, Read: Scripture, Textuality, and Cultural Practice*. University Park: Pennsylvania State University Press, 1996.

Kugel, James L. *How to Read the Bible: A Guide to Scripture, Then and Now*. New York: Free Press, 2008.

La Bonnardière, Anne-Marie. *Biblia Augustiniana*. 7 vols. Paris: Études augustiniennes, 1960–1975.

"The Canon of Sacred Scripture." In *Augustine and the Bible*, edited by Pamela Bright, Bible through the Ages, 26–41. Notre Dame: University of Notre Dame Press, 1999.

"Did Augustine Use Jerome's Vulgate?" In *Augustine and the Bible*, edited by Pamela Bright, The Bible through the Ages, 42–51. Notre Dame: University of Notre Dame, 1999.

LaCocque, André, and Paul Ricoeur. *Thinking Biblically: Exegetical and Hermeneutical Studies*. Chicago: University of Chicago Press, 1998.

Lancel, Serge. *Saint Augustine*. London: SCM Press, 2002.

Lash, Nicholas. *Believing Three Ways in One God: A Reading of the Apostles' Creed*. 2nd ed. London: SCM, 2002.

Legaspi, Michael C. *The Death of Scripture and the Rise of Biblical Studies*. Oxford Studies in Historical Theology. Oxford: Oxford University Press, 2010.

"Scripture: Three Modes of Retrieval." In *Theologies of Retrieval: An Exploration and Appraisal*, edited by Darren Sarisky, 155–72. London: Bloomsbury T. & T. Clark, 2017.

Levene, Nancy. *Spinoza's Revelation: Religion, Democracy, and Reason*. Cambridge: Cambridge University Press, 2004.

Levenson, Jon D. *The Hebrew Bible, the Old Testament, and Historical Criticism: Jews and Christians in Biblical Studies*. Louisville: Westminster John Knox, 1993.

"Historical Criticism and the Fate of the Enlightenment Project." In *The Hebrew Bible, the Old Testament, and Historical Criticism: Jews and Christians in Biblical Studies*, 106–26. Louisville: Westminster John Knox, 1993.

"Theological Consensus or Historicist Evasion? Jews and Christians in Biblical Studies." In *The Hebrew Bible, the Old Testament, and Historical Criticism: Jews and Christians in Biblical Studies*, 82–105. Louisville: Westminster John Knox, 1993.

Levering, Matthew. *Participatory Biblical Exegesis: A Theology of Biblical Interpretation*. Reading the Scriptures. Notre Dame: University of Notre Dame Press, 2008.

*Scripture and Metaphysics: Aquinas and the Renewal of Trinitarian Theology*. Challenges in Contemporary Theology. Malden, MA: Blackwell, 2004.

Lincoln, Andrew T. "From Writing to Reception: Reflections on Commentating on the Fourth Gospel." *Journal for the Study of the New Testament* 29 (2007): 353–72.

Lindbeck, George. *The Nature of Doctrine: Religion and Theology in a Postliberal Age*. 25th anniversary ed. Louisville: Westminster John Knox, 2009.

"The Story-Shaped Church: Critical Exegesis and Theological Interpretation." In *Scriptural Authority and Narrative Interpretation*, edited by Garrett Green, 161–78. Philadelphia: Fortress, 1987.

Locke, John. *Vindications of the Reasonableness of Christianity*. Clarendon Edition of the Works of John Locke. Oxford: Clarendon Press, 2012.

Lootens, Matthew R. "Augustine." In *The Spiritual Senses: Perceiving God in Western Christianity*, edited by Paul L. Gavrilyuk and Sarah Coakley, 56–70. Cambridge: Cambridge University Press, 2014.

Louth, Andrew. "Augustine on Language." *Journal of Literature and Theology* 3 (1989): 151–58.

"Inspiration of the Scriptures." *Sobornost* 9 (2009): 29–44.

Lubac, Henri de. *At the Service of the Church: Henri de Lubac Reflects on the Circumstances That Occasioned His Writings*. San Francisco: Ignatius Press, 1993.

*Catholicism: A Study of Dogma in Relation to the Corporate Destiny of Mankind*. London: Burns & Oates, 1958.

*History and Spirit: The Understanding of Scripture According to Origen*. San Francisco: Ignatius, 2007.

*Surnaturel: Études historiques*. Théologie. Paris: Aubier, 1946.

Luz, Ulrich. "Can the Bible Still Be the Foundation for a Church Today? The Task of Exegesis in a Society of Religious Pluralism." In *Studies in Matthew*, 313–32. Grand Rapids: Eerdmans, 2005.

"Hermeneutics of 'Effective History' and the Church." In *Studies in Matthew*, 349–69. Grand Rapids: Eerdmans, 2005.

*Matthew: A Commentary*. 3 vols. Hermeneia: A Critical and Historical Commentary on the Bible. Minneapolis: Fortress, 2001, 2005, 2007.

*Matthew in History: Interpretation, Influence, and Effects*. Minneapolis: Fortress, 2007.

"Reflections on the Appropriate Interpretation of New Testament Texts." In *Studies in Matthew*, 265–89. Grand Rapids: Eerdmans, 2005.

"The Significance of Matthew's Jesus Story for Today." In *Studies in Matthew*, 370–79. Grand Rapids: Eerdmans, 2005.

*Theologische Hermeneutik des Neuen Testaments*. Neukirchen-Vluyn: Neukirchener Theologie, 2014.

Lyotard, Jean-François. *The Postmodern Condition: A Report on Knowledge*. Theory and History of Literature. Minneapolis: University of Minnesota Press, 1984.

MacIntyre, Alasdair C. *After Virtue: A Study in Moral Theory*. 2nd ed. Notre Dame: University of Notre Dame Press, 1984.

*Three Rival Versions of Moral Enquiry: Encyclopaedia, Genealogy, and Tradition*. Notre Dame: University of Notre Dame Press, 1990.

*Whose Justice? Which Rationality?* Notre Dame: University of Notre Dame Press, 1988.

Mackinlay, Shane. "Eyes Wide Shut: A Response to Jean-Luc Marion's Account of the Journey to Emmaus." *Modern Theology* 20 (2004): 447–56.

Madec, Goulven. "*Christus, scientia et sapientia nostra*. Le principe de cohérence de la doctrine augustinienne." *Recherches augustiniennes et patristiques* 10 (1975): 77–85.

"*Verus philosophus est amator Dei*. S. Ambroise, S. Augustin et la philosophie." *Revue des Sciences philosophiques et théologiques* 61 (1977): 549–66.

Maier, Gerhard. *Das Ende der historisch-kritischen Methode*. Abcteam 901: Glauben und Denken. 2nd ed. Wuppertal: R. Brockhaus, 1975.

Maimonides, Moses. *The Guide of the Perplexed*. Chicago: University of Chicago Press, 1963.

Malcolm, Noel. "Hobbes, Ezra, and the Bible: The History of a Subversive Idea." In *Aspects of Hobbes*, 383–431. Oxford: Clarendon Press, 2002.

Mangina, Joseph L. "Hidden from the Wise, Revealed to Infants: Stanley Hauerwas's Commentary on Matthew." *Pro Ecclesia* 17 (2008): 13–19.

*Revelation*. Brazos Theological Commentary on the Bible. Grand Rapids: Brazos, 2010.

Margerie, Bertrand de. *An Introduction to the History of Exegesis*. Vol. III: Saint Augustine. Petersham: Saint Bede's, 1991.

Marion, Jean-Luc. *Givenness and Revelation*. Oxford: Oxford University Press, 2016.

*God without Being: Hors-Texte*. Chicago: University of Chicago Press, 1991.

*The Idol and Distance: Five Studies*. Perspectives in Continental Philosophy. New York: Fordham University Press, 2001.

*In the Self's Place: The Approach of Saint Augustine*. Cultural Memory in the Present. Stanford: Stanford University Press, 2012.

*On Descartes' Metaphysical Prism: The Constitution and the Limits of Onto-Theo-Logy in Cartesian Thought*. Chicago: University of Chicago Press, 1999.

"'They Recognized Him; and He Became Invisible to Them.'" *Modern Theology* 18 (2002): 145–52.

"Thomas Aquinas and Onto-Theo-Logy." In *Mystics: Presence and Aporia*, edited by Michael Kessler and Christian Sheppard, Religion and Postmodernism, 38–74. Chicago: University of Chicago Press, 2003.

Markus, R. A. "Augustine on Magic: A Neglected Semiotic Theory." In *Signs and Meanings: World and Text in Ancient Christianity*, 125–46. Liverpool: Liverpool University Press, 1996.

"Augustine on Signs." In *Signs and Meanings: World and Text in Ancient Christianity*, 71–104. Liverpool: Liverpool University Press, 1996.

"World and Text in Ancient Christianity I: Augustine." In *Signs and Meanings: World and Text in Ancient Christianity*, 1–43. Liverpool: Liverpool University Press, 1996.

Marsden, George M. *The Outrageous Idea of Christian Scholarship*. Oxford: Oxford University Press, 1997.

Marshall, Bruce. "Aquinas as Postliberal Theologian." *Thomist* 53 (1989): 353–402.

Martens, Peter. *Origen and Scripture: The Contours of the Exegetical Life*. Oxford Early Christian Studies. Oxford: Oxford University Press, 2012.

Martin, Dale B. *Biblical Truths: The Meaning of Scripture in the Twenty-First Century*. New Haven: Yale University Press, 2017.

*Pedagogy of the Bible: An Analysis and Proposal*. Louisville: Westminster John Knox, 2008.

Mathewes, Charles T. *A Theology of Public Life*. Cambridge Studies in Christian Doctrine. Cambridge: Cambridge University Press, 2007.

Mayer, C. P. "Prinzipien der Hermeneutik Augustins und daraus sich ergebende Probleme." *Forum Katholische Theologie* 1 (1985): 197–211.

McConville, J. Gordon, and Craig Bartholomew, eds. *The Two Horizons Old Testament Commentary*. Grand Rapids: Eerdmans, 2008-.

McCormack, Bruce L. "Historical Criticism and Dogmatic Interest in Karl Barth's Theological Exegesis of the New Testament." In *Biblical Hermeneutics in Historical Perspective*, edited by Mark S. Burrows and Paul Rorem, 322–38. Grand Rapids: Eerdmans, 1991.

McFarland, Ian A. *In Adam's Fall: A Meditation on the Christian Doctrine of Original Sin*. Challenges in Contemporary Theology. Chichester: Wiley-Blackwell, 2010.

Melamed, Yitzhak Y. "The Metaphysics of the Theological-Political Treatise." In *Spinoza's 'Theological-Political Treatise': A Critical Guide*, edited by Yitzhak Y. Melamed and Michael A. Rosenthal, 128–42. Cambridge: Cambridge University Press, 2010.

Milbank, John. "The Conflict of the Faculties: Theology and the Economy of the Sciences." In *Faithfulness and Fortitude: In Conversation with the Theological Ethics of Stanley Hauerwas*, edited by Samuel Wells and Mark Thiessen Nation, 39–57. London: T. & T. Clark, 2000.

"'Postmodern Critical Augustinianism': A Short Summa in Forty Two Responses to Unasked Questions." *Modern Theology* 7 (1991): 225–37.

Mildenberger, Friedrich. *Biblische Dogmatik: Eine biblische Theologie in dogmatischer Perspektive*. 3 vols. Stuttgart: W. Kohlhammer, 1991–1993.

Moberly, R. W. L. *The Bible, Theology, and Faith: A Study of Abraham and Jesus*. Cambridge Studies in Christian Doctrine. Cambridge: Cambridge University Press, 2000.

"What Is Theological Interpretation of Scripture?" *Journal of Theological Interpretation* 3 (2009): 161–78.

Morgan, Edward. *The Incarnation of the Word: The Theology of Language of Augustine of Hippo*. T. & T. Clark Theology. London: T. & T. Clark, 2010.

Morgan, Robert. "Liberal Theological Hermeneutics." *Journal of Theological Studies* 68 (2017): 212–29.

Morgan, Robert, and John Barton. *Biblical Interpretation*. Oxford Bible Series. Oxford: Oxford University Press, 1988.

Müller, Morgens. "Kierkegaard and Eighteenth- and Nineteenth-Century Biblical Scholarship: A Case of Incongruity." In *Kierkegaard and the Bible*, edited by Lee C. Barrett and Jon Stewart. Vol. 2: The New Testament, 285–327. Farnham: Ashgate, 2010.

Nadler, Steven M. *A Book Forged in Hell: Spinoza's Scandalous Treatise and the Birth of the Secular Age*. Princeton: Princeton University Press, 2011.

*Spinoza's Ethics: An Introduction*. Cambridge Introductions to Key Philosophical Texts. Cambridge: Cambridge University Press, 2006.

Nietzsche, Friedrich. *The Anti-Christ, Ecce Homo, Twilight of the Idols, and Other Writings*. Cambridge Texts in the History of Philosophy. Cambridge: Cambridge University Press, 2005.

"On the Uses and Disadvantages of History for Life." In *Untimely Meditations*, Cambridge Texts in the History of Philosophy, 57–123. Cambridge: Cambridge University Press, 1997.

O'Donnell, James J. "The Authority of Augustine." *Augustinian Studies* 22 (1991): 7–35.

"Doctrina Christiana, De." In *Augustine through the Ages: An Encyclopedia*, edited by Allan Fitzgerald, John C. Cavadini, Marianne Djuth, James J. O'Donnell, and Frederick Van Fleteren, 278–80. Grand Rapids: Eerdmans, 1999.

O'Donovan, Oliver. *The Problem of Self-Love in St. Augustine*. New Haven: Yale University Press, 1980.

"*Usus* and *Fruitio* in Augustine, *De doctrina christiana* I." *Journal of Theological Studies* 33 (1982): 361–97.

O'Leary, Joseph S. *Questioning Back: The Overcoming of Metaphysics in Christian Tradition*. Minneapolis: Winston, 1985.

O'Regan, Cyril. "*De doctrina christiana* and Modern Hermeneutics." In *De doctrina christiana: A Classic of Western Culture*, edited by Duane W. H. Arnold and Pamela Bright, Christianity and Judaism in Antiquity, 217–43. Notre Dame: University of Notre Dame Press, 1995.

Ochs, Peter. *Peirce, Pragmatism, and the Logic of Scripture*. Cambridge: Cambridge University Press, 2004.

ed. *The Return of Scripture in Judaism and Christianity: Essays in Postcritical Scriptural Interpretation*. New York: Paulist, 1993.

Oden, Robert A. *The Bible without Theology: The Theological Tradition and Alternatives to It*. Urbana: University of Illinois Press, 2000.

Ogden, Schubert M. *Faith and Freedom: Toward a Theology of Liberation*. Belfast: Christian Journals Limited, 1979.

Paddison, Angus, ed. *Theologians on Scripture*. London: Bloomsbury T. & T. Clark, 2016.

Paddison, Angus. "Who and What Is Theological Interpretation For?" In *Conception, Reception and the Spirit: Essays in Honor of Andrew T. Lincoln*, edited by J. Gordon McConville and Lloyd Pietersen, 210–23. Eugene: Cascade, 2015.

Pelikan, Jaroslav, and Valerie R. Hotchkiss, eds. *Creeds & Confessions of Faith in the Christian Tradition*. Vol. III, Part Five: Statements of Faith in Modern Christianity. New Haven: Yale University Press, 2003.

Placher, William C., and Amy Plantinga Pauw, eds. *Belief: A Theological Commentary on the Bible*. Louisville: Westminster John Knox, 2010–.

"Series Introduction" in *Mark*, by William C. Placher, *Belief: A Theological Commentary*, ix–xi. Louisville: Westminster John Knox, 2010.

Plantinga, Alvin. "Advice to Christian Philosophers." *Faith and Philosophy* 1 (1984): 253–71.

"Methodological Naturalism?" In *Facets of Faith and Science*, edited by J. Van der Meer. Vol. 1: Historiography and Modes of Interaction, 177–222. Lanham: University Press of America, 1996.

"Science: Augustinian or Duhemian?" *Faith and Philosophy* 13 (1996): 368–94.

"Two (or More) Kinds of Scripture Scholarship." In *Oxford Readings in Philosophical Theology*, edited by Michael C. Rea. Vol. 2: Providence, Scripture, and Resurrection, 266–301. Oxford: Oxford University Press, 2009.

*Warranted Christian Belief*. Oxford: Oxford University Press, 2000.

Poirier, John C. "'Theological Interpretation' and Its Contradistinctions." *Tyndale Bulletin* 61 (2010): 105–18.

Polk, Timothy. *The Biblical Kierkegaard: Reading by the Rule of Faith*. Macon: Mercer University Press, 1997.

Pollmann, Karla. "Alium sub meo nomine: Augustine between His Own Self-Fashioning and His Later Reception." *Zeitschrift für antikes Christentum* 14 (2010): 409–24.

"Augustine's Hermeneutics as a Universal Discipline!?" In *Augustine and the Disciplines: From Cassiciacum to Confessions*, edited by Karla Pollmann and Mark Vessey, 206–31. Oxford: Oxford University Press, 2005.

"Augustine's Legacy: Success or Failure?" In *The Cambridge Companion to Augustine*, 2nd ed., edited by David Vincent Meconi and Eleonore Stump, 331–48. Cambridge: Cambridge University Press, 2014.

*Doctrina christiana: Untersuchungen zu den Anfängen der christlichen Hermeneutik unter besonderer Berücksichtigung von Augustinus, De doctrina christiana.* Paradosis. Freiburg: Universitätsverlag, 1996.

"How to Do Things with Augustine. Patristics and Reception Theory." *Journal of Church Studies* 5 (2008): 31–41.

"To Write by Advancing in Knowledge and to Advance by Writing." *Augustinian Studies* 29 (1998): 131–37.

Pons, Jolita. *Stealing a Gift: Kierkegaard's Pseudonyms and the Bible.* Perspectives in Continental Philosophy Series. New York: Fordham University Press, 2004.

Popkin, Richard H. *The History of Scepticism: From Savonarola to Bayle.* Rev. ed. Oxford: Oxford University Press, 2003.

"Spinoza and Bible Scholarship." In *The Cambridge Companion to Spinoza*, edited by Don Garrett, 383–407. Cambridge: Cambridge University Press, 1996.

Porter, Stanley E. "What Exactly Is Theological Interpretation of Scripture, and Is It Hermeneutically Robust Enough for the Task to Which It Has Been Appointed?" In *Horizons in Hermeneutics: A Festschrift in Honor of Anthony C. Thiselton*, edited by Stanley E. Porter and Matthew R. Malcolm, 234–67. Grand Rapids: Eerdmans, 2013.

Potok, Chaim. *In the Beginning.* New York: Fawcett/Ballantine, 1997.

Press, Gerald A. "The Content and Argument of Augustine's *De doctrina christiana.*" *Augustiniana* 31 (1981): 165–82.

"*Doctrina* in Augustine's *De doctrina christiana.*" *Philosophy and Rhetoric* 17 (1984): 98–120.

Preus, James S. *Spinoza and the Irrelevance of Biblical Authority.* Cambridge: Cambridge University Press, 2001.

Project, The Scripture. "Nine Theses on the Interpretation of Scripture." In *The Art of Reading Scripture*, edited by Ellen F. Davis and Richard B. Hays, 1–5. Grand Rapids: Eerdmans, 2003.

Putnam, Hilary. *The Collapse of the Fact/Value Dichotomy and Other Essays*. Cambridge, MA: Harvard University Press, 2002.

*Reason, Truth, and History*. Cambridge: Cambridge University Press, 1981.

Radner, Ephraim. *Time and the Word: Figural Reading of the Christian Scriptures*. Grand Rapids: Eerdmans, 2016.

Rae, Murray. *History and Hermeneutics*. London: T. & T. Clark, 2005.

*Kierkegaard's Vision of the Incarnation: By Faith Transformed*. Oxford: Clarendon Press, 1997.

"Theological Interpretation and Historical Criticism." In *A Manifesto for Theological Interpretation*, edited by Craig G. Bartholomew and Heath A. Thomas, 94–109. Grand Rapids: Baker, 2016.

Rahner, Karl. *The Trinity*. London: Burns & Oates, 1970.

Räisänen, Heikki. *Beyond New Testament Theology: A Story and a Programme*. 2nd ed. London: SCM Press, 2000.

*Neutestamentliche Theologie? Eine religionswissenschaftliche Alternative*. Stuttgarter Bibelstudien. Stuttgart: Katholisches Bibelwerk, 2000.

Rasmussen, Joel D. S. "Kierkegaard's Biblical Hermeneutics: Imitation, Imaginative Freedom, and Paradoxical Fixation." In *Kierkegaard and the Bible*, edited by Lee C. Barrett and Jon Stewart. Vol. 2: The New Testament, 249–79. Farnham: Ashgate, 2010.

Ratzinger, Joseph. "Biblical Interpretation in Crisis: On the Question of the Foundations and Approaches of Exegesis Today." In *Biblical Interpretation in Crisis: The Ratzinger Conference on Bible and Church*, edited by Richard John Neuhaus, The Encounter Series, 1–23. Grand Rapids: Eerdmans, 1989.

*Jesus of Nazareth: From the Baptism in the Jordan to the Transfiguration*. New York: Doubleday, 2007.

Rawls, John. *Lectures on the History of Political Philosophy*. Cambridge, MA: Belknap Press of Harvard University Press, 2007.

*A Theory of Justice*. Rev. ed. Cambridge, MA: Harvard University Press, 2003.

Reno, R. R. "Biblical Theology and Theological Exegesis." In *Out of Egypt: Biblical Theology and Biblical Interpretation*, edited by Craig G.

Bartholomew, Mary Healy, Karl Möller, and Robin Parry, Scripture and Hermeneutics Series, 385–408. Grand Rapids: Zondervan, 2004.

"Series Preface" in *Acts*, by Jaroslav Pelikan, Brazos Theological Commentary on the Bible, 11–18. Grand Rapids: Brazos, 2005.

"Theology and Biblical Interpretation." In *Sharper than a Two-Edged Sword: Preaching, Teaching, and Living the Bible*, edited by Michael Root and James J. Buckley, 1–21. Grand Rapids: Eerdmans, 2008.

"'You Who Once Were Far Off Have Been Brought Near': Reflections in the Aid of Theological Exegesis." *Ex auditu* 16 (2000): 169–82.

ed. *Brazos Theological Commentary on the Bible*. Grand Rapids: Brazos, 2005-.

Ricoeur, Paul. "Esquisse de conclusion." In *Exégèse et herméneutique*, edited by Roland Barthes, Paul Beauchamp, Henri Bouillard, Joseph Courtès, Edgard Haulotte, Xavier Léon Dufour, Louis Marin, Paul Ricoeur, and Antoine Vergote, 285–95. Paris: Seuil, 1971.

*Freud and Philosophy: An Essay on Interpretation*. The Terry Lectures. New Haven: Yale University Press, 1970.

"From Interpretation to Translation." In *Thinking Biblically: Exegetical and Hermeneutical Studies*, edited by André Lacocque and Paul Ricoeur, 331–61. Chicago: University of Chicago Press, 1998.

"Preface to Bultmann." In *Essays on Biblical Interpretation*, 49–72. Philadelphia: Fortress, 1980.

*The Symbolism of Evil*. Boston: Beacon, 1969.

"The Task of Hermeneutics." In *Hermeneutics and the Human Sciences: Essays on Language, Action, and Interpretation*, 43–62. Cambridge: Cambridge University Press, 1981.

*Time and Narrative*. Vol. 1. Chicago: University of Chicago Press, 1984.

Rist, John M. *Augustine: Ancient Thought Baptized*. Cambridge: Cambridge University Press, 1994.

Rogers, Eugene F. "How the Virtues of an Interpreter Presuppose and Perfect Hermeneutics: The Case of Thomas Aquinas." *Journal of Religion* 76 (1996): 64–81.

Rowe, C. Kavin. "Biblical Pressure and Trinitarian Hermeneutics." *Pro Ecclesia* 11 (2002): 295–312.

Rowe, C. Kavin, and Richard B. Hays. "What Is a Theological Commentary?" *Pro Ecclesia* 16 (2007): 26–32.

Sanders, E. P. *Paul and Palestinian Judaism: A Comparison of Patterns of Religion*. Philadelphia: Fortress, 1977.

Sanneh, Lamin O. *Translating the Message: The Missionary Impact on Culture*. American Society of Missiology Series. 2nd ed. Maryknoll: Orbis, 2009.

Sarisky, Darren. "The Ontology of Scripture and the Ethics of Interpretation in the Theology of John Webster." *International Journal of Systematic Theology* (Forthcoming).

"Reading Augustine in Light of Gadamer: Reflections on the Character of Prior Understanding." *International Journal of Systematic Theology* (Forthcoming).

*Scriptural Interpretation: A Theological Account*. Challenges in Contemporary Theology. Oxford: Wiley-Blackwell, 2013.

"Tradition II: Thinking with Historical Texts: Reflections on Theologies of Retrieval." In *Theologies of Retrieval: An Exploration and Appraisal*, edited by Darren Sarisky, 193–209. London: T. & T. Clark, 2017.

Sarisky, Darren, ed. *Theology, History, and Biblical Interpretation: Modern Readings*. London: T. & T. Clark, 2015.

Schaper, Joachim. "Historical Criticism, 'Theological Exegesis,' and Theology amongst the Humanities." In *Theology, University, Humanities: Initium Sapientiae Timor Domini*, edited by Christopher Craig Brittain and Francesca Aran Murphy, 75–90. Eugene: Wipf and Stock, 2011.

Schindler, David L. Introduction to *The Mystery of the Supernatural*, by Henri de Lubac, xi–xxxi. New York: Crossroad, 1998.

Schleiermacher, Friedrich. *Hermeneutics and Criticism and Other Writings*. Cambridge Texts in the History of Philosophy. Cambridge: Cambridge University Press, 1998.

*Hermeneutics: The Handwritten Manuscripts. Texts and Translation*. Missoula: Scholars, 1977.

*On Religion: Speeches to Its Cultured Despisers*. 2nd ed. Cambridge Texts in the History of Philosophy. Cambridge: Cambridge University Press, 1996.

Schnabel, Eckhard J. "On Commentary Writing." In *On the Writing of New Testament Commentaries: Festschrift for Grant R. Osborne on the*

*Occasion of His 70th Birthday*, edited by Stanley E. Porter and Eckhard J. Schnabel, Texts and Editions for New Testament Study, 3–32. Leiden: Brill, 2013.

Schneiders, Sandra M. *The Revelatory Text: Interpreting the New Testament as Sacred Scripture*. 2nd ed. Collegeville: Liturgical Press, 1999.

Schüssler Fiorenza, Elisabeth. *Bread Not Stone: The Challenge of Feminist Biblical Interpretation*. Edinburgh: T. & T. Clark, 1990.

"The Ethics of Biblical Interpretation: Decentering Biblical Scholarship." *Journal of Biblical Literature* 107 (1988): 3–17.

Schüssler Fiorenza, Francis. "The Crisis of Scriptural Authority: Interpretation and Reception." *Interpretation* 44 (1990): 353–68.

Schweitzer, Albert. *The Quest of the Historical Jesus*. Mineola: Dover, 2005.

Searle, John R. *Speech Acts: An Essay in the Philosophy of Language*. London: Cambridge University Press, 1969.

Seow, C. L., ed. *Illuminations*. Grand Rapids: Eerdmans, 2013-.

Sheehan, Jonathan. *The Enlightenment Bible: Translation, Scholarship, Culture*. Princeton: Princeton University Press, 2005.

Sidgwick, Henry. *The Methods of Ethics*. 7th ed. Chicago: University of Chicago Press, 1962.

Smith, Wilfred Cantwell. *What Is Scripture? A Comparative Approach*. London: SCM Press, 1993.

Sommer, Benjamin D. "Dialogical Biblical Theology: A Jewish Approach to Reading Scripture Theologically." In *Biblical Theology: Introducing the Conversation*, edited by Leo G. Perdue, Robert Morgan, and Benjamin D. Sommer, Library of Biblical Theology, 25–48. Nashville: Abingdon, 2009.

Sonderegger, Katherine. *Systematic Theology*. Vol. 1: The Doctrine of God. Minneapolis: Fortress, 2015.

Soskice, Janet M. *Metaphor and Religious Language*. Oxford: Clarendon Press, 1985.

Spinoza, Benedictus de. *The Collected Works of Spinoza. Volume II*. Princeton: Princeton University Press, 2016.

*Ethics*. Oxford Philosophical Texts. Oxford: Oxford University Press, 2000.

*Theological-Political Treatise*. Cambridge Texts in the History of Philosophy. Cambridge: Cambridge University Press, 2007.

Stavrakopoulou, Francesca. "Materialist Reading: Materialism, Materiality, and Biblical Cults of Writing." In *Biblical Interpretation and Method: Essays in Honour of John Barton*, edited by Katharine J. Dell and Paul M. Joyce, 223–42. Oxford: Oxford University Press, 2013.

Steiner, George. "Critic/Reader." In *George Steiner: A Reader*, 67–98. Oxford: Oxford University Press, 1984.

"The Retreat from the Word." In *Language and Silence: Essays on Language, Literature, and the Inhuman*, 12–35. New Haven: Yale University Press, 1998.

Steinmetz, David C. "The Superiority of Pre-Critical Exegesis." In *Taking the Long View: Christian Theology in Historical Perspective*, 3–14. Oxford: Oxford University Press, 2011.

Stendahl, Krister. "The Bible as Classic and the Bible as Holy Scripture." In *Presidential Voices: The Society of Biblical Literature in the Twentieth Century*, edited by Harold W. Attridge and James C. VanderKam, 209–15. Atlanta: Society of Biblical Literature, 2006.

"Biblical Theology, Contemporary." In *The Interpreter's Dictionary of the Bible: An Illustrated Encyclopedia*, edited by George A. Buttrick, vol. 1, 418–32. Nashville: Abingdon, 1962.

Stock, Brian. *After Augustine: The Meditative Reader and the Text*. Material Texts. Philadelphia: University of Pennsylvania Press, 2001.

*Augustine the Reader: Meditation, Self-Knowledge, and the Ethics of Interpretation*. Cambridge, MA: Harvard University Press, 1996.

*The Integrated Self: Augustine, the Bible, and Ancient Thought*. Haney Foundation Series. Philadelphia: University of Pennsylvania Press, 2017.

Stout, Jeffrey. *Ethics after Babel: The Languages of Morals and Their Discontents*. Boston: Beacon, 1988.

*The Flight from Authority: Religion, Morality, and the Quest for Autonomy*. Notre Dame: University of Notre Dame Press, 1981.

"What Is the Meaning of a Text?" *New Literary History* 14 (1982): 1–12.

Strauss, Leo. "How to Study Spinoza's Theologico-Political Treatise." In *Persecution and the Art of Writing*, 142–202. Chicago: University of Chicago Press, 1988.

*Spinoza's Critique of Religion*. Chicago: University of Chicago Press, 1997.

Stuhlmacher, Peter. "Historische Kritik und theologische Schriftauslegung." In *Schriftauslegung auf dem Wege zur biblischen Theologie*, 59–127. Goettingen: Vandenhoeck & Ruprecht, 1975.

Stump, Eleonore. "Revelation and Biblical Exegesis: Augustine, Aquinas, and Swinburne." In *Reason and the Christian Religion: Essays in Honour of Richard Swinburne*, edited by Richard Swinburne and Alan G. Padgett, 161–97. Oxford: Clarendon Press, 1994.

"Visits to the Sepulcher and Biblical Exegesis." In *Oxford Readings in Philosophical Theology*, edited by Michael C. Rea. Vol. 2: Providence, Scripture, and Resurrection, 242–65. Oxford: Oxford University Press, 2009.

Swain, Scott R. *Trinity, Revelation, and Reading: A Theological Introduction to the Bible and Its Interpretation*. London: T. & T. Clark, 2011.

Swinburne, Richard. *Revelation: From Metaphor to Analogy*. Oxford: Clarendon Press, 1992.

Tanner, Kathryn. *God and Creation in Christian Theology: Tyranny or Empowerment?* Oxford: Basil Blackwell, 1988.

"Scripture as Popular Text." *Modern Theology* 14 (1998): 279–98.

"Shifts in Theology over the Last Quarter Century." *Modern Theology* 26 (2010): 39–44.

"Theology and the Plain Sense." In *Scriptural Authority and Narrative Interpretation*, edited by Garrett Green, 59–78. Philadelphia: Fortress, 1987.

Taylor, Charles. *A Secular Age*. Cambridge, MA: Belknap Press of Harvard University Press, 2007.

*Sources of the Self: The Making of the Modern Identity*. Cambridge: Cambridge University Press, 1989.

Thiselton, Anthony C. *Thiselton on Hermeneutics: The Collected Works and New Essays of Anthony Thiselton*. Ashgate Contemporary Thinkers on Religion. Aldershot: Ashgate, 2006.

Ticciati, Susannah. *Job and the Disruption of Identity: Reading Beyond Barth*. London: T. & T. Clark International, 2005.

*A New Apophaticism: Augustine and the Redemption of Signs*. Leiden: Brill, 2013.

"Review of Dale B. Martin's *Biblical Truths: The Meaning of Scripture in the Twenty-First Century*." Paper presented at the annual meeting for the Society of Biblical Literature, Boston, MA, November 19, 2017.

Todorov, Tzvetan. *Théories du symbole*. Collection poétique. Paris: Seuil, 1977.

Toom, Tarmo. *Thought Clothed with Sound: Augustine's Christological Hermeneutics in De doctrina christiana*. International Theological Studies. Bern: Peter Lang, 2002.

Torrance, Thomas F. *The Christian Doctrine of God: One Being, Three Persons*. Edinburgh: T. & T. Clark, 1996.

*Divine Meaning: Studies in Patristic Hermeneutics*. Edinburgh: T. & T. Clark, 1995.

Tracy, David. *The Analogical Imagination: Christian Theology and the Culture of Pluralism*. New York: Crossroad, 1981.

"Augustine's Christomorphic Theocentrism." In *Orthodox Readings of Augustine*, edited by George E. Demacopoulos and Aristotle Papanikolaou, 263–89. Crestwood: St. Vladimir's Seminary Press, 2008.

*Blessed Rage for Order: The New Pluralism in Theology*. Chicago: University of Chicago Press, 1996.

"Charity, Obscurity, Clarity: Augustine's Search for Rhetoric and Hermeneutics." In *Rhetoric and Hermeneutics in Our Time*, edited by Walter Jost and Michael J. Hyde, 254–74. New Haven: Yale University Press, 1997.

Foreword to *God without Being: Hors-Texte*, by Jean-Luc Marion, ix–xv. Chicago: University of Chicago Press, 1991.

"On Reading Scripture Theologically." In *Theology and Dialogue: Essays in Conversation with George Lindbeck*, edited by Bruce Marshall, 35–68. Notre Dame: University of Notre Dame Press, 1990.

*Plurality and Ambiguity: Hermeneutics, Religion, Hope*. Chicago: University of Chicago Press, 1994.

Treier, Daniel J. "Biblical Theology and/or Theological Interpretation of Scripture?" *Scottish Journal of Theology* 61 (2008): 16–31.

*Introducing Theological Interpretation of Scripture: Recovering a Christian Practice*. Grand Rapids: Baker, 2008.

*Virtue and the Voice of God: Toward Theology as Wisdom*. Grand Rapids: Eerdmans, 2006.

"What Is Theological Interpretation? An Ecclesiological Reduction." *International Journal of Systematic Theology* 12 (2010): 144–61.

Troeltsch, Ernst. "Historiography." In *Encyclopedia of Religion and Ethics*, edited by James Hastings and John Alexander Selbie, vol. VI, 716–23. Edinburgh: T. & T. Clark, 1913.

"On the Historical and Dogmatic Methods in Theology." In *Religion in History*, 11–32. Edinburgh: T. & T. Clark, 1991.

Van Fleteren, Frederick. "St. Augustine, Neoplatonism, and the Liberal Arts: The Background to *De doctrina christiana*." In *De doctrina christiana: A Classic of Western Culture*, edited by Duane W. H. Arnold and Pamela Bright, Christianity and Judaism in Antiquity, 14–24. Notre Dame: University of Notre Dame Press, 1995.

Vanhoozer, Kevin J. "Body-Piercing, the Natural Sense, and the Task of Theological Interpretation: A Hermeneutical Homily on John 19:34." *Ex auditu* 16 (2000): 1–29.

*The Drama of Doctrine: A Canonical-Linguistic Approach to Christian Theology*. Louisville: Westminster John Knox 2005.

*Is There a Meaning in This Text? The Bible, the Reader, and the Morality of Literary Knowledge*. Grand Rapids: Zondervan, 1998.

*Remythologizing Theology: Divine Action, Passion, and Authorship*. Cambridge Studies in Christian Doctrine. Cambridge: Cambridge University Press, 2010.

"The Spirit of Understanding: Special Revelation and General Hermeneutics." In *First Theology: God, Scripture & Hermeneutics*, 207–35. Downers Grove: InterVarsity Press, 2002.

"Theological Commentary and the "Voice from Heaven": Exegesis, Ontology, and the Travail of Biblical Interpretation." In *On the Writing of New Testament Commentaries: Festschrift for Grant R. Osborne on the Occasion of His 70th Birthday*, edited by Stanley E. Porter and Eckhard J. Schnabel, Texts and Editions for New Testament Study, 269–98. Leiden: Brill, 2013.

Vanhoozer, Kevin J., Craig G. Bartholomew, Daniel J. Treier, and N. T. Wright. *Dictionary for Theological Interpretation of the Bible*. Grand Rapids: Baker, 2005.

Vanhoozer, Kevin J., and Daniel J. Treier. *Theology and the Mirror of Scripture: A Mere Evangelical Account*. Studies in Christian Doctrine and Scripture. London: Apollos, 2016.

Voderholzer, Rudolf. "Dogma and History: Henri de Lubac and the Retrieval of Historicity as a Key to Theological Renewal." *Communio* 28 (2001): 648–68.

Volf, Miroslav. *Exclusion and Embrace: A Theological Exploration of Identity, Otherness, and Reconciliation*. Nashville: Abingdon, 1996.

*Flourishing: Why We Need Religion in a Globalized World*. New Haven: Yale University Press, 2015.

*A Public Faith: How Followers of Christ Should Serve the Common Good*. Grand Rapids: Brazos, 2011.

"Reading the Bible Theologically." In *Captive to the Word of God: Engaging the Scriptures for Contemporary Reflection*, 3–40. Grand Rapids: Eerdmans, 2010.

Ward, Graham. "How I Read the Bible." In *Theologians on Scripture*, edited by Angus Paddison. London: Bloomsbury T. & T. Clark, 2016.

Watson, Francis. "Does Historical Criticism Exist? A Contribution to Debate on the Theological Interpretation of Scripture." In *Theological Theology: Essays in Honour of John Webster*, edited by R. David Nelson, Darren Sarisky, and Justin Stratis, 307–18. London: Bloomsbury T. & T. Clark, 2015.

*The Fourfold Gospel: A Theological Reading of the New Testament Portraits of Jesus*. Grand Rapids: Baker, 2016.

*Text and Truth: Redefining Biblical Theology*. Edinburgh: T. & T. Clark, 1997.

Webster, John. "Biblical Reasoning." *Anglican Theological Review* 90 (2008): 733–51.

"The Domain of the Word." In *The Domain of the Word: Scripture and Theological Reason*, 3–31. London: Bloomsbury T. & T. Clark, 2013.

"Hermeneutics in Modern Theology: Some Doctrinal Reflections." In *Word and Church: Essays in Christian Dogmatics*, 47–86. Edinburgh: T. & T. Clark, 2001.

*Holy Scripture: A Dogmatic Sketch*. Cambridge: Cambridge University Press, 2003.

"One Who Is Son: Theological Reflections on the Exordium to the Epistle to the Hebrews." In *The Epistle to the Hebrews and Christian Theology*, edited by Richard Bauckham, Daniel R. Driver, Trevor A. Hart, and Nathan MacDonald, 69–94. Grand Rapids: Eerdmans, 2009.

"Resurrection and Scripture." In *The Domain of the Word: Scripture and Theological Reason*, 32–49. London: Bloomsbury T. & T. Clark, 2013.

"T. F. Torrance on Scripture." *Scottish Journal of Theology* 65 (2012): 34–63.

Welker, Michael. *God the Spirit*. Minneapolis: Fortress, 1994.

Williams, A. N. *The Architecture of Theology: Structure, System, and Ratio*. Oxford: Oxford University Press, 2011.

Williams, Rowan. *Arius: Heresy and Tradition*. Rev. ed. Grand Rapids: Eerdmans, 2002.

"The Discipline of Scripture." In *On Christian Theology*, 44–59. Oxford: Blackwell, 2000.

*Faith in the Public Square*. London: Bloomsbury Continuum, 2012.

"Historical Criticism and Sacred Text." In *Reading Texts, Seeking Wisdom: Scripture and Theology*, edited by David F. Ford and Graham Stanton, 217–28. Grand Rapids: Eerdmans, 2004.

"The Judgment of the World." In *On Christian Theology*, 29–43. Oxford: Blackwell, 2000.

"Language, Reality and Desire in Augustine's *De Doctrina*." *Literature and Theology* 3 (1989): 138–50.

"The Unity of the Bible and the Unity of the Church." *Internationale kirchliche Zeitschrift* 91 (2001): 5–21.

*Why Study the Past? The Quest for the Historical Church*. London: Darton, Longman, and Todd, 2005.

Wimsatt, William K., and Monroe C. Beardsley. "The Affective Fallacy." In *The Verbal Icon: Studies in the Meaning of Poetry*, edited by William K. Wimsatt, 21–40. Lexington: University of Kentucky Press, 1954.

Wisse, Maarten. "Hermeneutics." In *The Oxford Guide to the Historical Reception of Augustine*, edited by Karla Pollmann and Willemien Otten, vol. 2, 1126–35. Oxford: Oxford University Press, 2013.

Wittgenstein, Ludwig. *Philosophische Untersuchungen = Philosophical Investigations*. Rev. 4th ed. Chichester: Wiley-Blackwell, 2009.

Wolterstorff, Nicholas. *Divine Discourse: Philosophical Reflections on the Claim That God Speaks*. Cambridge: Cambridge University Press, 1995.

"Is It Possible and Desirable for Theologians to Recover from Kant?" *Modern Theology* 14 (1998): 1–18.

*Reason within the Bounds of Religion*. 2nd ed. Grand Rapids: Eerdmans, 1999.

"The Travail of Theology in the Modern Academy." In *The Future of Theology: Essays in Honor of Jürgen Moltmann*, edited by Miroslav Volf, Carmen Krieg, and Thomas Dörken-Kucharz, 35–46. Grand Rapids: Eerdmans, 1996.

Wood, Donald. "The Place of Theology in Theological Hermeneutics." *International Journal of Systematic Theology* 4 (2002): 156–71.

Yeago, David S. "The New Testament and the Nicene Dogma: A Contribution to the Recovery of Theological Exegesis." In *The Theological Interpretation of Scripture: Classical and Contemporary Essays*, edited by Stephen Fowl, 87–100. Oxford: Blackwell, 1997.

Young, Frances M. "Augustine's Hermeneutics and Postmodern Criticism." *Interpretation* 58 (2004): 42–55.

*Biblical Exegesis and the Formation of Christian Culture*. Cambridge: Cambridge University Press, 1997.

*God's Presence: A Contemporary Recapitulation of Early Christianity*. Current Issues in Theology. Cambridge: Cambridge University Press, 2013.

"The 'Mind' of Scripture: Theological Readings of the Bible in the Fathers." *International Journal of Systematic Theology* 7 (2005): 126–41.

Young, Frances M., and David F. Ford. *Meaning and Truth in 2 Corinthians*. Grand Rapids: Eerdmans, 1988.

Zac, Sylvain. *Spinoza et l'interprétation de l'écriture*. Bibliothèque de philosophie contemporaine. Histoire de la philosophie et philosophie générale. Paris: Presses universitaires de France, 1965.

Zachhuber, Johannes. *Theology as Science in Nineteenth-Century Germany: From F.C. Baur to Ernst Troeltsch*. Changing Paradigms in Historical and Systematic Theology. Oxford: Oxford University Press, 2013.

# Index


1 Corinthians, 85, 271
1 John, 28
2 Thessalonians, 196

Abraham, 10, 217
Acts (of the Apostles), 40
Angel, 85, 280
Anthropology, 50, 54, 76, 81, 83
  theological, 224
Anti-Semitism. *See* Judaism
Apostles' Creed, 120
Application. *See* Reading strategies, *applicatio*
Archaeology. *See* History
Auden, W. H., 153
Augustine, 189, 201, 215, 239, 268–69, 274, 280, 286, 301, 330
  blurring between disciplines of theology and philosophy, 78
  as commanding figure in Christianity, 146
  depiction of human life as a journey, 86
  and deuterocanonical books, 93
  on the importance of historical knowledge, 223
  on limits of human knowledge, 210
  on reader and text, 75
  on semiotics, 95
  and the Song of Songs, 100
  theology of, 64
and tripartite division of human beings, 83
Authority, 29, 162, 199
  disassociation from, 192
  religious, 177

*Barmen Declaration*
  as example of application, 322
Barr, James, 28–32, 259–64, 275
Barth, Karl, 142, 285, 337
Barthes, Roland, 236
Barton, John, 175, 336
  his biblical criticism approach, 356
Belief. *See* Faith commitment
Bible, x
  alterity of, 219
  ambiguity in the, 133, 277
  application of, 38, 43
  canon of, 93, 131, 215, 225
  claims of the, 121
  as collection of individual books, 93
  commentary on the, 257
  deuterocanonical books of, 93
  as direct personal address, 60
  as "face of God", 91
  geography of, 219
  history of reception, 33
  as literary art, 233
  as literature, 153, 216
  memorization of, 82
  as moral tool, 181
  nature of, 43, 45, 48, 267–82
  obscurity of, 219
  as past act of communication, 172
  as potential illustration of truth, 175
  as a sign of divinity, 206
  study of as like emprical science, 178
  as universally accessible, 233
  versions of, 146
  world of, 180
Biblical words. *See* Language
Brague, Rémi, 145
Brazos Theological Commentary on the Bible, 248, 252, 337

Buddhism, 73
Bultmann, Rudolf, 337

Cameron, Michael, 65
Catechesis, 82, 214
Christology, 79, 88, 115, *See* also Jesus Christ
Church. *See* Community, ecclesial
Community, 12, 23, 38, 40, 42, 44, 54, 162
  ecclesial, 55, 81, 107, 118, 188, 131, 214
  of faith, 199
  religious, 153, 180
  as source of reading strategies, 236
  synchronic/diachronic, 189
*Confessions* (Augustine), 85
Context, 8, 33, 36
  historical, 58, 111, 278, 299, 349
  literary, 278, 298
Creation, 88, 94, 98

Daniel (book of), 113
Demon, 102
Descartes, René, 160–63
Deuteronomy, 311
Doctrine, 33, 56, 101, 138, 144, 192, 220, 254, 355
Dogma. *See* Doctrine
Dualism, 56–58, 62, 243
  ahistorical, 244, 248–59
  of immanent frame, 246, 259–66
  soft, 263
Dupré, Louis, 182

Ecclesiology, 118, 138, 234
Education, 160
Eisegesis. *See* Exegesis
Emmaus, 49, 207
Epiphany, 209
Epistemology, 35, 105, 210
Eschatology, 84, 92, 204
Ethics, 105, 145
Eucharist, 49
Exegesis, ix, xiii, 5, 14, 21, 39, 71, 127, 139, 151, 200
  as complicating use of Scripture, 221
  as opposed to eisegesis, 346, 359
  distinct from naturalism, 183
  history of, 31
  levels of, 24, 252, 285
  practice of, 128
Exodus, 134, 272, 300, 311

Faith, 271, 275
  objective versus subjective side of, 202
  as opposed to credulity, 200
  privatization of, 30
  "pure," 201
  as receptive response, 206
  related to prejudice, 200
  as separate from daily life, 184
  without argumentation, 116
Faith commitment, xii, 1, 7, 18, 25, 35, 41, 56, 67, 78, 108, 139, 172, 181, 191, 209, 224
  as corrigible, 210
  as prerequisite to studying Scripture, 196
  as unnecessary, 167
Figural reading, 256, 321
Fish, Stanley, 234
Formalism, 234
Foucault, Michel, 92
Foundationalism, 162, 304, 325
Fowl, Stephen, 38–44, 53–54, 265–66, 290–92
Frye, Northrop, 154

Gadamer, Hans Georg, 109, 144
Genesis, 84
Gentile, 40, 135
God, 11, 122
  ability to discern, 204
  absence of, 40
  and humans in relationship, 86
  as human being, 125
  as love, 28
  as purely material, 163
  as source of all things, 45
  as tool, 77
  as transcendent, 72, 200
  as ultimate authority, 194
  as ultimate desire, 87
  as unnecessary to morality, 182

God (cont.)
belief in, 117
Christ as, 111
Christian understanding of, 214
death of, 7
delight in, 126
discourse of, 213
doctrine of, 1, 4, 288, 301
enjoyment of, 136
existence of, 46–47
face of, 204
identity of, 77
judgment of, 226
knowledge of, 209, 213
love of, 83, 91, 123
nature of, 1
perception of, 202
power of, 114
reader's orientation toward, 119
reality of, 2, 144
reduced to natural world, 163
in relation to, 56
representation of, 7, 47
revelation of, 92, 165, 206
self-disclosure of, xii
teachings about, 45
transcendence of, 77
understanding of, 99, 118
vision of, 204
will of, 84, 100
wisdom of, 114
Grace, 80, 203
faith as a gift of, 217
Griffiths, Paul, 80

Harvey, Van, 169
Hauerwas, Stanley, 252–59, 325
Hays, Richard, 221, 302
Hegel, G. W. F., 220
Heidegger, Martin, 109
Hermeneutics, xi, 8, 25, 34, 38, 67, 98, 105, 135, 143, 168
as circle, 121, 274, 325–26
as distinct in different religions, 217
first principles of, 188
as restoration, 68
of suspicion versus restoration, 312
Historical criticism, 6, 58, 146, 249, 253–54
Historiography. *See* History
History, 30, 34, 42, 56, 67–68, 72, 137, 201, 250, 255, 259, 277
of the Bible, 216
conflated with naturalism, 183
consciousness of, 63, 143, 171, 239
devaluation of, 159, 266–67
as domain of pure nature, 62
and historical distance, 218, 229, 280, 320
as important to theology, 186
importance in *explicatio*, 298
individual's placement within, 191
knowledge of, 59, 61
limitations of, 154
naturalistic view of, 298
questions related to, 293
and *Wirkungsgeschichte*, 33
Holy Spirit, 40, 199
gifts of, 124
in relation to signs, 271
work of, 227
Humanity, 107, 126
as independent from God, 165
viewed in light of God, 225

Illumination. *See* Revelation
Immanence, 260, *See* also dualism of the immanent frame
Incarnation, 88, *See* also Jesus Christ
Individualism. *See* Self, *See* Subjectivity
Inquiry. *See* Knowledge
Interpretation. *See* also Theological interpretation
aim of, 288–94
as power politics, 177
Isaiah, 124
Iser, Wolfgang, 80
Islam, 10, 217
Israel, 163
God's faithfulness to, 221

Jenson, Robert, 211
Jerome, 93
Jesus Christ, 12, 48, 88, 92, 104, 111
breaking bread with, 215

crucifixion of, 208
death of, 214
as depicted in Mark's Gospel, 302–3
humanity and divinity of, 89
humanity of, 115
incarnation of, 48, 134, 263
knowledge of, 79
life of, 120
as Lord, 253–55, 315
as physical being, 202
resurrection of, 208
revelation of, 230
signs pointing toward, 270
as Son of God, 202
as teacher, 114
transfiguration of, 36
John's Gospel, 270, 301, 323
Judaism, 10, 135, 209
modern, 217
relationship between Jews and Gentiles, 227

Kant, Immanuel, 201
Kaufman, Gordon, 6–7
Kelsey, David, 76, 155, 290
Kierkegaard, Søren, 58, 203
Knowledge, 203
establishment of, 115
of history as unnecessary for reading, 223
of truth, 122

Language, 6, 10, 22–23, 28, 30, 35, 43, 46, 76, 83, 89, 98, 102, 218
of the Bible, 127
doctrinal, 164
natural, 99
original biblical, 170, 199
about God, 54
relativity of, 171
semantics of, 133
theological, 142, 181
Literacy, 81
Liturgy, 50, 82, 214
Lubac, Henri de, 73, 139
Luke's Gospel, 49, 210, 214, 272, 300
Luz, Ulrich, 34–37

MacIntyre, Alasdair, 180, 212
Maimonides, 347–49
Marion, Jean-Luc, 46–51
Mark's Gospel, 303
Martin, Dale, 258
Mathewes, Charles, 149
Matthew's Gospel, 36, 124, 202, 211, 280, 302
McClintock Fulkerson, Mary, 234
Meaning, 22, 24, 42, 44, 172
Meaning/truth distinction, 171, 277, 305, 334, 341
Means/meant distinction, 261, 340
Metaphysics, 151
Morality, 201
as internally derived, 182
Mores. *See* Morality

Nadler, Steven, 179
Naturalism, 63, 72, 151, 198, 211
metaphysical, 351
methodological, 355, 359
as a presupposition, 168
Neighbor
love of, 123
love of God and, 119
New Testament, 93, 221, 230, 272, 300, 315
Nicene Creed, 12, 132
as example of *meditatio*, 314–16
Nietzsche, Friedrich, 69, 335

O'Donnell, James, 138
Objectivity, 30–31, 41, 46, 58, 66, 178, 201, 339, 341, 352
Old Testament, 28, 40, 49, 67, 93, 134, 209, 230, 272, 299, 315
*On Christian Teaching* (Augustine), 83, 86–91, 94–103, 107–8, 111, 121, 127, 137, 223
*On Eighty-Three Varied Questions* (Augustine), 87
*On Faith and the Creed* (Augustine), 83
*On Genesis, against the Manichees* (Augustine), 83–85
*On the Advantage of Believing* (Augustine), 119
*On the Greatness of the Soul* (Augustine), 82–83

*On the Immortality of the Soul* (Augustine), 83
*On the Instruction of Beginners* (Augustine), 98
*On the Literal Interpretation of Genesis* (Augustine), 84
*On the Lord's Sermon on the Mount* (Augustine), 124
*On the Teacher* (Augustine), 116
Ontology, 46, 72, 77, 94–95, 98, 106, 296, 311, 346. *See* also Reality
  naturalistic, 347–51
  prior to other concerns, 290–92
  related to function, 241
  as related to ontotheology, 46
  single-substance, 165
Ontotheology. *See* ontology as related to ontotheology
Origen, 139

Pantheism, 184
Passover, 134, 214
Pedagogy. *See* Education
Phenomenology, 38, 50
Philemon, 89
Philosophy, 16, 32, 45, 78
Postliberalism, 144
Postmodernism, 195
Presupposition, 351
  theological, 184
Pre-understanding. *See* Prior understanding
Prior understanding, 274–77, 319, 336

Rationality, 78, 160, 191
  hermeneutical, 188
  in relation to truth, 162
  procedural versus substantive, 162, 196
Reader, 2, 9, 63, 75, 78–79
  as active, 232–37
  ideal, 92
  implied, 80
  as important locus of interpretation, 190
  role of, 52
  self-conception of, 4
  transformation of, 50
Reader-response. *See* Fish, Stanley
Reading strategies, xiii
  *applicatio*, 318–24
  *explicatio*, 297–307
  *explicatio*, *meditatio*, and *applicatio*, 294–326
  interrelationship of, 325
  *meditatio*, 307–18
  *meditatio* as dialogue, 310–13
  in relation to interpretive criteria, 306, 317, 323
Reality, xi, 37, 42, 57, 67, 71, 80, 106, 144, 239
  depiction of, 45
  nature of, 43
  of an object, 179
  perception of, 55
  seen in light of God, 53
  vision of, 209
Reason, 143, 199
  critiques of universal, 195
  disengaged, 196, 224
  as independent of tradition, 163
  as tool versus body of beliefs, 167
Redemption, 75, 85
  of world through Christ, 228
Reference, 281
Reformers, Protestant, 179
Religion
  as superstition, 177
Reno, R. R., 222
Revelation, 23, 201, 218
Ricoeur, Paul, 295
Roman Catholicism, 49
Romans, 221, 228, 285

Salvation, 79, 168, 205
  divine plan of, 221
  economy of, 125, 193, 204, 226, 322
  as shared through the ages, 231
*Sapientia*, 121
Schleiermacher, Friedrich, 196
Schneiders, Sandra, 293
*Scientia*, 105, 121–23
Scriptural Reasoning, 217
Scripture Project, 9, 205
Secular, 7
Self, 108
  decentering of, 161

love of, 83
technology of. *See* Foucault, Michel
Semiotics, 68, 94–95, 104, 143, *See* also Signs
Septuagint, 93
*Sermon* 22 (Augustine), 91
Signs, 48, 75, 94, 96, 134, 201, 239, 247, 258, 264, 301
biblical economy of, 102
interpretation of, 111
as opposed to testimony, 240
as pedagogical, 112
privileged, 94, 269
whole Bible as, 272
Sin
burden of, 100
Skepticism, 106
Socrates, 203
Song of Songs, 100
Soul
as embodied, 103
human as embodied, 82
reorientation of, 86
Spinoza, Benedict de, 106, 157, 199, 329, 347–53
Stendahl, Krister, 340
Stock, Brian, 121
Subjectivity, 28, 30, 37, 39, 55, 128, 162, 202, 261
as determining Bible's importance, 181
and interpretation, 276
as spontaneous, 212
of theological belief, 344
Symbol. *See* Signs

Tanner, Kathryn, 233, 247
Taylor, Charles, xi, 105
Teleology, 125
Telos. *See* Teleology, *See* Vocation
Testimony
of others, 118
Theocentricity, 9, 76, 84
Theologian. *See* Theology
Theological interpretation, ix, 72, 328–29
movement, 6, 15
TIS as moniker for discussion of, 14
Theology, 260
as active, 33, 55
as aspect of selfhood, 37
consciousness of, 186
as data of Scripture, 157
description of, 28
as dismissal of history, 183
Liberation, 3, 23
as passive, 27, 54
Pottery Barn, 149
as presupposition of argument, 29
in relation to reading, 285–86
as separate from other disciplines, 194
Systematic, 2, 13, 53, 262
use versus mention of, 317
Time
independent of, 109
Tracy, David, 8, 50, 193
Tradition, 9–11, 41, 162, 199
Christian, 4, 6, 16, 214, 353
as counter-productive, 166
ecclesial, 238
Greek Orthodox, 36
as indulging in prejudice, 170
religious, 35
strands of Christian, 343, 362
Western, 34
Transcendence, 57, 342
absolute versus relative, 144
Trinity, 2–3, 12, 72, 94, 125, 143, 205, 229, 263, 271, 275, 277, 288, 303
economic, 315
as essential in theological reading, 211
immanent, 316
interpretive questions related to, 301
Truth
as residing within, 203
mediated access to at present, 210
of Scripture, 220
Tyconius, 64

Vocation, 78
Vulgate, 93

Williams, Rowan, 90
Wisdom, 78, 92, 117, 125
practical, 105

Young, Frances, 127

Lightning Source UK Ltd.
Milton Keynes UK
UKHW010729301121
394624UK00007B/223